Windrush ... *Britain*

Mike Phillips ... award-winning author of ... Formerly Writer in Residence at the Royal Festival Hall, he is currently Arts Foundation Fellow for thriller writers.

Trevor Phillips, a leading name in the world of broadcast journalism, is best know. as the presenter of LWT's 'The London Programme' and several BBC Radio 4 titles. He is an ITV executive, as well as running his own production company, and writes a column for *The Independent*.

id**e**a
Library Learning Information

To renew this item call:

0115 929 3388

or visit

www.ideastore.co.uk

TOWER HAMLETS

Created and managed by Tower Hamlets Council

WITHDRAWN

Other books by Mike Phillips

The Dancing Face
An Image to Die For
Point of Darkness
The Late Candidate
Blood Rights

WITHDRAWN

WINDRUSH

The Irresistible Rise of
Multi-Racial Britain

Mike Phillips & Trevor Phillips

TOWER HAMLETS LIBRARIES	
91000004500898	
Bertrams	16/10/2014
305.896	£14.99
THISWH	TH14001101

HarperCollinsPublishers

HarperCollins*Publishers*
77–85 Fulham Palace Road,
Hammersmith, London W6 8JB
www.fireandwater.com

First published in Great Britain by
HarperCollins*Publishers* 1998

Copyright © Mike Phillips & Trevor Phillips 1998

The authors assert the moral right to
be identified as the authors of this work

A catalogue record for this book is
available from the British Library

ISBN-978-0-00-653039-8

Set in Sabon and Frutiger by
Rowland Phototypesetting Ltd, Bury St Edmunds, Suffolk

All rights reserved. No part of this publication may be
reproduced, stored in a retrieval system, or transmitted,
in any form or by any means, electronic, mechanical,
photocopying, recording or otherwise, without the prior
permission of the publishers.

Mixed Sources
Product group from well-managed
forests and other controlled sources
www.fsc.org Cert no. SW-COC-001806
© 1996 Forest Stewardship Council

FSC is a non-profit international organisation established to promote the
responsible management of the world's forests. Products carrying the FSC
label are independently certified to assure consumers that they come
from forests that are managed to meet the social, economic and
ecological needs of present and future generations.

Find out more about HarperCollins and the environment at
www.harpercollins.co.uk/green

Contents

Dedication

For George and Marjorie, whose courage shaped the voyage.
For Jenny, without whose help it would have been impossible.
Also for Kwesi and Kip, and for Asha, Sushila and Holly.

Acknowledgements

Thanks to Sam King and Arthur Torrington, who initiated the Windrush Foundation. Thanks to Anne, Richard, Beverley, Joanna, Sharon, Rosie and Jan. Thanks also to David Upshal, who shared the bulk of the interviews with Trevor. And thanks to Andrea and Val, whose patience in this case was a greatly appreciated virtue.

Some of the interviews in this book were derived from research for the BBC2 series Windrush.

List of Illustrations

Introduction

'Listen, children. If you want to know how it felt to be where we were in that time, think about suitcases. A few years ago I was in Amsterdam looking out of a hotel window and I saw a black woman. Surinamese, I suppose she was, walking with two small children, boy and girl, holding on to her skirt, and she was carrying a battered old cardboard suitcase. Night was coming on and I had this feeling that they were desperate, looking for somewhere to go. Right there and then I was back in London, back in the old days. You used to see black families walking, humping these dirty great old suitcases with all their belongings, moving with all their belongings, or looking for a place to stay. Moving, always moving. Sometimes it was our family, and I can still remember in my palms and my fingers the agony of the weight, pulling along this suitcase nearly as big as me. We're talking about London, and it could be anywhere in the city; Islington, Brixton, Waterloo. Just find one of the big railway stations and put your finger down on the map. Sometimes I'm watching the news or one of these programmes about refugees and I have to switch off and let the feelings rest for a while, because that is the pain and the memory. Chips ebbing and flowing on a violent tide. That's how it was.'[1]

Our father arrived in Britain not long after the *Empire Windrush* docked at Tilbury in 1948. Caribbean immigration to Britain was a mere trickle then, but we now think about our family history as being bound up with that moment when he made his own crossing on a boat whose name none of us can remember. He would have been wearing a hat and a suit and an overcoat. In the old photographs, there is practically nothing to distinguish him from the men who walked the plank off the *Windrush*, and for us this recognition has become a reflex in which our imagination rushes to fill the gap between ourselves and those familiar images of the boat; the gangplank, the flock of tropical figures lining the rail. In our minds, it is the reality of

---

[1] Mike Phillips and Charlie Phillips, *Notting Hill in the Sixties* (London: Lawrence and Wishart, 1997).

arrival which has retreated, to be replaced by the myth of the *Windrush*.

It was a real boat, of course, carrying real passengers, many of whom we know personally, but over the last fifty years we have begun to view the *Windrush* and its arrival at Tilbury Docks with different eyes. We had been aware of it for a long time. Within a decade of its famous voyage in 1948, the *Windrush* had become a symbol of post-war immigration and, for a time, it seemed as if every TV documentary about race or migration had to begin with the image of a line of black men and women filing down the gangplank. As time went by new details emerged from the background: the white gloves and hats of women, beautifully turned out as if on their way to church or some other important celebration; the eyes of children, bemused and fascinated by sights they had never imagined.

Whenever we saw these pictures we felt a curious clash between nostalgia and irritation. The irritation was partly to do with the fact that these images were fixed, an unalterable statement about identity, asserting, over and over again, that black citizens, the Caribbeans and their children, were unreconstructed newcomers, aliens for ever. 'Just come over on the banana boat', was the taunt we had heard so often as children and, somehow, whenever we caught sight of the *Windrush* pictures through the cold, distanced eye of the newsreel camera, it was hard not to catch an echo of that gibe.

The roots of nostalgia were rather more difficult to disentangle. Perhaps it was the graceful awkwardness with which the *Windrush* people moved. Perhaps it was the hats and the unselfconscious stylishness of their dress. Perhaps it was the sheer innocence of faces unprepared for what they would encounter. But whatever it was that we recognised about them, it was also something that was part of ourselves. In recent years, catching sight of them unexpectedly on TV or frozen on the pages of a book, the *Windrush* people seemed to have come closer, instead of receding into the boundaries of their times. It was as if the *Windrush*, in spite of time and distance, had become part of our own story.

We have spent most of our lives in Britain. One of us arrived as a schoolchild at the beginning of 1956, the other was born during a snowstorm in London a few years earlier. Our passports declare us to be British citizens. Our children attend schools and universities in England. We perform a variety of civic duties. We are linked, both by kinship and by a complex network of intimate relationships, to other British citizens throughout the country. Behind the daily activity of our lives is a broad current of memory within which the sights and sounds, the people and the emotions that we associate with being British are a permanent implant, indelible. If our lives were to flash in front of our eyes most of it would be concerned with events and people here in Britain. Harold Wilson would be there, and

Enoch Powell and Ted Heath, and the shuffling queues in a dole office, and the sound of a Salvation Army band, and the naughty chirruping of the voices over the crackling radio airwaves when we switched on for 'Round the Horne', and the smell of wax on the floor of a public library, and the roar of the crowd at the Arsenal football stadium, and the antiseptic lines of beds in a ward at the old St George's Hospital, and a moonscape of rusted metal in Trafford, and the unexpected perfume of wild flowers in an abandoned railway bed.

Anything else would be surprising, because the idea of belonging to a country or to any specific place is underpinned by such acts of possession. At the same time, even in our own thoughts, there is an undercurrent of something daring about openly claiming the nationality which has become a fundamental strand of our identity as individuals. Our memory also encompasses a time when, as immigrants and the children of immigrants, our status as citizens was contestable, a matter of political will and argument. During the time when we grew up it was clear that to most of our fellow citizens there was an inextricable link between nationality, citizenship and race. Inevitably, the first question we were asked by new acquaintances would turn out to be, 'Where do you come from?' To be British was to be a white Anglo Saxon and, whatever that meant, it was not us.

On the other side of the coin we possessed a strong sense of being something more than what most people understood to be British. Our brothers and sisters and other close relatives were scattered throughout the world, working or being educated in widely separated continents. Sometimes our family gatherings felt like a meeting of the UN as we swapped experiences and arguments about daily life in half a dozen countries. Within our immediate family we could identify at least half a dozen different nationalities and, alongside that fact, ran the knowledge that if different choices had been made for us we could now have been citizens of some other country, our sense of what we are determined by a very different network of memories and emotions.

All this seemed both extraordinary and ordinary. It was extraordinary because it marked us out from the other Britons, who seemed to be so imprisoned inside a fixed identity that they carried everywhere, incapable of stepping outside the skin of 'their' island. It was ordinary because we shared our state of mind and our background with most of the families who had emigrated from the Caribbean region. But that was a long time ago.

There is no doubt that over the last fifty years the meaning we read into the image of the *Windrush* has undergone a radical change, but this is not simply a measure of how far our own perspective has shifted. Britain in

1948 was very different from the country in which we now live. To the majority of the passengers on the *Windrush* the arrival was a leap into the unknown, an adventure in which no one knew what they would find. In contrast, when we disembark from a trip abroad at Heathrow or climb off the ferry at Folkestone, we are entering familiar territory and simply coming home.

In the first months after arrival we had been grateful for our ability to escape what we had come from. Later on the impact of life in the outside world realigned our emotional maps and, during the worst of times in Britain, the regions from which we had travelled became transformed in our minds into idylls, lost paradises within which, in our memories, we still lived, and which, one day, we might physically reclaim. But after a couple of decades this dream began to lose its force and its meaning. Initially, within the idiom of our family, 'home' only ever meant one place, a small fishing village by the Atlantic shore: but almost before we knew it, the prospect of return faded and, along with it, the sense of 'home' as the place where we would feel most secure and comfortable. Instead 'home' became the distant spot on the map where we had our origins. Forty years ago such notions would have seemed alien, charged with a sense of moral terror and betrayal. But some of us had been born many miles away from 'home' and, for them, London or New York was the real 'home', the family's account of its roots almost mythical, no more than a piece of clan heritage that bound us together. Our loyalties had changed and our collective dreams were now more concerned with the future than with the past. Gradually, our world had shifted its centre. Today we look outwards from the cities of Europe and North America, and although we still talk of home, knowing exactly where we mean, it is now almost as far away from us as it is from our neighbours.

Bound up with this new distance, however, is a mood of assurance about our grip on where we are, the sense that we have taken possession of new ground, and this mood stems from something more than our right to enter the United Kingdom or our familiarity with people and places. During the second half of the century another gradual change had taken place in Britain which has fundamentally altered the nature of our relationship with it.

When our parents and their fellow immigrants arrived during the post-Second World War years, they felt themselves to be confronted by an exclusive and impenetrable image of British society, backed up by the ideology of race and racial superiority, which had for so long been an essential pillar of imperial power. This was a moral environment which steadfastly refused to acknowledge change, or the possibility of change, in the nation's self image. In the post-war reconstruction of British identity, for instance, the stiff upper lip had to be white, and it comes as a shock now to note the complete absence of black Caribbean or African participants in the plethora of British films about the Second World War. After all, the involvement of black colonials was a fact that was a part of our experience. One of our closest family friends, Ronald Hall, a dentist in south London, had flown in bombers throughout the war, and all the surviving photographs of our own father as a young man show him in uniform. We knew very well that those men had been part of the conflict. Our astonishment was, and still is, to do with the extent to which they had disappeared, had been expurgated from the story, as if they had never existed.

Looking back at those times from the standpoint of the present day, it is tempting to assume that the racial attitudes which prompted this kind of bowdlerisation are a thing of the past. We observe that the overt declarations of racist hostility which were commonplace in the fifties have, more or less, disappeared from public life in Britain. On the other hand, it is clear that racial hostility and exclusion are a routine part of British life, and few black British people can be in any doubt that the majority of their fellow citizens take the colour of their skins to be a characteristic which defines what they are and what they can do.

At the same time, paradoxically, among ourselves we never interpreted the racial discrimination or hostility that we encountered as 'rejection', largely because we never believed that 'acceptance' or 'rejection' was a choice available to Britain. Far from it. Our instinct told us that such notions were merely part of a racialised idiom, describing an identity which had long ago ceased to be relevant. For us the issue was a different one. In the last fifty years the minority to which we belonged had become an authentic strand of British society. If we were engaged in a struggle, it wasn't about our 'acceptance' as individuals. Instead, it was about our status as citizens, and it seemed obvious that if our citizenship was to mean more than the paper on which it was written, it would be necessary for the whole country to reassess not only its own identity, and its history, but also what it meant to be British.

To the people on the *Windrush*, who regarded their 'Britishness' as non-negotiable, the nature and extent of our commitment to this process, along with our interest in Britishness, would have been puzzling. Most of them had plans which were concrete, material and more concerned with their immediate needs. But, whatever their intentions, it is a fact that they were a crucial element in a network of events which altered major aspects of life in Britain today to the point where they would be unrecognisable from the perspective of 1948. It would be impossible to describe the country in which we now live without awarding a role to the Caribbean immigrants, their children and their grandchildren. In one way or the other, British identity presents a new and permanently altered appearance. The people who scrambled on board the *Windrush* or the *Reina Del Pacifico*, or any of the other boats bringing immigrants from the West Indies, would not have hoped for so much, and, certainly, could not have imagined how far and how fast they would travel. In hindsight, the moment of arrival captured by the *Windrush* has become a symbol for all those occasions when we, or any of the other black people who have become part of the British nation, stepped off our separate gangplanks.

Paradoxically, there had been groups of black people living in Britain long before this. Slavery and the vagaries of imperial adventure deposited substantial numbers in various parts of the country. By the time the *Windrush* arrived there were already black communities who could trace their ancestry back a couple of centuries. But on 22 June 1948 the *Windrush* sailed through a gateway in history, on the other side of which was the end of Empire and a wholesale reassessment of what it meant to be British. Before and after this historical moment, even simultaneously, the same kind of arrival was occurring in various other parts of the world, as settled populations shifted, driven by one kind of necessity or another. In the last half of the twentieth century this experience seems to have become universal, almost routine, and wherever we now travel we encounter over and over again the moment of the *Windrush* and the infinite variety of consequences packed within it. The echoes of migration vibrate everywhere we can name: the USA, Germany, France, Holland, Portugal, Spain, Italy, the Middle East, the Pacific Basin, anywhere in Africa, and in any territory in Europe east of the Oder.

From this perspective the spectacle of the *Windrush* has become a vital, necessary link between our nationality and the historical accident from which it springs, and, for us, the outline of the arrival and its consequences is also a journey which sketches out the shape of our identities.

For us, this journey was all the more urgent because, in the present day, the individual identities of these early migrants have disappeared from public view, or been reinvented to be served up in a form which is convenient for contemporary purposes. More often than not, for example, when we encounter versions of our own experience, its outlines are unrecognisable, buried under the surface of a narrative about racial threat, social conflict or some kind of nationalism. In much the same way, as the *Windrush* people recede into myth they also seem to have been transformed into objects, a block whose sole distinguishing characteristic is the colour of their skins. The result being that in many contemporary histories they turn up as a sort of sudden infestation whose numbers account for various social problems. At the other end of the scale, we are offered selective descriptions which identify them as an isolated, ghettoised unit of an African diaspora, whose 'blackness' makes them interchangeable with people in Africa or the USA.

Listening to the survivors of the *Windrush*, their stories, interwoven as they are with our own experience, remind us once again that they and their successors are a diverse group of individuals, shaped by a specific and peculiar history, moved by their own rational calculations, impelled by their own needs and ambitions; and linked together by the rich and complex history they now share with the people among whom they came to live.

Taken together, their separate experiences form a mosaic outlining the last fifty years of Britain's history. When we came to write the story, we were inspired, initially and always, by the desire to share the unique sound and rhythm of the heartbeat which echoes through it. Some of the narrative surprises us even though, in one way or the other, we have lived through almost all of it. By the end of the story, we knew much more than we had ever imagined about the toughness and spirit of the Caribbean migrants who came in 1948 and the following years. By the same token, we had come to a new understanding, both of ourselves, and of how Britain has developed in the years since the *Windrush* arrived.

Mike Phillips & Trevor Phillips

1

'We didn't have much job, you know, things like that, but plenty of people work for themselves, you know, and, like, cultivating. After you cultivate then you send a little crop to, you know, to the higher one. They ship it away, to go to England, Canada, you know, like banana. And what you're growing, you could ship away, you know. So, if you could put it this way, if you could make a few shillings for yourself, then you're alright, but if you couldn't make it, it was very hard. See, so that's the reason why I said to myself, I don't want to stop here to grow old and, you know, I want to travel and make something . . .'[1]

'I went to St Anne, stop at a sugar estate there called Richmond, and worked there for a while. And that was about fifty-nine miles from where I lived. I walked to go there, but you only have seasonal work in those places, because the sugar producing season, that only lasts about six months or thereabouts. You either go on further or return to your place. I returned. It wasn't very profitable, but at least there was something to do. And so as time went on, you travelled, get in where you can, but those days were hard days. I had left Jamaica before, I went to Panama when they were recruiting people for the Panama Canal, you know, when the war started. And that was all the war effort, because I had to work as a commissary there. And the money wasn't all that, but it was something. And people going away – that's the only way you see people. Most Jamaicans who have, at that time, had anything, they had travelled. They didn't make it at home because very few people could work and get well off, you know, with the wages they earned in Jamaica. Some people could do because, I mean, there are quite a number of people, if they earn £5, they still save something, it doesn't matter what, if you're made that way you could, but not everyone could.'[2]

---

[1] Interview with Lloyd Miller. Lloyd Miller came to Britain from Jamaica in 1949 and worked as a builder in Notting Hill. He is now retired and lives with his wife Marge in west London.

[2] Interview with Columbus Denniston. Oswald (Columbus) Denniston sailed from Jamaica on the *Windrush*. He was the first of the *Windrush* passengers, according to the contemporary press, to

A Part of Britain

The West Indies are a group of islands strung in a long flat curve through the Caribbean Sea, like a giant row of stepping stones which start at the southern tip of Florida and end close by the north-eastern corner of South America. Most of the islands are formed by peaks of volcanic mountains, which, as volcanoes go, are fairly recent in origin. The climate is tropical, with temperatures averaging about twenty-seven degrees. The region is one of amazing natural beauty, and if you were looking for a tropical paradise, this would be it.

Yet the area has had a chequered history. When Christopher Columbus arrived in Hispaniola at the end of 1492 he was greeted by aboriginal inhabitants – Caribs and Arawaks – whom he dubbed Indians. Within less than a century the indigenous populations of the Caribbean had been more or less exterminated by pandemics of new diseases against which they had no resistance, and by the Spaniards' insatiable demands for labour and tribute. Spain, Portugal, France, Holland and Britain had colonised most of the region by the middle of the seventeenth century; but during the turmoil of the Napoleonic Wars, Britain acquired the largest portfolio of territory. Exceptionally, Barbados was settled by English colonists in 1627 and a British expedition captured Jamaica in 1655, but most of the other islands – Grenada, Dominica, Saint Vincent, Saint Lucia and Trinidad – passed through periods of settlement and ownership by various European powers before finally coming under British control. Guyana, on the South American mainland, was ceded by the Dutch in 1814.

During this period the demand for cheap labour to cultivate the colonists' crops of tobacco, rice and sugarcane, was met by the institution of slavery. Ships set out from England with trade goods for the west coast of Africa

---

get a job. Under the headline 'Jamaica's Oswald Given Job', the *Daily Express* reported: 'Oswald M. Denniston – the first of 430 job-hunting Jamaicans to land at Tilbury yesterday morning from the trooper *Empire Windrush* – started a £4-a-week job last night. Wrapped in two warm blankets to keep warm, he settled in as night watchman of the meals marquee in Clapham Common, SW, where 240 of the Jamaicans are staying in deep wartime shelters. All of them sat down there to their first meal on English soil: roast beef, potatoes, vegetables, Yorkshire pudding, suet pudding with currants and custard. A bed and three hot meals will cost them 6s.6d a day. Most of the Jamaicans have about £5 to last them until they find work. Oswald Denniston, 35-year-old sign painter, got his job after making a speech of thanks to government officials. He called for three cheers for the Ministry of Labour and raised his Anthony Eden hat. Others clapped. Panamas, blue, pink, and biscuit trilbys, and one bowler were waved' (*Daily Express*, 23 June 1948). After leaving the deep shelter at Clapham, Oswald Denniston settled in Brixton, where he worked as a street trader until his retirement.

where they exchanged their merchandise for African blacks. The next stop on the notorious 'Middle Passage' from Africa was the West Indies, where slaves were exchanged for various products. The final stage of the triangle was the return voyage to England.

For most of the nineteenth century, following the abolition of slavery in 1834, the Caribbean population of Africans and European settlers was augmented by indentured labourers and traders from India, China and the Middle East. The routine condition of the region was multi-racial, polyglot; a crossroads of people, cultures and languages.

Nationalism, as a political creed, arrived late in the Caribbean. Up until the middle of the twentieth century, and after the departure of the *Windrush*, regional politics were almost exclusively concerned with labour conditions and rights. The separate countries of the British Caribbean did not yet exist as nations and there was no widespread nationalist movement. The dream of idealistic Caribbean politicians was a federation between the various countries, but, for most Caribbeans, whatever their origins, the territories in which they lived were simply a part of the British State. In comparison with African or European peasants the relationship that Caribbeans had with the land they inhabited was tenuous and tentative, and this was a feeling underpinned by every aspect of life.

Take saltfish, for instance. When you see it for the first time it has a singularly unappetising look, like a lump of cardboard encrusted with dirty grey grains of salt, but the Caribbeans love saltfish and it is an essential part of the region's diet. Its history in the Caribbean is also typical. Shortly after Columbus arrived in the New World, the Portuguese began fishing for cod off Newfoundland's Grand Banks. They salted the fish, brought it home and dried it into stiff, hard blocks which could be kept for months before being reconstituted by adding water. Since then salt cod, bacalhau, has been a staple Mediterranean dish. The Europeans took it with them to the Caribbean and saltfish became part of West Indian culture.

In the same way, most of the products routinely used by people in the Caribbean carried the hallmarks of slavery and a dependent colonial economy. Everyone who lived in the region knew that this was their history, and they also knew that each nation was a collection of people who had been assembled by an external power for its own purposes. Slavery had ended during the nineteenth century, but everything the Caribbeans owned, including the country itself, was conditional, a sort of tenancy in which the landlord was the Empire. In the circumstances national identity was, more or less, a legal fiction.

'I wouldn't say that we had our own identity . . .'

'As a young man, growing up in school, we always regarded England
as the mother country. And for that reason, she was regarded as a
parent who never often see the children, but the children think of
the parents abroad. We knew that Jamaica was being governed, or
ruled, by England and we accepted that. But further into that, there
was no political interest in anything except the fact that she was the
ruler of Jamaica, and Jamaica was a colony . . .'[3]

'I wouldn't say that we had our own identity. We were always
British. In Jamaica I can remember, when it was the Queen's birthday
or the King's birthday or the Coronation, everything was done the
way Britain wanted us to. We hadn't our own identity. It is only since
the last war and each country been getting independence that we
start having our own identity. England was "the mother country",
as they used to say, and anything the English did or the British did
was always right, you know. And even up to people like my
grandmother who would listen to the radio at six o'clock every
evening in the West Indies, World Service, and whatever was said
there had to be gospel, you know. You couldn't argue that with
everybody, couldn't say, "Well, that was wrong." It was said by the
BBC and it was from England, therefore it was right and you had
to agree to it and support it. It's as simple as that.'[4]

'I mean, I didn't have any strong sense of British identity. I never
really had it. But it's the only identity I had, because people from the
Caribbean are not from the Caribbean originally. We were taken
there, either slaves or indentured labour, or whatever. And I didn't
have any strong great feeling for Guyana. But, at that time, you
know, one didn't confront issues of identity. That came later in one's

---

[3] Interview with Euton Christian. Euton Christian joined the RAF in 1944. He took part in the
legendary battle of Manchester, when West Indian and African Americans together with white British
servicemen fought a 'pitched battle' through the centre of the city against white American troops
who were trying to impose segregation. He returned to Jamaica in November 1947, after signing
up for another four years in the RAF and, after his leave ended, embarked on the *Windrush*. After
leaving the RAF he settled in Manchester, becoming a town councillor and the city's first black
magistrate.

[4] Interview with Arthur Curling. Arthur Curling ran away from home in Jamaica to join the RAF
at the age of sixteen. He lied about his age and was admitted. He returned to Jamaica in 1946 but
could not settle down, coming back to Britain on the *Windrush* in 1948.

life. At that time you just accepted that you were slightly privileged but, at the same time, underprivileged.'[5]

'Grenada was definitely part of the Empire. England was certainly the only place to come after you've finished. It's like going to finishing school really. All the educators, the inspectors, and so on, came down from England. We didn't see England as a separate entity. For example, in my convent school we spent a lot of time knitting little bits of wool for people during the war, you know, the poor. We wept when the Catholic Church was bombed, we rejoiced over the statue of the Virgin Mary wasn't hurt, you know, so we were very much part of England. We didn't see there was any difference between Grenada and England. "There'll always be an England and England shall be free" used to be one of our school songs. Empire day was a big day in Grenada. So it was all part and parcel of what we were about, being part of England. So when England went to war, we were at war. There was no "if" about that. Young people of the right age were – what can they do? They were lining up to join up and go and defend the mother country. There was no problems with that at all. Grenada was certainly part of England.'[6]

'I knew more about England than I did about Jamaica. I mean, I knew absolutely nothing about Jamaica. For instance, I was taught in school that the black people in Jamaica were somehow better off than black people in South Africa, that although we were brought to Jamaica as slaves, this was somehow preferable to being free in whatever part of Africa we came from. And, of course, I was also taught that the person who freed the slaves was a white man called Wilberforce, so that one was always encouraged to believe that one must be beholden to white people for whatever happened. Whatever you became, it was due to the benevolence and goodwill of white people. What I'm really saying is that the whole imperialistic thing was drilled into you. Life might have been hard and tough, but you

---

[5] Interview with Cy Grant. Cy Grant came from Guyana and joined the RAF in 1941. He was shot down flying a mission over Germany and spent the rest of the war as a prisoner of war in Germany. After the war he qualified as a barrister, but, instead of practising, became an actor. During the fifties he was an international star, performing with such actors as Richard Burton and Joan Collins. Subsequently he became a household name as a result of his nightly appearances on the BBC's *Tonight* programme.

[6] Interview with Ros Howells. Ros Howells came from Grenada, arriving in Britain during 1951. She settled in south London, where she worked as a counsellor.

were grateful. You didn't complain about it. You certainly didn't blame white people for it. That's how it was. You've got this whole thing of the authority in Jamaica. The Governor was white, those in authority were white, the judges were white. The only people who weren't white were police officers, who were black. And, of course, on top of that, you're bombarded with images of the newspapers, of white people, and in cinemas, again, white people. So you're encouraged to love them, as it were. You're encouraged to cheer for the white goodie and boo the black baddie. That was my impression of it, that you're seduced into believing in their benevolence, in their goodwill. You're seduced into respecting them, never questioning what they did or why they did it. I didn't feel particularly Jamaican because you had no sense of what Jamaica was. I knew I was born in Jamaica, but in terms of having an identity called Jamaican, I didn't – no, I didn't have that.'[7]

'Jamaicans were always singing songs like "Land of Hope and Glory and mother of the free" and "Rule Britannia, Britannia rules the waves". The training that we had was typical British. And we accepted that, on a whole. Wholeheartedly I feel that, speaking as how I felt myself at that time, that we, as Jamaicans, were allies to Britain, whether we were miles or thousand miles away. And this comes to many of us joining the war effort. And this was a feeling to know that we were defending Britain. Because we felt that we were a part of Britain. We were part of Britain. And, of course, we were made to understand that we were British, so, therefore, we were compelled, in a way, to say, Well, we want to defend Britain in certain respects.'[8]

[7]   Interview with Vince Reid. Vince Reid travelled to Britain on the *Windrush* at the age of thirteen. In London he attended a secondary modern school and left without qualifications two years later. Subsequently he joined the RAF, served overseas in the Far East during the period of insurgency in Malaya, and achieved the rank of NCO before buying himself out. He later studied at Sussex University, then qualified as a teacher and taught in London until his retirement.

[8]   Interview with William Naltey. William Naltey came from Jamaica to join the RAF in 1943. He served as an air gunner with Coastal Command. After the war he joined the Civil Service. At the time the *Windrush* docked he was living in Wandsworth.

Labour Was Cheap

Throughout the first half of the twentieth century the West Indies produced a wide variety of tropical fruits, spices, sugar, coffee and cacoa. Petroleum was extracted from Trinidad and its surrounding waters, and industries included sugar, rum, tobacco and fruit processing, textile manufacturing and mineral refining. Tourism was not yet a major source of income and the role of the region in the imperial economy meant that prices and quotas were invariably determined by interests outside it.

In the circumstances labour was cheap and rates of unemployment consistently high. In most of the region, a substantial sector of the population was actually marginal to the cash economy, living instead by a complex system of barter. Within the Caribbean it became traditional for men and women to travel abroad to engage in seasonal labour, such as harvesting crops in Florida's agricultural industries. In addition, every large-scale project within easy reach – like the construction of the Panama Canal at the beginning of the twentieth century – attracted huge numbers of Caribbean workers. In the USA the great migration of blacks away from the South was also accompanied by a large-scale movement of Caribbeans into the Northern cities. For active and enterprising Caribbeans a high degree of mobility was a normal and routine fact of life.

At the same time the domestic life of colonial society was intensely stratified, still dominated by traditions inherited from the slave regimes in which skin colour and class were intertwined and indistinguishable. The memories of the *Windrush* generation are riddled with this sense of being trapped within insurmountable barriers.

At the bottom of the rung . . .

'The main source of work in my youth was from the sugar valleys, that's before we had bananas. And people worked in those valleys cutting cane from about six o'clock in the morning till about five-thirty on an evening, and then they went home and they purchased everything from the sugar valley stores, and so on. But the whole system in the Caribbean is based on two things: race and class. Because whether you like it or not, the French and indeed the British in the days of slavery had worked out a strategy of colours so that they classified people according to their colour, okay? The white people were on top, then there were the mulattos and the quatrains and the quintrains – you know, a quarter blood of white and black, or fifth blood of black and white – and so on, right down to the pure black African.'[9]

'In Jamaica, you had this kind of caste, because at the very top of the tree, as it were, you had white people. And as you came down, down to the bottom, you had the progressive grades of colour, so you'd have the white people at the top and then you'd have the sort of fair skinned people, and then, right down the bottom, you had black people. The more light skinned you were, you got some kind of kudos for that. Any opportunities going were given to you. And, of course, when you looked around in stores, most of the people who were the clerks and so on, were very light skinned. Very rarely did you see a black person, black like me, in those kind of positions. When you saw people doing hard work, it was black people. You never saw white people or light skinned people doing hard work. The lighter skinned people did less menial work and, of course, the white people did no menial work whatsoever. I never saw a white man work. In fact, I very often wondered how they lived, because they didn't seem to work. Well, I never saw them work, anyway, and that was my impression of what Jamaican society was. And I didn't regard myself as Jamaican, I simply regarded myself as a black person, even from as a child.'[10]

'There was English, then the kind of Portuguese people, then the coloureds and the Asians and then the black people came at the bottom of the rung. I was like them. In the so-called coloured class, yeah, people of mixed race. My father was a West Indian, my mother was Anglo Asian. So we definitely had privileges over the people of purely black descent. It's only when I came to England that I realised, fortunately, that I was, in fact, black. And people referred to me as black, you know. It seemed strange when I came to England.'[11]

'The Governor was white, the head of the Jamaica government really was white, the Financial Secretary and Treasurer was white. And you sort of grew up with, as long as these people did their three or four year tour of duty in Jamaica and they went back to

---

[9]   Interview with Ben Bousquet. Ben Bousquet came from St Lucia in the eastern Caribbean, and arrived in Britain in 1957. He settled in Notting Hill, became an active trades unionist, a North Kensington councillor and a prominent anti-apartheid activist.

[10] Interview with Vince Reid.

[11] Interview with Cy Grant.

England, another white man would come and take his post. So you just accepted the fact that these posts were just for white men.'[12]

'From my point of view, if you did not know better, it was alright, as long as you had law and order. It didn't matter whether you had education, welfare, food or not, as long as you did not disturb the peace. Only about two per cent of the population had higher education, if your parents had money, result in that the opportunities were very limited. And, to the best of my knowledge, I would say ninety per cent of the people were farming or farming industry. And in farming in the colonies, you do not control the market. The outlook was limited. Life was totally dictated by Britain. For example, if you wanted to buy a bicycle, you could not buy a Japanese Red Knight, although the Japanese would like to sell to you. The British Raleigh you had to buy, because the Governor would not allow the British traders to have Japanese Red Knight. Everything you did was geared to Westminster. There is a song to say that if you had a good cow, in the end it will go to Westminster; if you're a good cricketer, in the end, like Learie Constantine, you would come to England. So your whole outlook was British oriented, because they rule. The schoolbooks, the missionaries and everything was the British mentality. You could not be good on your own. Your good was not good. Your good had to be British.'[13]

Escape from the islands: Garvey, Moody and Pitt

The problems of race, class and identity in the Caribbean had another, more positive, aspect. In all the islands, as in British Guyana (Guyana) and British Honduras (Belize), the inhabitants were always conscious of being part of a structure that stretched round the globe. So the context of Caribbean life was never parochial. The imagination that young men and women brought to thinking about their future was shaped by the determination to

[12] Interview with Connie Mark. Connie Mark joined the WRAC in Jamaica and worked as a medical secretary until she came to Britain in 1954 to join her first husband, the professional cricketer Stanley Goodrich. Subsequently she worked for the NHS in west London until retirement.

[13] Interview with Sam King. Sam King came from Jamaica and joined the RAF, arriving in Britain in 1944. After the war he went back to Jamaica, then returned to Britain on the *Windrush*. He joined the Post Office and became active in local politics. He was elected to Southwark Council in the early eighties, becoming Mayor of Southwark in 1983.

make their mark on the world outside. The more talented they were, the more eager they were to propel themselves out of the region. Predictably, the network of ideas which fuelled the Civil Rights era in the USA or which influenced the first leaders of African independence were often the creation of Caribbean ideologues. For example, Marcus Garvey, the father of black nationalism and the best known, most influential black activist of the twentieth century, was born in rural Jamaica.

The career of Garvey, who became the most famous Jamaican in the world – that is, before the musician Bob Marley – was like a template for the ambitious Caribbean. Born in 1887, he qualified as a printer, led a strike at the age of twenty, then turned from union politics to public speaking and agitation about the racial barriers he encountered. Later on he travelled in Central and South America and started the Universal Negro Improvement Association (UNIA). In 1916 he moved to the USA, in time for the industrial boom in the Northern cities which drew half a million black people from the American South and the Caribbean. A charismatic speaker, he preached economic independence, pride of race and the need for black Americans to return to Africa. He was deported to Jamaica in 1927, but he never settled there again. Instead he moved to England and died in London in 1940.*

Garvey was extraordinary, but in at least one way he was a typical Caribbean. The normal trajectory for the talented young man in the colonial British West Indies was to leave. The sooner, the better. The labour force was, in any case, highly mobile; until the middle of the century, going abroad to study was a routine climax to an educational career, and the swiftest route to the higher reaches of any profession was through the portals of a British or American university. For blacks, however, career opportunities under a colonial administration were strictly limited and, as a general rule, those who were successful abroad did not come back.

The urge to leave the Caribbean wasn't always driven by a racial consciousness. Sometimes it was to do with a different kind of self fulfilment, which simply couldn't be achieved in the region. The sculptor Ronald Moody, for instance, came from the opposite end of Jamaica's social scale to Garvey. He was born in 1900 into one of the light skinned families of doctors and lawyers which Garvey regarded as the enemy. His family discouraged his artistic leanings and, taking the line of least resistance, he set out in 1923 to study dentistry in London. But visiting the British Museum one day 'he "turned left instead of right" and first encountered Egyptian art. He was transfixed by "the tremendous inner force, the irresistible movement in stillness, which some of the pieces possessed". At that moment he knew he would become a sculptor, no matter what sacrifice it entailed.' He qualified as a dentist and practised for a few years, but subsequently became one of the most highly respected sculptors on the international stage. He revisited Jamaica for the first time in 1963, forty years after he had left, and although his work was purchased by the Jamaica National Gallery and the country heaped him with its most prestigious awards for his art, he never returned there to live. He died in London in 1983.**

Garvey and Moody represented groups motivated by a specific kind of frustration, but they were also followed, at one time or the other, even by those people who might have expected, in the normal run of things, to achieve prominent status within the region.

David Pitt was born in 1913 in Grenada, and won one of the many annual scholarships which sent young Caribbeans to universities in Britain, and which was the start of a process of grooming them for high office. He studied medicine at Edinburgh and, after qualifying in 1938, went to the Caribbean with the intention of getting involved in its politics. He practised in St Vincent and Trinidad, rather than in Grenada, and became President of the West Indian National Party, which was formed in the hope of creating a West Indian Federation. The federation didn't happen and, after the war ended, he returned to Britain. Entering British politics in 1959 with a failed bid for the Parliamentary seat in Hampstead, he was created Baron Pitt in 1975 and died in London in 1995.***

The careers of these men demonstrate that the relationship between the Caribbean and the outside world was like a pump which pushed and pulled people round and out of the region. In the first half of the century 150,000 Jamaicans – about ten per cent of the population – left permanently for the USA and Central America. The Second World War accentuated this process. Before the war, getting out of the region required a more than average level of energy, qualifications or talent. For the average Caribbean the prospect entailed an initial investment which was hard to come by, years of hardship, and possibly, a permanent separation from family and friends. Recruitment to the armed forces during the war, however, made all these concerns irrelevant and threw down the traditional barriers.

For the young men who flocked to join the British Forces one reason to leave was as good as another. There was very little to hold them in the region while going abroad offered new prospects of adventure and advancement. They had no account of national self interest to inhibit them. In the atmosphere of the time patriotism was firmly linked with the need to defend Britain.

'When England was at war, we were at war'

'On my second trip to Buenos Aires, the night we left Sentas, on the way to Montevideo, the war started and as a coincidence one of our engines blew up that night, we all thought the ship had been torpedoed and we made for our life jackets. However, it was an explosion in the engine room and the ship stayed in Buenos Aires for three weeks for repairs. After the second week they put a sign up saying that all the British subjects had to take the ship to London because the Admiralty had called for the ships and the Americans – it was a British ship but a few Americans working on the ship – went back to New York. So that's how I happened to come here, working on that ship called the *Eastern Prince*. And I sailed into Woolwich docks, 26 October 1939. So I got here about six weeks after the war started and I served during the war in the Merchant Navy.'[14]

'I felt that I wanted to see a bit of the world, I couldn't have afforded to have gone to university, and joining the air force was one way of my getting out of Guyana and seeing the rest of the world. Purely and simply. I don't think it had anything to do with patriotism or anything like that. It was an adventure. I was a young man. And I think flying aeroplanes is always seen as very glamorous and I thought the opportunity presented itself for me to be a fighter pilot. Wonderful. So I joined up. There was no problems with that.'[15]

'England was being pulverised in the first stage of the war. If you stayed here, and heard about Coventry being bombed, you felt you had a duty, for one. Plus, one day at a dentist's chair, I picked up a copy of *Mein Kampf*, I was browsing through it. I came across a passage where Hitler described black people and Jews as semi-developed, anthropoidal, that sort of thing. Very derogatory terms. And, as a young man, I said, To hell to with you. If that's the way you think, I am going to fight this war. I am going to join

---

[14] Interview with Earl Cameron. Earl Cameron was born in Bermuda and came to Britian in October 1939 as a seaman and joined the Merchant Navy. Later on he toured with ENSA (the Entertainment National Service Association), entertaining the troops abroad. After the war he became the best-known black film actor in Britain, appearing in some of the most notable 'problem dramas' made at the Ealing film studios, such as *Pool of London*, *Sapphire* and *Flame in the Streets*.

[15] Interview with Cy Grant.

the Air Force and I'm going to shoot your tail off and come back home, and show you who's a semi-developed anthropoid – that's the sort of immediate movement I had. So, we left and went to England, joined the RAF there. That was that.'[16]

Wartime recruitment had introduced a new element to the region. In the hundred years since Emancipation resources in the Caribbean had failed to match expectations. So the moment the Panama Canal project was announced people from the islands began migrating there. In comparison with working in the USA, Central and South America, Europe had been a closed shop. People in the Caribbean were aware of being one element in a global structure managed by Britain, but they had always been on the receiving end. This time the message was different from anything that had gone before. Britain needed the Caribbean and its people. But it would be unjust to assume that the response of the region was the product of some unreconstructed feudal cringe. From the earliest days it was apparent that the threat Hitler posed in Europe was equally a threat to the Caribbean: and, in the circumstances, the people of the region understood that to defend Britain was to defend their own interests. In the present crisis everyone was in it together. At yet another level the concerns of the outside world broke into the everday life of the Caribbean; which affected everyone, even the children in rural villages.

'. . . the teacher would read you everything that was happening in the war. Some made sense, some didn't make sense, because there were just places, people fighting. What caused the war, we didn't know. I didn't know at that age. All I knew, England was fighting, and it affected us because commodities that we would have had – like oil, and other things – we couldn't get. You'd have to go and queue for oil. If you want flour or rice, or you want the oil, because that's important, you would have to buy so much rice, so much flour, and you'd get this much oil. People who couldn't get oil would ask

[16] Interview with Dudley Thompson. Dudley Thompson came to Britain from Jamaica in 1940 to join the RAF. He flew missions as a bomb aimer and navigator. He bombed Nuremberg during a 'fearsome' raid in which ninety-three British aircraft were shot down. In London he met and became friends with a number of personalities in the Movement for Colonial Freedom, such as Kwame Nkrumah, Jomo Kenyatta, George Padmore and T. R. Makonnen. As a result he was first chairman of the legendary Pan African conference at Manchester in 1945, at which the leaders of the anti-colonial movement began outlining their plans. After the war Thompson went back to Jamaica, but returned to Oxford as a Rhodes scholar in 1947. Subsequently he entered politics in Jamaica and became Minister of Foreign Affairs under the first Michael Manley administration.

whoever is going to get them oil, and with being small, nobody noticed me and they would send me several times, and I would buy rice, flour, oil and pass the bottles back. So, that was hard. Then the teacher said, they're fighting in Abyssinia, they're fighting in Egypt, they're fighting here, Britain is losing the war, what can we do? So, it said, every piece of scrap iron was to be collected and brought to this cove. We never used electric irons, they were flat irons – and I'm sure some of the good irons were taken up and put into the schoolyard as that.

'We were taught that Kingston had one of the world's six best harbours, meaning that the ships couldn't just sail in, they had to be piloted in and out. Then came the news submarines are seen outside Kingston, and there were nets, you know, out there, to prevent them coming in. Then came the news that the Zeppelins are flying, and everybody, it was just parrot fashion, "Zeppelins are coming, Zeppelins are coming." Then they say, When we toll the bell it means we must have a blackout, even up in the mountains, and that frightened me. And my grandmother, she walked with a limp, and I loved her dearly, and all I wanted to do, how could I save her? Could she run fast? And we had, like, a little hill, and it overgrown with bramble, and underneath there was a tunnel, and I would think of things to put in it. And, you know, at the first toll of the bell, I would lead her to it, and would stay there, and I'll protect her, you know. Because, don't forget, planes used to fly over, and we didn't know if they were enemy planes.'[17]

'Every school had a tin at the opening, and all the children would bring – in those days, you had pounds, shillings and pence, and halfpennies and farthings – and all your small change that you had, you would drop it in these tins. And then, that's when I learned to knit, actually. We knitted blankets to send here for the people that needed it. We knitted things for babies, booties and coats and things. We did a lot of knitting and we collected quite a lot. I mean, I would make cakes, for argument's sake, and the money that I made from those cakes, I'd put it in a little tin that the money would be collected and sent for the war effort. So, everything, all your mind was just the war effort, the war effort.

[17] Interview with Tryphena Anderson. Tryphena Anderson came from Jamaica in 1952. She landed at Liverpool and went to live in Nottingham where she trained as a nurse.

'If you look at a map, you'll see that Jamaica is the British island that's nearest to the coast of America, so we knew, when we were told that the Germans wanted to capture us, because it would just be a stepping stone to the coast of America. That is why the Americans had a big influence in Jamaica, they had a big camp, as it were, and they had a lot of soldiers there, because they were protecting their interests. Another thing is that a lot of things we didn't have in Jamaica, like, we didn't have oil, and in the country parts they needed oil for the lamps because there was no electricity. We don't grow rice, we got our rice from the then British Guyana, and a boat was coming to Jamaica, and that boat was torpedoed, so we were out of rice for a long time. And to tell a Jamaican not to have rice and peas on a Sunday, it wasn't the same having spaghetti and peas, you know, so we missed our rice. And if a boat was coming again, and that was torpedoed, we were short of oil for the lamps. And, of course, we improvised by putting the oil in a ordinary bottle with a cork, and every time it goes out we'd have to turn the cork over to ignite the thing, and a lot of people got their head and eyebrows and things singed, especially the kids, they have to be watching them.

'So we knew there was a war on. Plus the fact, we had a sign up downtown that said the names of people missing or people reported dead. And every time you go to the main street, which is King Street, today you might say a name, tomorrow you'd go and you might see one of your relations either dead or reported missing. And then I had to meet the troop ships coming back, as the senior medical secretary. And you see young men leaving hale and hearty, and you see them coming back from the war zones, you know, blind, one foot. One man came, he was a pilot and he was flying high over Germany, and all the tops of his fingers were frostbitten. And, you know, as a young person, like I was at the time, those things stick in your mind, because you can't imagine that anybody could get frostbitten and lose all the tops of their fingers, things like that. So we knew there was a war on and it affected us quite a lot.'[18]

'Papa was very involved in those things, you know, collecting scrap iron for Britain and helping the young men to be ready and enlisting them, and so on. So I knew it was happening, although I

[18] Interview with Connie Mark.

wasn't old enough to appreciate what it was all about. It was never seen as going out there to die, it was about going to defend England and coming back.'[19]

* Marcus Mosiah Garvey was born 17 August 1887 in Jamaica, and died 10 June 1940 in London. He organised the black nationalist movement of the 1920s in the United States. Garvey went to New York City in 1916 and began recruitment for his Universal Negro Improvement Association (UNIA). Its program was to unite black people through establishing their own country and government in Africa. Garvey was a magnetic speaker who dressed in a showy uniform modelled on the imperial administrators of the time, and led his followers in parades through Harlem. In 1921 he claimed nearly one million followers.

Although Garvey's ambition outstripped his capacity to realise his visions, black politics and culture both in Africa and the diaspora were deeply influenced by his work and his writings. He was a major influence on the first post-independence wave of African leaders, especially Kwame Nkrumah, and he was the primary inspiration behind the Rastafarian movement.

** Ronald Moody was born in Jamaica in 1900 into a family of doctors and lawyers. In 1923 he travelled to London to study dentistry at Kings College. By 1938 he moved to Paris, having held critically acclaimed one-man shows in Paris and Amsterdam. He became a fixture in the Paris art world, but in 1940 he and his wife were forced to flee, just two days before the Germans took the city. He spent the next year and a half on the run in Occupied France, and was eventually smuggled back to England by the Resistance. After the war ended he set up his studio in Redcliffe Square in London's Chelsea, where he spent the next thirty-six years. (Unpublished monograph by Cynthia Moody.)

*** David Pitt was born 13 October 1913 in Grenada. He attended Grenada Boys' School and, when he won the Grenada scholarship which allowed its holder to study abroad, he chose to study medicine at Edinburgh University. In 1938 he left Scotland with the stated intention of becoming involved in Caribbean politics. At the time, British Caribbean dreams of independence were wrapped up with the idea of a Caribbean federation. Like many of the trade unionists and intellectuals in the region, David Pitt was a passionate advocate of federation and, like his fellow idealists, he regarded the whole of the Caribbean, rather than just any one island, as his home and his political responsibility. But Federation was slow to be realised, and, disillusioned, Pitt sailed for England, after the end of the Second World War. By the fifties, he had established his surgery in London's Gower Street, close to what was then a major area of immigrant settlement around Euston and Camden Town. In 1959 he was selected to stand for Parliament in Hampstead. According to the electoral trends, he should have won. Instead he lost, and no one was in any doubt that he had lost because he was a black man. This view was confirmed years later when, in 1970, he stood in Clapham South, defending a Labour majority of 4,176 and was defeated by 3,120.

Pitt's failure at the Parliamentary polls, however, did not defeat him. He was elected in Hackney for a seat on the old London County Council a couple of years later, and when the LCC was replaced by the Greater London Council, he sat on the GLC from 1964–77, serving as chairman in 1974–5. In 1975 he was created Baron Pitt of Hampstead, the area where he had his first surgery. In 1977 he was appointed chairman of the Community Relations Council, accepted the chair of Shelter in 1979, and was elected President of the British Medical Council in 1985.

[19]   Interview with Ros Howells.

2

_____❖_____

'I didn't expect it, and I don't expect it in terms of material redress, but when I do see anniversaries like VE Day anniversary, and I see these victorious marches, I don't see enough of the people, sometimes not even mentioned, and it hurts me, because we lost some good men. We lost some very good friends out there who went out, you know. I saw Ashburn run right into a hill and blow up in a Spitfire. Roy Ashburn, a very good pianist from Jamaica College here. One day, it was a bright day, and they were flying in formation, he went right into a mountain, just blown up. There was Toro Tucker from Tucker's Avenue, one of the very first ones to join. There was Bunting from Biggin Hill, Battle of Britain. There was Baden, again, in Germany, immediately after the war, when the army of occupation was in Berlin, he was flying, and he just had an accident on the aerodrome itself, after VE Day, and died. And there was Billy – I could name a few of them – Billy Edwards. Billy Edwards, who was a policeman in Albon Town. He got shot down twice. He got shot down once in the sea, he was rescued. And the second time, of course, he just shot down, he was gone. We did our bit, we did our bit. And DFC and bar, I mean we all got medals and so on, but because of those men and quite a few more, I'd have liked to have seen a greater recognition of what the West Indies did to contribute. We fought as men.'[1]

'I very much doubt if I'd give myself up to what has happened eventually. They'd have had to drag me by the feet, screaming. I looked forward to the experience when I was young but, you know, I wouldn't do it now, and had my son been young enough now and he asked me if he should join the services, I'd probably tell him No. Although it may be better, but I'd tell him No. There are too many things that were happening and are still happening, although a lot of them are hidden, but they're still happening. But they need the bodies, you know, to take the place of those who are knocked off,

[1] Interview with Dudley Thompson.

so they would use the bodies like they did me. But I very much doubt
if I'd come here in peace time that anyone would have said, "Oh
come on, we welcome you into the RAF." They needed the bodies,
so they took us. Because I didn't know then what I know now, I
came rushing over. But I wouldn't do it today.'[2]

'We Did Our Bit'

The wartime experience of the Caribbean servicemen was complex and
variable, but it is also clear that it was that experience which was responsible
for the structure and the pace of Caribbean immigration. Over a period of
six years, there were two very distinct strands of recruitment from the
Caribbean.

The first group travelled to Britain to enlist during, or before, 1940 and
came from what could be roughly described as an existing officer class.
These were the children of the professionals and administrators, who, a
decade later, were going to create the pressure for independence. They
already represented a high level of social and educational achievement and
their motivation was strongly flavoured by the desire for adventure, as much
as by the desire to escape. Implicit in all their futures was the intention of
going abroad for their further education and, for some of them, the war was
a short cut. These were among the most talented, most energetic products of
the Caribbean population, and intensely conscious of their own worth.
None of them intended to leave their relatively comfortable homes and
careers merely to enlist. Instead, they set out to join the most glamorous
elite fighting force available – the fighter pilots of the RAF.

The Battle of Britain hugely enhanced the reputation of the RAF, but
even before then the pilots and their crews – the 'Brylcreem boys' – were
being touted as the finest, most admired examples of British manhood. On
the German side, Nazi propaganda extolled the Luftwaffe as the most
admirable of the Aryans and the competition between 'racial types' was an
underlying theme at that stage of the conflict. It was an atmosphere which,
both at the time and later on, made it unlikely that British propagandists
would be eager to advertise the multi-racial aspect of the gallant 'few'.

These early recruits had to be exceptionally qualified to achieve their goal,

---

[2] Interview with William Naltey.

and they were also obliged either to pass various tests or to acquire a prior training as pilots, then to make their own way to Britain before they could enlist. Once they were in the RAF, however, they had become members of a unique club and, as such, they were more or less exempt from racist difficulties, protected by their rank and by the prestige of their service.

'At the beginning nearly all of us who came, came over to fly, and, subsequently most of the West Indians who came over, came as ground crew. There were many, many thousands of West Indians here in the RAF. I think the majority were from Jamaica probably, and we didn't have so many ground crew coming from Trinidad, we had a few but not very many. The majority of the ground crew who came were from Jamaica. We had a few from Trinidad, one of them of course was Macdonald Bailey, the sprinter. But most Trinidadians came to fly.

'If you wanted to join the RAF, you could. There was a light aeroplane club which existed before the war, and that's where the training was done. And we also had a Fleet Air Arm contingent in Trinidad, and we did some lectures at the Fleet Air Arm, so that there was encouragement to that extent, see. The Fleet Air Arm helped, but 250 of us from Trinidad wanted to come and fly with the RAF.

'I remember, I think it was my *Kennedy's Latin Primer* and my *As You Like It*, I wrote my name on the flyleaf of these books: Flight Lieutenant P. N. U. Cross DFC. To me that was the height of anybody's ambition, to be a Flight Lieutenant in the Royal Air Force and to get the DFC. Most of my friends thought I was mad, but we were already involved in that, like almost every other colony in those days, Trinidad contributed a large amount of money to buy aeroplanes, and there was, in fact, a Trinidad squadron. I think they were Spitfires. It was a fighter squadron I know. Jamaica did the same and there was a Jamaica squadron, 139 Squadron of bombers, which I eventually joined. There wasn't any Jamaican on it. I was the only West Indian. It was a very cosmopolitan squadron. We had Poles, we had a couple of Indians, English of course, Welsh, Scottish and Scandinavians. We had a couple of Dutch. It was a very cosmopolitan squadron, so that we knew that Trinidad had contributed money to buy, equip the squadron of fighters. So to that extent we were involved in the war even before I came here. But we were not encouraged actively. We did not, in fact, get into the RAF until we got here. Then we enlisted. We came over as civilians.

'We were treated very well, people were welcoming. One thing is we were in uniform, you know, within the first week of getting here we were in uniform. And the whole atmosphere was completely different then, I mean not only towards black, but in the society generally. People were curious, children would stop you. Almost impossible to walk through a village without children stopping you to ask you the time, and you knew they merely wanted to hear you speak. I think there was probably a different attitude towards people who were flying in the RAF and those who weren't. I mean, you wore a flying beret so people knew you were flying, and this was a general attitude, particularly because of the Battle of Britain.

'There were one or two shocks. I remember we came over by boat and we landed at Greenock, and we were met by an RAF transport which took us into Glasgow and then we came down by train to London, and the first shock, there were a number of aircraftmen in this lorry which took us from the boat to Glasgow, and my first shock, being I suppose what you would call a gently nurtured middle-class Trinidadian, was the language. I mean I'd never heard it, normally, that sort of language being used, and that was the first shock, which shocked all of us, you know. Of course you soon got used to this. Four letter words were normal currency. There appeared to be only one adjective known to these people. Now of course it's widespread. Even children, even in Trinidad, speak that way now.

'Of the 250 of us who came from Trinidad alone, fifty-two were killed. One of them was in class with me at school. In my class I think there were about six or seven who joined the RAF and most, I think nearly all were killed, one of whom I was particularly close to because I did Greek at school and there were only ten of us doing Greek. And, this chap with whom I was friendly, we went to different navigation schools, he was a navigator also, but we ended up on the same squadron, and he was killed on the seventh operation. And I was flying that night too, that day really because we were doing low level daylights at the time, and he was shot down crossing the coast, the enemy coast. I was on Mosquitoes, Pathfinder Force, bombing and target marking pathfinders, and I did altogether eighty operations. I was very lucky, he was killed on the seventh and I went on to do eighty. That was sheer luck. I crash landed I think five or six, seven times I think altogether, including one we landed in a quarry at Swanton Morley. I suppose one felt, you know, the strange thing is that when you're really young you feel immortal. That may well be a defence mechanism, but you do feel immortal, and you knew that obviously the possibility existed, that every time you got up in an aeroplane and flew over Germany you wouldn't come back. That possibility always existed. But the young feel they will live for ever. I still don't feel my luck will run out. I know it will one day, but I've always felt I have been lucky, and I've always felt lucky. It may well be when you're young this is a defence mechanism, you know. You know you're immortal, though deep down you know you're not.

'I didn't have mixed feelings, I thought it was regrettable it had to be done, but it had to be done so one did it. I think there was always a feeling, this feeling which I have and I can only speak personally, that, my young daughter always points out there is no such thing as a just war, but there is such a thing as a war for a just reason. And I felt, you know, I was doing the right thing, according to my own feelings, in trying to stop Hitler. I never felt I'm going to the aid of the mother country. Some people did but I would say the majority of us didn't. Reasons differ, but certainly for myself, you know, you're young, this was a tremendous adventure and you were doing it for the right reasons. Maybe that, I suppose we'll always be romantics at heart, I think I probably still am, but no question about it, I think it was worthwhile. It's extremely difficult, it's so, so very personal, what I did find, including the sort of British that we met here, there was never the feeling for what I've read of the First World War, that you were saving the world for democracy. I don't think there was that feeling, not overtly anyway. Deep down, maybe, you felt there was a way of life which could have been imposed on you which you didn't want imposed on you. But I don't think we felt that the end of the war was going to bring an upsurge of democracy and all men are brothers. You felt it during the war but you knew deep down it wasn't going to last; and there was, after the war, you knew there was going to be a dog-eat-dog kind of world.'[3]

'Well, I was earmarked. I was recruited from Guyana. Four Guyanese men were chosen. When things were getting pretty bad in England, they were losing aircrew, they started to recruit from the colonies. Prior to that they did not want black airmen, the Air Force

[3] Interview with Ulric Cross. Ulric Cross came from Trinidad, joined the RAF and flew bombers during the war. He was featured in a BBC wartime propaganda film as Flying Officer Ulric Cross. He flew eighty missions and crash landed seven times. After the war he qualified as a barrister and worked as a talks producer for BBC radio. He went to Ghana in 1956 when it became independent to work in the Attorney General's Office, then to Cameroon as Attorney General. Subsequently he went to Tanzania as a High Court Judge and Dean of the Faculty of Law at the university. In 1974 he returned to Trinidad as a High Court Judge.

definitely did not want black people flying in the Royal Air Force. A very good friend of mine, a fellow called Sidney Kennard, who was a pilot, had a pilot's licence in America before the war, had applied to join the RAF just after the war broke out, but they didn't want him. They said, "We don't recruit men of colour, obviously." And his father was an English doctor, white English doctor. Married an African West Indian woman. But when things got bad they changed the policy very rapidly and they started recruiting from the colonies and four Guyanese came over at the time that I came over to join the Air Force.

'I started off training. You've got to study things like navigation, whether you're going to be a pilot or whatever, you have to do basic navigation. And I was flying Tiger Moths for a while. And just before I completed my flying course, I was told that I was going to be made a navigator. At the time it didn't seem sinister at all to me. I really wanted to be a pilot, a fighter pilot. But, at the same time, what happened is that the old crew of observer in the Air Force was split into bomb aimer and navigator, so they needed a whole category of airmen to fly. And, because I had done particularly well as a navigator in my navigation courses, I was pulled off and put on a navigator's course. Which didn't please me very much, but, you know.

'I was shot down on my third mission. We were shot up, having bombed, and were coming back to England and we could hear there was a battle going on. Then we were attacked by two German fighter planes. And, at one point, we caught fire in one wing. And you could hear them, the mid upper gunner reporting fire on the starboard wing and gradually the fire spread right we were like a blazing comet. The pilot was trying to get the plane back to England, and he asked us what we felt. You know, by then we coming over Holland. He said, "You know, we can probably make it back to England, if she doesn't blow up." But after about ten minutes or so, he said, "I don't think we going to make it." So he turned back. And as soon as he turned back, the plane just started screaming down. And everyone was dashing to kind of positions to exit the plane. There's a hatch in the nose of the plane. Well, the plane just blew up and suddenly I found myself falling, you know. Strange sensation. But instinctively you know what to do. You release your parachute. But then the next sensation is of just swinging in space. And searchlights. It's very strange trying to recall that stuff.

'I was captured by the Germans, but what happened is that I landed in a field in Holland near a town called, believe it or not,

Arnhem. It was the longest day of the year in 1943. And it was quite bright and light and I lay out in the field in the corn or whatever it was there. And the next evening I saw a farmer working, and I went and attracted his attention, he recognised me straight away as Air Force, you know, because I had a uniform on, and they took me to a barn and the farmer and his wife came, fed me. And the entire village came and were looking and asking questions about the war. And then, about two or three hours later a Dutch policeman turned up and said he had to take me in because if he didn't these people would all be shot. And so he took me away to his home, made me more tea and about eleven o'clock that night the Germans drove up and took me away. And I was put in solitary confinement for about a week before I was dispatched to a holding camp.

'At the time I was not anxious. I didn't think about being a West Indian or that didn't come into it, I must say. But I was apprehensive because I was being interrogated all the time, pulled out every day, asked the usual questions. What is your name, your rank, squadron? Things like that, which you never gave. And then pushed back into solitary confinement.

'And then one day I was pulled out in a bright summer day and a press photographer came and took a photograph of me. And I was pushed back into the cell. Eventually, I was sent off. But when I did eventually get to a camp, months later – to an officer's camp because by then I was an officer in the Air Force – someone showed me a photograph of myself in this German paper. A member of the Royal Air Force of unknown race. And I still have a copy of that photograph, with a clipping from the newspaper with my photograph in.

'Well, suddenly the whole racial thing came into it. But, a strange thing, I was interviewed by the Commanding Officer of this particular camp and he was a strange man because he was very smart. Seemed a very refined German officer. You couldn't believe that he would have been in charge of a prisoner of war camp. You would have thought he would be at the front because he was such an elegant and polite man, and he questioned me. And I told him that I was from Guyana. He said that he had been to Guyana and that kind of changed how the Germans looked at me throughout, I think, because every time he saw me he kind of saluted. Which is quite nice. But I was a long time being in a prisoner of war camp, two years. But I read a lot and made many good friends. Friends I have today. The only racism that I encountered was from an American. American I don't

know what, he was a corporal or something like that who happened
to be in this holding camp. And he called me a nigger one or two
times, but I got nothing from the Germans. They didn't single me out
for any special treatment.[4] The guards were really despicable,
miserable creatures. We kind of felt very superior to them. No, no,
those guys, they shouted at everybody but then again, we were in
an officers' camp.

   'You're not mistreated as an officer, but of course there was
shortage of food. And sometimes you were very hungry. And it got
pretty dodgy towards the end of the war when the Russians
advanced, because the Russians actually came and liberated our camp.
The Germans had suddenly disappeared one day, and we were force
marched. It's a long story actually, let me pick it up. We were
evacuated from the camp that we had stayed in for the best part of
two years before the Russians actually came. And we were marched
through the snow for about a week, sleeping in kind of barns along
the way. I mean, put in a huge open kind of a prisoner of war camp
where there were thousands of prisoners from every single
nationality. There were Poles, Americans, you name it, from all over.
And then that's when things really got very bad. And then eventually
the Russians came and overran the camp. The night before they
actually came to the camp, the Germans had all disappeared. And
then it was pretty tough because we were in the centre of the fighting,
and we had to make out we had to go out foraging for food and
things like that. It was pretty grim the last bits of the war. And, in
fact, I had to escape from there, you know, from the camp,
unofficially. I left unofficially. It's a long story. I was a prisoner of

[4] Paradoxically, the Germans appeared to have treated the captured black RAF officers in more
or less the same way as their white colleagues. The only hint that their capture might have been
used to put over a characteristically Nazi propaganda message is the caption under Cy Grant's
photo in a German newspaper identifying him as being of 'unknown' or unclassifiable race. In the
circumstances this comment seems like a miracle of restraint, but none of the black RAF flyers seem
to have found anything to the contrary. According to Ulric Cross, 'Two of my friends were in fact
shot down and captured and were in prison camp. Cy Grant was a prisoner of war for some time,
and another friend of mine who died recently, Johnny Smythe, he was from Sierra Leone and he
married a West Indian, we were very friendly, in fact I met him when he came back from prison
camp and we studied together. We did law together, he also is Middle Temple, and he was also a
prisoner of war, and they say they were quite well treated as prisoners, there was no problem. They
were both officers and, you know, under the Geneva Convention officers cannot be made to work
in prison camp. I think the Germans were, for obvious reasons, fairly punctilious. There may be
exceptions about treatment, certainly of RAF officers, because I mean, you know, they didn't want
their own people treated badly when they were captured.' Ironically, it seems that the black RAF
prisoners of war were probably in greater danger of being badly treated by their American liberators
than by their German captors.

war for two years and, in a sense, that was the best thing that could
have happened to me because it turned out to be a kind of university
for me.'[5]

'I went to England in 1940 to join the Royal Air Force. There
were a few of us that were slipping away, because you couldn't go,
they were not recruiting from the colonies. In the early part of the
stage, in fact, it was difficult to get into the RAF. It was very difficult,
oh yes. You'll be surprised to know, it's not very well known, but
it was a stipulation in the early part of the war, for the first two,
three years of the war, if you joined the Royal Air Force, "Are you
of pure European descent?" Dr Moody's son, Major Moody,
eventually, Rondel, who was born in England, his mother was
English, he went to an English public school, he was an officer in the
cadet force. He was turned down for the Royal Air Force because
he was not of English descent. And I could name quite a few, it was
quite stipulating, "Are you of pure European descent?" They
changed it later on, because there were many people in the colonies
that wanted to go. In fact, there was a tremendous *impasse* at one
stage, the early stage, between the governors of the colonies and
the Colonial Office and the War Office, because the governors
found it difficult, in fact, embarrassing, that they had people who
wanted to fight and England was telling them No. But it changed
later on.

'Well, when I went to London it was 1940. Recruitment was
pretty hot, quite a few people going on. And when I came to the
questionnaire, "Are you of pure European descent?" I put, Yes. One
fellow, a sergeant who was in charge of the station, came up to me,
one of the old fellows, seasoned fellow from the last war, says, "Are
you of pure European descent?" I said, "Yes, take a blood test, try
it . . ." Oh, he's a difficult fellow. So I got in.

'Towards the end I did flying for the Pathfinder Force, where
you didn't count, each mission was on its own. There's one that
stands out very well, more than one, but there's one that always
comes back, and it's Nuremberg. I think it was '43. On that day we
lost more aircraft from the Royal Air Force than at any other day
up to then, I don't know if any after. But we lost, I think it was
ninety-three aircraft that night. It was a very bad night. Somebody

⁵ Interview with Cy Grant.

got wind that we were coming and they waited for us. And I remember it particularly because I lost a very good friend, Vivour, who was a Nigerian. We had been very close together, and then I had the difficulty of telling his intended wife, his fiancée, the difficulty, that he wasn't coming back home. I never forgot.

'At the early stages, we were very welcome, everywhere. We wore distinctive badges, you know, Jamaica, or Trinidad, as the case may be, and we were received, because there were so many – not just West Indians, you had Poles, you had France – and it was, "This is the gang come together to fight." We were very well received everywhere. And you are very, very impressed by those people who, every night, went down into those underground places, and slept there every night and came up with a joke on their mouth every day. It really impressed me, the fact that these are people who I'm fighting for – fighting with. Later on, towards the end of the war, it varied, you had a very different composition there. You had, instead of a few hundreds, you had thousands, and tens of thousands, coming from British Honduras, coming from other parts there. You had munition workers who are civilians, and you had the civilian forestry men, some forestry men came from British Honduras and Belize. So, with the multiplicity of them and people, I would say, of a low educational standard, things got quite different, they were not so well received, there were quite a few racial incidents took place."[6]

Given all the circumstances, this elite group of recruits would have been best suited to cope with post-war conditions in Britain, and their presence might have made a substantial difference to what happened over the next decade, because they possessed the self-confidence and the skills to have provided a buffer against some of the worst difficulties their countrymen encountered later on. Ironically, this was also the group which was the least likely to remain in Britain because they were eager to return and change the political landscape.

In comparison, the second group of wartime recruits came by different routes and emerged into a different environment. In 1943 and, more urgently, in 1944 the nature of the conflict changed. The emphasis shifted to the invasion of Europe. What Britain needed was support staff to service and maintain the front-line fighters while the invasion and bombing raids went on. So the second wave of recruitment was very different in tone.

[6] Interview with Dudley Thompson.

Ground crews were recruited in the colonies and came from a broader social spectrum; from rural communities comprising farmers and artisans. This was an unprecedented opportunity for them to travel abroad and to change the entire course of their lives. This time recruitment was by invitation and, instead of in hundreds, they came in their thousands.

The environment into which they emerged was that of the skilled and semi-skilled 'other ranks', focused on the military camps in which they did their training. By then life in Britain had settled into a grim routine, but the new recruits were greeted with more or less the same warmth as their predecessors had been. There was a notable difference, however. Their arrival coincided with the presence of large numbers of American troops with formal and established patterns of racial segregation and discrimination. In general the British population distanced itself from the American traditions of racial segregation and largely resisted its imposition, but, for the Caribbeans, the atmosphere created by the Americans was a fatal inhibition against any prospect of easy integration within civilian society. The result was that the experience of these later recruits was narrow and specific, largely confined to the services and to contacts with pockets of the working-class community.

'I think Jamaicans had the most support with personnel coming here from the Caribbean, from that area of the British Caribbean countries. We had about five to six thousand who had joined voluntarily in the ground crew, and about 300 air crews, plus the army, the British West Indian Regiment, and other individuals who had been attached to regiments in Britain. And don't forget we had also a number of young women who had joined the ATS[7] when they had started to recruit women to come along, and also the Women's Air Force. So there were quite a number of people who came over to support Britain at that stage.

'Well, I joined up just after eighteen years old. And it was announced in the Jamaican papers and also broadcast that they like to have young men to come along, to join the Air Force. So I went and volunteered, as so many of us did. There were no conscription, by the way. We were all volunteers, you know, nothing to say that we had to go. So I volunteered and a number of us did that at the same time and we had an adaptable test, by the way, to see whether you could take up any position as a tradesman or various senior position in the

---

[7] Auxiliary Territorial Service. Formed in 1939, the ATS was a non-combatant unit recruiting women for jobs such as radar operators, cooks and searchlight operators.

ground crew. I wasn't a member of the air crew, I was a member of the ground crew. I signed up as a teleprinter operator myself. I was in the printing business, I suppose it just came naturally, I went in as a teleprinter operator in the signals section. And then I came to England after that, we waited in Jamaica before we were transported here, because there were a lot of U-boats in that area at that same time, from Germany, coming into the Caribbean seas. So we had to wait quite a long time before we could travel to Britain.

'Landing in Liverpool we got off there and we met quite a few people who were standing on the dockside and waving and things like that. Then we travelled down to various other stations. In the first place we came to a camp for training, which was giving you all the various unarmed combats and various physical techniques of warfare, the training of the different type of ammunitions you're supposed to use. And that was for about three months. We called it the square bashing period. You had to drill regularly and do various exercises. Now we, at that moment, had not really met a lot of people from the public. We were now meeting people who were preparing our lives in the army and the air forces and the different type of things that you're expecting to do. However, eventually we had a visit to a place called Hunmanby Moor, which was a little village in Filey [Yorkshire]. And we begin to talk to a few people and some of them were running away from us. Some of them looked at us strangely. And that gave us the impression that these people were not used to us. There were a number of people asking where we from? What are we doing here? And how do we have Air Force uniform? They didn't realise there were people in the different islands who are British. So that was something that gave us another outlook now to say, well, we were not being recognised by these people, they don't know what we are doing here.'[8]

'I came to England in June 1944 as a member of the Royal Air Force. I was recruited in Jamaica, and spent about two weeks on camp before they were able to find us transport to take us across from Jamaica to Britain. We spent about a fortnight in what we would describe then as "shark infested waters" in the Caribbean and in the

---

[8] Interview with Laurie Philpots. Laurie Philpots joined the RAF and came to Britain at the age of eighteen in 1944. After the war he lived in Nottingham and qualified as a linotype operator. In the late fifties he moved to Welwyn Garden City, then worked for the Mirror Group in London's Fleet Street until his retirement.

Atlantic, before we landed in Virginia, United States, where we spent about a fortnight recuperating from our hazardous journey across. And then we had to make the journey from America to England now. It was just as traumatic, you know, every so often you've got emergencies, as if the enemy was launching torpedoes at you. But we landed here safely, on 1 June, Liverpool, without any incident.

'The buildings were terribly bad and dirty, the people they're a mixture, depends on where you are and where you go. You find a variety of reactions, different places, different counties, different towns. At first, we were looked upon as a kind of a curio, something that people have never seen and they want to have a good look at it. People might have seen the films, might see films of a black person in Africa, or America, but they never actually touched one or spoke to one. The few that they see in England is more or less those that they saw who are working on the docks in Liverpool or Manchester or Swansea or what, but they never actually see a crowd of black people in RAF uniform, walking down the street or in a bus, you know. So they were more or less curious to find out if really what they think is true of us. So, reactions were, you know, varied. I can say for sure that the people in Lancashire accepted us very, very well. I don't know if it is because of a tradition that they have, but we had no difficulty in going about in Manchester, or, for that matter, parts of Lancashire. They were quite helpful and cheerful and willing to give you any assistance that you need.

'Well, other parts of England, I would say, is different. If the people are used to seeing people of our sort, then they respond, if they don't, then they're a bit drawn back. I don't know if it is maternal instinct or not, but we find that the women were more cooperative and more than the fellows, the fellows more or less want to fight.

'I was involved once in, nowadays they would call it a brawl, or the police might describe it as an affray. It wasn't that bad. But we were confronted one day in Manchester, in the city centre. And there was a punch-up between British soldiers, West Indian RAF and Canadians and American soldiers and the Canadians were on our side. And we all had a punch up. We don't know how it started. I don't know if it was over a girl or not, I really couldn't say. But we were all in this mêlée in the centre of Manchester. And, I don't know, nobody got really hurt, anyhow. But I was involved in it.'[9]

---

[9] Interview with Euton Christian.

*   *   *

'Well, seventy-five per cent of what we saw on arrival in England is what we were expecting it to be, but the other twenty-five per cent was something strange to us, you know. And then, well, being in the Forces then, well, we didn't have to do much about civilian life, the mixing, because we arrive at Liverpool docks and then we got the train right up to Filey in Yorkshire where we had our initial training.

'They realised there was a war on and we'd come to help and the treatment was good. Colour, everything, it doesn't worry most of them you come over. You're coming to do something. They realised that you're being patriotic, because that was one of the main reasons why I come over when we heard about patriotism, what it is to love, and devotion of your country, it was good. They made us to feel as if we were at home. See, it was good. Not like what it is now. You know, those people, they went out of their way to do things for you, make you happy.

'I can remember one occasion, I was hitchhiking all the way from Tibenham to London for the weekend. I got a lift to Colchester in an Army lorry and after I got there this man came along in his Bentley with his wife, you know. "Come, a lift, come in here, man", and we were talking and we were talking all the way to London. Oh my God. That man, it made me feel so well to know that you're coming over to risk your young life, you know, in the war, to help us and all that. And we reach London, I say, "Well, sir, the nearest Underground will do me, because I can find my way." I was staying at the YM at Rondel Street, you know, off the Strand. He say, "Now here, man, you tell me exactly where you're going", and he took me right outside the YM. To that I said, "Thank you very, very much." Just like that. But now you wouldn't see anything like that. So those days you know they help you. People I remember on some unit where we were stationed, people send letter inviting you, because I can never forget this, it was at Hatfield. There was a little unit, we were an attachment there, and they wrote a letter to the Adjutant and asked – well, they call it the West Indian Regiment, you know – invite them to come at their homes for tea, you know? Invite you home for tea, 'cos they say, "Oh, we are all one. You're coming to England to help us, we must make you happy." But after a while, you know, all that changed.'[10]

---

[10]   Interview with Cecil Holness. Cecil Holness joined the RAF from Jamaica in 1944 and after the war re-joined for another four years. He went back to Jamaica and returned to Britain on the

* * *

'Now, the farm that I grew up on, it's a banana and coconut plantation. My father has been head man on it for many years, actually until he retires. But I never work on the farm myself. I have an engineering workshop background, and it was that kind of background I had from which I eventually joined the Air Force and come over here. I was twenty-three years old, and that was in 1944. When I came over I think I was rather lucky that I was posted into Fighter Command after I finished my training, and my unit was 17 Flight, 5015 Airfield Construction Squadron. And we were more or less a mobile unit. We had our own transportation, take our own equipment around with us wherever we go. And, consequently, we were a little unit on our own, a little team. We spent between four or five weeks on a camp, finish our job, and we move on. And so we were able to form what I would describe as a very good team relationship with that small group of people.

'I think it would be totally untrue for anybody to try and pretend that racism never existed in the service. But I suppose I escaped that, in a number of ways, during the war years. The short period, we were never settled at one unit too long for me to form too great a tie, where I spend a few weeks, we move on, spend another few weeks, we move on, and we are constantly on the move. As a matter of fact, I remember the very first unit that I was posted to, that there were five of us West Indians in that unit. And before we joined the unit, the Commanding Officer had the whole lot of them on parade and let it be known that if they don't make us welcome and feel like one of the team, he will come and have them hanged from the flagstaff himself, and there must be no nonsense about it.

'And I was particularly fortunate, because there was my corporal, a chap by the name of Frank, Corporal Frank Wheeler. He became almost my surrogate older brother. As a matter of fact, we kept in touch with each other over the years until he died, about a few years ago. I even go to his funeral. And, I remember, I was in a spot whereby I was placed in the guard room. And Wheeler was there at least twice a day to come and see that I was alright, and how was it, that I shouldn't be there, and vice versa, you know. So all these are part and parcel of what you experience.

Windrush. His wife Claire was the daughter of West Indian parents who had lived in Britain since the First World War, when his father-in-law had joined the British Army. He settled in London after leaving the RAF, worked as a motor mechanic and is now retired.

'It was in Nottingham, here, where I met my wife and her family. I couldn't ask for better. And there's a fascinating thing, my mother-in-law, the first time I met her, gave me a good telling off for keeping her daughter out until eleven o'clock at night. What kind of a young man am I? I should see her home much earlier than that. And she lived till eighty-nine, and actually die in the arms of my children, myself and my wife. My wife's father, he, as well, I couldn't ask for better. Her brother, and his wife and family, I couldn't ask for better treatment, either.

'And, then, I also met a family in a little village known as Weldon, in Northampton, the Raynes family. They are about the first family home in Britain that I spent some time with. And I'll never forget our meeting, another Jamaican and I, we left camp and was going to Kettering. We missed our bus. And there was a churchyard nearby, we went in there, just to walk around and look. You go in there, you get more historical information than you can imagine. And we walk under a lovely tree, and there were two graves there, nothing to indicate, and a wooden cross, and we stood looking at it. And I heard about that, "Oh, it's two Germans buried there." And we look up, and I said, "Why are they there?" And there was a lady and a girl, they understand, they said, "Well, their plane was shot down and they were Germans, their plane was shot down and, after they were pronounced dead, the villagers asked if they could take the body and look after it." And I promptly asked her why do you do that sort of thing? They said, "Well," the lady said, "well, we feel sure that if two of our sons, boys, were shot down over there, there would be people who'd know that they are somebody's son, and they would be prepared to do as much as we did." And then she invited us home for tea. And I shared many a happy evening with that family while I was stationed there. And we kept in contact for many, many a long year. I even went back, my wife and I, some years ago, to find those two graves, but by then, the verger told us, he took us to this spot and showed us and said they'd removed them to the cemetery somewhere in London and re-buried there.'[11]

'I came to England in 1944 because I'd joined the Royal Air Force. Nazi Germany was rubbishing Europe and the world and we, as a part of the British Commonwealth, which was Empire then,

---

[11] Interview with Eric Irons.

thought we should help the mother country. We were British.

'I was shocked when I came to England. We arrived in Greenock and it was winter. I came off the troop train and I stepped into about three inches of snow. And it remained on the ground for about one month. It was shocking. I remember the sergeant looking on, and I looked back to see and to examine, he said, "Move! It is snow."

'I can remember, on the troop train, the Salvation Army gave us a cup of tea and a bun, and I can always thank the Salvation Army for that. And when I see them today, asking for a penny, if I have two pennies, I give them one.

'I was fortunate. I met and worked with an RAF friend, Harry Challis. He invited me home. And right away, I became a part of the family. I met another fellow, Seagraves, from Nottingham, they invited me home. Once I was in Bulwell – which is, by the way, the banks of the Trent – I made myself useful. Mom and Pop had a shop at Mansfield Road, Nottingham, and I would lay the fire and clean the house and things like that before they returned. As a matter of fact, in 1946/47, the very bad winter, and the miners were on strike, there was no coal. We were breaking down fences or orange boxes. And I took a pram, because some women were going to Bestwood Colliery to get coke, and I went there and got the coke and, when Mum came back, the fire was laid, of course, coke, not coal, and made myself useful. So I was a part of the Seagraves family until this day. The same thing happened to Harry Challis, now lives at Shrewsbury. After fifty-three, fifty-four years, I'm a part of their family, they even called their grandson Sam.'[12]

'When I left Jamaica it was as a wireless operator/gunner. When I came here I tried to re-muster as a pilot, but they said, "You have to wait at least a year", and it wasn't really what I came for. I wanted to be involved, and they said again, "If you want to be involved early, you have to drop the wireless operator part and just become a gunner." So I dropped that too and became a gunner. So there I was, a gunner with Coastal Command. That meant submarine hunting and German shipping, you know, rather than bombing Germany, which was Bomber Command.

[12] Interview with Sam King.

'I am not sure that there was ever racism in the crew with which I served, but it had to be kept well hidden, naturally, because, well, they're ten of us whose lives depended on each other in case trouble ever came up. So, you know, I couldn't afford to make an enemy of you, or you of me while we were in the same crew. So from that point of view we more or less existed together as a sort of family, you know. Most of us went out. For example, I was in the Azores and on our days off the whole crew, except for one – and he was my very good buddy, we came from Jamaica together, he wouldn't go – but we all went into town, we had our drink and our food and enjoyed life together. And on the same island where we were there was also an American base, and they would invite members of the crew or peoples generally from our side over to enjoy there what they had. And believe me they had plenty.

'They shared the same base with us, you see, and they would come over and visit us and they would invite us over. Their invitation was much more enjoyable than ours, because they had everything. You would hardly think there was a war because they lived like civilians in America. Even the movies that they had were the most up to date because they'd bring them straight over and show them, even in England, you see. So ours was, perhaps, two, three years old; theirs was the most up to date. So it was a pleasure being invited by them for anything.

'Now, the Americans did not believe in their black troops enjoying the same things that they had in exactly the same way. They have ate the same food, but not in the same mess. You know, they'd see the same movies but I remember going to one of their cinemas once and I said, "Well this very strange, I don't see any black people here." So they said, "Look·behind you", and there they were up in a kind of crows nest, all of them, all the black troops. And yet here were I, sitting in the front with American officers. Huh? Hard to explain. They have funny ideas. They would treat me as a human being, but their own, you know, they'd probably kick him out if he came into where they were. Hard to understand how people behave like that, but naturally it is something with which you grow up and I suppose it's hard to get rid of.

'I was in Belfast once and we wanted to go to a dance hall. I were told that down the road there is one, you see. So off we went, and the fellow on the door said, "I am sorry, you can't come in." I said, "Why not?" He said, "Well, if I let you in and the Americans come along and they see you, they'll probably have a fight, or if they don't have a fight, they won't come and use our facilities any more." I said, "So what, it's nothing to do with us." Said, "This is the RAF, not American." Anyway, along came two American SPs – you know, patrols, the people who play policemen – anyway, along they came and they looked as though they were ready for trouble. Anyway, they came and this fellow said, "These two fellows want to go in." So they looked. "Ah well, sorry, there's nothing we can do about them", and they walked away. Now, as you can well imagine, if they were their own, they'd probably break their heads and throw them in the bushes, or something like that. I don't know if they were told to treat us differently or whether it was just a natural thing.

'Again, I was in Glasgow going to a dance hall and I was going up in the lift with this American black serviceman, we're chatting away and suddenly he disappeared: I'm talking to myself. Then I notice that two American officers had come into the lift. Now I'm still in the lift. They haven't said anything to me. But they were laughing at the way this fellow suddenly jumped out of the lift and disappeared when they came in. You know, they had great fun thinking, "Oh, see, see that bastard jump out?" I couldn't understand it you know, it was something new to me until then. It took a lot of getting used to, I assure you.

'The only West Indian I was likely to meet on a regular basis were those who were in the flying service. Otherwise there were very, very few blacks that I would see on the stations to which I went. There was just this one other, and we happened to be in the same crew, and we were the only two on the squadron at the time. He went on to rejoin the RAF. When we all went out together he didn't used to go. He didn't. No. No. And you wonder why? Well, that's because he was as black as your trousers, and I think he was conscious of it. Nobody stopped him, he could do what he liked because we, as I say, we worked as a crew; we lived as a crew; on the station we sat and drank as a crew. But I think, now that it comes back, I didn't think about it at the time, but he must have been more conscious than I was of the problems that he could have. But nobody stopped him. He just stopped himself.'[13]

At the time there was practically no formal contact between the two different groups of West Indian servicemen. Even after the conflict had ended the

[13] Interview with William Naltey.

members of the first group – the professionals and officers – are notable for their absence in the public perception of what was to become the black community. This was partly to do with the social atmosphere of the time. More importantly, their numbers had shrunk significantly. The casualty rate, considering their relatively small numbers, was high, and the survivors were eager to carry on where they had left off on their career path.

3

After the war economic conditions in the Caribbean worsened. European reconstruction was the immediate priority of the major economic powers, and the boom associated with wartime bases – increased shipping and a high demand for raw materials – faded away. To the men who were returning from the war, life in the Caribbean seemed slower, smaller and poorer than it had before, with even fewer opportunities for advancement or self expression, and governed by the same oppressive structure of imperialist control. They had been to the centre of the world, bombed it, and watched their friends die in the conflagration. They knew what it felt like to live in London and Leicester and Lancashire. They had seen new and surprising possibilities, and it was now impossible to control their aspirations in a Caribbean colony. For example, the carefully nurtured structure of ideas which bound together race and class in the Caribbean colonies was exploded by the servicemen's very first experiences in Britain. White Englishmen and Englishwomen were exactly the same kind of human beings as black Caribbeans.

'I'd been a colonial all my life here, in Jamaica and, in fact, not even in the city of Kingston, in the country. So the view in the colonies is that the white man is on top in every respect. The civil servant seniors are all European. Governor lives in King's House, you never see him. And King's House is the Governor's residential, just next to Buckingham Palace in the hierarchy of things. You hear about that. And after Buckingham Palace comes Heaven, that's the order of things, you see what I mean. So, when you leave, you leave with that sort of setting in your mind. And you're used to seeing the white man boss. When you go to England, you find that it is not like that. You get a sudden immediate shake-up when you find an Englishman that can't read and write, you know, it shakes you. And you go and you find a coal heaver, you know, at the place, working, and you don't expect to find that. So you get a psychological change, a change over, that this is the real world.'[1]

[1] Interview with Dudley Thompson.

*   *   *

'English people you see out in Jamaica, you see them as people who are highly intelligent, and I always assumed that because of my background, the sort of thing that I'd been taught in school about England, England would be teaching people here about the colonies, where I am from. And I was shocked at the gross ignorance when I came here, so few people, the only thing they knew of Jamaica is Jamaica where the rum come from, and they haven't got any other idea about the place.

'I remember we landed in Scotland, and while on the train several things struck me, the first time I see white children poorly clothed. And when we stop along the siding, will be asking us for cigarettes and nylons, and that sort of thing. To see a white child begging from us, it was something I'd never dreamed of.'[2]

The Real World: After The War

Revelations of this sort had all kinds of repercussions. For political radicals like Dudley Thompson these new insights intensified the urgency of the post-war campaign for independence. For the typical Caribbean of the time the logical answer was to escape. In those days the answer to the question, 'Why leave the Caribbean?', was another question, 'Why not?' And to that one there was really no answer.

In the present day, popular and 'common sense' accounts describe this first group of Caribbean emigrants as having been 'brought' to Britain, rather as if they were naive and passive, manipulated by unseen puppet masters. Nothing could be further from the truth. If they were moved by anything it was their own drive to escape the boundaries of colonialism, allied to a unique combination of historical circumstances, the most important of which was to do with the logistics of travel.

Up to that point, and in spite of the colonial linkages, passenger travel directly between the Caribbean and Britain was expensive, difficult and sporadic. The normal route would have been via New York and across the

[2] Interview with Eric Irons. Eric Irons grew up on a farm in Jamaica, joined the RAF and came to Britain at the age of twenty-three. He stayed in the RAF after the war, serving in Malta and Egypt, then settled in Nottingham and worked at the MOD's Central Ordnance Depot at Chilwell. Subsequently, he worked for the WEA and, in 1962, was appointed as a magistrate in Nottingham.

Atlantic. In the aftermath of the war, however, there were a number of former troop ships ploughing across the seas, taking up and depositing servicemen and civilians in various parts of the Empire. The *SS Empire Windrush*, by way of the Atlantic and the Mexican Gulf, was the first to pass through the Caribbean in 1948.

'Well, Jamaica was a colony and, having been to the library and read a few books, I did not want to live in a colony. So I asked to be enlisted again into the Royal Air Force. They said that I had to be married to an English girl – I don't think I would do that just to stay – or if I was going to a college or university here. So, I was shipped back on the *SS Allemanzora*. When I went back to Jamaica it was shocking. Men who had been Home Guards, men who were working in the American factories and farms, men who were on the Panama Canal, and all of us, I would say 30,000 men were thrown back without any planning. It was bad and, having examined the situation, it's not a question of producing. I am from a farming background. You may have produced bananas, but if they don't buy them, they're just rotten. And I decided that my children would not grow up in a colony, so I came back on the *SS Empire Windrush* on 22 June 1948.'[3]

'What caused me to be on the *Windrush*, is that I – by virtue of signing on [in the RAF] for a further four years – was due some home leave. I went over there in November 1947. I took a ship from Bristol, and this shipping company asked me the colour of my skin, the colour of my hair, what shade I am, and all that nonsense. It's a fact. So, I suppose it was to segregate me on the ship, I don't know. But because, in those days, shipping was very hard to come by – you know, not many boats knocking about . . . with the war – well, they all got knocked off in the Atlantic. But this was 1947, everything was a bit quieter now. But I still got these forms. I can recall being very, very annoyed, but I had to answer these ridiculous questions. Anyway, I went home. I was supposed to be there for two months, they couldn't find me a ship to come back for four months, so I've stayed six months.

'So, this *Empire Windrush*. I was told it was a captured German trooper, and they must have dug it out from somewhere. And they

[3] Interview with Sam King.

send it to Jamaica to collect all the West Indians who were on leave then from Barbados, Trinidad, Guyana. So they all assembled in Jamaica where the ship was, to take us back; if not, we would spend another six months on leave again, and they've got to pay us for it there. So, the ship had a capacity of about four, perhaps five, six hundred. And the RAF was only about three – two, three hundred people – so they had extra capacity. So they say, well, sort of make some money, they offered these extra berth capacity to the people who wanted to come to England, because they could just come, you see, no stopping them, no immigration control. They could just come if they wanted. So people came over and they paid, I think, £28 to come over, to fill up the space of the ship.'[4]

There had been a brief hiatus during which many of the servicemen ended their service working in some kind of liaison role with the armed forces or the Civil Service. When the *Windrush* people arrived they were greeted by black ex-Army Civil Servants like Johnny Smythe and Ivor Cummings. Ulric Cross worked for the Civil Service and the BBC before becoming Attorney General and a High Court judge in independent Africa and the Caribbean. Dudley Thompson came back to Oxford as a Rhodes Scholar, became part of the movement for colonial independence and, later, a government minister in Jamaica. Cy Grant became a household name on TV in Britain and an international screen actor. The general pattern was one in which most members of this group resumed their studies and, influenced by the anti-colonial current of the time, began preparing to replace the British rulers in the Caribbean and Africa.

'Well, I came off flying in November '44, before the end of the war, and I went to the Colonial Office. The Colonial Office had set up a department to deal with the further education and training of colonials who were in the war, after the war. And I headed that department, as a liaison between the Colonial Office and the services and, in fact, I was one of the beneficiaries of that system in that I did law as a result of that. And quite a lot of people, certainly a lot of Trinidadians I know – I guess Peter Byner did architecture, his brother did medicine – a lot of people did professions, mainly.

'Well, as part of the job, when West Indians were charged, you know, I would go up sometimes and defend them on charges, those

⁴ Interview with Euton Christian.

who were in the RAF anyway. I was not a lawyer, but any officer can defend anybody on a charge if he's chosen by the person to defend them, and I did that. Not very serious offences. One or two, there were one or two serious offences. I remember defending some people on a charge of mutiny, and they were acquitted on the charges of mutiny but they were found guilty of conduct to the prejudice of good order and discipline, or something like that, which is not all that serious, but on the whole there were not very many charged. But I used to visit lots of West Indians on camps, and visit them, you know, just to reassure them there was somebody in London looking after their interests, and also persuading them to take advantage of the further education and training schemes which had been established.'[5]

'After the war I stayed on for a short while, I worked as what they called a liaison officer. I used to sit on court martials and also defend West Indian ground crew who were still in the Air Force and they were, you know, there was all this friction between the white and the West Indian airmen. Always friction. Jealousy with women and things like that. And there was always kind of cases to defend. And there was a small unit of us who acted as liaison officers to either sit on court martials to see that justice was done, or you had to defend, which was quite a nice job. That introduced me to law and I studied law after that. And I was qualified to go to the bar in 1950.

'I thought about going back when I qualified. And in fact I did go back to look at the situation in Guyana. But, again, the same old story, I was disenchanted with Guyana. I did not like the way law was being practised, and I came back to England hoping that I'd find work as a lawyer in some capacity. But that was impossible. In those days I couldn't have afforded to have gone into Chambers. It would have been very difficult. You know, barristers find it very difficult to make out. And then I started trying to find jobs as anyone with legal qualifications, any job. I kind of applied for jobs, newspapers. But never got a response. Never. Well, I mean, you can draw your own conclusions, why not. It was okay for me to be an officer in the Air Force, but I couldn't get a job anywhere. And so I went into the theatre, instead. Well, they say the two things are quite similar, anyway.

[5] Interview with Ulric Cross.

'Attitude changed completely. I mean, in England, during the war, of course, if you're in a very small village, walking down in a little English village and a little child would see this black person, you know, and you would always hear, "Mummy, Mummy, look, there's a black officer there", you know, a black guy. And, of course, when I first walked in to an officers' mess heads used to turn. But, you know, it became commonplace. There were people from all over the place, and then the Yanks were over here. Things did change, though. I mean, I must say that wearing an officer's uniform protects you and during the war people have a different sense of camaraderie. We were all in it together, fighting a war. But after the war you did notice attitudes were completely different out of uniform. If I walked in to, say, a saloon bar in a pub, conversation just died.

'I have always had a very strong sense of who I am, you know, I really have. I feel that my life has been very privileged that way. It has affected me, yes, because I couldn't get a job, and I had to go into the theatre. But I didn't mind it, actually. I mean it didn't really affect me at any great, fundamental level. I knew that racism existed and, you know, my life has made me more aware that it exists and it still exists: although things have changed considerably since the fifties. Considerably.'[6]

'The latter part of the war, I was influenced by the Pan-African situation, the Pan-Africanists in London. And the men that I came upon were Kenyatta – Jomo Kenyatta, who was then a student at the London School of Economics – and there was also Forbes Burnham from Guyana. There was Barrow, who was in the RAF and who stayed over. Those were men who later on all became prime ministers in the various colonies. So I became very politically inclined, and to see what was happening here. Michael Manley came over later, too, he was among the lot. So I was very, for the first time, awakened to the political movements taking place in the West Indies.

'Then there was a 1945 charter, the Atlantic Charter, which promised self government to all of the colonies. I left as a colonial. And growing out of that colonial status now to self government. And as to just what form that self government was going to take took a few years to work out. And I came back when that was

6 Interview with Cy Grant.

being worked out and political parties are being formed, so that was a great part of our thought during that time, '45 right to '50. No, in fact, we were given an offer, we were given an option of staying on, at least in the officer rank, I don't know what happened to the others. We were given an option, and they were very, very good. It wasn't a small job, you know. Those of us who were up in the rank. I mean, I was just about to get a substantive rank as squadron leader, and they said, in five years you'll be so-and-so, and the pay would be good. But I personally felt that I'm not a born soldier, I'm not a born military man. If there's a war, I'll fight, but I'd like to find my own way outside, and I came home and study, so I didn't have any thought of staying on in England for anything at all. I come home to Jamaica. I was twenty-three when I left and twenty-eight when I came back.'[7]

Unlike the Caribbean officers and professionals like Dudley Thompson and Ulric Cross, the bulk of the servicemen who had arrived in 1944 had very little to which they could return. The war had ejected them from their environment and their new experiences had made it practically impossible for them to go back to their former lives. On the other side of the coin they now had a vision of a life in which they could use their abilities and skills to good effect. Every kind of logic dictated a return to Britain, and the *Windrush* was a relatively insignificant factor in that movement. In any other circumstances, of course, the *Windrush* would have kept on sailing with its complement of sixty Polish women.[8] Caribbean immigration would have been sporadic and smaller, at least until the intensification in 1952 of border controls in the USA. But even then, without the post-war skeleton of ex-servicemen who had already pulled thousands of friends and relatives in their wake, the impetus towards Britain would have been much less powerful, and British social history over the next three decades would have looked very different.

'Well, when we first came over here, we were more or less welcomed because we were in the uniform of the King. But when the war in Europe ended and the war in Japan ended, some of the other people tend to say to themselves, well, you come over here to help us to win a war, now the war is over, isn't it about time you go back? That

---

[7] Interview with Dudley Thompson.
[8] See Ch. 4, p. 53.

sort of attitude. Because, really and truly, this country doesn't like strangers. And they don't like foreigners, put it that way. It's a fact of life. I can say that because I've got fifty years' experience of this country. This country don't like foreigners. Americans even worse. So, when the war was over, they were saying to themselves, Well, okay lads, you've been over here now for two or three years, you won the war for us, go back home now, isn't it about time you go back home? That was the message. It wasn't spelt out but that's what it was.

'But we didn't feel like foreigners, far from it. We came over here voluntarily and when the war was ended we could remain here indefinitely, they couldn't send us back. Mark you, thousands of us were repatriated, but, technically speaking, we could avoid being repatriated, because we were then British subjects and we could stay here indefinitely. But if you weren't repatriated, then you would waive the right to any repatriation if you wished to take up the option after. There wouldn't be an option afterwards. Thousands of us were repatriated, but I wasn't one of them.

'Well, when the war ended in Europe and Japan the tempo of the dismissals or the resignation from the services were tremendous. Men were leaving because their time was up. And the services had, what you call, an idea, wherein one would have to rejoin, or the manpower situation would be acute. So the Air Force ask us, some of us, if we would like to stay on for a further three or four years, because they were losing men so rapidly that they couldn't afford to maintain the standard of service that the Air Force needed still. So they asked some of us West Indians if they would like to sign on for a period of years. The option was either for three years or four years. Well, I personally opted for four years; some for three years. We were given a bounty at the beginning and a bounty at the end. I think I got £36 at the beginning and about £40 at the end. And I did four years. But at the end of my four years, or towards the end of my four years, the situation was just as acute. So they enacted an Act in Parliament compelling us to remain a further twelve months. It was a fact. They couldn't break the contract, so they have to enact an Act of Parliament to force us to stay for a further twelve months, so that the shortage wouldn't be as effective as it would otherwise have been.'[9]

⁹ Interview with Euton Christian.

4

EMPIRE MEN FLEE NO JOBS LAND:
500 HOPE TO START A NEW LIFE TODAY
Five hundred unwanted people, picked up by the trooper *Empire Windrush* after
it had roamed the Caribbean, Mexican Gulf, and Atlantic for 27 days are hoping
for a new life. They include 430 Jamaican men. And there are 60 Polish women
who wandered from Siberia, via India, Australia, New Zealand and Africa to
Mexico, where they embarked in the *Empire Windrush*. The Jamaicans are fleeing
from a land with large unemployment. Many of them recognise the futility of
their life at home. (*Daily Express*, 21 June 1948)

A Happy Ship:
A Great Voyage

The Cook's Tale

'I'd seen them before, you know. I'd been out there before, had been
called out there. In Kingston I believe there's the hotel just outside
the docks where we used to go swimming, allowed us to go in there
and swim in the pool. I think it was ten pence or something, a shilling
or something like that and they had a bar there and we was all
drinking. So our attitude was, you know, hail fellow well met. Cheers,
how are you? Didn't make no difference to us, you know. With
seamen we've seen it all before, haven't we? Where I come from,
Custom House in Cardiff, seen it all before. We had coloured living
in Custom House for years and years. Indian seamen used to walk
past my house regular at times, you know. I was brought up seeing
that. It didn't worry me.

'Actual fact it was an ex-German ship. Apparently, from stories
we was told, that it was sunk and it was refloated and brought on
as a troop ship but we took troops away – more or less we brought
them home from abroad, you know, not taking them away but

bringing them home. The last of the troops, 'cos India had got its independence, then we brought the last of the British troops home from there, from Karachi and Bombay. The last trip was going to be to the West Indies – 'cos it was gonna be a short trip I decided to do one more trip on it.

'My ones were going out to the colonies, you know, they were taking passengers out – cargo as well, I mean full of cargo, you know. Sheep and everything like that from New Zealand, full up on cheese and that. So the passengers were supplementary to it really, you know, they was cargo passenger ships. Could have two or three hundred passengers I suppose, but a lot of them – say at the end of the war and just after the war – they was all immigrants going out to Australia and New Zealand, loads of them, all settling down for a new life out there. I suppose they thought of the sun and all that, you know, that tempted them. But the *Windrush* basically was a troop ship. Taking troops from here to there, bringing them back. I think we had some Arabs on for some sort of reason. Oh when we was coming back from India with the last of the British troops we was bringing some Arabs back as well who got off at Suez, you know. The others during the war were troop ships, but after the war they converted back straight away. Troop and cargo boats, you know.

'As for the *Windrush* itself, you know, I've always had a soft spot for it. Don't ask me why, it's just I liked that ship. I liked all ships, but I liked that one. That will always stick in me memory that *Windrush*. Anybody mentions *Windrush* that's the first one. I even follow a horse now that's called Windrush!

'It wasn't me last trip to sea, you know, it was just the last trip on the *Windrush*. I'd done four or five trips which was usually what I done, three trips and then have a change, just for a change. Usually with the same company, you know, the New Zealand Shipping Company, so the Rangitiki, Rangitane, Rangito – they're all different Rangi boats.[1] Well I suppose in a sense I followed me father 'cos he was on all them – the old Rangitane and Rangitiki, Rangitane. He was on the old ones, I was on the new ones, you know, so I probably followed him in a sense without realising it, you know.

[1] Ships of the same shipping line had identical prefixes; 'rangi' here referring to the same New Zealand line.

'Well it's hard to explain to someone who hasn't been to sea, you know, to be fair, because going to sea was a life for us. So a ship was a ship is a ship, sort of thing, you know. So the *Windrush*, in comparison to say the Rangitane or Rangitiki of the New Zealand shipping company's passenger ships, was on a par with that size wise, but not so comfortable because of the age of her I suppose and where she'd been and that and what she was built for. Whereas Rangi boats of the New Zealand Shipping Company they were built for running out to the colonies. But a comfortable ship, you know, there's no doubt about it, it was a comfortable ship. Much as it made you sweat it was a comfortable ship and I suppose being a happy ship made it different, you know, that you didn't notice other things about it 'cos you was contented on board.

'We was limited to the kitchen. You wasn't allowed to just wander around everywhere, you know. So except for them coming down to our cabin, we didn't really go to theirs or where they was sleeping, so I didn't really see them. Every ship it's a job and that's it, you know. You're involved with your job so therefore you're not involved with passengers as such. You're down in the kitchen there sweating, so the only way I got involved was because I used to feed the shore boatswain in Kingston, in Jamaica and he said his nephew was coming on board. So he'd sent a letter, and the steward brought me this letter and I read it and it was saying about his nephew coming on board; would I keep an eye on him and put him right. The first morning that they come on board they're all up for breakfast and that's when I got the letter to say about this chap wanting to meet me, so I went round to where they were serving the breakfast through their mess hall and to say the sight of some of them, their eyes were rolling, you know, they all looked ill, being sea sick and not used to being at sea they wasn't, and that struck me as funny in a sense, you know, that was all. Said to the chap, "We'll see you later on." "Oh, I'll see how I feel." Couldn't take it. That was the funny part with them. But they soon got over that. But that happens to everybody when they go to sea first, you know, get sea sick. They're nearly all sick and you start rubbing them up the wrong way talking about fatty pork and all that.

'So that's how I got involved with these three chaps. Formed a band on board, 'cos they used to take me down the cabin, have a few drinks and all that, laugh and joke. Oh they were brilliant too. I should imagine they must have come over here and must have gone somewhere, you know, 'cos they were a good band. I don't remember five or whatever it was, but these three I know. One of them played – I think one played guitar, one played a saxophone and I'm not sure what the other one played, but they used to play in the cabin and we had two other chaps in our cabin with us, you know, but they took it in good part, they didn't bother. So we used to have a little jazz session while we was having a drink till about eleven o'clock at night and we'd say right, that's it now 'cos we used to be up at five in the morning. But they used to come down more or less every night.

'And then she broke down, coming home she broke down, had to put into Bermuda for repairs and, which is our wont, we'd go out for a few beers in the pubs and they put a dance on in Bermuda and it was for all the coloureds really, you know. So we got on the way back from the pubs we're walking past this big compound and the gates were open, we looked in and there's the band, the three lads we knew up on the stage, playing. They spotted us and we spotted them, waved come in, see. We was the only two white fellas amongst the lot. But we had a good dance and we got up on the stage singing, a few more beers and that. The next thing I knew I woke up in the morning, about four o'clock in the morning in some café, upstairs in a café. Anyway they got us back to the ship eventually and that's it. Once the repairs were done then we got on the way again. They seemed to enjoy it anyway. In fact they called us into the dancing hall. They must have been friendly otherwise they could have just waved us by, couldn't they? We still had them down in the cabin, having drinks and all that and then once we got to Tilbury more or less that was it, finished, and I didn't see any any more. Didn't see anybody and I've never met anybody since that was on it.

'They were passengers and that was it, you know. They got off the ship, we got another lot of passengers on and we're off and gone again. So it was passengers, you know. Didn't matter about anything else. That's our attitude anyway, or it was my attitude, you know. And we got on fine with them. Got on fine with them out there as well, laughing and joking. We used to try to talk like them . . . all this business you know. I used to yell back the same thing, you know, a laugh and a joke, yeah. But they were great, yeah. That reminds you of these things, you look back and your memory tells you all these things. We had a great time. I enjoyed them.

'Remember getting to Tilbury. Faint recollections, 'cos as I say it's years and years now, en it, fifty years now. But I remember getting to Tilbury and I know it was June or July or something like that, you know. They were feeling cold. You could see they were feeling cold. We were probably looking out the porthole of the kitchen seeing them go down the gangways and that, you know, suitcases and that, and they looked cold. But from what I can remember it wasn't cold to us, but it was cold to them. Probably it's because they was all tensed up to what they was going to, what was gonna happen to them. So probably that was more or less – call it a fear I suppose, you know, that made them look cold. I suppose we said, "Oh, look at them, they look frozen", but that was just an aside, sort of thing, you know. Amongst people. But they did – they certainly looked cold from what I remember of it. But it wasn't cold. No, it was quite a warm day really. But not like they'd been used to. Wait till the winter comes, you know, 'cos it's bound to affect them in the winter. Can't remember what the winter like in them days but used to have some cold ones.

'Takes some getting used to, you know. Specially the way they'd come over, you know, they was looking for jobs weren't they really, and there was plenty of jobs 'cos we had no men. Menial jobs. Often wondered how they all got on, you know, used to often think about them and wonder how they got on.

'There was rationing, wasn't there? Clothes rationing, food rationing. They had to get used to all that. One egg here, one egg there, sort of, so coming over to the country at that time was hard, very hard, especially if you've been used to, say, going up and buying a bag of sugar if you wanted it or some fruit if you wanted it. They had none of that over here. Just nothing. Just your bare necessities rationing wise.

'Well, it was unusual, in a sense it was unusual, but when you realise what it was for, we did, you know, because during the war we lost so many men that we could understand it. Well, it's only a personal opinion but how would we have got going again after the war? It wasn't me, I wasn't ashore, I was at sea, but – factories, tubes, railways, nursing. Can't make up all them thousands of dead just like that, can you? So someone had to do it. As I say, to my mind, my way of thinking, thank God they come over or else this country would still been in debt to America. So we've got on our feet and that was it. Surprising really, what a country has to do after a war like that, you know, 'cos it was a bad time. We had thousands, millions killed. Someone had to do the jobs afterwards. We wanted people over to do jobs, you know. It's a natural thing to us. Well, it wasn't to some people, I know, they objected, a lot of them objected.

'To me they were people and they was over here for a job. I had my job, I was at sea so I didn't get involved with that, you know. Don't like it so I didn't get involved with it. There was, obviously, you hear it now even. It's all wrong, you know, but I was talking to someone the other day if I knew anything about this and first words was like there always was, Took our jobs. I said, "Did they?" Then I explain to them, you know, how all the men we lost, all these jobs had to be done. This country would never have been on its feet without them. "Oh, when you put it like that, yeah, I see it different now." Surprising. But nobody explained it properly, unfortunately. If it had been explained to people a bit more sensibly I don't think it would have been so bad.

'But we was used to it, you know, colour means nothing, never has done to me. I don't think it ever will. I don't think it does to a majority of people who come round from dock areas, you know, live round dock areas, Cardiff or anything like that, you know, used to them. So it didn't worry us. But you do hear people, yeah. Can't push it under the carpet. The main thing was taking our jobs, but if they only suddenly thought, you know, they wasn't taking anybody's jobs, they was filling jobs, you know. They wasn't *taking* anybody's job. But it's got to be explained to people, you know, which it wasn't. There was suddenly this influx, you know. This was the country. As I say to people, it's all your grandfather's fault. If they hadn't have pinched their country we wouldn't have it now. Which is fair enough, isn't it? And it was rife, and I should imagine it must have been hard work for them to settle down in a place.

'When you see coloured people I used to say, did your family come over on the *Windrush*, I used to ask, wherever I worked you know, British Telecom. No, never met anybody that come over on the *Windrush*. I thought, it's surprising this, they've all moved up north. Yeah, and no one lives around here now.

'It was a happy voyage. Happy trip. We had laughs, so, you know, the whole trip was a happy trip in a sense, which basically every trip was for me 'cos I loved the sea, you know, I loved being at sea. But that stuck in me mind, the *Windrush*. Not just for that trip but for the other trips prior to it, you know. I had a good time on her. She was a happy ship.'[2]

[2] Interview with Arthur Coats. Arthur Coats came from Cardiff and was the cook on the SS *Empire Windrush*. The journey from Jamaica, which ended in June 1948 at Tilbury, was his last voyage on her.

Meanwhile, in the House of Commons: 500 men in a boat worry Mr Isaacs

'I DON'T KNOW WHO SENT THEM'

A shipload of worry for Mr George Isaacs, Minister of Labour, will arrive at Tilbury on Saturday week – 500 West Indians, all seeking jobs in Britain. Mr Isaacs confessed his worry to MPs yesterday. He said he does not know who sent the men. 'All I know,' he added, 'is that they are in a ship and are coming here. They are British citizens and we shall do our best for them when they arrive.'

But MPs did not allow the mystery of 500 British citizens to rest there.

Mr Stanley (Tory: Bristol, W.) asked: Will you find out who is responsible for this extraordinary action?

Mr Isaacs: That is already being done. I wish I knew, but I do not. Those who organised the movement of these people to Britain did them a disservice in not contacting the Labour Ministry and giving it a chance to take care of them.

Mr Hughes (Soc: Ayshire, S.): Will you let them see the housing conditions in Scotland? Then they will want to go back to the West Indies.

Mr Driberg (Soc: Maldon, Essex): Will you instruct your officials to meet the ship and help them find work in undermanned industries in the interests of production and welfare?

Mr Isaacs: They will be met at the ship and told how to register for unemployment. The arrival of these substantial numbers of men under no organised arrangements is bound to result in difficulty and disappointment. I have no knowledge of their qualifications or capacity, and can give no assurance that they can be found suitable work. I hope no encouragement will be given to others to follow them. (*Daily Express*, Tuesday 8 June 1948)

'We were Passieras . . .'

'About a fortnight, ten days before the *SS Empire Windrush* arrived in Kingston, Jamaica, there was an ad in the *Gleaner*, which is the national paper, to say that there is a troop ship going back to England with about 300 passage berth on, for £28.10. I arrived shortly at the office of the agent, and I was shocked. There was a great queue. Eventually, I arrived with my document and I paid the £28.10, and my passport, et cetera, et cetera. Waited about a week, five days, and on 24 May 1948, we arrived to board the *SS Empire Windrush*.

'Well, the average Jamaican who came on the *SS Empire Windrush* on 24 May was not the destitute. The destitute man did not have £28.10. In my case, it cost three cows. The average Jamaican did not have three cows. And I think you'll find, in statistics, the people who are destitute, he might stow away, he hasn't got the passage. They were the people like myself, Holness, Christian and others, were looking for hope, betterment. Yes, one or two might be unemployed, but they were from a family background of support. So, they were above average as far as income was concerned. And they were people who were thinking ahead. Columbus, when we got to Mexico, he got off the ship, because somebody was selling melon and he could speak Spanish and bought the whole tray load or cart load of melon. And let's assume he bought it for ten X, he came back and cut them in four and sold them for a lot of money, and that's why we call him Columbus. He's still trading in Brixton Market today, almost fifty years on. But to the best of my knowledge, let's say 500 people were on the boat, also including the stowaways, I would say three-quarters of those people were tradespersons. Again, about a third were ex-service. I'd worked on aircraft, I've worked on all propeller driven aircraft that you can think. So, three-quarters of us, I would say, were skilled.

'So I was never apprehensive, I know where I was coming, because I'd lived in England, in the Royal Air Force, and I had been from Folkestone to Aberdeen, and once the Blue Mountain was behind us and I did not see it any more, I know where I was going. There was hope. People were concerned, especially those people who have never been out of Jamaica before, but there was an attitude of comradeship. We were Yard People, we didn't use the word Yardie, we used the word Passiero. We were Passieras, we were going to club together and we were going to survive.

'It was, by the way, a former German troop ship, actually made for the SS. It was very clean, very nice. We had dinner, some people were sick, and we had a few stowaways, so the stowaways would use the sick peoples' tickets to get lunch. And we cooperate, we had a little entertaining like boxing and bowl, and, by the way, I boxed in the Royal Air Force, and some of the people in the ring that were fighting, I'm not stupid enough to go and fight with them. Then you have dancing, but I know nothing about ladies, because I wasn't looking ladies, I was looking work. So, people like Holness would know about ladies. The main thing was to survive, to land in England.

'You had to start washing your own few shirts you had, because the stowaways, by the way, shirts were dirty around their necks. So we decided – and Sam King made that decision, by the way, I was not a leader, never was, but there are different times you had to make decisions – when they caught a stowaway, because his shirt neck was dirty, I let it be known that the stowaways should not steal shirts, but people should give the stowaway his shirt. They wash their shirt and they add clean colours, and it worked.

'After about a week, people were asking questions about England. About eight of us had been in England before, and I said, "Well, I'm not going to answer questions here and there." In the evening, about five o'clock, we went below deck and we discussed England. Jamaicans left on the SS *Empire Windrush* to seek a living. And I tried to explain to them that there is no problem finding work in England, but you had to have documents. They said, "Well, I'm not going to England about documents, I am going to work." I said, "You have to have a ration card to get food, because food is rationed. You have to have a National Insurance Number to pay tax, et cetera, et cetera." And it took me a long time. And I didn't do a good job, because I think about two days before we were landed, somebody said, Sam, you know, I'm not worrying about them papers, I just want the work.

'About five days out, one evening, about six-fifteen, I saw a man crying on the leeward side. He said, "They're going to send us back." I said, "What rubbish are you talking about?" And he told me that he heard on the six o'clock news that if there was any disturbance, they were going to send us back. By the way, HMS *Sheffield* was on the skyline, a pocket British battleship. And I got two wireless operators, they're former wireless operators, they have sparks on their jacket. I got them to play dominoes by the wireless operator window. And whatever was happening in Westminster, tick, tick, tick, tick, we knew. And the message went out, peace and love.

'Now, Yard People work together outside of Jamaica total. So there were no disturbance, and we organise ourselves and we arrive. When we arrived, Flight-Lieutenant Smythe, which was an RAF officer for the Minister of the Colonies, were on board. He put a leaflet out that we will have difficulty in England and we shouldn't have arrived and all kinds of things, and encouraging us to go back. One man asked me what to do about the paper. I said right to that place, put it in the dustbin. Smythe is an African, he's not a Jamaican, so how he can tell me? Secondly, if he was even English, I'm not going to listen to an Englishman. I am going to England to seek a living. So, we ignored that. There were great consternation in Westminster, say about three days in, and the Right Honourable Creech-Jones stated, Don't worry about it; these people are only adventurers, they will not last one winter in Britain. My friend, you touch me. I'm here fifty winters, I'm among the living. They did not want us. And what is important for us to tell the nation, and especially the young people, we survive.'[3]

The trader, a pretty boy, and the only child

'Nine out of ten of all the men who left Jamaica, they claimed they were coming here for five years. Well, I mean, England, to us, was a seat of learning, and people always take it, because most of the people who had become, you know, professionals, they cut it here. They came to England to be trained. So, to us, that was a Godsend opportunity. Just go up to Kingston and catch a boat. We had a departure time, and we went up to Kingston and caught it. It took me about three days to wrap up everything in my case. Ah, people there laughing, joking, and a lot weeping, you know, their loved ones leaving, some think they would never see them again and all that sort of thing, because, remember, it was just after the war.

'But people were glad that their relation – whether it be a husband or sweetheart, a brother, or any relative – going abroad, because that's the only thing Jamaicans had, you know, to export, was manpower. And they were glad if a relation going abroad, they would be helped one way or another, they always look forward to that.

'Well, me, myself, I play cards the whole journey. We stopped at Cuba, I didn't go ashore. This is where, the fellas, they came alongside the ship and sell things, fruits and drinks and things like that, and I bought up some stuff, and sell it back to the chaps as we travelled. I had a good time. A woman stowed away, so we paid for her. That was the only thing that was rather strange. I can't remember anything as strange as that. On the boat it was just, you know, how it is. A load of men. I doubt if there were half a dozen women. I think about one wife. Oh, I can remember a fellow from my town, two brothers and a sister, they were coming to work with Tate and Lyle, the sugar barons. They were coming, they had acquainted in Jamaica, they worked at the hotel where they stayed, so they came over here.

'The main thing is to earn money. And quite a few of the young men claim they're going to spend five years. Well, I suppose, one or

3 Interview with Sam King.

two of them managed that, but the rest of them finished up like me and they're a working citizen. There was a lot of work about.'[4]

'Well, as far as I can remember, and I wouldn't say this a hundred per cent, but as far as I can remember you had a variation of people. You had a lot of fellows who came who went in the farm work from Jamaica to America. You had a lot of people who were ex-servicemen like myself. You had a lot of people who just decided to come to look and see. But at the same time you had some characters on board. We had a calypso singer by the name of Lord Kitchener. We had another singer by the name of Tony Bennett. People like that, but they were characters in their own way. Then you had fellows like myself who were, what? He's a pretty boy. All you're interested in is getting dressed and looking around and seeing things.'[5]

'I was thirteen when my parents brought me. My father worked the railway as a labourer, and my mother worked in a match factory. They were church people, those thrifty people. And one of the ways in which you could accumulate large sums of money was something that they called "pardner". You put in so much money, and you've had a draw. I think that's how a lot of people were able to get that £28. It was an awful lot of money. And I think a lot of people, because of the opportunities they perceived were going to open up to them, would sell what they had, and, of course, they had "pardner" schemes, where a lot of people were in churches, you had credit unions, you know, so you'd partner. That's how they got the money. I suppose he thought, well, you know, being a labourer in England couldn't be any worse than being a labourer in Jamaica. In fact, it would be better, because at least you would get more money for doing the work. And that's why they came.

'For me it was a massive adventure. I mean, I'd never been outside of Kingston, let alone, you know, this massive journey to England. I had no idea where England was or how long, you know, it would take to get there. I'd never been on a train, I'd never been out of Kingston. And here I was stepping on this huge ship which was going to bring me to this place called England. I was thirteen years old and, I remember, you know, all these people on the ship and the officers on

4   Interview with Oswald 'Columbus' Denniston.
5   Interview with Arthur Curling.

the ship were white and, you know, the crew were white. And it was fairly exciting, because I'd never been anywhere before. And going to undertake this journey I had no idea what's going to happen to me and my parents. As far as I was concerned, I didn't have any idea about how long we're going to be in England or anything like that.

'It was single men. I think there might have been a couple of children but, no, they were overwhelmingly adults. In fact, off hand, I can't think of any other person of my age on the boat. I think the next youngest person to me must have been about nineteen. Obviously, some people had been to the UK before and they would talk about England and, you know, people were also looking forward to work, because, of course, in Jamaica there was not a great deal of work for people. So a lot of people were looking forward to coming. There were carpenters coming, people with all kind of different skills who were coming, and were looking forward to, you know, earning money and working and earning money to look after their people back in Jamaica. So there was a kind of general excitement and optimism.

'One of the things that I liked on the boat, they had some boxers that came over – like Leftie Flynn, who was a very good fighter, Pal Silver, Brendon Solus – I used to like to watch them box, you know. And that was exciting, because I quite liked the idea of myself being a fighter. But a white guy was bringing them over, called Dale Martin. Dale Martin Promotions. And that was about the most exciting thing on the ship, except when we went to Bermuda. And we disembarked and went in the cinema and we were told we had to sit in a particular place, you know. And, of course, Jamaicans, although you had this kind of hierarchy of colour in Jamaica, this was a new experience, to be told that you couldn't sit where you bought your ticket to sit, you had to sit in a particular place. And, of course, this led to a fight, and we were, you know, told to leave the cinema and sent back to the ship. And, of course, the other thing was people were saying that there's a British warship that was shadowing the *Windrush*, and there was talk that they might blow us out of the water, that they might sink the ship. Because there was some people didn't want black people coming to England. And there was this fear that they might very well sink the ships, so that there was an element of danger. Whether it was real or not I don't know, but that's what people said, that there were certain hostilities and there was this warship that was shadowing the *Windrush*.'[6]

---

[6] Interview with Vince Reid.

Lord Kitchener: The singer and the song

'I always wanted to know the mother country, and I was so happy when I got a break from a promoter, asked me to go to Aruba. Then I decided to go to Jamaica. I spent a couple of months in Jamaica working at the Shoehead Club in Kingston. Then, after a while, I started getting a kind of homesick. It was very funny, that it was a homesick, but not homesick for Trinidad. So I said, "Well, I want to go out of Jamaica somewhere around, either America or England." Then, fortunately, there was a talk about a boat will be leaving Jamaica soon for England, called the *Empire Windrush*. I was happy. I went to my boss, Mr Clifford Reid was the person. I told him, "Look, I have to leave your job because I want to get to England, and it's a nice opportunity for me." He didn't like it much, but, of course, he saw my way. He said, "Alright." He said, "Okay, I'll give you the freedom to go." I think it was £28, as I remember, was the cost of the journey from Jamaica to England.

'And then we all boarded the ship, and we left Jamaica, moving towards Havana. While we're on that ship, we heard that there's a lot of stowaways on the ship, so we continue. Reach Havana, pass Havana, and going towards Bermuda. While we're going to Bermuda, a woman stowaway was discovered, and she started crying, because she thought they would want to put her in prison. So, the purser of the boat said, Well, if you all get together and get some dollars, some pounds, you can save this lady the embarrassment. Pay the fare for her, and then she'll be free. So we all gather and gave a concert on the boat. And we got the money, paid the money to the purser, and she was free to travel to England.

'When we reached to Bermuda, we spent three days in Bermuda, having a nice time, a wonderful time. And we left there for England. While we're going to England, saw so many strugglers, I see a lot of young fellows, who they say, Well, I stowaway – I'm a stowaway. And they had nothing to eat, and we used to help them out with a bit of food. So it continue like that. And the boat reached Tilbury, the water was brown and red. Well, it's the time I really realised that people are really brave. All those stowaways jumped from the ship into the water and started swimming ashore. And I was wondering if these fellas are not afraid of alligators, because that water seemed to me that it must have some kind of reptile in it. Anyway, they went ashore, and we took the train from Tilbury to London. About a week after, I went to a place called the Paramount, where they could dance, there was a lot of dancing there. To my surprise, many of the stowaways were in the Paramount jiving, dancing and what-have-you. I had to laugh, I couldn't believe it. A man just stowaway and, after a couple of days, he was in a dance hall jiving and dancing around.

'But entering England, when the boat had about four days to land in England, I get this kind of wonderful feeling that I'm going to land on the mother country, the soil of the mother country. And I started composing this song, *London is the Place for Me*.

'And I composed that song. And it had to be a famous song. Eventually it came up as a famous song. *London is the Place for Me*. And that is when I composed that song. The feeling I had to know that I'm going to touch the soil of the mother country, that was the feeling I had. How I can describe? It's just a wonderful feeling. You know how it is when a child, you hear about your mother country, and you know that you're going to touch the soil of the mother country, you know what feeling is that? And I can't describe it. That's why I compose the song. Imagine how I felt. Here's where I want to be, London. So I sung:

> London is the place for me, London that lovely city.
> You can go to France or America, India, Asia, or Africa.
> But you must come back to London city.
> I said, London is the place for me. London, that lovely city.
> You can go to France or America, India, Asia or Africa.
> But you must come back, to London city.
>
> London is the place for me. London this lovely city.
> You can go to France or America, India, Asia or Africa.
> But you must come back to London city.
> London, this lovely city.
> You can go to France or America, India, Asia or Africa.
> But you must come back to London city.'[7]

---

[7] Interview with Lord Kitchener. Aldwyn 'Lord Kitchener' Roberts is a Trinidadian and one of the best known and loved calypsonians in the Caribbean. After working in various parts of the region he embarked on the *Windrush*, settling later in Manchester. He returned permanently to Trinidad in 1962.

Panic in the Civil Service, but Attlee remains ice-cool

In later years the response of the contemporary authorities to the *Windrush* sailing has tended to be characterised according to whatever political purpose is being served. One popular account described the government as actively having 'brought' the migrants to do 'the shit jobs'. In 1948 all the evidence indicates that this was clearly untrue and, later on, the recruitment drives in the Caribbean were precisely targeted and involved far fewer candidates than is generally supposed. Another contradictory account describes the government as stricken with racist anxiety and doing everything in their power to stop the migrants. This too, is apocryphal.

What seems closest to the truth is that the Civil Service went into paroxysms of anxiety. It was, after all, a Service which, for the last decade, had run a tightly controlled, amazingly disciplined bureaucracy. Every aspect of life was subject to some sort of control. Every last ounce of food was allocated and monitored. Every resource analysed and weighed. This was the real problem. The issue of race might have reinforced the Civil Servants' agitation, but their primary motivation was distress at the advent of a group of workers about whom they knew no details, whose movements were completely unregulated and who couldn't be controlled by official sanctions. The exchange of letters between the Colonial Office and Government House in Jamaica testifies to the Civil Service irritation at being caught unprepared. Minor elements in the House of Commons took this view, as the exchanges on the floor demonstrate, but the senior politicians on all sides had bigger fish to fry. In the end Attlee's letter rebuking his correspondents for overreaction, seemed to be justified by the almost audible sigh of relief which emerges from the final Colonial Office report on the *Windrush* passengers.

TELEGRAM FROM THE ACTING GOVERNOR IN JAMAICA TO THE SECRETARY OF STATE FOR THE COLONIES (11 MAY 1948): 'JAMAICAN WORKERS FOR THE UNITED KINGDOM'

I regret to inform you that more than 350 troop-deck passages by *Empire Windrush* – your telegram MAST 972 refers to – have been booked by men who hope to find employment in the United Kingdom, and that it is likely that this number will be increased by another 100 before the vessel leaves. Most of them have no particular skill and few will have more than a few pounds on their arrival.

2. Public announcements on the difficulty of obtaining work have

not discouraged these bookings and only 40 persons have, so far, provided information such as was sent with my savingram No. 802 of 3 December 1947. This is being sent by airmail and every effort is being made to secure similar information in respect of the remainder in order that it may reach you as long as possible before the vessel arrives in the United Kingdom.[8]

LETTER FROM THE COLONIAL SECRETARY'S OFFICE IN JAMAICA TO THE COLONIAL OFFICE IN LONDON (29 MAY 1948)

My dear Cummings,[9] . . . You will now have had our Saving telegram No. 325 of 24 May which gives you the information which you will require on as many workers as have provided it; in the next day or two I shall telegraph the number that finally embarked. I am sorry that there has been delay in letting you have this number, but the fact is that the Royal Mail themselves did not seem to know the precise figures and I am badgering them for it as hard as possible.

We are very sorry indeed that you and your staff will be put to all the trouble which the arrival of this large number, who are mostly unskilled and who will have little money with them, will involve. It is an appalling thing with which to be saddled, but, as you know, it has been quite impossible to prevent their going, which is symptomatic of the conditions here. I hope that you will be able to cope with them without too much trouble.[10]

FROM THE PRIVY COUNCIL OFFICE TO THE COLONIAL OFFICE (15 JUNE 1948)

Your memorandum on the immediate situation does not deal with the underlying reasons why these 417 Jamaicans decided to come to this country and who instigated and organised the movement. The Lord President hopes that to save time in any discussion that may be necessary, the Secretary of State will be ready to throw light on these matters, and to explain what he is doing to ensure that further similar movements either from Jamaica or elsewhere in the Colonial Empire are detected and checked before they can reach such an

[8] PRO CO 876/88.

[9] Ivor Cummings was a principal in the Colonial Office. He was himself of mixed race origins, his father a Sierra Leonean and his mother a white Englishwoman. He was a central figure in the decisions and arrangements made within the various Civil Service departments with regard to the migrants' reception. He was a fastidious, elegant man, with a manner reminiscent of Noel Coward – he chain smoked with a long cigarette holder and addressed visitors as 'dear boy'.

[10] PRO CO 876/88.

embarrassing stage. Otherwise there might be a real danger that successful efforts to secure adequate conditions for these men on arrival might actually encourage a further influx.[11]

OUTWARD TELEGRAM TO THE OFFICE OF THE ACTING GOVERNOR IN JAMAICA FROM THE SECRETARY OF STATE FOR THE COLONIES
(16 JUNE 1948, 19.30 HRS)

Most immediate.

Essential I should know whether decision of Jamaicans to travel by *Empire Windrush* to England was of their own motion or can be attributed to any form of local organisation. If the latter, can you say who was responsible?

2. We are doing what we can to deal with them on arrival.[12]

INTERNAL MEMO FROM W. H. HARDMAN, MINISTRY OF LABOUR (19 JUNE 1948)

There is no logical ground for treating a British subject who comes of his own accord from Jamaica to Great Britain differently from another who comes to London on his own account from Scotland. Nevertheless public attention has been focused on the 400 or so men who are coming from Jamaica and who will arrive in London on Tuesday. A political problem has been created to the embarrassment of the government and to our Minister in particular. In these circumstances it is necessary to see whether any extraordinary measures can be taken that would help solve the problem. If only they could be dispersed in small parties, then even though they did not get immediate employment, they would cease to be recognisable as a problem.[13]

LETTER FROM THE MINISTRY OF TRANSPORT TO IVOR CUMMINGS AT THE COLONIAL OFFICE, CC W. H. HARDMAN AT THE MINISTRY OF LABOUR (22 JUNE 1948)

Dear Cummings, I refer to my conversation with you on Saturday about the possibility of further West Indian personnel availing themselves of the opportunity of coming to this country in the

---

[11] PRO CO 876/88.

[12] ibid.

[13] PRO LAB 8/1816.

Empire Trooper, which is due to sail from Trinidad about 19 July. I understand that the Colonial Office have given a free hand to the Governor as regards booking her troop-deck accommodation.

Our view is that if it is considered undesirable on general policy grounds that these people should come to this country unless they have accommodation and work already arranged, action must be taken by your department and/or Ministry of Labour to deal with the matter. We would not be prepared to take the responsibility for refusing passages unless your Minister, or he and the Minister of Labour, would stand up to any criticism.

I think you suggested when I was talking to you that what we really needed was an immigration policy in this matter, and in that I entirely agree with you. I do not think, even if we took action in this way in this case, that refusing passages to people who are otherwise entitled to come to this country is a legitimate long term policy.[14]

LETTER FROM CLEMENT ATTLEE, PRIME MINISTER, IN REPLY TO A LETTER FROM A GROUP OF BACKBENCHERS (5 JULY 1948)

I am replying to the letter signed by yourself and ten other Members of Parliament on 22 June about the West Indians who arrived in this country on that day on board the *Empire Windrush*. I note what you say, but I think it would be a great mistake to take the emigration of this Jamaican party to the United Kingdom too seriously.

It is traditional that British subjects, whether of Dominion or Colonial origin (and of whatever race or colour), should be freely admissible to the United Kingdom. That tradition is not, in my view, to be lightly discarded, particularly at a time when we are importing foreign labour in large numbers. It would be fiercely resented in the colonies themselves, and it would be a great mistake to take any measure which would tend to weaken the goodwill and loyalty of the colonies towards Great Britain. If our policy were to result in a great influx of undesirables, we might, however unwillingly, have to consider modifying it. But I would not be willing to consider that except on really compelling evidence, which I do not think exists at the present time.[15]

14   PRO LAB 8/1517.
15   PRO CO 876/88.

'To find a job, to find a home'

'Opportunity. Opportunity. You see, strange as it might seem, or as it might sound when the war was raging, the people in Jamaica – although they were restricted somewhat by the effects of the war – things weren't so bad. But when the war ended, things became worse. For what reason, I can't explain exactly why. And the people were trying to get away, because they were prepared to be restricted during the war years, but now the war is over, and things get worse, they said, Well, no, you know, I can't stand this. So the opportunity came for them to come on the *Windrush*, and to grasp that opportunity, and they came.

'For the civilians it was, "I wonder what is going to happen? I wonder if I'm going to get a job? I wonder if I'm going to get somewhere to live?" It was uncertainty. Some people knew where they were going, very few, mark you, very few. Nobody knew exactly what they were going to do. But we, in the Air Force, we know we're going back to the base. The ex-RAF fellows who were stowaways, they were here already for two or three years, so they knew exactly where they're going to go and where they're going to live and how they're going to get a job. Jobs weren't difficult to find. Jobs were very, very easy to find, so that wasn't a problem. The problem was housing, accommodation. That was a bugbear.

'So the mood on the ship was, I wonder what is going to happen; I wonder if so-and-so is going to happen to me, that sort of thing. Which is a natural reaction for any strange traveller to a strange country such as this. They expected to come here and to find a job, to find a home. And in about four or five years, they earn enough money to go back. But a lot of people said that – ninety-nine out of a hundred say that – but they never achieve that goal, working here for four or five years to go back, because nobody gets rich in four or five years anyway, but that is always what they say. Well, I'm not going to stay over here for long, you know, five or ten years and then I'll go back. They spend here five, ten, fifteen, twenty, and it's twenty-five and they're still here, because they never earn sufficient to enable them to go home and start out something for themselves. It never happen, it never happen. And ninety-nine out of a hundred had the same idea, that they're not coming over here into this cold country to live indefinitely; a short period, get some money, go back home. But it never happened.'[16]

---

[16] Interview with Euton Christian.

5

New Labour, New Nation

Citizenship, nationality and the meaning of Englishness in 1948

Memory suggests a uniform picture of Britain in 1948, most often summed up by the phrase 'post-war austerity', typified by stories about bread rationing, armies of the homeless squatting in unheated accommodation, private grief and public disaffection. It was certainly true that the years following the end of the fighting had been extraordinarily tough on the British, and report after report details the 'scenes of squalor and misery'.[1] A typical observation in the spring of 1946 describes a squat in London:

> A bus conductor, two women, and three schoolchildren, driven desperate for somewhere to live, camp out in a large dilapidated room without light, water and without fuel for a fire. Sullen and dirty faces swollen with colds, an orange box scraped dry of all but coke-dust, two saucepans on an unmade bed, a spirit stove on which bacon was frying, and a green teapot shaped like a racing-car on a strip of newspaper many times ringed.[2]

These were among the immediate consequences of wartime devastation, but the most painful manifestations of post-war austerity were easing by the summer of 1948, and that year was a watershed in the process of transforming Britain. Labour had won the first post-war election with a huge majority, and, during the next two years, had put in place the basic elements of the Welfare State. The essential services had been nationalised, and the National Health Service had been created. Under the premiership of Clement Attlee a firm outline of the country's goals and how to achieve them had emerged over two years of hectic legislation.

1947 – which the then Chancellor, Hugh Dalton, described as his 'annus

---

[1] George Beardmore, 'Civilians at War: Journals 1938–46' (Oxford, 1986). Cited in Stephen Brooke, *Reform and Reconstruction* (Manchester: Manchester University Press, 1995), p. 121.

[2] ibid., p.122.

horrendus' – had been a year of financial crisis and disaster. In comparison 1948 saw a restoration of direction and confidence in the government. This was partly due to the firm grip of the new Chancellor, Stafford Cripps, who imposed a wage freeze and continued strict rationing. The average citizen was limited to a weekly ration of thirteen ounces of meat, one and a half ounces of cheese, six ounces of butter and margarine, one ounce of cooking fat, eight ounces of sugar, two pints of milk and one egg.

On the other hand, during the first part of 1948 there was relative industrial peace and a wide acceptance of the government's stern domestic policies. A year later, a series of unofficial strikes and, notably, a prolonged dispute on the London docks was to open up a renewed sense of crisis, but for the moment unemployment had disappeared, there was a massive regeneration of industry. Production had risen dramatically, exports were surging. In 1948 all the indications were that Britain was performing more successfully than at any time since the First World War. So, for the majority of the British, austerity was balanced by a sense of there being considerable achievements in progress.

For the working classes the sense that everyone was suffering equally eased the pain, while there were significant concessions in the domestic economy. Food subsidies, for instance, kept the cost of living at an acceptable level, while irritating regulations like clothing rations were abandoned in Harold Wilson's 'bonfire of the controls'.[3] In any case, 1948 saw a remarkable rise in the choice and availability of leisure industries. Football, cricket, cinemas, dance halls and holiday camps were all booming. For the middle classes the age of labour-saving devices and Ideal Homes was about to arrive. On the page of the *Evening Standard* which reports the docking of the *Windrush* an advertisement features a grinning housewife announcing, 'My home is Hoover cleaned'.[4] Infant mortality rates went down and various indices showed that the population was becoming healthier and, paradoxically, better fed, than it had been for a long time. At the moment when the *Windrush* landed at Tilbury Britain was experiencing an unusual period of equilibrium.

A significant part of this sense that the country had achieved a new settlement was the fact that the government had at last solved the problem of India. India had become an independent country in 1947 and in the following year the British Nationality Act divided British citizenship into

[3] Harold Wilson was President of the Board of Trade in 1948, and announced a list of deregulation on Guy Fawkes night, 1948, giving rise to the more popular name.

[4] *Evening Standard*, 21 June 1948.

two categories: citizenship of the United Kingdom and Colonies, and citizenship of independent Commonwealth countries. Citizenship of the first category implied possession of the same rights throughout the Empire, and the Act extended these to citizens in the second category. In effect it meant no change in the status of citizens of the independent countries joining the Commonwealth, because the motive behind this piece of legislation was concerned with retaining Indian membership, and, for the moment, it fitted in neatly with British beliefs about the nature of their relationship with the former colonies.

The juxtaposition of the Nationality Act and the arrival of the *Windrush* was a pure coincidence, but the two events seem to fit together because the Act itself enshrines what became a classic uncertainty about how to define the nature and the boundaries of British citizenship. The problem was partly to do with the way that the concept had evolved within the framework of imperialist expansion.

In the heyday of Empire the award of British citizenship was more or less simultaneous with the acquisition of new territories by Britain. From the point of view of the colonies, British citizenship was a symbol of British power and ownership rather than the seal of an individual's contract with the State. In any case, British citizens were not signatories to some mutually agreed charter of citizenship. Instead, they were subjects of the British sovereign. So the touchstone of citizenship was not acceptance of a schedule of rights and duties. It was allegiance to the symbol of the Crown.

What made the citizens of the United Kingdom different from any other British subject was that natives of the British Isles saw themselves as being at the head of the hierarchy of British nations. The idea which underpinned this role and held the whole structure together was a belief in the racial supremacy of whites born in Britain. Throughout the heyday of the Empire this idea developed mystical overtones, linked as it was with the notion that the British had a destiny to rule over 'lesser races'. For a time in Britain this belief in the divine right to racial ascendancy was assiduously fostered and propagated by a wide variety of means, from children's fiction to government propaganda. Although it was clear that it was the middle classes who took up the White Man's Burden and set out to accomplish the 'civilising mission', it was also clear that racial supremacy was a potent myth which permeated through all levels of the society. The war had added another dimension to the British self image, marinating it in Churchillian rhetoric about the heroic bulldog spirit.

By 1948, however, change was in the air. It was to be almost another decade before the Suez adventure killed off the British dream of universal potency, but the loss of India, the uneasy muddle in Palestine and the increasing disaffection in Africa and the Far East created doubts, even for those citizens who knew and cared little or nothing about such places.

Debating the Nationality Act in the Commons a fortnight after the *Windrush* docked, the Home Secretary, James Chuter Ede, made what amounted to a ringing repudiation of the past. He said:

> I know there are also some who feel it is wrong to have a citizenship of the United Kingdom and colonies. Some people feel it would be a bad thing to give the coloured races of the Empire the idea that, in some way or the other, they are the equals of people in this country. The government do not subscribe to that view. We believe wholeheartedly that the common citizenship of the United Kingdom and Colonies is an essential part of the development of the relationship between this Mother Country and the Colonies. We believe and we hope it will be understood that citizenship of the United Kingdom and Colonies means that when we talk, for example, of the development of the Colonies, etc., we recognise the right of the colonial peoples to be treated as men and brothers with the people of this country.[5]

On the surface speeches of this kind appeared to be a symptom of the Labour Government's democratising purpose. Attlee and his colleagues, however, while convinced of the necessity of modernising the colonial relationship had no intention of changing it fundamentally, and no interest at all in altering its racist tone. A couple of years later, one government minister, Hugh Dalton, was still capable of describing the colonies as 'pullulating poverty stricken, diseased nigger communities'.[6]

In the circumstances the debate on the Nationality Act was actually the beginning of a trauma about citizenship, race and nationality which swiftly became associated with the arrival of Caribbean immigrants. It was to dog British politics for the rest of the twentieth century.

One strand in the argument is defined by the figure of Enoch Powell. During the Second World War Powell spent two years in India and 'fell head over heels in love with it'.[7] But his love of India was inseparable from its imperial role.

---

[5] Parliamentary Debates (Commons) 453, 7 July 1948. Cited in Stephen Brooke, *Reform and Reconstruction* (Manchester: Manchester University Press, 1995), pp. 125-6.

[6] Dalton Diaries, 27 February 1950 (Dalton papers. 1/38). Cited in Ben Pimlott, *Hugh Dalton* (London: Jonathan Cape, 1985), p. 577.

[7] Enoch Powell, *The Times*, 12 February 1968.

The concept of self-determination, both personal and political had no place in Powell's mind's eye, nor in the parody of Late Victorian India he identified with. On a journey through Bihar, he was struck by a 'blinding revelation': 'I was the only Englishman within, thirty, forty, maybe sixty miles, and that this was a part of the natural order of things.'[8]

For the next twenty years Powell's views about citizenship developed into a precise reflection of British anxieties about how to redefine citizenship in the wake of imperial collapse. He opposed the Nationality Act on the grounds that 'the Crown is the great link which binds the Empire together in a common loyalty. But the British Nationality Act of 1948 took away allegiance to the Crown as the basis for British citizenship. Citizens of the Indian Union were expressly given all the rights and privileges of British subjects, though repudiating the King as their sovereign.'[9]

By the mid-fifties Powell was declaring that the British Empire had been 'self deception', 'delusion' and a 'hallucination'.[10] Ten years later he had arrived at a coherent statement about English nationhood. This turned out to be a romanticised pre-Raphaelite vision.

On 22 April [1964], in a speech to the Royal Society of St George, he proclaimed his vision of England. The power and the glory of the Empire had gone, but in the midst of the 'blackened ruins' there remained, 'like one of her own oak trees, standing and growing, the sap still rising from her ancient roots to meet the spring, England herself.' It was the task of his generation to reclaim their English heritage, to rediscover that earlier generation of Englishmen who had lived before the 'expansion of England', and had been untainted by Empire. In language reminiscent of his most bathetic poetry, Powell led his audience back to the 'brash adventurous days of the first Elizabeth': 'there at last we find them in many a village church, beneath the tall tracery of a perpendicular East window and the coffered ceiling of the chantry chapel.'

He asks these imaginary Englishmen a rhetorical question:

'Tell us what it is that binds us together, show us the clue that leads through a thousand years; whisper to us the secret of this charmed life of England, that we in our time may know how to hold it fast. What would they say?'

His own answer lapses into pastoral excess:

'They would tell us of that marvellous land, so sweetly mixed of opposites in climate that all the seasons of the year appear there in their greatest perfection;

[8] Jonathan Rutherford, *Forever England – Reflections on Masculinity and Empire* (London: Lawrence and Wishart, 1997), p. 107.

[9] *Birmingham Post*, 6 November 1952. Cited by Rutherford, op. cit. p. 109.

[10] Rutherford, op. cit. pp. 111-12.

of the fields amid which they built their halls, their cottages, their churches, and where the same blackthorn showered its petals upon them as upon us.'

This sentimental, rustic wonderland is embodied in three enduring principles of Englishness; its unity under the Crown in Parliament, its historical continuity and its racial homogeneity. The political institutions of England have evolved out of this pastoral idyll, like works of nature.

'The deepest instinct of the Englishman – how that word "instinct" keeps forcing itself in again and again! – is for continuity; he never acts more freely nor innovates more boldly than when he most is conscious of conserving or even of reacting. From this continuous life of a united people in its island home spring, as from the soil of England, all that is peculiar in the gifts and the achievements of the English nation.'

And what binds and symbolises this 'continuous life' is the 'English kingship'. This, Powell declares, is England's unalterable truth which no 'Hanoverian' or 'Headships of Commonwealths' can undermine.[11]

Four years later Powell made his famous 'Rivers of Blood' speech in which he pictured the recent black and Asian immigrants as alien invaders. In a sense this was the logical climax to his reading of British identity, and his nationalistic outline of citizenship had an enormous influence throughout the rest of the century. At the same time, during the post-war years, there were other elements redefining British citizenship and identity in a very different, yet oddly complementary fashion.

Most of these were focused in the persona of Clement Attlee who made a point of emphasising the divide between himself and the Conservative heirs of imperial tradition. During the first post-war election Churchill, trailing the rhetoric of imperial history and Britain's global importance, travelled around in a cavalcade surrounded by an entourage. In contrast Attlee was driven to his rallies by his wife in their Hillman Minx; at lunchtime he unwrapped a packed lunch; and his vision was about 'well-planned, well-built cities and parks and playing fields, homes and schools, factories and shops'.[12] An almost Chaplinesque figure, his image was that of a little man from the suburbs. In the phrase which was frequently quoted against him, he was 'a modest little man, with plenty to be modest about'.[13]

Attlee's image outlined English identity in a way that deliberately challenged the pretentious mythology of the Empire-builder.

[11] ibid. pp. 124-5.

[12] Extract from a radio broadcast in 1945. Cited by Francis Beckett, *Clem Attlee. A Biography* (London: Richard Cohen Books, 1997), p. 214.

[13] A popular quotation, dubiously attributed to Winston Churchill. The most reliable counter-claim names journalist Claud Cockburn as the originator.

Soon after the election he insisted on travelling from Westminster to his constituency by train and bus. He boarded a bus and started rooting around in his pocket for the fare, as he had done dozens of times before. By the time the bus got to the East End it was overrun by photographers clambering over the seats, and in Stepney the police begged him to send for an official car for his journeys to and from Downing Street. He agreed reluctantly, protesting that he could not justify taking his official car when petrol was rationed.[14]

Here was a new picture of what it meant to be a British citizen, focused on cooperation and the sharing of mundane difficulties within the domestic arena. This was a developing concept which, instead of demanding allegiance to a pre-determined authority, redefined citizenship in the context of mutual agreement with the State. It was a view which had been endorsed by Labour's massive post-war election victory, and the implications were repeatedly spelled out by the government's ideologues.

The next step is for the people to run the old and new institutions of our society, participating at all levels as active members – workers, consumers, citizens of an active democracy. Full employment, a rising standard of life, social justice and equality of opportunity for individuals to fulfil all their great and as yet untapped capacities, social ownership of the keys to social power, joy in life and pride in work, democracy in the community and democracy in industry – these, the purposes of democratic socialism, should become the common purposes of peace linking people together in a free and integrated society.[15]

Working from this blueprint, Attlee presided over a government which changed British society more radically than at any other time this century. Between the ending of the war and the arrival of the Windrush the post-war Labour Government managed the reconversion of a wartime economy, revolutionised industrial relations, created the Welfare State and set in motion the dissolution of Empire.

The urgency of the legislation was dictated by the mood of the country. For most of the electorate the dreams of Empire were irrelevant: citizenship was an expression of their material living conditions and its meaning could only be described in terms of immediate and concrete improvements.

A new conflict between different ways of describing the nation and its citizens was shortly to be provoked by the Caribbean immigrants, but for

14 Beckett, Clem Attlee. A Biography, pp. 209-10.

15 Michael Young, 'Small Man, Big World' (London, 1949), p. 4. Cited in Brooke, Reform and Reconstruction, pp. 136-7.

the moment the *Windrush* and its passengers excited very little interest and there was certainly no hint that their arrival would be a central feature in the future of British debates about nationality and citizenship. Public comment, therefore, tended to focus on their exotic origins and manners, but, even so, the West Indian arrivals were not the only exotic residents in the post-war landscape. For instance, the front page of the *South London Press* for 27 August 1948 featured a story about 'dusky Rannie Hart',[16] leader of a band which played in the saloon bar of the Queen's Hotel that week, and most of whose members had arrived on the *Windrush*.* The top of the page, however, is dominated by a photograph of women in Austrian folk costume, dancing 'at the Brixton club for Austrian brides of British ex-servicemen'.

There was nothing remarkable about the presence of the Austrian women, apart from their colourful costumes, because there was nothing unusual about the importation of foreign workers in 1948. Equally it seems that there was nothing objectionable about the prospect that they would settle permanently in Britain. The Polish Resettlement Act in 1946 cleared the way for resettling Polish soldiers and their families; and there were similar concessions to admit various stateless and displaced persons, along with European Volunteer Workers from Germany, Austria, Italy and Belgium. In the four years after the war Ministry of Labour permit holders totalled over 300,000. In comparison the arrival of a few hundred Caribbeans was pretty small beer.

This public perception was soon to change. During the following decade, independence became an established fact in West Africa and, in 1956, the Suez crisis finally dispelled any lingering delusions about the limits of British power. The arguments about the nature of British citizenship relocated themselves within the domestic arena and swiftly focused around the role and the status of the Caribbean immigrants.

[16] *South London Press*, Friday 27 August 1948. The tone of this report is remarkably matter of fact and friendly in comparison with the hostility which, only a short time later, crept into the style of journalistic commentary on West Indians.

* JAMAICANS PLAY EIGHT TO A BAR IN BRIXTON

Dusky Rannie Hart, aged twenty-two, of British Guiana, pressed a trumpet to his lips in the saloon bar of the Queen's Hotel, Pulross Rd, Brixton, on Wednesday night and played out of sheer delight.

Customers stopped talking and drinking to listen. Then, impressed, they applauded vigorously.

Rannie Hart is leader of a fourteen-man band, eight of whom played at the Queen's Hotel on Wednesday, most of whose members came from Jamaica on the *Empire Windrush* about a month ago.

They started playing in the Queen's because the licensee, Dennis Snow, who served in the merchant navy during the war, met Rannie in Georgetown, British Guiana, and extended a 'look me up' invitation if he ever came to England.

Rannie has toured South America as a trumpeter and played with Ken ('Snake Hips') Johnson, the Brixton dance-band leader who was killed in the Blitz.

He entertained British and American troops in British Guiana during the war.

'We're all musicians – it's in our blood,' he says. 'We don't mind where we play so long as we can.'

They are hoping to popularise calypso singing, at which they are adept, through their star performer, Lord Kitchener, a twenty-five-year-old former nightclub vocalist from Trinidad.

Another Jamaican, Frederick Geo Ogilvie, has for the past month been engaged on his duties of sanitary inspector for Camberwell Council.

Mr Ogilvie was chosen from among several applicants for the job because of his knowledge of the work. Yet he only started to learn about public health after being demobbed from the RAF.

Encouraged by a service friend, himself a sanitary inspector, he took the special government training course and qualified with excellent marks. Salary for his new job is £420 a year.

6

450 ARRIVE – GET PEP TALK: 'THINGS WILL NOT BE TOO EASY'

Four hundred and fifty Jamaicans crowded the rails of the *Empire Windrush* as she anchored in the Thames last night. They sailed as refugees from their island's unemployment problem, and have provided a new problem to the Colonial Office and the Ministry of Labour here. Loudspeakers called the 450 work-seekers to a pep talk by Mr Ivor Cummings, a principal officer of the Colonial Office, who welcomed them. They were told: Things will not be too easy.

Some of the men were resentful. But when they learned that the Colonial Office had only heard of their coming 12 days ago, they switched the blame to the Jamaican Government. An ex-RAF man returning to seek a welder's job said: 'Now we know how much our government cares for us.' (*Daily Express*, 22 June 1948)

'But the only thing after the war finish and people see us, the first thing they're asking you, "When are you going back to your own country?" And those are the things I didn't really like, because they say, Well, you come, you do your little bit in the war, England has won the war and now it seems as if they don't want you any more. That's how I look at it probably, I could be wrong. But I didn't like that. Anyhow, the first thing, "When are you going back to your own country?" '[1]

'I suppose you can say racism crept up on me, although some other people may have seen it straight away. But it is something that crept up on me very slowly. Just after the war was over, I was on a bus and there were two service people in front of me, one a woman. And she was saying, "Isn't it about time they went back to their homes?", and it was the first time that it hit me that, you know, that people were putting up with us, that they didn't really want us, but we were a necessary evil. But, apart from that, I didn't experience much problems with people.'[2]

'1948, 1948, 1948. There was a fellow living there from Jamaica who went down for five months holiday. He was down there for

---

[1] Interview with Cecil Holness.
[2] Interview with William Naltey.

quite some time and he came back on the *Windrush* and he told me about this ship that brought all these people from the West Indies, the bulk of them, I think, from Jamaica. Even one or two Bermudans happened to be on the ship. And it was the first time in the history of England, anyhow, the West Indies, that so many people came at one time. I don't know what numbers there were but how many, three or four hundred? Yes, and he was very excited about it and I was too because I thought this was good, very good. We should bring from our parts of the world the way of life that we know, we're not gonna do any harm.'[3]

'Things were changing. Although things were still rationed, they were re-building the cities and all that. But the attitude of the people was changed, people were more aggressive to you. In short, they are trying to say that you shouldn't be here. But there's another side. I would say a third of the people in Britain still had imperialist ideas. People from the colonies should be planting bananas and chocolate and whatever it is. Another third, I would say, did not really matter as Arsenal win on Saturday. The other third, they were just nice, ordinary people.'[4]

A Mixed Reception: 'Britain Is No Paradise'

A LETTER FROM THE HOME OFFICE

15 Portman Square
London, W1
E.M.2543/1948
Ambassador 1212

16 December 1948
Dear Wilson,
    We had hoped that shipping restrictions would have prevented any further influx of British West Indians. The termination of

---

[3] Interview with Earl Cameron.
[4] Interview with Sam King.

troopship sailings will, we think, minimise it, but I am afraid we must expect small parties from time to time. We have today been advised by the Colonial Office that a party of some thirty Jamaicans is expected on the SS *Raina Del Pacifico*, due to dock in Liverpool on Saturday next, 18 December. We understand that about nine have accommodation and employment to go to, but little is known about the remainder.

We should be glad if you would ask your people to consult with Mr Charles Owen, the Colonial Office representative in Liverpool, as to the best way in which men who need to obtain employment may be advised to register for it. We do not want any special steps taken to find the men employment, but simply that they should be informed of the facilities offered by the Local Office and how best they can make use of them.

If any of the men have accommodation to go to outside Liverpool, they can be given free railway warrants and travelling allowances in accordance with U.I.C.C.7.

H. J. Wilson Esq.

North-West Regional Office

Manchester, 3.[5]

Very few of the migrants could guess what problems they would encounter or the course their lives would take. Most of them thought they would be back in Jamaica in a few years with money in their pockets, and they had no way of predicting the future. Their only source of information was the men who had served in Britain during the war and who sailed with them, who could tell them about documents and bureaucracy and, of course, about things like the chimneys. Arriving at Tilbury the first thing all of them noticed was the chimneys, because the only time chimneys were seen in the Caribbean they signified factory buildings. When the migrants saw the chimneys on the houses it seemed the country was covered with factories, and they kept on saying, 'This place has got a lot of work', which, in an upside down sort of fashion, was true enough. But these things which struck them so forcibly were just part of how different it all was, not just the chimneys, but the look and the smell and the smoke and the dirt covering everything. It was going to be strange for everyone, because what the servicemen couldn't tell them, and what they wouldn't find out for themselves until they left the army or the Air Force, was what it was like to live outside

[5] HO 213/714 Public Records Office.

the protection of the military camps or the uniform, in amongst the civilian British. This was a different kettle of fish, when you came to housing, for instance. Work was no problem. They'd come to find work and there was plenty of work. Any fool could see that. Accommodation and getting on with people was going to be something altogether different.

In 1948 the result of wartime production meant that Britain was still a tightly regulated, even regimented society. The anxiety of the Ministry of Labour at the news that there were 500 colonial workers arriving unexpectedly was largely to do with the fact that no formal arrangements had been made and the West Indians were not part of official calculations. Their numbers were insignificant, but they were coming into an arena where almost every single facet of life was subject to some kind of control. The officials who greeted the *Windrush* were under no illusions, either, about the conditions which its passengers would face in civilian life.

Ivor Cummings, who led the boarding party of officials at Tilbury, was himself the son of an African father and an English mother, and had spent the preceding decade smoothing out the petty conflicts which surrounded the presence of the black servicemen.[6] Such matters had been manageable during wartime, but his own experience of black people who had been born and grown up in Britain would have been instructive about some of the difficulties that the Caribbeans would face in civilian life.

In the circumstances the *Windrush* passengers were relatively fortunate. By the time the boat arrived at Tilbury the Ministry of Labour, the Colonial Office and the local authorities had set in motion the kind of procedure they'd been accustomed to operating throughout the previous war-torn decade. First they briefed the new arrivals, then they classified them, then they transported them to their pre-arranged destinations.

The Jamaicans – and others with them - have been sorted into two groups: Group One: 82, who are volunteering for the Forces, will go to a Wimpole Street hostel (cost to them £1 1s a week). Group Two: 104 who have friends in England. Group Three: the rest with no contacts, who will go by motor coach to deep shelters on Clapham Common (cost 2/6d a week).

[6] Ivor Cummings addressed the migrants in a tone of patronising kindliness which exactly echoed the spirit of the time. 'I now want to address my friends who have nowhere to go and no plans whatsoever. I am afraid you will have many difficulties, but I feel sure that with the right spirit and by cooperating as I have suggested above, you will overcome them.' On the surface he maintained an iron neutrality as befitted a senior Civil Servant. But in conversation with Mike Phillips in the seventies he revealed that, at the time, he was desperately anxious about the migrants' prospects. He himself had been denied a commission at the start of the war because of the stipulation in the King's Regulations, which stated that H.M.'s officers had to be of pure European descent. This was abandoned shortly after, but by then Cummings had already joined the Civil Service.

The ship will not berth until 7 a.m. and all non-official communications with her have been barred by Transport Ministry officials and military police. Reporters were refused permission to go on board from a launch.

Footnote: Three men reported as stowaways as the anchor was dropped near Tilbury. They had eluded several searches. This brings the stowaway total to six, including one woman. (*Daily Express*, 22 June 1948)

The Shelter

'Well, when we arrived at Tilbury, a few people, political people, mostly Communists, you know, tried to befriend us. Burnham was just qualified. He's dead now, Burnham, he was President of Guyana after he went back, and a doctor, I forget what was his name now, a white man, he was a Communist, they come to meet us and tried to talk to us and that sort of thing. But all it needed at the time was who hadn't got any place to go to, wants somewhere to go, and that was uppermost in our minds. So I just went through the crowd and hear that to go into this place, Clapham South, I didn't know what the feeling was ashore, but I just followed the crowd, really. When we came to Clapham South, knowing that we were going to stay there temporary, everybody felt alright. The shelter was quite ordinary. It wasn't a family home, it was like a soldier's thing, as it was intended. Just like a camp, only it's down in the ground, small beds, well, the necessary convenience, apart from that it's only a place to sleep for a few nights. And when you got work, you had to leave. You had to go in by midnight, I think, I'm not quite sure, but you had to go in. You couldn't stay out all night. Paid two shillings a night for it, and that was cheap. But it was a good arrangement really, the hard up people coming, you know.

'I did not know how many people were there, but there was quite a few. But most of them didn't stay long at all. I, myself, I was only down there just over a week, call it two weeks, or something like that. Well, the truth is, I don't look for socialising. I was gambling on the ship from the time I left Jamaica, so if I can find people to play cards, I'm quite happy, used to be. That is all I am. And two things, a gambler don't suffer, he doesn't suffer from stress, 'cos he always have something to think about, whether you're going to win or not. And you never ever feel left out, because there's always somebody to try to win your money. The boys used to, you know, go outside and stand up by the Common there, congregate there and all that sort of thing. And gradually, some of them had friends to come and take them to the Labour Exchange and that sort of thing, 'cos you weren't restricted, you move about as you please. And very soon, the number was down to just a few.

'I remember a man came to me from the Ministry of Labour and asked me, "Can you get a few of the boys to go to the mines?" And I said, "Yes." It was the Ministry of Labour man asked me, because the fuss they were making of us and that, I thought I'd thank them, and they give me a job. I started working the same night, see that the fellows get food, because the WVS people provided food for us, 'cos everything was rationed in those days, so it wasn't easy to just get food like that.'[7]

'I came to Tilbury and then we're coming along on the coach, because they brought a coach and took us to Clapham. Was it Clapham North or Clapham South? One of them, the one beside Balham. What was strange is when we have to go down, because we'd never been down in the earth like that, something strange. But then, after a while, you get used to it. It wasn't bad, you know, because that place is a very big place, because one evening we was walking, I never reach the end of it. We was walking along, and we walk and walk and walk, and there was bed two sides, until we get to the end and turn back. But it wasn't bad. The things were clean, and we get food to eat down there, and things like that. But I've been in worse places than that. I don't know if it was two hundred or a hundred and fifty, there was quite a few of us down there. But then gradually we dispersed, because some of them, the Army come down and recruit some, the RAF come down and recruit some, everybody got different places. The coal mines, people come down and recruit some at the time, things like that. And they are spread several ways, several places.

'But then they sent us to London Bridge, which in those days, you get a medical at London Bridge. We went to London Bridge, we get the medical, and they send me to Orpington. So I used to have good fun at Orpington, because, when, in the evening, when I'm going home, if I went into a coach – because in those days they don't have a carriage like now, you have compartment coaches – and if I go into one compartment, I can fall asleep in that because nobody will ever come into that coach, that compartment. So I'll drive from

7   Interview with Oswald 'Columbus' Denniston.

Orpington as far as London Bridge, and when I reach London Bridge somebody might come in my compartment. So always I had a free compartment all the time. Nobody come in my compartment. When the train pull out, I'll just lay down and that's that. But after, say, a couple of years, that's changed, people come in my compartment. But in 1948, '49, nobody would come in that compartment.'[8]

DRIBERG TELLS THE JAMAICANS BRITAIN IS NO PARADISE

Forty Jamaicans who came to Britain on the *Empire Windrush* and are now staying in the Clapham Common deep shelters, were given a public welcome to Lambeth at the Brixton Astoria on Wednesday by the Mayor.

Among them were law students, dockers, potential chemists and scientists, who had left their homeland because of the difficulties of getting employment there.

One member was Norman Hamilton, a 24-year-old ex-RAF, wireless operator – one of the many who served in the Forces in Britain during the war. He comes from Kingston the capital.

He said, 'I visited London many times when I was here last and like the city a lot. We were completely disillusioned when we were demobbed in Jamaica after being assured that jobs would be awaiting us. There was nothing at all. We look to Britain for a brighter future.'

At the Brixton Astoria to greet them was Lt. Col. Marcus Lipton, Brixton MP with Mr Tom Driberg (Malden) and John Lewis (Bolton).

Col. Lipton, who had stated in the House of Commons a few hours previously that south Londoners would make them welcome, repeated the pledge and urged them to regard themselves as honoured visitors.

'We want you to regard this country as your second home. I hope it will not be very long before each of you is provided for in a dignified fashion.'

Another MP who questioned the Colonial Secretary about their welfare, Mr Tom Driberg, warned them frankly that Britain was 'not a paradise'. 'You have been warned that there may be difficulties caused through ignorance and prejudice, but don't let it get you down. Try and stand on your own feet as soon as you can.'

In charge of the party was Mr Colin Bryant, who is studying social welfare at the London School of Economics, and volunteered to show his countrymen round. He said that the welcome had deeply touched them. (*South London Press*, 25 June 1948)

---

[8] Interview with John Richards. John Richards came from Jamaica on the *Windrush*. He had been a farm worker in the USA before setting out for Britain. Subsequently he joined British Rail where he worked until his retirement.

The shelter provided an invaluable breathing space for the new arrivals. At the same time they found themselves at the receiving end of a formidable line-up of patronage and welfare. Caribbean students like Forbes Burnham and Colin Bryant, turned up from the LSE and Oxford. The Women's Voluntary Services [WVS] distributed food. Officials from the Ministry of Labour and Colonial Office interviewed, categorised and recruited them. Various church groups came to minister to their spiritual welfare. One of the migrants married a church worker he met in the shelter soon after. National and local politicians passed through and made speeches.

The official reception followed the logic of the previous decade, and inserting the migrants into the paper world of the bureaucracy presented few problems. This was a society which had run a wartime economy, then transformed it in a couple of years. The Labour Exchange nearest to the Clapham shelters was in Coldharbour Lane, and that was where the migrants went for their documents and permits.

> 'Within days some start working, and within one month, all have got jobs and left the shelter. And because they worked very hard in the factory or office or wherever it is, all of our people had employment. And the employer could not get enough workers, resulting that when my brother came, normally you arrived in England, say, Monday, you have your documentation by Tuesday, Wednesday, you were working.'[9]

In the circumstances, the authorities were laying out a welcome mat. At the time the Berlin airlift was in full swing. The guerrilla war in Malaya was entering a new and more deadly phase. A crippling dock strike was about to erupt. As a whole, British society still possessed a grim stoicism and intolerance of deviance inherited from the war years. After their interlude in the Clapham shelters the migrants were about to encounter very different experiences. The issue of where they could live and what sort of housing they would occupy, was, to a large extent, out of the control of the authorities. It proved to be a fault line which sketched out the nature of the black community and also began to determine the style of relationships over the following three decades.

---

[9] Interview with Sam King.

'I must find a place ... I must find a place'

'So you come off, and we leave the deep shelter, and they put us at Hounslow Square, at the hostel. And then we used to leave from South Kensington to Victoria and take the Orpington train. And then, when we leave Hounslow Square, went to West Cromwell Road to live in Earl's Court, and then still have my job, and, after I leave West Cromwell Road, I live at Nevern Square, off Warwick Road in Earl's Court. And then I leave Nevern Square, live up Pennywern Road in Earl's Court. You move around a lot because people didn't give you a lot of time. You say thirty bob a week, somebody would come and say two pounds. And, of course, when your wages is about five or six pounds a week, to pay two pounds, that's a lot, so you've got to go around and look, because in those days, it's either two or three of you in a room, in those days, as a black man, it's very hard to get a room, you wouldn't get one. They always put on the board, "Black – Niggers not wanted here", on the board, you know, these boards out there, "No Niggers" or "No Colour", things like that. So it's very hard to get a room.

'I get kicked out once, and at that time, Lyon's Corner House used to open all night. You go into Lyon's Corner House and then you buy a cup of tea or a cup of coffee, and then you have it there, you see, and then you nod off. And the guy comes, "You can't stay here, sir", so you buy a next cup of coffee, and that's how you work it. Because, at that time, I didn't have a place to go. It's a funny thing, you don't realise how a roof is so handy over your head until you walk out of work and you're going home, aren't you? But if you leave here and don't have nowhere to go, it's that time life's really tough with you. But it didn't take long. A chap named Albert Halthornes get me a room and I stayed there for a while, then from there, from Penywern Road, I went to Gower Street and lived in Gower Street for quite a while. And then I went to Tavistock and Westbourne Park.

'And then when I leave, I have a friend of mine named Helen Clark who have a place in Tavistock. So Helen say I can come, because no need to have the whole house. And then I went to Helen and I stayed at Helen until a friend of mine says an old lady who have two flats, he had one and I took the flat from him. The flat wanted papering. Well, we said we're going to paper the flat. Well, we didn't know how to paper, we didn't know how to do papering. So, what we do, you know a roll of paper, we opened a whole roll, and then we didn't know how to cut a length, but we would plaster it, and then put it down, and cut the length down. We didn't know you must cut the length before you do that. And there's about six of us, we buy lots of paper because they used to have little, what they call them, firkin, little barrel of beer, and we buy that, and we buy some VP wine. And, you know, there's about six of us was there, and we're drinking the beer and drink that wine, and we never put up a roll of paper, we never put up nothing. We got to sling the whole lot away. And then a chap come round, as a matter of fact he was a coal man, and he had an idea what to do.

'Just when we got married, 1949, and I saw this advert, you know, in a shop window about rooms to let and then when I phoned this lady, she say, "Oh yes, come around, it's all here, you'll get the room." So when I arrive, I rang the bell and this white lady she came out and I said, "Good afternoon, madam", and the moment when she answered the door you know it's like as if she's so frightened because she didn't expect to see a black man. I said probably she might know it was a foreigner by my accent, but I made myself quite clear to her, she could understand me and she said, "All right, come into the room." And then, just like that, she said, "No, I haven't got any room to let." No, first of all she say, you know, in that nice sugary way to say, "Oh, I'm so sorry. You are just five minutes late. The room is taken." So I said to her, I said, "Madam, do you see that telephone kiosk down there?" She said, "Yes." I said, "That's where I was phoning from and I did not see anyone come to your door like that." So she paused for a while and said, "Well, I don't want black people." I said, "Why not say so?" I said, "You'd have saved me all that trouble of making all my own way here." She said, "We don't want any black people." I say, "You should let me know." I said, "It's your place. I can't force you to let me your rooms", you see, and just like that. That's one thing I can never forget.'[10]

'I couldn't get a room to live in. It took me a long time before I find a little room and when I do find a little room, it was very restricted, I couldn't take no visitors, I couldn't do anything. Islington, that was the first room I had. And I wasn't allowed to take no visitors at all, even the couple of friends that I know, they couldn't come and meet, we got to meet in the street. And you couldn't take a girlfriend there, the female couldn't go in the male apartment, neither the male go in the female apartment. So if you want to meet up, you've got to meet around the street, see. And sometimes, when the winter is on, because winter was winter, you see, snow was two, three inches high, off the ground, and them days it was cold. I even had a friend, and I take him into my flat to visit me. And the landlord get about three big police and he put me out right away, right away, he put me out. Then, from there, I've got to go down to a little hostel.

'The police said, all they can tell me is a hostel down in EC1, there's a hostel down there. I can go down there, and if I pay I can stop in there. Now, when I got down there, all I could hear is people coughing. So I paid the money for the one night, I never go back. Then I start walking around, walking around, you know, so I must find a place. I must find a place. And I was sleeping from Brixton to Warren Street, where there is a big dance hall. It closed down now. I was walking from Brixton, walking, in the morning, from Brixton, to Warren Street, morning and evening, just walking around, 'cos them days you couldn't hang about in the corners, the police would have gone with you, so you just keep walking. Anyway, I was doing that for nearly two or three months, couldn't get no place. I just walk around, come down, go to dance hall, the Paramount, and then just walk the streets in the night, just walk about. I tell you, that was the old life, I was young and strong, I didn't sleep, wouldn't worry me. I might have a little nod in the dance hall, right, that would do me, because, you know, when you're young and strong you don't feel it. Strong will power, you know. So it never worried me.'[11]

'I was sent to one place, and the fellow took all the time in the world to show me around it, say, "Well this is the room, that I have for rent." Then, having shown me around the house we went outside and we sat smoking a cigarette. Then he said, "Well, I can't rent you the room, you know." So I said, "Well, why not?" He said, "Well, if I let you have it, the rest of my tenants will go." He said, "I have nothing personal against you, but that's the way it will be." '[12]

[11] Interview with Lloyd Miller.
[12] Interview with William Naltey.

For most of the new arrivals these were typical and characteristic experiences, and they more or less determined the major features of Caribbean immigration over the next decade. Caribbeans would keep on coming, because there was plenty of work to be had, and no one was in any doubt that they had a legal and moral right to do so. When they arrived, they would have to cluster in those places which were prepared to accommodate them, and where the *Windrush* passengers had already established a foothold. In much the same way the experience of Vince Reid, the only teenager on the boat, foreshadowed the issues which would bedevil the education system in Britain over the next fifty years.

'I don't know how, we stayed one night in a hotel in Victoria, but my father knew some people who were quite willing to put us up. And it was over in Valetta Road. And then we eventually got a room over in King's Cross, in Argyle Square. And that's where, that's where we lived, all three of us in one room: two adults and a young boy in one room, that was it. You couldn't get any place to rent. I mean, you had usually notices, about "No Irish" and not even "No Blacks", but "No Niggers". I mean, this is 1948, you know, and already you had those things in shop windows.

'So we were forced to live in one room, all three of us. You can imagine the tension, two adults and a thirteen-year-old boy in one room. It was horrendous. But that's how it was. I had no sort of personal impression of how I'm going to be received, because, as I say, I was a boy. And I wasn't expecting anything. But how I was received was when I went to school, first of all, I was a subject of curiosity, which is quite surprising when you think that you had black soldiers in England. And, you know, people would come up and rub your skin and see if it would rub off the black, and rub your hair and, you know, it's really insulting. And, of course, there was always the latent violence, you know, people want to fight you. Fortunately, I was quite big and could handle myself, so that didn't persist very long, because they couldn't deal with me on that basis. But, even at that time, one was very aware of hostility, quite serious hostility, you know, being beaten up, even at that time.

'I was the only black child in the school. And, funnily enough, one of the other things about the school was they didn't even give me a test to see – it was a secondary modern school – they didn't even give me a test to see which grade I should be put in, you know, they just put me in the lowest grade. Then they had a sort of end of year examination and I moved up into the top class. But I remember a teacher, teaching Shakespeare and the soliloquy from *Julius Caesar*. And this teacher said, "Who can explain what this soliloquy means?" So I put my hand up, you know. And, of course the way I spoke then is not like I speak now, I had this funny Jamaican accent. And this teacher just rolled around. I felt so ashamed, that he was basically mocking me, you know, and I felt so ashamed. And I stopped, I really basically stopped going to school, because I felt so angry and ashamed. It still hurts to this day, you know, because it was bloody upsetting. And that was what it was like. You weren't expected to know anything and they just took the mickey. And that was then, 1949, '49, and it still hurts.

'It was fairly demoralising. I mean, you go to a secondary modern school, you come out with no kind of certificates whatsoever. I remember when, at fifteen, I left school, and I actually wanted to be a tailor. And I went along to the youth services thing, and this bloke just laughed. Want to be a tailor? You know, no way. So I ended up in the Post Office as a junior postman. And I didn't want to be a postman, so, eventually, at the age of about sixteen, you could become a boy entrant to join the Royal Air Force. And given the kind of conditions in which I was living, I thought, well, it's a way out. So that's what I did, I went and joined the Air Force, signed on for twelve years, in fact. Bought myself out after three years, 256 days, for £250, which was a lot of money in those days.

'I mean, I would have to go in anyway, because you had National Service at that time, so I thought, rather than wait, I could go in and perhaps learn a trade, which I did. I was trained as a radio mechanic. And in fact, my entry, I was the first one to be trained as what they call a ground wireless fitter. And I was the first one in my entry to be made an NCO. I was a corporal when I was about nineteen. So, although the whole thing had been humiliating to some extent, I wasn't exactly demoralised, 'cos I always had this belief in my own ability and nobody was ever going to eradicate that. So, of course, going in the Air Force and becoming one of the first to be made an NCO reinforced that opinion of myself.'[13]

Another exception to general rules was the calypsonian Lord Kitchener. Kitchener's role was extraordinary because he became the voice of the Caribbean culture the immigrants had brought with them. Like all calypsos

---

[13] Interview with Vince Reid.

his songs were topical and loaded with double entendre, but it was the language he used – the Trinidadian dialect and his ability to highlight what it meant to be Caribbean – which made him an icon within the group of arrivals from the *Windrush*. After the publicity given to the actual docking of the boat, the *Windrush* slipped, for a time, out of the national consciousness. If anyone beyond the relatively small circle of people who encountered its passengers knew anything about who they were or what they were like, it was through Lord Kitchener's songs. But, unlike his colleagues, Kitchener had to begin by creating his own audience.

'Well, it's my time now, to get around. I'm a bit confused, because, you know, I'm new in this country, so I want to know what I'm going to do. My work is calypsonian. A friend of mine told me that I can get a job in a pub at Brixton. I went to Brixton and I started on this job. I started singing. While singing, a customer came to the microphone, took away the mike from me, told me he can't understand a word that I'm saying. And I just stood there, just looking around. So, eventually, the boss of the pub came and whispered something in my ear, meaning that I would have to stop work because the customer doesn't understand what I'm saying. Oh well, they were all white, no blacks in the pub on that night, all white. So, I lost my job. I started looking around and asking about work.

'I met another friend. He told me I can get a job in a place called The Sunset Club. I went to The Sunset Club, and there was a mixture of people. And I started singing this song. "Kitch come go to bed, I have a small comb to scratch your head." Of course, the Caribbean people understood the song and they explain it to their white friends. So, most of the people understood the song, and then the song became very popular. It was so popular until I was in three night clubs in one night. One here, one there, and the other one. So I'm working through the night. And this went on for quite a while. So, after this, I had no more worries. I was living like a king at that period.'[14]

[14] Interview with Lord Kitchener.

7

———◆———

'Cricket lovely cricket
at Lords where I saw it
cricket lovely cricket
at Lords where I saw it
Yardley did his best
but Goddard won the Test
with those little pals of mine
Ramadhin and Valentine'

Lord Beginner

'Don't forget 1950, that's the year we won the Test at Lords.
Ramadhin and Valentine and the calypso. I think that changed the
whole face of cricket. It was no longer the quiet game where you
sat on the terraces and gently clapped when somebody scored.
Caribbean people took over and we brought the steel band, we
brought the calypso. In fact the cricketers were adored. They were
very, very popular. They were entertained. They were treated
like royalty, actually. But they were seen as distinct from the
immigrants coming to Britain.'[1]

'It is 1950. The West Indies won. And I was about going
home, about twenty voices said, "Sam, you can't go home, man.
Beginner going to make a song." I said, "What?" They said,
"Just come." We sat down on the grass and Beginner says,
"Cricket, lovely cricket," and someone said, "Put Ramadhin in,
man." And he put Ramadhin in, and he went over it, and in thirty
minutes he wrote the song, "Cricket, lovely cricket, at Lord's,
where I saw it. Yardley won the toss, but Goddard won the Test,

[1] Interview with Ros Howells.

with those little pals of mine, Ramadhin and Valentine." I was
there. That was history.'[2]

Cricket, Lovely Cricket

The Caribbean migrants kept on coming, but the ships were few and far
between and the numbers of men and women were tiny. The *Orbita*, which
sailed later in 1948, for instance, only carried 108 passengers, and until
1951 the total in any one year never reached one thousand. In 1951 the
census figures showed that there were about 15,000 people born in the
West Indies resident in Britain, 4,000 of them living in London. Even if
this was an underestimate it is clear that in 1950 the Caribbean presence
in the country was relatively insignificant. Public awareness had peaked
with the docking of the *Windrush* and, for a couple of years, subsequent
arrivals sparked no concern at all. Within a matter of months the newspapers had lost interest and confined themselves to the occasional story
about crime and drugs. For most people the West Indians had conveniently
disappeared into an isolated urban underbelly comprising an anarchic,
floating population which was easy to forget.

On the other side of the coin, the Caribbeans were more or less crushed
by the country's indifference, coupled as it was with casual discrimination.
The adjustments they faced went deeper than differences in the weather,
styles of speech and clothing. It was the colour of their skins which ensured
their isolation and began to shape their relationship with British society.
This was no trivial irritant because, when all the other factors were taken
into consideration, it was the West Indians' colour which the British nation
took to be the characteristic that defined their status and potential. In turn
the racial attitudes the Caribbeans encountered confirmed and intensified
their sense of isolation.

'You're not thinking of your skin, but you feel other people are
thinking of it. And every little thing that you do reflects on your
reaction. Like, if you get on the bus, and there's an empty seat, you
sit down, and somebody comes in, pass and go down the back and
didn't sit with you, you're saying, maybe they want to sit on the

---

[2] Interview with Sam King.

back. But when the bus fills up and you find you're the last one to have somebody beside you, then you know something is wrong. Come on, be yourself, be strong.

'I came from such a bright place, so much sunshine, so much colour, it was very depressing that time of the year. They didn't know anything about us. Some people ask you where you came from. Jamaica. And you could have come from the moon. They don't know where it is and you have to tell them, you know, it's in the Caribbean. And a lot of them would talk behind your back. Darkies, you know. You weren't a person, you were a darkie. And after a while I became indifferent.

'I wish I could be back home so bad it hurts, tears came into your eyes, because you missed the sort of freedom and companionship that you used to have, you know, with your own kind. One day I was on a bus, and I was upstairs and I was at the corner of Parliament Street, and I saw a black man. Although I was used to the very small community, I just felt, if only this bus would stop, I would get off it and just run and hug him, and find out, you know, where he came from. Because you feel lost, you know. It wasn't so much open hostility. When you're back home, you know when somebody's angry with you, and this is blatant, you can see it in the speech, you can see it in their action. But instinctively, you built something up in you that tells you, this people or this group doesn't like me. And the first thing you think, it's because you're black. But can you imagine writing home to come back?

'What am I going back to? Where am I going to get the money from? Just after your board is taken out, you get just under £8 a month. And then you have to live off that. And all of us that came from Jamaica always know that you must make a sacrifice, too. Even out of that money, if it's even two pounds, you would still buy a postal order and send it home.'[3]

As yet, there was no widespread sense within the country that the presence of the migrants was to be an arena of political conflict. However, early in 1950 the Labour Government suddenly experienced two serious crises which, in hindsight, seemed to be announcing the nature of the debates which would come to dominate argument in Britain around the question of citizenship and nationality.

[3] Interview with Tryphena Anderson.

One crisis was about Europe, and about Britain's relationship with the Continent. It concerned the plan outlined by Robert Schuman, the French Foreign Minister at the time, for a coal and steel community to integrate heavy industry in Europe, and which would include the German Federal Republic. The Schuman Plan split the Western Alliance and prompted passionate debate between the parties, without stirring up any great excitement among the British electorate.

In contrast, the other crisis of the year focused on race and became a cause célèbre. This was the case of Seretse Khama, heir to the hereditary chieftaincy of the Bamangwato people in the British protectorate Bechuanaland, later Botswana. Khama studied law in England and married Ruth Williams, a white English woman, in 1949. His uncle Tshekedi seized on his marriage as an instrument in pursuing a long-standing rivalry, and soon the South Africans were involved, lobbying the Foreign Office to prevent the accession of Seretse and his white wife on their borders. The line taken by the Secretary of the Commonwealth Relations Office, Patrick Gordon Walker, who described the marriage as 'irresponsibility', was rigidly hostile, and he began preparing to oust Seretse. This now seems cruelly ironic, given that, during the next decade Gordon Walker's political career would be ruined by the public perception that he was 'soft on blacks'.

At the time Clement Attlee, not a man to utter opinions lightly, protested: 'In effect we are invited to go contrary to the desire of the great majority of the Bamangwato tribe, solely because of the attitude of the governments of the Union of South Africa and Rhodesia. It is as if we had been obliged to agree to Edward VIII's abdication so as not to annoy the Irish Free State and the USA.'[4]

In spite of various objections, however, the Cabinet voted to depose Khama. He was forced to renounce his claim to the title and was exiled from his country for six years.

The Cabinet may have seen its treatment of Khama as a necessary political and diplomatic strategy but throughout the colonial world it was viewed as British endorsement of South African racism. And, although it had no direct connection with the situation of the migrants in Britain, they saw it as the official counterpart of the racial barriers they encountered daily. The ugly exercise of British power over Khama's private life had been a reflection of imperialist relationships which also referred to life in Britain.

Identity was the issue. Back in the Caribbean the migrants had been

---

[4]   Memo from Geoffrey Cass to Patricia Llewellyn-Davies, CRO, 22 January 1950. Cited in Kenneth Morgan, *Labour In Power 1945-1951* (Oxford: Oxford University Press, 1984).

brought up to perceive British power as part of the natural order of things, but they had also believed that British citizenship made them part of the show. After a few months in Britain it was impossible to maintain that illusion. The first clue about their status was the widespread ignorance about the Caribbean. Caribbean education had focused on the geography, economy and history of Britain. This was more than a simple cultural cringe. It was part of a quasi constitutional balance in which British power was tolerated in the framework of the assumption that the Empire, whatever else it did, was an internationalising project where the rights and obligations of citizenship were interchangeable, both in Britain and in its outposts. But, once in England, the migrants immediately discovered that people were confused about where the Caribbean was. Some of them thought Trinidad and Barbados were places in Jamaica, and they kept on asking where the migrants had learned to speak English. This was a revelation demonstrating British indifference to the constitutional bargain which had formed a corner- stone of Caribbean identity. More importantly, it was a sign of the process by which the Caribbeans would come to feel deprived, stripped of the most vital part of their being.

The country they arrived in had been the first and the most thoroughly industrialised nation in the world, and the war had intensified the social effects of industrialisation. In comparison the Caribbean economies were based on agriculture, cottage and workshop industries. A craftsman could turn his hand to anything, from planting and harvesting to carpentry and tinkering with engines. The biggest cities, like Kingston, resembled market towns doubling as administrative centres rather than the industrial cities of Europe. As a result the unifying themes of the Caribbean were based on a collective sentiment which originated in families or small autonomous communities. For example, one of the institutions the migrants brought with them was the 'pardner' system.

'Pardner' was a way of saving and amassing capital for immediate needs. A group of people would contribute a fixed sum of money each week which would be held by a banker. Each week one person would be entitled to a 'hand'. In a group of twenty contributing £10 a week, the hand would be £200. At the end of the round, the order could be reversed, so that the last and first hand went to the same person. This would double the hand, yielding £400. This meant that members of the group could receive a rela- tively large sum of money at regular intervals for a small outlay.

'Well, I was no spendthrift, I save, because we already have a saving bank, you know. British Rail have a savings bank, and you put a certain amount of money away, and pardner, that's West Indian business. Okay, I'll give £5 this week, he give £5, he give pounds, he give £5. They start, you will get £30. Next week, you give the same amount, your draw, you get £30. You know, and that's the way it go. And it go round. So if you get £30, you would save £30. And there you go. And in those days, it's about £200, £300, to deposit on a house. The most was £400 in those days. You get to a stage, for the first, you will accept three people into a room, after a while you only accept two people. And then you advance from this stage again where you alone want a room, you don't want to share with nobody. And then you move to the next stage, you get yourself a flat, and then after you get yourself a flat, then you get yourself a house, if you can do it. I did move up. I move along, from a room to a flat, until I bought my own place.'[5]

This was a model of social organisation which depended on a high level of personal knowledge, mutual trust and friendship. By contrast social organisation in urbanised Britain was on a mammoth scale and depended on a network of depersonalised contracts guaranteed by a legal framework instead of relationships between individuals. Coming from environments where the nature of community allowed each individual a social role, the West Indians were worse than isolated. The points in the moral and social compass which told them who they were and what life was about had disappeared, and they had become anonymous.

In the two years after the *Windrush* the Caribbean migrants were to canvass a variety of solutions. But if they had been searching for a symbol which would announce their presence to the public at large, and at the same time assert their individuality, they could not have found a better one than the cricket tour which arrived that summer. Cricket still occupied an important role in the culture of British superiority. Cricket meant Englishness, and the spread of the game throughout the Empire was merely taken, in England, to mean that everyone else recognised the superior virtues of being English. Popular commentators like Neville Cardus described the national character in terms of the game. 'The laws of cricket,' he wrote in 1930, 'tell of the English love of compromise between a particular freedom and a general orderliness, or legality.'[6] It was the sort of statement that everyone believed and which had been an important aspect of the mythology

[5] Interview with John Richards.

[6] Christopher Martin-Jenkins, *The Spirit of Cricket: A Personal Anthology* (London: Faber & Faber, 1994), p. 5.

of Britishness in the Caribbean. It had become a fundamental element of Caribbean identity, partly because the culture of imperialism had relentlessly fragmented and erased local and traditional games and rituals – both in the Caribbean and throughout the colonised world – and replaced them with an internationalised process governed and orchestrated from London.

Like the Empire, cricket and its rituals belonged to everyone within its reach, but the English were its masters. That is, it was the only game in town, but to play it you had to accept and propagate all the English assumptions of imperial mastery. On the other hand, the rules also meant that it was the one arena in which colonials could dispute on equal terms with the metropolitans. Given the fixed nature of the relationship, every time Britain faced one of the colonies on the cricket field the game became a confrontation within which a variety of strains and contradictions were exercised. For black and Asian colonials such confrontations provided a unique and solitary opportunity to challenge established beliefs about racial superiority.

In 1950 when the West Indies team beat England at Lords for the first time, Caribbeans all over the world celebrated, but in England the victory had a special significance. It was also the first time that West Indians living in Britain had announced their presence to such effect, shouting, singing and rattling tin cans in the stands. There were only a few dozen of them, but the ripples they caused can be deduced from the fact that, at the end of the match, a file of policemen emerged to form a solemn line along the boundary. 'Unnecessarily', sniffed the MCC diaries of that year. On the other hand, the sheer exuberance of the West Indians' celebration was to do with the sense that this was an event which had an importance that went beyond the confines of the ground.

'Fifty years ago, when England came to the West Indies, there was an article in *The Times* . . . These people are very nice and jolly, but they will never understand the finer points of cricket. Their slip fielding was shoddy, et cetera. I have got the clipping, you wouldn't believe it. But this is 1950, we're at Lords. And, at the end, we won. Here, at the headquarters, Ramadhin, bowling the ball, and it will go on, like Shane Warne, forty-five degree angle. And Goddard was the captain, and he did a very good job. And there were not many West Indians there. I would say thirty at the most. Now, after that, the British people, realising that the minority people from the colonies here had beaten them at cricket, we were not as stupid as a lot of them assumed or wanted us to be stupid. And even in the factories, gradually, it start permeating, that if you teach these people machinery, they will be good machinists. And in the Forces, a few of us were engineers or whatever it is, and then they realise, if you give them the opportunity, they will be good non-commissioned officers, and if they had the education, they'll be officers. Yes, it was a milestone for the people from the colonies.'[7]

'That was quite sensational. As a matter of fact, that gave us the impetus of forming a West Indian cricket team in Nottingham, which was called the West Indian Carib CC. In 1951 we formed a team. The year before was '50 when the West Indies first beat England at that time. So that was quite an achievement to look back and see. That was well taken up by a number of people.'[8]

'It was very important, we didn't have anything else, did we? That was very important for us. We loved that, we enjoyed it. It was good, because it's new. We never beat England, they always thrash us. We beat them in the West Indies, but now we beat them up here. And, as far as I know, must be the first time we beat them up here. That time we have a good side, very, very good side, disciplined side. In those days I go from Old Trafford and Nottingham, you know, one of the first games. Then they come to Lords, the second one, then we go to Birmingham, Edgbaston. And we go to Leeds. But I go to all the Test matches. We go up by train sometime, we hire a van and things like that, but we go there, support them all the time. It was no problem. I thought it was great.'[9]

The match was front page news in Britain, and attached to every commentary or report was a description of the West Indian supporters and the style of their celebration. After that afternoon, few people in Britain could fail to be aware of the presence or the individuality of the West Indians. From that point onwards, the cultures and customs the migrants brought with them, or invented, were to become a clearly identifiable strand in the progressive development of British identity; and in much the same way as the few dozen who turned up at Lords, the West Indians in Britain were fated to have an influence which far outstripped their numbers.

[7]   Interview with Sam King.
[8]   Interview with Laurie Philpots.
[9]   Interview with John Richards.

'I went there, with a guitar. And we won the match. After we won the match, I took my guitar and I call a few West Indians, and I went around the cricket field, singing. And I had an answering chorus behind me, and we went around the field singing and dancing. That was a song that I made up. So, while we're dancing, up come a policeman and arrested me. And while he was taking me out of the field, the English people boo him, they said, "Leave him alone! Let him enjoy himself! They won the match, let him enjoy himself." And he had to let me loose, because he was embarrassed. So I took the crowd with me, singing and dancing, from Lords, into Piccadilly in the heart of London. And while we're singing and dancing and going to Piccadilly, the people opened their windows wondering what's happening. I think it was the first time they'd ever seen such a thing in England. And we're dancing in Trinidad style, like mas,[10] and dance right down Piccadilly and dance around Eros. The police told me we are crazy. So, we went a couple of rounds of Eros. And from there, we went to the Paramount, a place where they always had a lot of dancing. And we spend the afternoon there, dancing and having a good time. At that time, I am living in a place called Bayswater.'[11]

[10] A Trinidadian word, probably a corruption of *mass*, referring both to the period before the carnival and to the jumping up in the streets. Also short for masquerade, referring to the practice of dressing up and playing a role, which is fundamental to the carnival. To 'play mas', or to 'play ole mas', is to participate in the carnival, to dance around, play tricks, be a joker.

[11] Interview with Lord Kitchener. There were at least two calypsonians at the match, Lord Beginner and Lord Kitchener. Lord Beginner composed the best-known song, *Cricket, Lovely Cricket*, while Kitchener led the dance from Lords to Piccadilly.

8

'I sold dope, right? I posed as an African prince with my friends and we go to Bond Street and we steal diamond rings and thing like that, right? But these are not me, man, you understand? That's not my life, you know. I do these things as a means of survival and nobody can say, Well, you should not survive, no? Otherwise I wouldn't be here. I mean, if I'd conformed to them and let them subject me to all the bullshit, I mean, what kind of shape would I be in? My head would be fucked up. But, you see, I'm a man, and I'm nobody's tool or nobody's slave and I've got no superiors, right? I'm not responsible for anyone holding themselves below me, right, but I'm a man and this is my story, and I'm a man who is black. I'm not a black man. I'm not the Englishman definition of who I am, I'm my own explanation of myself, yeah? I'm my own actor and my own director and I star in my own movie. I don't need anyone directing my shit, you know. And this is my life and this is the way I am, this is what I think about things, hmm? And I'm not afraid to die, so I can live anywhere I want. That's the secret of life.'[1]

'One wrote, sent back photographs and tell me he's walking on a diamond pavement. So, you can understand we would like to come and walk on this diamond pavement as well. It happens one night we were coming from the West End, and I turned to him, I say, "Vinny, where is this diamond pavement that you told us about?" It was raining and the light reflection looking down Bayswater Road, it seems as if the pavement, where they used to make it with broken glass or anything like that were in the concrete, so it glitters when the rain washed off. So he said, "There it is. Good question you asked. There's the diamond. Here, man."'[2]

---

[1] Interview with Johnny Edgecombe. Johnny Edgecombe arrived in Liverpool 1949 as a merchant seaman. He lived in Notting Hill and ran various enterprises on both sides of the law, but is most famous for his romance with Christine Keeler, which sparked off the Profumo scandal. He was jailed for firing a gun at Keeler. He now lives in London with his family.

[2] Interview with Alfred 'King Dick' Harvey. Alfred Harvey came to Britain in 1954 as a stowaway. He now lives in London.

Cowboys of Notting Dale

Even before the war London was rearranging its population in patterns which are now familiar. In August 1948 the *South London Press* commented that in south London alone, 'the inner circle of boroughs within five miles of Charing Cross have lost 365,000 people since 1931. This area includes all Battersea, the northern part of Wandsworth, Lambeth as far down as Brixton, the bulk of Camberwell and part of Deptford.'

The major motivation behind the population shift was the degeneration and decay of the inner city areas and the sheer nastiness of the environment in sizeable pockets of the city. Some districts were more notorious than others for the crime, violence and prostitution which traditionally accompanied their rotten housing conditions. Such spots as the Jago (in the East End), Hoxton, Hackney and Notting Dale, were skirted round by respectable folk, abandoned by the upwardly mobile working class, and inadequately policed. When Mark Strutt, grandson of the Honourable Edward Strutt, inherited a parcel of houses in Notting Dale from his grandfather in 1948, he described them as being 'filled with prostitutes, burglars, murderers and negroes'.[3]

In a city where landlords were largely unwelcoming and the housing stock depleted, these were the districts where migrants found it easiest to be accommodated and from which they found it difficult to escape. The association had immediate consequences, because from that time onwards the migrants were to be identified with the unsavoury reputations of the places where they lived. The mythology of urban vice which had been constant for a century, following the Ripper murders in the East End, transferred easily to an unpopular foreign group. For instance, during the same period, the Maltese resident in London acquired a fearsome reputation as violent pimps, due mainly to the activities of Sunday newspapers like *The News of the World*, which gave Maltese criminals front page headlines and printed numerous stories about Maltese gangs. In much the same way, within a few weeks of the *Windrush* arriving, what public opinion there was about the migrants, patronisingly tolerant at first, had swung towards deep suspicion and outright hostility. As with the Maltese, it was the sexual threat the newcomers presented which attracted the most attention. Within a few months, local newspapers like the *South London Press* had promoted

---

[3] Shirley Green, *Rachman* (London: Michael Joseph, 1979).

the *Windrush* migrants from benign human interest stories about 'dusky' musicians, to the objects of popular complaint.

WEST INDIAN IMMIGRANTS DRIFT INTO CRIME: MINORITY SET PROBLEM FOR POLICE

A minority section of the 400 West Indians who arrived in this country a few weeks ago to look for work and a new life in Britain, are becoming a problem for police, churchmen and welfare organisations in south London. Many of the West Indians are skilled workers who quickly found jobs and homes, but others, reinforced by some who had come to this country earlier, are drifting into crime, vagrancy and other anti-social activities.

When they arrived in this country they were accommodated in the deep shelter at Clapham Common, and those who have not found jobs or whose activities are questionable have not moved far from that area.

Police have been called upon to investigate a growing number of complaints and incidents, and reports have been received showing that some of the West Indians are congregating in unsavoury haunts known to be the meeting places of criminals.

A fortnight ago, a sixteen-year-old Battersea girl, who was missing from home for three days, told the police that she had become friendly with a coloured man and gone to live with him. After smoking a cigarette which she believed was drugged, she remembered nothing more until she woke up in a strange house with a second coloured man. Dazed and distressed, she escaped by climbing down a stack pipe and returning home.

The mother of another south London girl who was missing for a week said she believed her daughter had been enticed away by coloured men whom she met in a café.

Writing in his parish magazine, the Rev. D. R. Blackman, rector at St Paul's, Deptford, says: "I am very distressed about the West Indians that we see about here. They have nowhere to live except common lodging houses and tell me how unhappy they are because they have no place of their own where they can be during the day. It would be a good thing if they could have a hostel fixed up for them where they could live together. I wish something could be done for them, for they have estimable qualities and are worth caring for, if only for the sake of the Englishman's good name." (*South London Press*, 2 November 1948)

West London's Notting Hill was where many of the recent migrants had settled; or, more precisely, Notting Hill and Notting Dale. However, after the riots in 1958, which made the district notorious as a centre of racial conflict, the distinction was forgotten and the whole area was called Notting Hill. Increasingly, and all through the fifties, there were West Indians all over London: in Clapham going through south London to Brixton; in Euston moving north to Finsbury Park, Holloway, all over Islington and up to the borders of Hackney in the east; in other major cities like Nottingham, Birmingham, Manchester and Leeds. But Notting Hill was the headquarters which caught the public imagination even before the 1958 riots. After the riots, events like the Profumo affair – when the Minister of Defence, John Profumo, was impeached for lying to the House about his relationship with a woman he met in Notting Hill – and, later on, the annual Notting Hill Carnival, made sure that, for a couple of decades, it was Notting Hill which shaped public perceptions of who the Caribbean migrants were and what they were doing.

When the migrants arrived after the war, the district still carried distinct echoes of its murky past. In the nineteenth century Notting Dale was still known as the Potteries, named after the area's gravel pits and the Norland Pottery Works on Walmer Road. It was also known as the Piggeries – the district had 3,000 pigs, 1,000 humans and 260 hovels. At the end of the nineteenth century its nickname was the Guilt Garden and it was designated a Special Area because of its poverty, outbreaks of cholera and high mortality rates. Round about that time, the street fights were prompted by religion and politics: 'Who are you for? The pope or Garibaldi?' was the signal for a whacking, and this was an echo of more violent times when the boys from Hammersmith and the boys from Paddington Village pitched battles on the waste ground between Westbourne Grove and the brick field, which lay towards Shepherd's Bush.

At the beginning of the 1950s the area was still a massive slum, full of multi-occupied houses, crawling with rats and rubbish. The people who lived there were poor. Their wages were low or they were unemployed. The men worked for the railways, for London Transport, the Post Office and in various factories. The women had domestic jobs in cafés, hospitals, packing at Lyons. There were local industries, small, backstreet industries situated under the railway arches. Lots of the people who lived locally also worked locally or had service jobs in the wealthier parts of Kensington. In some parts of the district there were pockets of Poles, Irish and blacks, competing for jobs and living space with the natives. Mostly born and bred in the Notting Dale area, these natives, like the immigrants, were at the bottom of the ladder; young couples with children or poor families waiting on the Borough housing list.

'I used to live in a house, and there were nineteen children and eleven grown-ups in nine rooms. It didn't have a bathroom and two families used to have to cook on the landing. One used to cook in their room and the other family I don't know how they used to do the cooking. One toilet. One toilet.'[4]

All these people were trapped in an area of 'traditional' deprivation. The devastation of this west London district was not the result of bombing, so the mythology which the wartime and post-war propagandists assembled around the East End passed it by. Unlike Pimlico, Notting Hill was not stocked with loveable rogues. Its decadence was too visible and too ugly. And, unlike the East End's acres of crumbling Victorian warrens, Notting Hill contained a stock of large well-built houses, which put it low down the list of priorities for rebuilding and redevelopment.

'Most of the buildings consisted of large houses, which originally were meant for the middle class, but which had become very, very dilapidated and run down and were in multiple occupation. There were lots and lots of people and even families, in a big house, and so you get a situation in which there would be twenty people sharing a toilet, sharing a bathroom, sometimes three or four women from different families trying to cook in the one kitchen. So, it was a run-down area, and it had always been an area of a floating population, always been an area in which a single man looking for a job would get himself a furnished room and then perhaps move on. Originally it was colonised by workers who were building the railway, building the Great Western Railway, Paddington, and so ever since those days you'd had a rather anarchic floating population.'[5]

The geography was crucial. Notting Hill was at the end of a highway which led west, straight as an arrow, from Soho in central London down to Shepherd's Bush Green. At the start of the route, therefore, there was an area which was famed as the vice capital of Europe, renowned for its gambling, drinking and prostitution. The short stretch from Piccadilly to Marble Arch gave easy access to the high-class brothels and tarts' flats which spilled over from Mayfair's Curzon Street. Marble Arch was a gateway to Hyde Park, which hummed with couples having sex on the grass or in the bushes. Opposite the park, across Bayswater Road, were the servicemen's

[4] Mike Phillips and Charlie Phillips, *Notting Hill in the Sixties* (London: Lawrence and Wishart, 1997), p. 26.
[5] Interview with Mervyn Jones. Mervyn Jones was a staff reporter on the *Tribune* in the fifties. He covered the Notting Hill riots in 1958.

clubs, which, all through the previous decade, had furnished a steady stream of clients for the army of prostitutes who lined the Hyde Park railings every few yards along Park Lane and all the way down Bayswater Road, through Notting Hill, and along Holland Park Avenue as far as Shepherd's Bush.

It was the scale of the spread that was staggering. When Dr Alfred Kinsey[6] visited London in 1955, he said he had never seen so much blatant sexual behaviour out in the open, and he claimed to have counted a thousand prostitutes at work in the West End one Saturday night.[7] When the police carried out a raid on Holland Park Avenue towards the end of 1958, they counted, in the space of one half hour from ten to 10.30 p.m., seventy-three prostitutes operating in the short stretch between Notting Hill and Shepherd's Bush. Twelve women were arrested that night, but only four made an appearance in court. One of them had failed to appear a few months previously and she was fined £2 and ordered to forfeit £2 for the offence. The rest had disappeared into the warren of streets between Holland Park and Notting Hill.[8]

The district was a well-established offshoot of the Soho vice empires. For West Indians who were holding on to jobs with long hours and low pay, struggling to save enough to bring a family over from the Caribbean and find somewhere more salubrious to live, the district was appalling, the rotten housing conditions compounded by the hostility they encountered in the streets and often at work.

'There was always a bit of anti-immigrant feeling, and I just think, whereas a Pole walking down Westbourne Park Road would be, you know, a white person walking down Westbourne Park, you wouldn't know he was Polish unless he opens his mouth and said he was. A West Indian or an African were very obviously from somewhere else. So I think there was some hostility towards new immigrants and very much with West Indians, at one stage. Well, immigrants are always accused, whoever they are, of taking people's jobs and housing, and girlfriends, yes? There was that sort of general hostility. I think that it wasn't very personalised. I think where West Indians knew white families, got on well together, 'cos once they

[6] Dr Alfred Kinsey was an American biologist best known for his seminal works of research, 'Sexual Behaviour in the Human Male' and 'Sexual Behaviour in the Human Female'. Kinsey was a synonym in the fifties for modern (and perverse) sexual values.

[7] Paul Ferris, *Sex and the British: A Twentieth Century History* (London: Michael Joseph, 1993), p. 157.

[8] *Kensington News and West London Times*, 21 November 1958.

knew people and saw people and talked to people, they were accepted. But it was this sort of propaganda type hostility, you know, that they were doing things to the local community and taking away from the people living there before, which is not true, but that's the things that were said. There was always racialist people who would, you know, attack West Indians verbally, et cetera, and say things about West Indian families. As for hostilities in every way – I mean, attacking them – there was occasions, obviously.'[9]

There were a number of migrants, however, who were relatively untroubled by the character of the district. These were young single men who had come, like all others, to find work and opportunity, and who found it in the customs and the habits of areas like Notting Hill. For them the aura of vice and violence was pure excitement, and it gave them the space in which they could create a bohemian culture based on gambling, sex and music, in more or less equal parts. Within a few years they had constructed a network of clubs and gambling joints which rivalled Soho; and the district was a testing ground in which they lived wild and free, uninhibited by laws and respectability. To be an immigrant anywhere else in London meant that, out in the open, you ran a gauntlet of hostility until you were safely forted up behind your own locked doors. It was only in Notting Hill that there was a public life. Clubs, restaurants, cafés, music, street corner talk. This was the work of the immigrants, many of them bad boys who set out to make Notting Hill a playground in which bad boys could have fun.*

And there was Two Gun Cassidy

'Number one the reason I left south London is because the army wanted to conscript me so I had to come back in the [Ladbroke] Grove and hide. So from then, until 1961/62 I'm not clear about the date, when they did an amnesty for everyone, then I come back from being a ghost. So all that time I had to live by knowledge. This is why most of the gunslingers in the Grove, I know them. The ordinary working man, them kinda flat cap guys used to buy them Kangol caps and the Sunday-go-to-Church people we never meet.

'You see, people cannot visualise what used to happen in those days. Now the whole of the Grove – let's say the square from Portobello Road

⁹ Interview with Mervyn Jones.

up to Chepstow Road, coming up Talbot Road, coming back down West-bourne Park Road, and if you want you can sweep up Great Western Road down Tavistock Crescent, down to Portobello Road – that whole area there was total slum! You see Powis Square and Colville Square all them places with all them yuppy now. I'm talking about rats big like cats. All around Tavistock Crescent I remember the guy lighting the light with a long stick, a gas light, that lil' ha'penny step going over to St Ervan's Road. And it had a toilet underneath.

'You had a lot of shebeens, you call it that, a social situation of which there was nothing because of the no-coloured policy, no blacks, no coloureds in homes, entertainments, there was nothing really for black people so you had to create your own social environment. The Jamaican people created particularly ska and bluebeat. And a chap called Fullerton was a tailor and bought his first house in Talbot Road. He had a basement and we used to have blues dances and stuff. Everybody used to get down there and get down. You had people like Duke Vin who used to play with big speakers. It had the blues and right next door to the blues Bajy opened a café upstairs with a club downstairs. That's in Talbot Road. Now at that time Michael was still living in Powis Square, right in the basement. Now if you don't pass there for the day, something wrong. You had a certain club that a lot of us never got into called the Montparnasse that was on Chepstow Road, the corner of Chepstow and Talbot, but round the corner was the Rio on Westbourne Park Road. Then you come further down, then Larry was in a place there with Johnnie at the corner of Ledbury Road and Westbourne Park and that was called Fiesta One. And right next door it had the Calypso. That what I call there, is no more than about 800 yards square. Then when you leave there you come to the corner of Colville Road and Elgin Crescent and some Barbadian guys have a club in the basement. Then Sheriff had his gym/club.

'It was a wild life. Sometime you don't reach the West End. I used to hit the Grove like about four o'clock of the evening and leave there about quarter to five in the morning. Then Totobag had a place, number 9 Blenheim Crescent. It had another one at the corner but we didn't used to get in that one so much on the corner of Blenheim Crescent and Kensington Park Road. That was for the real real heavy heavy white guys and them. They had a gamble house in St Stephens Gardens and they had another gamble house in Lancaster Road.

'On top of that too, the Grove was very explosive because they didn't like Trinidadians at all. The Dominicans and the St Lucian and all them guys they didn't like Trinidadians because, you know, we used to wear too much nice clothes and all that. That's number one. Number two the

Jamaicans found out that the Trinidadians wasn't afraid of them because one night a Trinidadian stab Weatherman in the middle of he head. Because Weatherman was supposed to be the biggest devil amongst the Jamaicans.

'And there was Two Gun Cassidy! About that time I like about twenty and those guys like about thirty-six, thirty-eight. And when you see gambling happen and they got their hand on my money, I have to defend my money. Because that's the only way you could exist. Because I not working as such. You can't work. Most of these guys, a lot of them was poncing. I'm talking about big money – these guys had it. When you look back most of them guys used to get £30 a night from a chick. A bus man never even himself get £12 a week in them days. So you see what them guys was turning over.

'Danny lost forty-four houses. He owned forty-four houses round the Grove. A guy conned him out of forty-four houses. Danny, he went to the *Cleopatra* film and he came back here and he fancied himself as a director. He signed up all these houses, and bredip, bredip, the guy gone. You see all guys like Danny. £99 a night.

'Sometimes we gambling in Bell Street and one of the pots would be £150. In them days! £5 a stake. Right. You could buy yourself back in the game at one pound higher than the highest man so if you're sitting down and its seven handed or five handed, everybody set in a fiver. So three gets knock out the first time, they buy themselves back in. That's fifteen plus the twenty-five already. That pot reach forty-five already, you know. If you think of the Klondike, that's how we used to live.

'The police didn't take kindly to it. A lot of things made them annoyed. The music was too loud. They didn't like blacks period gathering in any kind of situation, and the selling of drinks which was outside the law, because you couldn't get a licence. So you had to break the law. All this got under their wick. The shebeen didn't survive, well they survived in a sense. The police used to regularly raid them, kick their boxes in, kick their speakers in, but that aggravated the blacks no end and gave them the determination to persevere and the whole police hatred came out of that.

'You see, I came over here and ninety per cent of the people I met were either ex-seamen, or ex-villains from home, a lot of them running away from a lot of different charges and sixty per cent of them stowaway and come here. So I'm not talking about any bourgeoisies or pseudo intellectuals or whatever. I'm just talking about these guys who are just here. The majority of Guyanese are pickpockets. They're what we used to call flat foot hustlers. It had about thirty or forty of them. And then there was a younger Trinidad crowd which was well wicked, because that whole crew, about twelve or fifteen of them, you tamper with them then you've got problems on your hands. It was like living in a frontier town.

'And when it comes to the ladies they would be lined up against the railings; Bayswater Road, against the Dorchester keeping their bodies warm from the ventilating systems. They worked in Park Lane, they worked in the park behind trees, they worked everywhere, in the Bayswater Road, the East End, all over the place. They lived all over. Not only blacks, white people with white husbands. Nobody cared until blacks decided to get into the game. When blacks got into it and were earning money they realised. Hold on, a black guy with white women. Most of the men took the money and gambled it, natural showing off, these guys with lots of girls making white £5 notes for them. Buying cars and expensive suits from Alexanders and Berg. Blacks can't get a job anywhere in England. Everywhere you go the white folk are saying, "Sorry, there's no vacancies" and all of a sudden you find this black person, lots of blacks owning cars. That annoyed the police no end because the police think, "How come these people doing it?" When they realised that they were doing it through prostitution then they brought in the law.

'When I was first here you either had two kind of women. You either caught one straight out of the pub or straight out of approved school. That was our level of communication because our only social outlet was the pub. If you didn't go to the pub you go up West End to a club like the Abalabi or the Grenada. Real dives. You meet up with some chick who has just run away from some approved school or borstal. We didn't know anything about how old they was or whatever. You couldn't catch a woman who was working at Marks & Spencer, I don't know anybody from my peer group at that time who had a woman from Marks & Spencer. You might have catch one from Woolworth's and the odds of catching a nurse was getting better.

'All we used to do them was in the name of sex and love. Or sex and lust, whichever one. And they well used to look forward to that. Even up to then we were still living with a frontier mentality. Nobody ever settled. The majority were not thinking about putting stamp on your card and looking towards a pension.'[10]

This part of the Notting Hill story outlined and dictated the shape of racial anxiety about sex in England for the next couple of generations. At the

[10] Mike Phillips and Charlie Phillips, *Notting Hill in the Sixties* (London: Lawrence and Wishart, 1991), pp. 52-5.

opening of the sixties it was part of the rhetoric of public hostility against the blacks. For many, the prostitutes they encountered were the only people to show them any generosity of spirit, to give them a friendly smile or a helping hand. But in the stifling atmosphere of the times, the association which developed was seen as a demonstration of working-class degeneracy on the part of the women, meeting with the legendary and indiscriminate lust of black men.

In a short time the degenerate tag was extended to characterise any relationship of any sort between blacks and whites. But the bohemian life-style the Caribbeans created in Notting Hill had a number of consequences. It attracted the rich, famous and the boldest spirits in café society. It offered a stage to the renaissance of racist politics in Britain. It helped to motivate the race riots in 1958. It gave a setting to the most notorious political scandal of the century, the Profumo affair. It focused urgent attention on housing conditions in London. It shaped and dominated the relationships of the migrants with the rest of the country for more than two decades.

The memoirs of King Dick, Gigolo

'Hearing about *Windrush*, people coming to England, seek better life, work for a few years, we decided to try our luck to England. Quite a few of us came here. When we look in Jamaica they were building a prison in Jamaica by the name of Fort Augustus. No work, nothing to do. When you stand up and you look in it, and you say that's the prison Bustamante[11] is building for us. We got to find somehow to counteract that. So we happens to run away from it. But if we did remain in Jamaica, it's a certainty a lot of us would wind up there.

'Some people had money to pay their fare. I did pay my fare once, but I went and draw it back. I was more adventurous and decide to stow away. There was five. Two was Duke Vin and Socco.[12] The night when we were in the wharf they were there. Then suddenly they were missing, so I said to my other two friends, "We can't afford to let them go to England and tell the boys that they leave us on the wharf, so we got to go on this ship, because they were here and they're missing now." So, that give us more impetus to go on the ship. Well, eventually we went on and we hide ourselves. About

---

[11] Sir Alexander Bustamante was leader of the Jamaican Government during the forties.

[12] Duke Vin and Socco were two of the most famous DJs and sound system men in London during the fifties and sixties and, as such, pioneers of the black club-scene.

five days after, I don't see them. So I turned to a crew member, and say, "You got some more men down there." And he went down, find two, but wasn't two that I knew. I'd say eventually five of us were stowaways on this boat. Well, when we came, we got twenty-one days. I did nineteen, then we came out. So when I come out, somebody said to me, "Duke Vin and Succo, they're here." So I says, "How comes? And they didn't ride on that boat?" Well they didn't. What happened was the police saw them on the wharf and run after them and they run into the woodland. That's the time when we were looking for them and didn't see them and say they gone on the ship. Well, if they didn't do that, we probably wouldn't get on that ship because we didn't want them to come here to tell the rest of our friends that they leave us on the wharf.

'So when they came, the ship that they came on, when they reached England, immigration come and see that their papers was right and thing like that, the skipper just say, "Oh, you're in London, you're in England now, so get off my boat", and throw them off. They didn't get a day in jail. So they happens to leave Jamaica after us, but they know England before us because we had us to do nineteen days. I did mine at Brixton Hill.

'When I came out, to be honest, I didn't get much problem. I was one of the fortunate one that when I came my friend was already here, and he had a flat in Warwick Road, so I went there and I never really had any problem in finding place to live or anything like that. I didn't have to go and look anywhere to live, like it was there waiting on me to come to it. Work was easy too.

'We had freedom to go about, we had freedom in making parties, anything like that. Gambling was at Totobag's, the headquarters, number 9 Blenheim Crescent. We had everything there. We had restaurant, gambling, everything was there. Drink. Then we had another place, Westbourne Park Road, 51 Westbourne Park Road, we used to gamble a lot there. The barber come in and trim you and thing like that, so you know, we were all right. But I stopped gambling because I'm always a loser. And when I lose I inclined to fight, no one seen and call me, so I don't see why I should go and lose my money and then fight after, so I just stopped gambling.

'6 Powis Square was a shebeen where I get to know a lot of people, society people. Right. Seen them, not knowing who they are until I asks them, but we've seen all film star and people like that on there. Now when certain people are there and you go, you can't make any entry, like they just come in say, "All right, there is £50, now here's £100, don't let in anybody, just we." And all we know that, if you was to go on Cambridge Road you'd see where they park their Rolls Royce and their Bentley and thing like that and take cabs, come in. You see them going in the cab. They come and drink, smoke, eat, 'cos all those things were on there: smoking, drinking, eating. Music. That was the attraction, and then it was a dive, innit? When you're locked in, you're locked in. It's only the police could come in really, and I can't remember the police ever come to that place. It's more a society clique like, used to want a dive, that's where they come. It was clean, true, but I think good sex was the thing that really attract them to us. Yeah, I think sex played a great part in it. Stamina. Don't know, that's why they call me King Dick. That's my name. Differently from my right name, my nickname is King Dick. Well, the Dick gone now, but the King still remain. A girl gave me that name.

'I've seen some things that you wouldn't believe it, in the gambling house. A man would come in there and look on the boys. If you looked clean and healthy and thing like that, he just call you and ask you if you want a job. "What is the job?" "You like to have some sex with my wife?" And that's it. Plenty of that used to happen. Like walking down Bayswater Road, Sunday evening, you're nice, and you just see a big car pull up beside and, "Are you busy?" "No." And next thing you know, they take you to some posh house and you going to have sex with some posh white woman. One told me, "When you see me on the street, don't you talk to me." That's true. See her one day in Oxford Circus, and when she saw me she recognised me all right. And that's all I got. Didn't talk to her.

'You know I think we were really fit human beings. Yeah, we do get money, quite a few time. £100. A lot of money in those days. Yeah, more than one time. We called a gigolo, something like that. I don't want to call her name but I have been with famous film stars. I remember one night I was in Shaftesbury Avenue and I saw this couple. One can hardly talk English. The one who could talk English a bit fluent, asked me, "Where do I find a strip club?" So I look at the woman and I said to her, "A beautiful woman like you, what you want a strip club?" And we went to one in Windmill Street, and then he turn to me and he says, "Roaring Twenties, what about Roaring Twenties?" I says, "The Roaring Twenties, I don't think you will like it. There's a few whites, more black." So he says, "Take me there, I've been hearing about Roaring Twenties, I want to go." So, we went on Carnaby Street and stop at the Twenties. They didn't feel like going in, so he turned to me and says, "From here to Piccadilly." So I says, "Go down there, take right hand, take left, and that will lead you back into Piccadilly." And they wouldn't leave me alone. They want me to take them back to Piccadilly. So when I go back to Piccadilly, I say, "Here's Piccadilly." And at Piccadilly they used to have some two per cent lager, that's all those restaurants used to sell, so went on there and they buy six bottles. So, having a bite, the woman turned to me, she says, "Where you live, tenement or your own place?" I say, "Tenement." She says, "Me, you, him, can go your place?" So I say, "Yeah." And we went to Charing Cross and we get a cab and I were living in Balham at the time, and we went there and it was sex. And they pay me. Well, I won't call any name, but a famous, very famous star. I had feelings I can still remember, nearly fifty years. I don't know why I had that feelings, but she was so beautiful, and that man she was with put me in all different position just to look at me.

'Another one was Sarah Churchill. Yeah. I don't know, probably she was a nymph. She never satisfied one man – two – three. She come to the gambling house, and her chauffeur would be out there with his cap over his face fast asleep and she's in there gallivanting herself. So, it's somebody who I knew. She took three of us one night. She was living in Maida Vale, Carlton Vale or one of those Carlton, and she had some jewellery on mantelpiece, and one man start to pinch the jewellery. But then one was getting ready to go and have sex with her, and when she look at his underpants she said, "Get out. Get out." And she ran us out, I understand, but then one of the bloke had taken some jewellery off her mantelpiece. I know I didn't, 'cos, I mean, like an exhibitionist me, I like her watch me 'cos to me I was so good at my job, you know. Anyway I think about it, I think I'd always get money for it, 'cos you got some woman out there, the only thing they can't get from their husband is good sex. Everything else, so you know she don't want a man to really live with or she just a Miss, but she have all the comfort apart from good sex. A lot of women out there. If it was pure men here a lot of us would go back home, 'cos the men hated us. The women, they seems to fancy us, so I would say white women let us stay in Britain. Yeah, they are the main cause for a lot of us, especially boys from my syndicate. But I don't know about today. I don't know what these young boys are getting up to, but I were pretty young when I came here. I've seen some things you wouldn't believe.'[13]

* Another factor in the style of this group was the fact that they were not, in this period, inhibited by the presence of the wives, mothers or sisters. In the Caribbean the origins in slavery, the mobility of the male labour force and the habit of social organisation based on family units or small communities, gave women an authority which meant that some aspects of Caribbean manners and behaviour were dominated by older women, in particular. There were only a few women on the *Windrush*, and over the next ten years the proportion of male to female migrants was more than two to one, only evening out in 1958. In any case most were coming to join husbands or fiancés, or train in occupations like nursing, with restricted access and freedom of movement. This left a large pool of unattached young men, more or less free of all the social limits which had previously constrained their behaviour.

[13] Interview with Alfred 'King Dick' Harvey.

9

―――●―――

'Everybody gathers, we didn't have cars and such to take everybody, so they get the trucks and they put the lot in, and everybody's going to come. My friend from school, she came down from the north side of the island and stayed with us. And everybody come, they bring you gifts, gifts of money. And then they do a lot of cooking, things they can eat on the way. And they bring large handkerchiefs, because they're going to cry, you know. And I was glad, I was sad, and it was an excruciating pain. You're going away. And everybody gets in this truck. You're in the front, they're trying to make you happy, and they were sad, because these are the people that you know. So, we drove down. It wasn't like one of these excursions we used to go on, where you're singing, "Riding along on the crest of the waves". There was no waves. It was all the people wanting to hug you, touch you.

'Then we get to Kingston to the airport. The tears start to flow, and then I had to move away, and I don't think I've ever dragged my feet like I dragged them that day. I was nineteen.'[1]

'Nobody tells you the truth and nobody tells you everything. When I came, I saw everybody going into their little houses, and then nobody spoke to you. That never happened in Jamaica. As long as you met somebody in the street – whether you'd met them or not – it's good morning, good evening, and hello. And you find you'd be saying to somebody, good morning and good evening and they never answered you, and then you felt stupid after that, so you stopped saying good morning and good evening.'[2]

'I wanted to know what sort of people could be the way they are. I mean, they would tell you, Come round, but they don't mean come round. I couldn't understand that.'[3]

[1] Interview with Tryphena Anderson.
[2] Interview with Connie Mark.
[3] Interview with Jessica Huntley. Jessica Huntley came from Guyana in 1958 to join her husband, Eric Huntley. Both were committed political activists in the region and did not intend to stay very

Riding Along On The Crest Of The Second Wave

The great bulk of Caribbean immigration to Britain effectively began and ended in less than ten years between 1955 and 1962. Migration to the USA had been traditional up until that point, but the McCarran Walter Act in 1952 put strict limits on the number of migrants who could enter the USA from the Caribbean, leaving Britain as the only industrial nation to which the British Caribbeans had access. It took a couple of years before the penny dropped in the region, but migrant numbers climbed after 1954 and half the total of Caribbean migrants to Britain arrived before 1960.

There was a precise relationship between the number of migrants and how much work was available. In the recession years, numbers fell. The number of arrivals decline through 1955 to 1959 and then climb up again to a peak in 1961. Migrants already in Britain communicated efficiently and continuously with their friends and relatives in the Caribbean, so that news of a labour shortage in a particular sector would bring an almost instant response from the Caribbean. News about a shortage of jobs would be a signal to postpone travelling.

After 1961 other factors took over in influencing the numbers. This was the year that the Commonwealth Immigration Act introduced a system of employment vouchers which limited the intake of migrants and there was a rush to get in before legislation closed the doors. After 1961 the arrivals tended to be families – women and children and dependants of people already in Britain. It was the period of the fifties which established the character of the black community in Britain, and which dictated the events and trends which were to dominate its identity and the structure of its relationship with the rest of the country.

The facts and figures of Caribbean migration in the fifties throw up a series of features which yield a revealing portrait of the black community and what happened to it.

---

long in Britain. In the sixties she founded the independent publishing house and bookshop, Bogle L'Ouverture, and published a stream of works from Caribbean and African writers, including Andrew Salkey, Walter Rodney and Linton Kwesi Johnson. The Huntleys were part of the Black Parents' Movement which had its origins in the campaigns over educationally sub-normal schools and the 'sus' laws, meaning 'suspected person', which allowed the police to stop and search during the eighties. They still live in London.

Jamaicans came first and in the largest numbers, partly motivated by the size of their involvement in the war effort, and because they had the largest population in the Caribbean. They were largely self motivated. Legend has magnified the number of Caribbeans who were recruited to government sponsored schemes, fuelling the argument that Caribbean immigrants were 'brought' here, but their numbers were actually insignificant. The largest block of sponsored workers came from Barbados to work for London Transport and the railways, but between 1955 and 1961 only 4,449 arrived, a relatively insignificant number. On the other hand, the news of these sponsored schemes, together with the recruitment drive conducted by various political luminaries from Britain, spread around the Caribbean like wildfire and, like a vacuum, the British labour market began sucking in everyone within its reach.

'I was church secretary. If you had a quarrel with your wife and things wasn't working and you want to see the minister, you either had to see him at church, or you couldn't get to him unless you get past me. And so I would be arranging things, if people want to borrow money on their house and they want somebody stand security for them and all the rest of it. So when a British politician was coming, I was one of the people that was called, and I went with the minister to be briefed. It was at Government House. He was only there for forty-eight hours, but he addressed the nation and we had *The Argosy* and *The Chronicle*, *The Guardian* and *The Times* here, the big newspaper, and a half sheet of advertisement to work for Lyon's Corner House and the different hospitals and so on. It was an opportunity for the country to serve the motherland. There was an opportunity for work and development and to education and to create a better life for yourself and your family. We didn't see any further.

'What does young black people in those days see in white people? I mean, now, I would say that I see the devil in most of them, but then it was, you know, you trust them: they knew it all, they told you what was right and all the rest of it. But at that stage I already had my doubts because I had two overseers had come down from England who didn't know the job, but they were the overseers and it's the black men that had to do the job for them. So I already had doubts that all of them were on the level, and I said that to some people that maybe things is not as easy as he's making it out. But, who wanted to hear that? I half didn't believe it myself, but I was just a bit sceptical, you know, that it can't be so easy.

'But this politician told us all about the colleges and how you can study and the nurses had an opportunity to train and he's outlined the jobs and so on, and Lyon's Corner House and the tea and so on, and catering and what kind of life you could have. He made it sound very attractive. Yes. That's the word. Somebody said to me at that time that it was a bit like the Gold Rush, because, many years, when I was much younger, I understand that when they had found gold and diamond our schoolmasters had left and go to the diamond field to try and make their fortune. And this old lady said to me that this was like the diamond rush when she saw how people were leaving for England. But the station was in Barbados and so the papers will come down from Barbados to Guyana and we'll fill them up. And of course they have to come to either get a solicitor to do it or somebody like myself that wouldn't charge them anything, or the minister, and then it goes back to Barbados and the tickets come down, and all the rest of it.

'It's like a hire purchase agreement that they used to sign because they had to pay when they come here, they had to pay back some money. Or they borrowed the fare there and so people would send a pound to buy clothes for their daughter and set them up, or the wife sometime pawn everything – even to her marriage ring – to get her husband an outfit, and so on. And you know what black people's like: you have to have nice underclothes and all this sort of thing. And you got to buy your trunk and all these wonderful things to come. And they'll borrow money on the house. They went from all strata of life. Teachers left to come to England. Lots of young women that wanted to be nurses and men that wanted to become doctors that felt that if they offer as male nurses – because I could remember this discussion so well – in church these two brothers, and they were twins, and one wanted to be a doctor but had failed exams, and my minister say that this is an opportunity if you go and be a nurse, a male nurse, you can then study from there to become a doctor. A doctor that we know very well came in that route, and he worked as a male nurse and went on to study. He's very famous today. So lots of people took that opportunity to come and be trained and went on.

'British Rail I remember because I really like this boy so much, and he want to be a train driver. He was teaching and he wanted to be a train driver! And I said to him, "You're mad! You want to go to England to drive a train?" And he says, he was just fascinated when he go in the pictures and see all these big trains, you know, he wanted to drive a train! He came, he end up being a minister in the Methodist Church! Oh my God, he left the Church and leave teaching and come to England for British Rail because he want to drive a train – he want to drive a train. I mean, in my snobbish Guyanese, a train driver was nothing in comparison with a school teacher. I mean he could be headmaster soon. "You want to drive a train?" When I met him here he was training for the ministry. He had come out of the train. He was fed up of shunting trains as he said, so then it was, of course, he went and offer for the ministry and when I came here he was in his last year training as a minister. Yes, lots of people had a way out. A lot made it.'[4]

The migrants were coming from everywhere, but most of them came from Jamaica, and the bulk of Jamaicans came from rural parishes – Clarendon, Manchester, St Anne's, St Mary. Kingston was still a small city in the late forties and fifties, an 'urban aggregation with a rural underbelly'.[5]

'In some instances, they came from the bauxite areas, where bauxite was discovered. And the bauxite companies acquired their land, because Jamaica has had, since emancipation, a very strong and independent peasantry, so people owned land and they could, in fact, sell that land to the bauxite companies to get the money for their passage, you know. The thing made a lot of sense.'[6]

They were people who were, in Caribbean terms, skilled, semi-skilled or eminently qualified to become skilled workers, but whose potential was clearly limited in the Caribbean environment.

'The people who are going are usually very sensible people, in fact, the sense of adventure, very ambitious, very energetic. I remember many young women migrated to go and study nursing. And I

[4] Interview with the Reverend Sybil Phoenix MBE. The Reverend Sybil Phoenix MBE came to England from Guyana in 1956. She worked in the fashion industry for a time, but became famous as a source of help and advice for young black women in south London. She started the Moonshot Club, a youth and community centre which was then burned down by arsonists. She was ordained and made an MBE during the eighties.

[5] Interview with Professor Rex Nettleford. Professor Rex Nettleford came to Britain from Jamaica as a Rhodes Scholar in politics at Oxford. He is now widely acknowledged as the leading intellectual, cultural critic and creative artist in the Caribbean. He is Pro Vice Chancellor of the University of the West Indies and also the founder, artistic director and choreographer of the National Dance Theatre Company of Jamaica.

[6] Interview with Professor Rex Nettleford.

remember filling out several forms for many of these young ladies who, in fact, couldn't get into the local nursing school in Jamaica because they didn't have the school certificate as it then was, but British hospitals took them. Later, in the fifties, we had a group of young tradesmen, many of whom were trained in youth camps, and as soon as they left these youth camps they migrated, and many of them went to England. So England inherited lots of masons and carpenters, that kind of person. It was a real loss to Jamaica, though we didn't realise it at the time.'[7]

The overwhelming majority of migrants were men. In 1953 the total of 2,300 Caribbean migrants was 73.9 per cent male and 26.1 per cent female. The balance did not even out until 1958. Two years later, in 1960, it had shifted again. That year the intake was 56.3 per cent male and 37.8 per cent female (with 5.9 per cent children).

The positions they came to occupy in the labour market were closely related to demographic and social changes in Britain itself. The suburbanisation of the inner city population, along with the high take-up of skilled workers involved in the reversion to industrial processes, left substantial gaps in the bottom end of the market into which the migrants moved. The efficiency of communication between the migrant groups, the result of the personalised, intimate character of Caribbean social organisation, also dictated patterns of settlement. At the end of the fifties any migrant could have predicted where to find specific groups of Caribbeans. Jamaicans in Clapham and Brixton. Trinidadians in Notting Hill. Vincentians in High Wycombe.

'If you look at the areas north of the Thames, you can pick out almost a kind of archipelago: Dominicans and St Lucians around Paddington, across the Montserratians around Finsbury Park. Chain migration and differentials in times of arrival produced this sort of differentiation within the Caribbean pattern. High Wycombe, for example, had a high proportion of Saint Vincentians. People from Nevis particularly concentrated in Leicester and also in Leeds. You can pick out these effects of family connections, island connections, village connections quite strongly still in the map. Of course it doesn't affect so much the children, but the first generation, people born in the Caribbean, still show the continuity from that very early

---

[7] Interview with Professor Rex Nettleford.

settlement pattern. There were very, very good lines of communication between the Caribbean and Britain. The responses, for example, to shifts in the demand for labour were typically felt within about three months of happening, and people coming from the Caribbean who were questioned all had addresses of friends to whom they were going when they came. So it's quite clear that there was a very, very precise flow of information, and flow of money, particularly in the case of dependants coming. People knew where they were going, and so essentially what you had is sort of recreation of the family and village and island patterns. Of course, facing a fairly hostile environment, having support, having people who knew a little bit about the system, partner systems and so on, they were very important in facilitating the ability to find accommodation and to find work in Britain.'[8]

By 1955 the characteristics of Caribbean migration were set and established. No doubt that the push/pull factor which propelled people out of the region had been magnified, but the migrants were not simply moved by forces beyond their control. The move was also a choice – a planned and calculated risk. By 1955, everyone in the Caribbean knew that England was a cold place and that the English were unwelcoming; but at the time this was not a huge disincentive to Caribbeans. The seasonal migrants to the American South, for instance, understood and lived with the rules of segregation. In the Spanish speaking islands it took time to learn the language. In many ways the English would be more like the devil they knew. By that time, also, the gamble was cushioned by the presence of countrymen who had already made the trip and survived. The point was the possibility of a new, improved future; and there was still no question in Caribbean minds that the worst England threatened was better than the limitations of their own environment. In any case, work was plentiful, and there was no doubt that, at least from that point of view, they were needed.

Even so, Caribbeans were no more prepared for what they would find when they arrived in England than their predecessors had been. If they had arrived in Lisbon, New York or Rio de Janeiro, they would have taken what they saw as a matter of course. But all their ideas about Britain had been acquired in the context of a grandiose imperial imagery. When they encountered the reality of British life, it was a salutary and dislocating experience.

---

[8]   Interview with Professor Ceri Peach. Professor Ceri Peach is an Oxford Professor of Geography and the author of a number of landmark studies about West Indian migration.

'I got a mixture of genuine affection and a lot of curiosity. I always remember going into my first Dewhurst butcher's shop when I was about seven, and this big, large lady looked at me. She kept looking at me, and then she said, turned to the butcher, and said, "Oo, I could eat him." I'll always remember Dewhurst butcher's shops. I was terrified. It was after the war when I came back to London and I lived in Forest Gate, then I found myself the only black youngster throughout the whole of my schooling, in Odessa Road Primary School there, and then I went to a secondary school in Forest Gate, again the only black person throughout the whole of my schooling. There were times though when I was there, as a youngster, there were certain roads I couldn't go along, like round the Romford Road. I'd be pelted with bricks and bottles. "Get out, blackie, nigger, nigger, nigger", there were roads and places I knew instinctively I wasn't going down.'[9]

'I was blown, I was shocked, I couldn't believe what I saw. I arrived in Paddington and it was all very grey and dismal and these little white men were coming up to take our suitcases and I couldn't believe it. In fact, we travelled with a friend who stood there stunned, and I think all during his years as a student here he never recovered from that because it used to be one of his strongest stories. He used to say, "I couldn't believe this man coming and calling me 'sir'." But what was most striking, I think, was the age of the people. At that time there were old men working on the stations, and on the buses there were old men or old women. There weren't very many young people. And then we began to realise that the war had taken its toll of the young people between eighteen and probably thirty-five. Quite a lot of them had died or they'd come back injured from the war. So you had a country that appeared, in those places anyway where I noticed, that they seemed to be all old people, and there were very few people who didn't have a story of having lost someone or knew someone who lost someone, or telling you stories of streets that had been bombed. So although it was 1951, the war was still very much part of what was happening in Britain, and people were

---

[9]   Interview with Paul Stephenson. Paul Stephenson was born in 1937. His father was West African and his mother came from a mixed race English family. In 1963 he initiated a boycott of the Bristol Bus Company because of its refusal to hire black workers. Subsequently he worked for the CRE and sat on a number of quangos, including the British Sports Council and the Press Council.

living in prefabs, and that was quite strange. You couldn't understand why were they living in what we saw as huts.'[10]

'So many little things horrified me when I first came here. I couldn't understand how all the houses in a street could almost be the same. There didn't seem to be any individuality. And when I saw things like bread being delivered, bread literally was left outside the door with your milk, and I was horrified. And then, what surprised me most of all was the child care, because at home, when we were fighting for self government and independence, we talked about Britain, we said, you know, children are taken care of, provisions are there. And then, of course, you had to take your child to a childminder, surprised me a lot, you know. And, of course, the cold, you didn't realise how intense that cold is, and I knew that there were a couple of people who came with me who went back the first Christmas. We just couldn't take it. And the unfriendliness of people, that surprised me, 'cos it's like a shock wave, you know. I couldn't believe the lack of humanity. And I don't even want to use the word "prejudice" because it's a new word, you know, the unfriendliness and the coldness and the mask, like, is given for a smile. And that deep down, there was this hatred that they have of you. I mean, I was just horrified at things like that, I couldn't believe it at all.'[11]

'And as the train was sailing in I saw this white woman, as my minister would say, looked like the devil. He used to say that these white women when they paint themselves they look like the devil and he used to warn us not to do it, we will go to hell. So in those days you used to wear the beehive, and she had a big head of hair on top and well painted, her lips was red and her eyes blue and all the rest of it, and she was sweeping the platform. And I went like that, "Uri, Uri, look at her sweeping the platform." I mean, I'm only accustomed to seeing white women who's painted devils but do nothing, they don't even sweep their own home! They have six of us to do it for them. And I just elbowed Uri to look at this woman. I don't know what I'd expected but that was my experience of sailing into Paddington, and there was this white woman, a broom in her

[10]   Interview with Connie Mark.
[11]   Interview with Jessica Huntley.

hand – I'd never seen a white woman with a broom in her hand before – sweeping the platform.'[12]

'I didn't feel that I was coming to a place that was totally strange. I felt I was coming to a home away from home. Having said that, when I, together with the others, boarded the boat train at Calais to come to Victoria, the train travelled up on the south coast, and I saw a lot of houses with smoke billowing from the chimneys, and my impression was, Good God, what a lot of factories! 'Cos I had never seen a house before with chimney pots bellowing smoke. And in those days, it wasn't any clean air, it was just burning coal and smog and all the rest of it.'[13]

'The first shock in England when I came in was that all the bomb sites were still there. You went to places like Moorgate or in the City of London itself, there were all these bomb sites, half shell, half buildings were still there. Nothing had been done about that, and that was the main shock. The second shock was that it was unusual for people to respond if you said hello or good morning. You know, from the Caribbean where you came from a society where people responded when you said hello to somebody or good morning to somebody. Over here it was different. They didn't answer or they shied away, and if you spoke to somebody on the underground, they were busy reading their papers and you didn't get a response. You never got that. That was the second shock, you know, because I was accustomed to people speaking just naturally and easily and sociably. And that type of thing we found very difficult to adjust to. It was unlike anything that I've ever come across before.'[14]

In view of the Caribbeans' surprise about routine aspects of British life, it is clear that no one on either side fully understood the consequences of immigration, either for the migrants themselves or for the country as a whole. For instance, the issue which dominated the experience of all the migrants throughout the fifties was, on the surface, simple – finding some-

[12]   Interview with the Reverend Sybil Phoenix.

[13]   Interview with Ivan Weekes. Ivan Weekes came from Barbados in 1955. He settled in Notting Hill, living in a Rachman property and later on becoming a tenant of the Notting Hill Housing Trust. He served as an alderman on the Kensington and Chelsea Council during the seventies, and was one of the first black people in recent times to be appointed as a magistrate.

[14]   Interview with Ben Bousquet.

where to live. The paradox was that while there was a massive shortage of labour in Britain, which fuelled migration, there was also a massive shortage of housing which was causing social conflicts even before the migrants arrived.

Take prefabs, for instance. Prefabricated houses were a temporary answer to the shortfall. They looked like large huts, and they consisted of mass produced units which could be put together quickly like a giant lego set. They met immediate needs, but the problem was so severe that prefabs were around a lot longer than anyone intended. Towards the end of the next decade, getting rid of the last prefabs had become an urgent political issue.

In later years the government of the time has been repeatedly condemned for its *laissez-faire* attitude to Caribbean migration. But, in the circumstances, it is hard to see how they could have acted otherwise. In the matter of housing choices were strictly limited, and after the migrants arrived they were on their own. Access to council housing was tightly controlled by residence requirements, so the migrants were thrown back on the private market. This provided the perspective from which they would have their first close-up view of British society. But the experience did not discourage the Caribbeans from coming. On the contrary, the pace of migration speeded up between 1950 and 1954. After all, Caribbeans believed that they could survive anything. They prided themselves on their toughness and adaptability, but there was no way of predicting the extent to which the initial problems of housing would block the potential for progressing beyond their first footholds. In the short term so much energy and so many resources had to be devoted simply to the business of finding shelter, that many of the ambitions with which the migrants arrived had to be shelved. Skills they already possessed had to be abandoned, and the dreams and visions which had given them impetus were swamped in the daily desperate grind of survival. In the longer term, the immigrant community that emerged from the conflicts of the fifties was traumatised and embittered, a mood which inhibited and hindered their own ability to negotiate the problems of the following decades.

'We moved from place to place, I can't tell you the amount of places we lived, and then we saw this flat advertised, and we went to look at it and I didn't know about coal cellars. So this man had done up the coal cellar, and so you had a bedroom and a kitchen. So the kitchen was under the coal cellar bit to the footpath, when people passing you could look through the grill and see male or female. So every time you light the gas, after about ten or fifteen minutes the water start streaming down the wall. I cooked my first Christmas dinner in this country under a male umbrella. I just went out and bought an umbrella, put it up over the cooker so that it was all right. So when I start to cook I open the umbrella, put it up and then nothing drop on me or in the pot.

'I really got a very bad cold and things was difficult and so the minister came and see me and he said, "Oh my God, what are you doing in this coal cellar?" And apparently he went back and told people in the church what was happening. And this Sunday morning this woman came up to me and virtually in tears, you know. And said she was so very sorry, holding on to my hand, and said, "Oh, Sybil, I'm so very sorry, and really I know yourself and Joe is all right, but I've got the children to think of and nobody in my street yet has taken in any coloureds, and I'm sorry I can't really let you all a room. I really have to think of the children and the family, and I'm really sorry, I don't know what to do." I just yank my hand out of hers and said, "I didn't ask to come and live at your house." That was my church sister. But nobody on her street had taken in any coloureds yet, so she was afraid or ashamed to let to coloureds because she have the children to think of and the family to think of. So she couldn't let us the room.

'The nice houses we lived in, we had to leave early in the morning and they didn't let us back until seven or eight o'clock in the night. Or you lived in the Rachman[15] places where there was eight of you sharing one cooker, and you come home and you don't know where all these people come from. The two of us have a room, but there's half a dozen men trying to cook on this cooker when you come home. So I went out and bought a pressure cooker. This was in Ladbroke Grove. Because we came to Shepherd's Bush and we moved, lived all around Shepherd's Bush, Blythe Road, all around there. And so I went and bought a pressure cooker so that I can put everything, so I can put the meat at the bottom, the vegetables on top, make a custard and put in that as well and I have got a meal. The whole meal cooked in the pressure cooker. And so what I will do is to cook the night before, so while we're sitting down looking at television in a night and sewing, I would be cooking the meal. Because you come home in the afternoon and you put your ten pence, five pence

[15]   Peter Rachman was a west London landlord associated with the intimidation of tenants and ruthless evictions.

in the meter, and somebody will even move your pot over when you've gone back in your room, and you come back, there's no money in the cooker but your pot isn't cooked. So the cookers used to line up on the stairs where you go up on the platform there, they would put cookers there.

'Or I've lived in place where that is the bath there, and three cookers on the other side of the bathroom. So what they do is to cover the bath, they got a sheet of board over the bath tub, and that's your table. Everybody rest things on there and the cooker's on the other side and you're drawing water from the sink in the bathroom. I've lived in houses where the bath and the toilet is there and that's the only place you can get water, 'cos there's no water in your room. In the nice houses that you live in where the house is posh and so on and they might just take two of you in, or one if you know one room they're letting, the only place you can get water is in the toilet and bath. So you can all put your kettle under the bath, the tap in the bathroom, and that's where you fill your kettle. That is the sort of places that we lived in.

'In those days you'll see the sign up that they want ladies that are in business, and you go and they'll tell you, "I would let you all the room, but you can't come in before six-thirty, seven o'clock in the evenings." And we lived there right through the winter and I think it was the February she gave us notice to go, she wasn't going to have us in the summer. But the house was warm, it was good during the winter. But we had to leave home six o'clock in the morning. Half-past six, if I'm there half-past six, she's knocked the door to get you out. One day I had forgot something, or was going on this course and I knocked on the door and she wouldn't let me in. She came to the door and said, "I'm sorry, you can't come in, I've got visitors." And I said to her that I'd left the thing for this course and she asked me to tell her what it was and she said, "If you go down the road and wait I'll get it for you." And she went to the room and got it and she came out, the door locked, and she came down the road and gave it to me. She had visitors so she couldn't have me in. She was a nice Irish lady.[16]

'To go out and get rooms, you find a few of the Eastern Europeans, like the Ukrainians, they would let rooms to black people, but there were always rules and conditions and whatever. You can't have a bath till the weekend. You can't wash your clothes in the bath. You can't do this, you can't do that. They couldn't wash their clothes in the bath but they'd let you wash in the kitchen sink, yes, that was alright, but not in the bath. And we wouldn't understand, you know, what was happening. Then the few West Indians who came here first, they bought houses, and now they were letting rooms. And as people started to come in, you find not only was one sharing a room, but two sharing a room, three sharing a room, four sharing a room, and I don't think people minded that. You'd say, "I'm a girl", but then, you might come and they say, "That's your bed, doesn't matter who you are." But that soon disappeared, because more people started buying, then you find just one person sharing a room. But the conditions – not really gross, but I don't think a lot of people were used to that. I certainly wasn't used to that.

'When we started buying houses there was a lot of resentment from the white people. They talked about overcrowding, but what they didn't realise, that whatever we lived in back home, most people either lived with their parents or their parents owned their own smallholding, and you shared whatever accommodation you have with your own. And it's the same thing, while other black people came over here, while providing housing for themselves, they were also looking for making a bit of money. And who's against that? And each person was now, what we would say, copying what each black person was saying. I want my own house, to work towards it, and immediately they're buying. And, if you buy in an area, sometimes you could be there, people won't speak to you, you know. And white people would openly say, "I don't know where they get their money from to buy houses, you know, how they come here – we've been here all this while and we can't buy a house, and they come and started buying houses." '[17]

'I remember, once I went to look for a house or a flat, and I went in Haringey, and it was a Greek woman who owned this flat. And it was a very nice flat. And I paid down my deposit. And when I went back to take my suitcase a woman was there, a white woman was there, and she was telling her, "Don't give the nigger this flat, it's too good for them." And, of course, we had an altercation because

[17] Interview with Tryphena Anderson.

I was able to talk for myself, you know. And I did, and I said to the landlady that I paid my money, I don't want it back and, if she dared, what was going to happen. Just empty threats really. But, you know, this woman came in, because she was white, this flat was a nice flat, it was a new flat, nothing spectacular about it, it's clean. And she felt that it was too good for me.

'Then we lived in another place where the landlord took the fuse out of the lights, so that when you came in and it's winter, the place is dark, you know, you've got to walk up some narrow stairs. Those days there wasn't electric heaters, these were paraffin heaters, we lived on paraffin heaters. We had a paraffin heater in the centre of the house, and you had a kettle on there, so in the mornings, when you woke up, you could do your business, you know. And the thing about it, they didn't want you to live in the place, the houses were so dowdy. I remember the skirting board was dark brown, and they had some hideous wallpaper. And smoky, you know, very, very smoke-filled the houses were, that we lived in, anyway. And, so, of course, once we decided to send for our children, then we had to seek proper accommodation to have them, because they've been used to space. And it would have been very hard for them. Because we lived in a place in Wood Green, oh, we lived in a lot of places. And when my children came, my mother brought them, and I phoned up every ten minutes or fifteen minutes to find out how they were. And my mother said, "You'd better come, these children playing the calypso so loud", and even she was conscious, you know, that they were playing it so loud. When I asked the time to go, when I go home, and you get to the street, well, you hear Sparrow[18] coming through the window. And, of course, the landlord complained about it, but why they were saying, Why can't you play your music loud? So you knew, therefore, that you had to have your own place for them, and of course, we wanted to have that, once we decided that they are here, to make proper provision for them, which we did.'[19]

'People were very, very mobile. We lived in Waltham, in Haringey, Hornsey, Finsbury Park area, and, most probably, in about a couple of years, we must have changed ten times. Fortunately, there was accommodation available, so that you were able to leave one flat or one room and go to another. So even though there was discrimination, because you would see that advertisement, that board at Finsbury Park was really a historic place for black people. Large board, you don't see them now. Some tobacconists and confectioneries have still got them, a large board outside Finsbury Park tube station, because there was no weekly advertiser or no *Loot* in those days, that was the *Loot* or weekly advertiser for the whole of the district, and so you've got jobs, you've got accommodation. And you would telephone for a flat or a room, mostly, and the person would say, "Yes, it's vacant, come and get it." And then you'd get there, it was so obvious that when you got there, as soon as she saw your face it's gone. But one survives. So that's why one of the main dreams and plans of our generation when we came over was to own your own place. Because once you've gone through that kind of experiences from landlords, you worked very hard to buy your own place.'[20]

'When I came, I found me and my husband and this baby in one room. I couldn't believe it. And I said to him, "Is this how I'm expected to live?" Anyway, he was living in a house, just a bachelor's, and we heard about another room – in those days it was just rooms, but you never see them 'cos somebody's always in, so you always have to wait 'till the person leaves for you to come in. And then my husband came and said to me, The house hasn't got a bath. And I said, "I'm not going to live in any house without a bath." And when I went back, the landlord, where we were, he laughed his head off. He says, "Look, my dear, most of the houses here don't have baths." Because what they did in those days, they used to take the bathroom and rent it out as a bedroom to make money, you see. So, he laughed at me and said, "You don't refuse a room because the house hasn't got a bath."

'Anyway, in the end, we did get a room in Chelsea that had a bath, but we could only bathe on a Thursday night 'cos there were so many tenants, you only had one night to bathe. And the bath was in the dining room, and it had a bit of plank over it, so when it

[20] Interview with Eric Huntley. Eric Huntley came from Guyana in 1957. An anti-colonial activist who intended to return to Guyana after a breathing space of a few years in Britain, he settled in north London and worked in the Post Office, then in insurance sales, as well as being engaged in the work of the publishing house Bogle L'Ouverture and the Black Parents' Movement. He now lives in London and edits *Caribbean Watch*, a magazine devoted to ecological concerns in the region.

was the bath, the plank was a stool, a chair, for people to sit to eat at. And if you drop one drop of thing in the landlord's or the landlady's kitchen, you'd be in trouble. So anyway, my husband and I said we couldn't be bothered with that. But in those days you had the Fulham Baths, so we used to go to that. But there was a little room outside, and I can tell you, you can get a good bath with a pail. 'Cos we used to go outside and we used to put warm water, sort of tepid, and then my husband would throw the water on me, and I would soap up my skin and I rub it up, and when I think I soap it up enough, he would throw the water at me again and wash the soap off. So we used to have some lovely baths with the pail, I can recommend it. And, of course, I did the same to him. So that was much less a trauma than going into this bathroom where you can only go on a Thursday night and when they were finished eating and things like that. I called it the one room syndrome.

'Say you were a white person, you would get a whole flat for £1.25 a week, a whole flat, and some of them got front and back gardens, if you're lucky enough to get a ground floor. But we were obliged to pay £3 and £3.50 for one room. And at that, you had to cook outside. In the passageway they would have this stove, and maybe three, four people are to use the one stove. It was a rat race really, 'cos if you put your money in, you make sure you go and put your food on right away, so that you can use the money that you put in.

'It was a rat race. We used to have these paraffin lamps that we used to keep in our room, but some of them have some little holes in. So, you know, in Jamaica, we have to have our rice and peas every Sunday, and the rice and peas take long to cook in those days, I don't know where they got those peas from, you had to cook it overnight. So while the room was getting warm with the paraffin stove we would put our pot on a saucepan and with the peas and cook the peas overnight, so that would save us even having to use the stove that was in the passageway. Because the landlord those days wanted to make all the money they could make, so all the rooms are rented, so there wasn't even a kitchen, the kitchen was in the passageway, and that's where the stove was.

'So it was the thing, to buy houses. Sometimes a whole family would put together and buy a house, that 'cos they found it cheaper than just renting a room for £3, 'cos maybe in those days the rates those days would be about roughly £50 a year, so it was cheaper to buy a house. And then they were making money, and they were exploiting their own people, 'cos the average white person didn't want to rent a room because they didn't want their neighbours to see a coloured person coming out of their house, 'cos their white neighbours look down on them. So, even if they would have rented the other room cheaper, they were afraid, because you would be an embarrassment to the white neighbours.

'I never had an English landlord. But the West Indian, we were our worst enemies. We used to exploit our own people. I mean, in those days, we didn't have the Commission for Racial Equality, so even if you want to move, you go and see signs, room for rent, "No Irish", "No Coloureds", "No Children", "No Dogs", £3 per week. No, £2 per week, 'cos it was less than what the West Indians would charge you. But, you know, what was the point of going, you were coloured, and they said No Coloureds, but they could have put these signs up because there was no law, like there is now, to take them to court or stop them.

'Well, I had a friend of mine, we worked at the same hospital, that's the National Hospital for Nervous Diseases. She lived near to me, and we used to literally play a game. And we'd go and see this thing, the one that said, "No Coloureds", "No Irish", we didn't go to that one, but we just went for room for rent. And I used to go first, that's it, I went first, "Oh Madam, I'm so sorry, but we have just let it." "Oh, I forgot to take the notice out of the board." You know, excuses. And then she was waiting around the corner, this was in West Kensington, and then she would go and she would say, "Hello, how are you? I'm looking for a room and I saw on the board, by Castletown Road." "Oh, do come in." And then I would run around just the same time, and just as she was coming out I would go up and said, "How is it you have told my friend that you still have a room and you only just told me that you didn't have one?" I says, "It's your house, and you do what you like, but I just thought I'd let you know that I know that you're playing games."

'This was when I worked at Maida Vale Hospital, and I was secretary to the senior pathologist. And hospitals have notices, and this woman rented a room or a flat, whatever. And she happened to come through to me, and she said, "You know, I've got a flat to rent, and it's quite nice", and she told me the price and she gave me the address. She says, "But there's only one thing, I don't think I want to rent to any coloured people." So I said to her, "That's most unfortunate, because you're speaking to a coloured person", you know. And she said, "Oh, oh, I'm so sorry, I'm so sorry." I told my boss about it, and he was mad, he was mad. And, of course, he told the hospital secretary, the secretary's office, and her name was deleted from the list of people there. And she had the cheek to say, "Oh, but you don't sound coloured", you know. But you got accustomed to things like that, after a time, it's like throwing water at a duck's back, 'cos you couldn't do anything about it, you just have to accept that people are nice and people are prejudiced. And you're not in homeland, you tell yourself, so you got to put up with all these prejudices.

'I think what helped a lot of us was that we were brought up as Christians, and you pray, and if you read Corinthians, it tells you, you do good to those who abuse you and you pray for those who hate you, and from you're a child that's stuck in your brain. I'm not saying that I walk with a Bible under my arm or that I go to church every Sunday, but I still have the Christian thing in me. I was brought up as a Christian and I think that helped it quite a lot to survive; pray for people that really hate you.'[21]

'It was shocking, the accommodation. When I eventually came on the scene, I was involved in starting an organisation, at 1a Pennyforth Street, that's where we kept all our meetings. And, therefore, people in difficulties, they would come and seek advice and what help they could get. You go along some part in Nottingham, you would see signs put up, "Rooms for rent, no niggers need apply", that's not unusual. And you have people, some of them who were working, and when they asked, "Have you got any rooms for rent?" The first thing they ask, "What shift you work?" It means, when you're working from two to so-and-so, somebody else will be sleeping in your bed while you're away. And that is the sort of conditions that existed. I used to, at meetings, I described the conditions of the houses, I used to call it the houses with rubber walls, in that they pack in as much people as they can in these houses and charge them, at the time, very, very high rent. It was very, very, very bad.'[22]

If the hostility the migrants faced had been totally uniform, their existence would have been impossible, and the stream of arrivals would have dried up. But even apart from their own network of friends, relatives and the wider group of previously settled migrants, there were Caribbeans who had

[21] Interview with Connie Mark.
[22] Interview with Eric Irons.

arrived during the First World War, one of whom became Oswald Dennison's father-in-law. There were established activists like the brother of the sculptor Ronald Moody, Dr Harold Moody, who ran a large medical practice in London, and in 1930 had founded the League of Coloured Peoples. There was also a large pool of refugees and migrants from other parts of the world: Poles, Austrians and East Europeans, who had no interest in supporting a colour bar. Above all, the migrants were frequently aided by individual whites.

> 'When we went to Walthamstow, we were looking for a house to
> buy, and we were living in Muswell Hill, travelled to Walthamstow
> just like a foreign country, actually. And when we didn't know
> where we were going – there were no A to Zs in those days – and
> we got a bus to Blackhorse Road. And we asked a white woman
> who was on the bus for the road we were going to, Haroldstone
> Road, and it began to rain, and she came out and she used her
> umbrella to shelter us, and walked with us to Haroldstone Road.
> Now that was a very unusual kind of experience, and so it sort of
> balanced the feeling of alienation or animosity which was obviously
> there.'[23]

Most migrants could relate a similar experience, but they were much too infrequent to alter the general tone of the atmosphere. Paradoxically, the sheer brutality of the conditions they faced motivated the migrants into establishing themselves in the landscape faster and more stubbornly than they might otherwise have done. Even though most of them had begun with the intention of returning to the Caribbean, what impelled them had not been simply the search for work or money. Going abroad meant improving your lot in life, not only financially but in every other way. The effort needed to survive in Britain precluded that kind of personal progress for a number of years; so for most of the migrants it was impossible to return. The job was unfinished. As time went on the changes in themselves, in the environment from which they had come, and in the country where they now lived, began to make it more and more difficult to retrace their footsteps.

> 'Well, as time went by, I get closer and closer to England because
> I started looking for family, because I started courting, and then
> getting married, married at Wandsworth. So, I never give any more

---

[23] Interview with Eric Huntley.

thought of going once I started having a family here. And, as I say, my mother had died, I had nobody there. My sister still alive, but, it was quite alright for me to make a home here once I met my wife. Well, I don't know whether I was belonging to it or not, I felt I was here to stay.'[24]

'I don't think it's possible to profile a typical West Indian immigrant, but I think it is possible to be accurate about their intentions. None of us intended to stay. I certainly didn't, you know. I was in a slightly different case; I'd come to go to university, so you might have thought that I might go back and be a lawyer or go into government Civil Service, or teach at the university. I should go back, I didn't want to go back either. But none of us admitted that. And I think if I draw on my own experience, I cannot tell you when I decided I wasn't going back. I fooled myself, not this year, next year, and not next year, but perhaps the year after I'll feel like it. I went back home, I liked what I saw. Well, I'm going back just to wind up things, and the year after that. So, the point at which you actually acknowledge to yourself you've taken the decision to stay on, as a sort of open ended, long term basis, the decision was probably taken three or four years before. And I suspect that's true of many, many families. They had no intention of staying. And, in a way, they didn't know whether the negative aspects of their experience would be so great that they wouldn't stay or couldn't stay. They thought perhaps the British might likely chuck them out when immigration reached a certain point. So, you know, they couldn't commit themselves like that. But they began to put down roots very, very quickly, of course. And, you know, the more roots you put down, the harder they are to pull up. You don't quite know when that tip over point arrives when you are on this side.'[25]

'I came to England because I got married and my first husband, Stanley Goodrich, was a fast bowler and he represented Jamaica and all the Islands, and he was a professional cricketer and he played

[24] Interview with Oswald 'Columbus' Dennison.

[25] Interview with Stuart Hall. Stuart Hall arrived from Jamaica in 1951 as a Rhodes Scholar to Oxford University. In the sixties and seventies he became a leading figure among radical sociologists, a recognised leader in the interpretation of the new schools of Continental philosophy, and founder of the New Left Review, a highly influential journal of the British Left. He went on to head the Centre for Contemporary Cultural Studies at Birmingham University, subsequently becoming Professor of Sociology at the Open University.

for a team in Seaham Harbour in Durham. Well, he left me when I was seven months pregnant and, while he was away, his daughter was born. He wanted to see his daughter, that's why I came to England, for him to see his daughter. I came by air, by the way, with a three-month-old daughter. And I came with a suitcase of clothes hoping to go back in a year. Well, what it is, you're on a contract, and while you're under contract they keep renewing it and renewing it and renewing it, and then by the time you're here certain years, you think, well, you want to go back but you haven't got the amount of money for the fare, that if you go back, what are you going to do? And it just goes on and on and on.

'I personally want to go back for good, and I did go back for a bit, but, my husband changed his mind and he didn't come to join me in Jamaica, and my daughter, after a time, didn't like Jamaica at all. She couldn't stand the weather and she couldn't stand the people and she couldn't stand the food. And she was getting on seven, eight, and she couldn't read and write. I brought her back to England because she grew up in England and she missed being here, so I really came back for my daughter and my husband's sake, I was quite happy staying there.'[26]

'I think what most West Indians who came to England in the fifties made of the England which they came to was this: We've come here, we will work a while, we'll save some money and we'll go back home. It was just supposed to be a temporary gap, because we never came here with any intention of doing any other thing than to save some money, to educate our children and to return home. What went wrong is there's such a thing called time where people change, where the home which you left may not be the home which you could go back to, where the system itself changes, where you yourself change, where you start to have the children and those children begin to have children of their own. So, and that's changed. That's what happened. For some people, they might have said, "Yes, fine, I've made a life here and I will stay here." Quite a lot went back, and some went back and returned because they couldn't fit in. But this is the thing about life, about being a human being, that you will do things as it happens, and according to what happens to you within that period of time.'[27]

[26] Interview with Connie Mark.
[27] Interview with Ben Bousquet.

Postscript: *The exception to every rule*

'Well, I went to England in the fifties – 1954 – and, of course, I was looking for a better life. I was a young man, and I wanted to see what the outside world was like, and it was a good thing that I did go to England. I do all sorts of jobs. I can remember my first job in England was to work in the park. I then go on, of course, to dig the street up, you know, and from there, the sheepskin factory, the rubber factory, the bakery. I becomes a haulage contractor, I own a number of trucks. And you name it, I've done it, in England, and I enjoy it.

'Well, I could remember, I saw a lot of West Indian folks buying properties, and I tried to find out, you know, a little bit about it, and they would not give me the details. They suggested it was a difficult job, you couldn't get into it. But I was living at one of my relations' property, and I did some calculations very quickly, and see, of course, what they were doing. They were buying these houses, renting them out to their fellow West Indians, and were making a package. So I decided to buy a part vacant property in Forest Hill. And the first one I bought I started to do the same thing, rented a part of it, and within about – what was it? – two months, I bought the next one. Within about three months, I bought four properties. And then, within forty-five years, I own, of course, the most property as any black man in the country. Something like just over 400 houses, all over England.

'Well, the heart of doing this, and a lot of people didn't sort of realise, I go along and I will buy, say, five houses, for £5,000. I'll go to my bank and I will get the £5,000 – a hundred per cent mortgage. I would convert those houses – if they're four storey, I'll probably put them into four flats. And then I would sell one flat for, you know, what I paid for the five houses. And I still retained the freehold of the property. And then, if I want to buy the next ten houses, I'd then go back and use that property as, of course, the collateral to buy. So, to me, it was really a game. Understand the tricks, how you do it, the timing, and, believe you me, it was great.

'I had no problem with the banks, because you go to your bank manager and you prove to him that you're very honest, straightforward and hard-working person, trustworthy, simple. Our bank, of course, used to tell me that his limit was, say, £3,000. So, he tells me he could let me have three. So, I use up the £3,000. So I form a next company, and I pick up a next £3,000, and I form ten companies, and, of course, I pick up, of course, I mean, ten threes, you know. So, I never have any problem at the time. I could remember once I was buying some properties for somewhere in the region of about half a million pounds, and I had no money in the bank, and I want the properties. And I went and signed a contract. And the people said to me, "Fine, when you're going to complete?" Twenty-eight days. I went to my bank manager and said, "Now, look, I've signed a contract for this half a million." He said, "Oh, my God, Jo, you're going to let me lose my job, man." I said, "No, you're not going to lose your job." Because I then go away and I pre-sell about a third of that property, for three quarters of a million, and my lawyers send the contract on to the bank. So, the bank manager loves me because he knows that he can rely on me, and as I grow in business, doing very well, and the folks get to know me, I becomes a part of the English family. They get to love me, I love them, you know, I go anywhere, and it was great.

   'As far as I'm concerned, Britain is my home. My first house in England were at Forest Hill, and then I moved to Ravensbourne Road, it's just off Stanstead Road. And my third home that I live was in Bromley, a fabulous house, you know. It's like a twenty bedroomed place overlooking the Sanctuary Park Golf Course. Lovely, beautiful, Rolls Royce, everything. You name it, Jo Whitter did make it.'[28]

---

[28] Interview with Jo Whitter. Jo Whitter came from Jamaica in 1954 and became the first black property magnate on a large scale. He returned to Jamaica in 1980 and went into business there, but he still owns substantial property in Britain and his five 'English kids' have remained here.

10

'I think perhaps the biggest problem that I faced was knowing very quickly where to go and where not to go; where you weren't welcome, where your face wasn't welcome. Where hostility could be violence, for instance. Teddy boys were rife in south London – Walworth Road and the Elephant and Castle. It was getting connected very quickly to be certain that you weren't stepping down the wrong alley, going in the wrong street, being in the wrong place in the wrong time because I felt very often instinctively that there were places where you had to avoid, and I think that was proved to be right by people who would get their heads beaten in and had very difficult experiences. And for me that was new, but at the same time I think it was very much part of growing up – growing up very quickly.'[1]

'I think it was cold. I think it was lonely. The main thing I remember of my parents in Dudley was walking around and nodding to other black people who I didn't know. "Who was that?" "Oh, I don't know. It's just somebody, you've got to show your respect. Just to say Hello, it's good to just incline your head." And it was this thing of everybody knowing that we were all going through the same tribulations and just nodding. It was a nod of recognition of who we were. So there was, at first, a loneliness, and as people got to know each other, a network of people grew via the church, via bingo, via dominoes, via the pub, people in the same situation grew close. You grew your circle of friends, and I think that's what happened, eventually.'[2]

[1] Interview with Sir Herman Ouseley. Sir Herman Ouseley came to join his family from Guyana in 1957. He went to school in south London and later worked in local government, eventually becoming chief executive of Lambeth Council. Subsequently he was appointed Chairman of the Commission for Racial Equality. He was knighted in 1997.

[2] Interview with Lenny Henry. Lenny Henry was born during the fifties to a Jamaican family in Dudley. After school he became a stand-up comedian, achieving enormous popular success on television. He is the best known and most influential black entertainer in Britain.

It Was All Fairy Tales

A letter from Mike Phillips to Kwesi Phillips: From the past, to the present

Memories are made of this. The decade of the fifties exists in the shadow of the following decade, which they talk about nowadays as being colourful and exciting, a time of explosive liberation, and, in comparison, the fifties are described as being drab and colourless. But, of course, the way you see the world around you depends on where you're standing at the time, and that isn't how I remember it at all. For a start there always seemed to be some world shaking event happening, or just about to happen. There was the Korean War, the guerrilla war in Malaya, the explosions in Algeria, the Mau Mau in Kenya, the Suez Crisis, the Soviet tanks crushing Hungarian revolt, the Cold War, the independence of Ghana, the start of the Civil Rights struggle in the USA, the threat of the nuclear holocaust and the triumph of Fidel Castro's revolution in Cuba. These things didn't happen nightly on TV, the way they would nowadays, but there were plenty of pictures in the paper. And when you went to the cinema, sitting in the dark, the newsreels which they showed just before the film started attacked you with images that made you tense up and grip the arms of your seat. It was the sudden quality of it – the soldiers marching, the angry faces, the relentless tanks rolling – which made you feel as if all these terrors were about to burst through the screen into your world. The point was that you knew that there were dramatic changes taking place in the world all the time, and somehow those changes seemed part of our lives and the way we lived.

Listening to the voices of friends and relatives talking about what happened to them during that time, the phrase that Connie Mark used occurs to me over and over again. Nobody tells you the truth and nobody tells you everything. It isn't that they're not trying, but it's probably impossible. For instance, you ask someone about finding somewhere to live, and you hear a hundred stories about insults, insecurity and appalling conditions. Fleeting between the words like fish in a pool are another hundred stories about happiness and despair and change and love.

This must be what gives my memory of those times such a

slippery, elusive quality. I knew that I was surrounded by all kinds of threats, hostility, even hatred, but when I think back to how I felt, what I remember is excitement and promise, and the thrill of discovery.

The smell in the air was something burning, and it was sharp, almost chemical, like tar melting to a liquid in the sun. It made you think of steam engines and funnels puffing vapour, and when you looked up you could see long grey feathers of smoke wavering upwards into the sky. Coal fires burning. After a while it got so that you didn't notice it any more, except for a short time at the end of summer, when you could tell the season was changing because the first sign of autumn was this smell, coming from nowhere, until you looked up and saw the thin plumes of smoke growing out of the chimneys.

I couldn't avoid thinking about who I was and why I was here, because someone was always asking. I'd bump into a man or a woman in the street, or trip over someone's bag, and if it wasn't the first thing they said, it might be the last thing: the inevitable question, 'Why don't you go back where you came from?' The odd thing was that there wasn't a single moment I can remember when I wanted to go back. I can't remember, either, any of us even discussing it as a realistic option. Going back was for people who were too old to take it any more, or for babies. Every time you went out was like walking into a freezing day with a cold wind blowing needle sharp bits of ice right in your face. That's what it felt like, but, as it happens, that's not what I remember. The things I remember go like this:

There were names on the front of the buses and, reading them, I would try to imagine the places: Stamford Hill, Bethnal Green, St Johns Wood. In my mind a countryside emerged, in which wooded fields sloped down the sides of round green hills. It couldn't be far away, I thought.

James Dean was everywhere on the cinema posters, leaning against a wall in his red jacket with the zip up the front. I was just like him, I knew. Young and misunderstood, a crazy, mixed up kid. The dark of the cinema flickering with the reflection of the giant faces was a refuge, a passage to escape, dreaming of California. You could stay there while the programmes ran over and over again, until the lights went on and they played God Save The Queen. Then you had to go. While they filed out I used to sit, nerving myself up for the dash home, which by that time of night was dangerous, a gauntlet. In the street I moved like a cat, every sense tuned up, taking a different route every time. One night a gang of boys erupted out of an alleyway, yelling and waving chains, but I was fast, some sixth sense warning me the moment before I saw them, and I got to the High Street pulling away and leapt on the platform of a double decker, clinging to the pole, my legs sweeping out behind me as I scrabbled for a foothold.

Most nights there was no trouble. I'd reach the top of our road, and I'd see my father standing under the lamp post, straight and tall like the soldier he used to be, staring out into the night. When he saw me he'd turn around and go back into the house. We never talked about it, partly because, for most of the time I knew him, he was at work or asleep.

When I wasn't at the cinema I listened to the radio. I was hoping that I would learn something, mostly about the boys in my class. It wasn't that I didn't understand them – although I didn't, but that didn't matter all that much – it was the sound of the voices I wanted to learn. I wanted not to be noticed, because being noticed meant you were going to have a fight with somebody. One day I was fighting this kid. I don't remember his name, but he had an Elvis haircut and he worked down the market at weekends, so he was tough, and his game was to come up behind me and mutter 'Nigger' out of the side of his mouth, and the third or fourth time it happened I turned round and banged him one in the face. Before it could go much further one of our teachers came in and stopped us. Then after he'd ticked us off he took me down the gym, made me put on a pair of boxing gloves, and said he'd teach me to box. He did this with all the foreign boys, so we were all in the boxing team – me, Kenny Cardozo, a couple of Greek kids, and Coppelotti, who became a policeman later on – which is true, although no one believes it when I tell them. Anyway, I didn't learn much from the radio, except maybe to drop my aitches and aspirate the letter t, but I guess I would have learned that in any case, just from going to school.

One evening I went to a dance at school and danced with this girl, and for the next few weeks I kept seeing her on the way home because she went to a school nearby. We smiled at each other, and sometimes we sat together on the bus. I liked her, and, in any case I'd just hit puberty, so we'd exchange some awkward words about the last film I'd seen or what she was going to do to her hair, then I'd go home and think about the conversation and what I should have said. Her name was Valerie and she had dark hair and blue eyes and real breasts you could feel bumping against you when you danced, and she occupied most of my thoughts. She was a lot bolder than me too, the way thirteen-year-old girls are. She'd come on the bus and she'd go to her friends, 'There's my boyfriend', and she'd plump herself down next to me, while I cringed in embarrassment, thinking that everyone was staring. And the problem was more than embarrassment because it was obvious to me that sooner or later some big Ted would be sitting behind us and take it into his head to grab me off the bus and give me a good kicking. So she was scary, in that way, as well as in all the other ways girls can be scary when you're thirteen or fourteen.

Her best friend lived near Clements, who was one of the boys in my class, and one day Clem told me that Val's parents were going out for the evening that Friday and we were invited round. It was a strange prospect, partly because I'd never been out with a girl before, and, of course, I'd never been in a white person's house, and I kept wondering what it would be like. They lived in a prefab off Hornsey Road and her parents were friendly, and when they shoved off we put some records on the record player and jived. Bill Haley and Elvis Presley is what I remember, but then it had to be. In a couple of hours her parents came back and we went home. That would have been that, except for Newman, who was in my class and up to that point had been relatively friendly – that is to say, he'd never been abusive, or offered to fight, and when we met in the street he'd smile. What I didn't know till then was that he fancied Valerie and, after Clem had told everyone where we'd been that Friday night, Newman was in a rage. He cornered me at lunchtime with half a dozen of his mates and a crowd of other boys drawn by the news he was going to do me. I saw them coming but there was nowhere to go, and they held me up against the wall while Newman punched me. He kept talking to me, using the most obscene words he could think of: 'I bet she loved it, you black bastard', I remember him saying and the rest I wouldn't repeat even if I could remember. But oddly enough I haven't forgotten the look of his tormented eyes staring out at me while he punched and slapped at my face.

If all this sounds like nothing but the story of anger and conflict and confusion, think again, because at the bottom of these events it is now obvious to me that there is a process of discovery going on. It's not a simple process, the sort of thing that you hear being described as two lots of people meeting and getting to know each other's odd customs and strange habits. It's a lot more complicated than that. I think that the most important part of what we learned wasn't so much about unfamiliar cultures and manners, it was about ourselves. And, on the other side, I had the sense that the reactions of the English people we met were moved and shaped by the feelings about themselves which they brought to the experience. I think this was what I saw in Newman's eyes while we fought and he shouted the filthiest things he could think of about a girl he liked.

Sometimes what was happening seemed obvious. Take our mother, your grandmother. She was working, for the first time in her life outside our home, in a workshop sewing furs, with a Jewish couple who owned it and an Irish lady named Peggy. The couple were refugees from somewhere in Germany, and Peggy had migrated from Ireland with her family, and they all appeared to be fascinated by each other, to judge by the way they talked all day. In the evening my mum would tell us, at length, about life in Nazi Germany or about Peggy's latest row with her husband. 'Tea in bed,' she would say, laughing. 'That's what she wants. Tea in bed!' These were among her closest friends all the time she was in England. Sometimes I went to meet her when she had something to carry home, or when I was passing at the right time, and, walking home I used to listen to her talk with a feeling of surprise. She had never, in my experience, talked so much and so freely. It was as if she was turning into a different person, bigger and more aggressive. She laughed a lot too. She liked the female comedians she heard on the radio, like Peggy Mount and Kathleen Harrison, but Alma Cogan made her scream. Alma Cogan sang a song called 'Pickin' a Chicken With You'. I don't think it was meant to be funny, but it reduced my mum to hysterics. Later on, thinking about her, it always struck me that I'd probably never seen her so happy as in those times when her life was changing so much.

For me this was a clue about how to read the memories of other migrants who had lived through the same times. When you hear what they say, it begins to be clear that there are several different stories hidden in the words. First is the story about what happened to them. There's another about how the events affected the way they felt about themselves and about the circumstances they were in. Then you realise that various kinds of potential are emerging as they react to the events, and inside that framework you can feel them becoming different people. On the other side of the coin, the character of the white people they encounter steals through between the lines: confused, angry, vacillating between fumbling insecurity and *downright fear. The movement between all these elements in the memories of migrants begins to tell us another, bigger story, which is the story of a sort of dialogue, in which they're trying to extract from the experience a set of guidelines about how to cope with changes over which they had no control.*

'Biggest shock was, one, the cold, and two, having gone to church for the very first time – so elated, so delighted that I'm coming from an Anglican church back home, I went to join in worship, and so I did – but after the service I was greeted by the vicar, who politely and nicely told me: "Thank you for coming, but I would be delighted if you didn't come back." And I said, "Why?" He said, "My congregation is uncomfortable in the company of black people." You could just imagine what that meant to me. And I went home, I didn't say anything to anybody for months. That was my biggest shock. I was the only black person in that congregation that Sunday morning, and my disappointment, my despair went with me and I didn't say anything to anyone about it for several months after that. But the people with whom I was sharing living accommodation belonged to a Pentecostal church; first in my lifetime that I heard of the Pentecostal Church, having been brought up in an Anglican church as a youth back home. Very loving, kind, affectionate people, and I began to go to church with them and I've never looked back. I accepted faith in the Pentecostal Church in 1959 and, thank God, until this day I'm one of its ministers.

'It was a common experience, more so with the Anglican Church and other mainstream churches too, but most of all with the Anglican. A sense of isolation. Nobody really cared. And therefore people soon had to form partnerships and groupings together to survive, offering support in every shape or form, and the black churches, Pentecostal churches emerged, and that support was beginning to come forward. Comfort, counselling, healing, when people depressed, contact for people back home, advice in particular, loneliness, the loneliness that people feel from separation, and even financial support. And that time, because we begin then to pool our resources together, even at that early stage in something that was commonly known in Jamaica as "pardner". It's known by other names in other parts of the West Indies, and people begin to pool their resources together, to send for their loved ones and relatives back home, that's building the family base. The Church provided that, not least the spiritual support and a sense of camaraderie that

that brings, the togetherness. And then you will find people gather
in their own bedroom, in their living rooms and start worship there,
and it was a meeting place, it was a bringing together of people
where common ideas could be shared. And then we begin to hire
halls, rent halls, for worship and so on and so forth, and so the
membership grows, because it brings together people from various
parts of the West Indies where that camaraderie was shared. And
it grew and grew till we could no longer hold prayer meetings and
day worship, Sunday worship, in bedrooms and dining rooms. When
we begin to rent halls and then the membership grow.'[3]

   'And this shipping company, there was a board by Finsbury Park,
under the bridge, and there were hundreds of accommodation –
notices, work, et cetera. So I went up and I got the job and I was
at this typing pool, and there were about five of us there. And then
one evening, the manager said to us that the bosses are coming
down from the City. Well, I don't understand what the City is, you
know, 'cos living in London, I thought that was it. And then he
came and inspected the premises and to see what everybody was
doing, and so on. And then, ten minutes after he left, the man who
took me on, he called me in the office. And he said, "I'm sorry,
Jessica, but the directors don't want any niggers to work in their
offices." And he himself was very, very sorry, because my work was
good and whatever. And I said, okay, and I just left, what else could
one have done? And the man I learned, subsequently, with one of the
girls, that he got the sack for employing a nigger. And that was it.
   'Then I went to Haringey, an office of the Minister of Pensions
of National Insurance, and I went temping, and the manager
interviewed me, he gave me tests and whatever, and I did that, he
was happy. And he said it was just a temporary job, and I said, Fine.
And I left and I came back home. And we lived by that time on
Whiteman Road itself. And then ten minutes after I got there, the
door knock, and the landlady said to me, she was a Greek lady, she
called out, she said, "A white man here for you." And I said, "Oh,
my God. Which white man . . . to see me?" And it was the man
who interviewed me, you see. And he said, "I'm terribly sorry, Mrs
Huntley, but the job is really very temporary, it's only for a week."

---

[3]   Interview with Carmel Jones. Carmel Jones came from Jamaica in 1955 and joined the Pentecostal
Church in 1959. He became a Pentecostal Minister, and then Chief Executive Officer of the Pentecostalists' umbrella organisation, The New Assembly of Churches.

And I said, "Well, I don't mind, even if it's a week, I will take it." He said, "But it might be less than a week." And I said, "It doesn't matter if it's less." I said, "I'll work for two days. If there's no work, for a day." And I spent five days there. And what happened was that when the staff heard that I was taken on, as a nigger – by that time, "nigger" was not even going out, but between "nigger" and "coloured", you know, they were floating between those two terms – and they really didn't want me to be there at all.

'But, you know, I ended up there being Assistant Treasurer of the union and things like that. But I had a lot of problems with the staff. There was a Scottish woman, and I thought we were very friendly until, I can't remember which of the Royalties had a son, and the lunch hour I came in, and she said, "It has arrived, it has arrived." And I said, "What has arrived?" She told me. And I said, "Well, I have two." And she took off on me, I'm telling you. "Why the hell you don't go back to your own country? Why black people have to come here?" And I tell her she must go back to Scotland, too. I mean, I gave as much as I got. But that was the kind of experience I spent five years dealing with. It wasn't easy. I was always given memos, one after the other. There were always complaints. But the guy who was the supervisor was a young person, and we got on very well together. Because most of the women then, in particular, and the men, they were there because during the war years there were no qualifications needed, and now they resented anybody who came in at their grade or higher.'[4]

'I think most Trades Unions, like most Churches in England, they didn't want to have very much to do with us, and they didn't particularly want us to join the places where they were powerful because they had something called the closed shop, where jobs went from parents to sons and daughters and they wanted to keep that going. So they saw black people coming into the organisations where these things were possible, where they could join the Union, as a threat. So the Trades Union movement did not come up to us with open arms, neither did the Church. The forms that took was that in the local places of employment – whether it be in the Post Office, whether it be in the railways, whether it be London Transport, you know the places which we first went into, even to a certain extent,

[4] Interview with Jessica Huntley.

the hospitals – it was almost made impossible for you to get a job. And if you did get the job it became impossible, almost, to actually join the union. Normally the Union would go to the person who got the job and ask them to join, but you know the black people that didn't happen, you used to have to go and look for them and ask them for you to join. So they made it in that way by not approaching you, you knew that they didn't want you. And I think it always became incumbent on us to make sure that we joined, you know, so we made the initial move, not the union. We joined the Trades Union movement; the Trades Union movement didn't come looking for us.

'One of the places I can remember was Euston Road railway, when there was some trouble there between the black staff and the white staff over a lack of representation. I know at Smethwick there was a problem again between the union and the black people. And that was going almost right up to the sixties, you know, and we were having difficulty with the unions, because the shop stewards saw if they brought black people into it, black people might actually question things. Or we might want things done a totally different way. So they saw us as opposing their power bases. We were not particularly welcome.'[5]

'I had applied for a job in a library, a local library. And, in those days, the library would take in the young people who have applied and then present them to the committee about a month or so later and have them confirmed in their posts. But I wasn't called in at all, and they couldn't fault my qualifications for the job. I was probably more qualified than any of the others in terms of having had my basic training, and what happened was that they had a big discussion with the staff to find out whether they would work with a black person, and when I went to the committee they'd all had experience of working in the library which I didn't have, and I had to go through an interview. And quite frankly that interview was quite amazing because people were complimenting me on my English. Well, I'd never spoken any other language, and some of the people who were speaking to me were not, in my opinion anyway, speaking good English themselves.'[6]

[5] Interview with Ben Bousquet.
[6] Interview with Ros Howells.

* * *

'That was about 1950, late 1950, I came down this way. So, one day, I can never forget, my friend and I was going out, and we meet this little boy, and he was a brave little boy, he come over, he said to me, he says, "Where's your tail, then?" So, we didn't rough him or anything, I called him over, I said, "Come here, son. Come here, sonny boy." I said, "Look, we are all human beings, I'm no different from you. It's only the colour of the skin, the same blood." A little boy of about eight or nine. He said, "My Mum said you have got tails and my Dad said so, too." So, I said, "When you go back, you tell your mum and dad they are wrong." I talk to him nice. And he says, "Yes, right, because you haven't got no tails, have you?" I don't know how he make it with his mum and dad. It was all fairy tales. Oh dear, oh dear.'[7]

[7] Interview with Lloyd Miller.

11

Marge and Lloyd

'Well, I had a friend, and my friend came, Betty, her name was. She said she was taking me out for the evening, on a Friday evening. We was going to this dance over in the Lyceum. We was on top of the bus. And my friend, she had a boyfriend, and her boyfriend brought a friend, and that was Lloyd. And when I looked out in the bus, and she said, "There they are, on the corner", I said, "You must be joking. They're black people." Never met a black person before, never in my life. Anyway, we had already got there, so I thought, Well, I'm game for anything. We went to the dance hall, with Lloyd and Dexter, that was his friend, and we had a great time. I'd missed the last bus home, me and Betty, so Lloyd said, "Right, here's the taxi fare, go home. Get a taxi and go home." So I thought, Well, that's nice of that man to give us the taxi fare. So eventually we used to come back to the Lyceum nearly every weekend and we used to meet up and things was going fine, we was courting and everything, you know. Until my family found out. My family hit the roof. They hit the roof. So, it was like one big argument. I left. And I knew what time Lloyd used to come from work, so I met him at Euston Station. He didn't know I was going to be there, with my case. So he said, "What's happened?" I said, "Well, family, you know, got to know that I'm going out with you, and they've told me I must get out and blah-blah, and here I am." And from that day, we've been together since. I was seventeen. I was nineteen when I had my son. They wanted to put him away, 'cos my brother was my next of kin, 'cos I'd lost my mother and father, and my brother was in control, was supposed to look after me. My brother brought in this big old sergeant-major, she looked like something like that. And they was going to take my Roy away. And I said, No way. 'Cos it was black, and 'cos he wanted me to come home, and I said, No. I discharged myself in case he come back. And never spoke to my brother for years and years. And when the race riots started, I took my boy down to my family to see whether they would look after him while the riots was on. They refused point blank. So, just have to get on with it, and it really made me hard, you know. 'Cos you would have walked along the street and you'd have people spit at you, 'cos you've got a black baby. It was very, very hard. And Lloyd was in hospital for four years, 'cos he had a bad back, and it really made me hard. But we survived. Been married now forty-seven years. And we're still together.

'We was living in rooms. We lived in Hazelwood Crescent, then we went to Rillington Place,[1] and very airy scary, but we didn't know what was happening there, 'cos that had all happened before we went there. And from then we bought a little place up in Portobello Road. And compulsory purchase came in and the council had to re-house us, and from then we sort of gone on from there. Up in Willesden there was a house for sale up there, and I never took Lloyd with me, 'cos I had a funny feeling. But, anyway, the house was for sale, and we was to go up there and sign some papers, and as soon as they see Lloyd, they put the price up. Didn't want to know. That was that. There was no nobody you could complain to, nobody. Not in them days.

'Roy was what you call a street urchin. I used to lock him in his bedroom, but he's going out the window, and he's gone. He came in crying one day 'cos some boy had hit him, and his father run him out the house. "Don't you dare come in here and say somebody had hit you." And from then on that boy always used to be in fights, 'cos they used to call him black boy, and he never liked that. He grew up very hard. Very tough. Which, I think, me and him survived, really, 'cos it made us hard and tough. When Roy started school, I used to get a job and go to work, it'd be about three or four days, but I find I'm not in a job because I was married to a black man. And I went from job to job, and it always seemed to follow me, I don't know why. Until eventually I gave up and I done early morning cleaning. Well, the workers then knew everybody more or less, and I was a machinist, and I used to make clothes. And they never used to speak to you, and it made your life very uncomfortable. 'Cos sometimes Lloyd used to meet me from work and, of course, when they found out I was married to a black man they would never speak to you, and they made your life very, very difficult.

[1] Rillington Place was the street where Dr Christie murdered several women and entombed them in alcoves behind the wallpaper. The area was redeveloped and the street no longer exists.

'And there was no unions in them days, and on the Friday when you got your wages, you used to get your cards, and that was that, you were out. When you used to ask why you're going, they never told you why you was sacked. Is it my work? You know, I asked the question. No, they would never tell you. But then, eventually, the penny dropped, 'cos it was going on into other jobs, that was that. You know, people make life very uncomfortable in them days. I had a friend called Inge, and she got married to Joe, and they was getting on in life and that, and she fell for a baby, who's called Raymond, and he wasn't actually dark, he was very light, but her family got to find out that she was married to this coloured chap. And Inge was very, very nervous, she couldn't stand worries or anything like that. And apparently her family come over and had a talk to her, and she just walked off and left Raymond. And his father brought him round to me in his arms and said that his mother had left him and gone back to Germany, would I look after him? And from that day to this, he's with me, and I brought him up. She just never had the bottle, put it that way. And she went back to Germany. She got in contact with Raymond and he went down there to see her, but I was a little bit upset, but things worked out that he came back. And he hasn't seen her since.

'It wasn't very common, was it? But it was eventually becoming common. I knew about three or four that was married to coloureds when I lived in Stoke Newington, and when I moved down this way I met different people, and there was about three or four of us married to coloured men then. So it wasn't very common. That's why the people never liked us, because we more or less lived all round this area, the four of us. We used to meet every day, you know, and take the children out, they had children like I had children, well, one. And that was all the contact we had of people, because white people would never speak to you. As they used to pass you, they used to spit. It was terrible. It was no joke. And I still see them people today, and they speak – 'cos they're old, they're my age now – and they still speak, and they say, "Hello, Marge, how's Lloyd?" You know, life has gone round in a circle. But they never remember what they used to do to me years ago, but I remember it, and I'll never forget it.

'It's my brother had to break first, and I didn't break. We used to pass each other on the street, never looked at each other. He was disgusted with me and I just had to fight on and live my life. And eventually, about, maybe ten years, he invites us down there or he comes here. But I've still got that feeling there that they gave me a hard life, my own family. Lloyd's family, they was great. They accepted me into the family. But my family never. And I wish I could forgive, but I'll never forget. I've still got that feeling. Now, they are very, very nice to us, every minute, every day, they would be on the phone. Well, it's only out of conscience, isn't it? I needn't have suffered the way I suffered, and that's the way I look at it, 'cos I really did have it hard, I really did. God only give me one, if I'd had two or three, well, I suppose I still would have managed. But my own family did give me a hard time, 'cos they've missed a lot of my life and missed a lot out of my son's life.'[2]

[2] Interview with Marge Miller. Marge Miller was born and brought up in London. She worked as a machinist and cleaner in west London, and is now retired.

12

'I was a bit naive at the time, I wasn't quite sure what was going on. And a lot of people were like that, they weren't quite sure what was going on. I remember, I was staying in Ledbury Road, which is in North Kensington, just watching. And this is what lots and lots of people were doing, they just came out their houses, stood on their doorsteps, waiting to see what was going to happen, because it had been in the press. And there were groups of white youths going round at that time, looking for black people to beat up. Eventually, some of the black youths got together to protect themselves. But the thing I noticed most, that there were these characters in the crowd who were stirring things up, like wandering round saying, "Let's get the black bastards", and this sort of thing, and, that, at the time, struck me as strange. They weren't working class, they seemed to be a bit from somewhere else – not from the area – and that went on for several days, if I remember correctly. But, eventually, it fizzled out, you know. It didn't completely fizzle out, because Mosley went on to run for the election in the area, and there were still problems from groups. But the general, where everybody was out on the streets and that, only lasted for a short while, as I remember it.'[1]

'It was late August, but it was cold, it was full of smog, and you couldn't see your hands sometimes. So, somebody could well ram a knife in you on a morning at the bus stop, as easily as they could at night, because the whole environment was putrid. And I used to feel not only frightened but wondering what's going to happen next. I could get bumped off. I used to work in Park Royal at the time and you would get on a bus and the atmosphere on that bus was electric. You could cut the air with a knife, the tension. People would talk in whispered tones: "You hear what happened last night? You hear who got shot?" That kind of thing. And people would look at you, like spears, daggers. Bloody blacks. People would spit at you.

[1] Interview with Eddie Adams. Eddie Adams has lived in Notting Dale since he was born in 1936. He was a Teddy Boy in the fifties, worked at Fords in Dagenham, Essex, then at the local Law Centre until retiring.

Nobody spit at me personally, but I know that happened. And the way you feel always lost. If you went to sit down beside somebody on a bus, they'd shuffle up. But then somebody would look at you, see that you're as frightened as hell, and say, "Oh, mate, take no notice of them, we're not all the same." I think that's important to say. That was my experience. "Take no notice of them, we're not all the same." And just those words gave me two things: hope and comfort. And I proved from that, in 1958, that people are not all the same. And those words stayed with me for years, so that even now, when the going gets rough, I know what that Cockney woman said to me on that number 17 bus, "We are not all the same, take no notice of them." [2]

The Nottingham And Notting Hill Riots

Another letter from the past

Sometimes history is like flying over the landscape in a plane. You can see the general features, but the details are missing. What looks like a gentle slope or a short walk from where you're sitting is actually an insurmountable barrier. In much the same way, most of the history that you may be told about the events that black people lived through in the fifties are packed together in a simple formula, which, on closer inspection, doesn't make any sense at all. For instance, here is what one historian says about the Notting Hill riots in 1958.

Britain's imperial chickens came home to roost with the flaring of racial tensions from the 1950s, associated with New Commonwealth immigration. What precipitated violence was the impending introduction in 1961 of strict immigration controls, provoking a deluge to beat the ban. Indian and Pakistani arrivals in Britain, running at a mere 3,000 in 1959, leapt to 48,000 in 1961; West Indian immigration, around 16,000 in 1959, jumped to 66,000 in 1961; Cypriot immigration quadrupled in 1960–61. The great majority of immigrants initially

---

[2] Interview with Ivan Weekes.

settled in London, and a few areas – Brixton, Notting Hill, Camden Town and Southall – bore the brunt. London's first race riot erupted in Notting Hill in late August 1958, when white mobs attacked the homes of blacks, smashing windows and throwing petrol-bombs.[3]

Reading this, what stands out is the oddity of the dates. If the impending introduction of an immigration ban in 1961 followed by a 'deluge' precipitated the violence, then why did 'London's first race riot' happen in 1958? This was well before there was any serious prospect of restricting immigration, and before the numbers of migrants arriving showed any significant increase. Ask yourself why the riots only took place in one location. Why not Brixton or Camden Town? In his next paragraph Porter describes the 'race riots' that occurred over twenty years later in Brixton and Tottenham as if they were the same sort of events, taking place within the same social context, fuelled by the same causes.

All this is mistaken, and spotting these mistakes is crucial because, if you are working from a crude distortion of the facts, it becomes impossible to approach any true understanding of what happens next. This, in its turn, makes it very hard to arrive at sensible decisions about your present identity and direction. Another problem is that distance imposes a generalised identity on disparate groups, muddles one happening with another, lumps opposed individuals together on the basis of superficial resemblances, and assumes that discernible emotions and attitudes were the same thing as the motivation behind events. It is healthy to regard with suspicion any narrative which ties the past together into a rational and coherent account – including this one – because the truth is that people cannot help reshaping history according to their own needs as individuals and according to the needs of the time.

For example, when black people now discuss the Notting Hill riots there is a lot of talk about 'fighting back'. Most of those with opinions will have been nowhere near Notting Hill at the time, perhaps not even have arrived in Britain, or not yet have been born. If you have been listening to these stories since the event – as we have – you would realise that such expressions only begin to be used halfway through the next decade, after extensive reporting about Black Power in the USA and after the impact of visitors like Malcolm

---

[3] Roy Porter, *London: A Social History* (Harmondsworth: Penguin, 1996), p. 354.

X. Round about this time stories also appear about black American servicemen coming to Notting Hill to join in the 'fightback'. One man claims to have been a member of a secret organisation of ex-servicemen preparing for guerrilla warfare. There is even a story about black American servicemen driving a truck into the area with a machine gun in the back and parking it in Cambridge Gardens ready to spray the crowd with bullets when their white aggressors attacked. Needless to say, no one used such language or told such stories at the time because that is not how it was.

By the middle of the fifties, 'Teddy Boy' had become a generic name for working-class delinquents, or working-class young men who merely looked like delinquents. They had got that name because they had, apparently, adopted what was said to be a version of Edwardian dress – long jackets, sometimes reaching right down to the knee, tight 'drainpipe' trousers which fitted so close at the ankles that they had to work their feet into them with care, a string tie, which looked like a black bootlace tied in a bow, and shoes which came to a point and were called 'winklepickers', or shoes with thick synthetic soles, which, at one point, were called 'brothel creepers'. The whole ensemble was topped off with a well greased mop of hair, with a lock falling over the forehead. In the early fifties it was called a 'Tony Curtis', but when Elvis arrived on the scene the hairstyle became a little more floppy and greasy, and took his name for good. Not every Teddy Boy wore the full regalia, but all of them had at least one of the elements. The trousers were obligatory. Every boy had his mother unpick the seams of his old trousers and sew them up again, narrower. It was the first manifestation of youth culture to sweep across the country, but, unlike later youth movements, it was never captured by entrepreneurs and resold as a commodity. It remained firmly working class, symbolising rebellion, and the worst Teds were proud to be mad, bad and dangerous to know. Later on people focused on the style, but it was really all about culture. The Teds belonged to a generation which ten years earlier would have been fully occupied trying to kill the enemy, but conscription had come to an end, so unlike their older brothers and their fathers, there was no institution within which they could test their courage and aggression. Mostly they fought each other and smashed up furniture. The culture was all about territory. Each group of Teds controlled a patch of the city. Sometimes they fought battles by arrangement. At Alexandra Palace, for instance, there would be fights between the North London Teds, and, afterwards, the police would pick up a selection of weapons, from flick knives and bayonets to old revolvers.

The aggression was traditional. Part of the style came from the wave of movies about juvenile delinquents which were exported from Hollywood round about that time. The most popular films had names like *Blackboard Jungle, Four Boys And A Gun, Rebel Without A Cause.* Most of them would climax in a gang fight, with boys circling each other with deadly intent, knife blades flickering. Violence was part of the style, and most nights Teds would be out looking for a punch-up, but they first became headline material in 1956 during the first showings of the film *Rock Around the Clock* when they started dancing in the aisles, then progressed to slashing the seats with their knives and beating up the rest of the cinema's patrons. By then they were a routine part of life in every working-class district, and at school on Mondays there would be an excited buzz about what the local Teds had been up to that weekend. One story went that they had thrown a girl over the balcony of their favourite cinema in Islington's Upper Street. It was the sort of thing they did. Sometimes it sounded as if they thought they were actually in a movie, acting out the kind of theatrical wildness they'd picked up from the cinematic imagery of juvenile delinquency.

'I remember that particular night, I was travelling with a little attaché case in my hand and a book I was reading. And these Teddy Boys were on the tube, lots of them. And you know those little things, those little swivel things that are hanging from the roof of the tube, they were swinging on those like circus clowns. Swinging on them and kicking the thing and coming nearer to me. And once they'd got to me, of course, all the indigenous people got up, because some of them were elderly people and they were frightened. And two of them sat next to me, one on either side. And the first one went, "Nigritta, Nigritta, Nigritta, Nigritta, Nigritta, Nigritta." And the other one went, "Catch a nigger by the toe, when he hollers let him go." That's what they were saying. And I just kept on reading the book. And then they got up, and one fellow put his hand on my head – like that – and they went on, up the tube, terrorising whoever they could.'[4]

The affray in Nottingham which sparked off the Notting Hill riots was not a sudden and unpredictable event. Considering the prevailing atmosphere of the time, the routine mood of public irritability and anger which sur-

---

[4] Interview with Rudy Braithwaite. Rudy Braithwaite came from Barbados, arriving in 1957, and is now a self employed osteopath.

rounded the migrants, it was not difficult to guess that something of the sort was going to happen somewhere. Public behaviour was generally rude and disgruntled, but the same or similar things could be said about various periods in Britain over the last fifty years. It was more than that. If you were a migrant, every argument or dispute you got into – in the street, at school or at work – however mild, was likely to begin or end with the question: "Why don't you go back where you came from?" People were not always so direct or unpleasant about it, but it was an attitude informed by the sense that black people should not have been in the country at all. There was also the sense that when an individual said this, they were conscious of being backed up by a vast and popular consensus.

It was an awareness fed from a number of sources. In 1948, for example, the newspaper stories about migrants were mostly human interest, patronising and friendly. Within a few months they had turned into stories which represented the migrants as a threat, often regurgitating urban myths about drugging and abducting young women. By 1955 there was a steady drip about the possibility of government action to halt 'the problem of West Indian immigration',[5] or about the pressure that the migrants put on housing in various districts.[6] This was an accurate reflection of attitudes on the ground, because the gossip and rumour which filled the pages of the local newspaper was only the tip of the iceberg. Only a few years earlier an essential element in managing social policy had been an official focus on scapegoats and domestic threats – black marketeers, spivs, smugglers. The same structure of social disapproval translated easily into a widespread hostility towards the immigrants. It was a pattern established over the previous decade, everyone grumbled, and everyone who had an opinion was convinced that 'something should be done', but no one knew quite what that 'something' should be. The exception was the range of right wing politicians, in and out of Parliament, from declared fascists like Sir Oswald Mosley to closet racists like Duncan Sandys and Sir Cyril Osborne, who offered their publics a clear explanation of what was going on, which drew on the idiom of the war years, and was combined with new focus on race.

The ideology of whiteness wasn't a new idea in Britain, but during the fifties it was reinforced and stimulated by events abroad. Britain was still the hub of the Empire and, for many people, the news from abroad struck an urgent personal chord in a way that is now difficult to imagine: the independence of Ghana; the guerrilla war against the Mau Mau in Kenya;

5 Daily Express, 19 January 1955.
6 Daily Express, 20 January 1955.

the struggle against racial segregation in the American South. All these events were accompanied by fiercely contested debates and, increasingly, they revolved around the issue of race. White settler propaganda about African atrocities and barbarism along with the sex obsessed polemic of the Southern segregationists, became a hot topic of saloon bar gossip. New words like 'trash' and 'nigger hunting' were imported from the racial front lines abroad and rapidly became part of a new racialised idiom. Every public confrontation, however trivial, in which migrants were involved, was suddenly underscored by a deep current of racial resentment and hostility.

'You would find incidents on buses, and on tubes. I remember, one morning, there was a fight going on. This black woman was standing at the entrance of the tube, and her umbrella so poised on the thing, and this white lady stepped on to the tube and kicked it away. And the black lady, she was a Jamaican lady, said, "Well, look, I expect you to say sorry when you do something like this, you know. And you are not saying sorry." And the woman says, "What do I say sorry to you for? You black whatever-it-was." And the woman took up the umbrella and started beating her with it, and that was a battle on the tube. I got off, because I could see the whole thing threatening to develop into an attack on anybody who was black present. I don't know how that woman ever fared, but that was what it was like. You felt surrounded all the time, in those days, in those years. You felt that you were an intruder and, truly, you were a foreigner. You were an outsider. You did not belong, but you had to bear it.'[7]

Confrontations of this kind happened daily all over the country, wherever migrants lived and worked. Before the Second World War racial abuse would not have been unusual in certain streets and districts, but there had always been sanctions against public harassment of blacks and foreigners in the wider society. Something had changed, however. At the start of the fifties racial superiority had been an incontestable plank in the platform of ideas about the Empire and imperial destiny. By the time the decade was halfway through, the idea of race had become a personal threat, one of the demons which stalked the changing post-war world. In the short term sexual terror became the medium by which racial conflict spread through the social landscape.

---

[7] Interview with Rudy Braithwaite.

'In Manchester, that was in my student days, I was walking with my duffle bag on my shoulder, and this woman had just come out of her boyfriend's place, you know, and she was walking down the street in front of me, on Alexandra Road. I was walking along a few paces behind her. And he came out, you know, he ran across the street. I wasn't even thinking about her. And he ran across the street. "What you getting up to? What you up to? Is he bothering you?" calling the woman by name. And I was looking at him in amazement 'cos I didn't know what he was talking about. As a matter of fact, I didn't connect that he was referring to me giving her some kind of harassment. Because that is the one thing that I would never indulge in. And, on the other hand, she was a big woman, to me, and he ran across the road. "If I catch you, interfering, I'll give you a couple of fists in your mouth", and that sort of thing. And he went on, you know. And I was looking at him in amazement, because I couldn't work out what he was talking about. And so I stood there and listened to him, and I thought to myself, Well, he probably is a little bit funny in the head, I mean, he's not right, you know. And then he ran back, he tiptoed back across into the place, you know. And I think the woman had told him that I didn't interfere with her. And he just ran back across the road without saying any more.'[8]

The 1958 riots might have been predictable, but they were not inevitable. Race was the trigger which set them off and kept the passions burning, but the causes were due to a number of complex elements. Remove one of those and the riots might well not have taken place. Imagine an overloaded lorry with faulty brakes speeding round a blind curve. Add another, similar lorry coming the other way and an accident is likely. When you add a cow strolling across the middle of the road, an accident becomes almost inevitable. But it takes an element of blind chance for all those elements to come together in the same time and place. In that sense the riots were an accident which the merest shift in any one of the circumstances might have averted. Later on it became received wisdom, especially on the political right, to describe them as a spontaneous and inevitable reaction to the mere presence of the migrants, and, of course, this was an argument which narrowed the range of explanations to the issue of race and racial conflict. The result was that subsequent public discussion of the riots focused on ending Caribbean migration, while ignoring the other trends and conditions which the disturb-

[8] Interview with Rudy Braithwaite.

ances had highlighted. In the long term every political debate about every
issue in which migrants were concerned has been haunted and shaped by
the distant prospect of uncontrollable eruptions of white fury. For instance,
the rhetoric which allowed Enoch Powell to set the political agenda ten
years later drew its credibility and its power from the widely accepted belief
that a species of berserk racism had been the unique cause of the '58 riots.
At the other end of the scale, the events of that year drove the Caribbean
migrants into a defensive posture, and planted the seeds of a marginalised
culture which was, in many ways, the mirror image of the racialist framework which shaped it.

'I was threatened, frightened inside, but I know I must go to work.
And, even at work, you find some strange people in every nationality,
I'm not just saying in the white people, who had no sympathy. Like,
there's one lady, and she was really anti and, really, I don't even think
she was anti, but she was on the side that was anti because that
was the ruling side, because we were a minority in this small hospital.
She would come up and she says things like, the Teddy Boys were
out last night, and they're saying that they're going "black burying".
And I was stupid then, I thought they were picking blackberries,
but, no, it was to kill blacks, you know. Black burying. And going
home on the buses, my husband then said, you know, Don't be
afraid, we'll come and meet you, or I'll meet you at town. And you
could see them, you know, running across the streets, and you're
really afraid, 'cos they're shouting, "We're going black burying." And
still you have nowhere to go, you just have to hope it would calm
down.'[9]

The first disturbances were in Nottingham, which was the nearest town to
one of the big camps where West Indian servicemen had been received back
in 1944, and was therefore one of the places to which they had returned.
The city used to be famous for making lace, and in recent years had started
earning its living with a little light engineering. But in 1958 Nottingham
was suffering a local recession. Factories were going out of business and
redundancies were climbing. The centre of the city had housed generations
of workers, but with the drift out to the suburbs most of it had degenerated
into an enormous slum. In the middle of this swath of decay the area round

[9]   Interview with Tryphena Anderson.

St Ann's Well Road was immediately recognisable as the sort of district which had become home to the Caribbean migrants.

I saw small, cooped up terrace houses with decaying brick-work, broken windows and inadequate sanitary arrangements. In these hovels which are due to be pulled down under Nottingham's slum clearance scheme, two thousand coloured tenants live in crowded, unhealthy conditions . . . Side by side with these houses were secondhand furniture shops, fish and chip shops, pubs, pawnbrokers and a host of other small shops of the type to be found in working-class sections of all English cities. There was a decaying, crumbling air about the whole district.[10]

Around St Ann's black men were, more or less, legitimate targets in the constant interplay of local gang fighting. A lone black man late at night was a safe target because, even if the police got involved, they were likely to treat such affairs as routine faction fights. In any case, the local hooligans and Teds were buoyed up by the self righteous feeling that they were on the cutting edge of a popular consensus – that they were only dishing out what the blacks had coming to them. For many of them the harassment of black people was the first opportunity they had had to insert themselves into public life, to become part of the wider community with a recognised social role – guardians of the race, protectors of women and children, a last line of defence against the creeping invasion of aliens. The same pathetic sense of a fantasy, licensed by the attitudes of their elders, steals into many eyewitness accounts of the Teds' bullying behaviour.

It was apparent to me that these white hoodlums around the St Ann's Well Road district – for that is the only way to describe these Teddy Boys – had appointed themselves a law unto themselves. Armed with daggers they issued fascist directions to coloured people. They shouted, "Don't walk in groups or you will be attacked." The white kids who usually played with coloured children in the empty sites in the back streets stayed away. They walked by with their mothers without acknowledging the coloured playmates. These mothers looked at the dark-skinned children who were merrily chattering away oblivious of all the bother around them. I saw hate in the eyes of those English mothers. Walking along St Ann's Well Road I could feel the eyes of hatred staring at me every time a group of English youths passed by. There was arrogance in the way they brushed past me, laughing and cocking their heads up in the air, hoping that I would make a wrong move. They did the same to an elderly coloured man near the corner of the road. In fact, they approached every coloured person in that same cocky fashion. The only reason they didn't start a fight was because it was early in the

[10] Edward Scobie, *Tribune*, 5 September 1958.

afternoon and police cars and policemen on foot in groups of three were patrolling the streets. On three occasions English people on St Ann's Well Road ignored me when I asked for directions on how to get to my hotel. They walked away from me without answering. I just wasn't welcome in the St Ann's Well Road district. Neither were the 2,000 coloured people who lived there.[11]

In the summer of 1958 there was a self-imposed curfew for black people in St Ann's. Being caught out on the streets late at night was simply dangerous. The incident, which local legend blames for setting off the chain of events leading to the riots, happened when a black man had to visit the late night chemist to get a prescription filled for his wife. On the way back he was waylaid by a group of Teds, who the police were, as usual, unable to locate. In hindsight the truth of the story is not relevant. What matters is the fact that the Caribbeans in Nottingham were thoroughly fed up with the pressures and restrictions imposed by neighbourhood bullies. In the normal run of things they might have been reluctant to back up the sort of young black men who habitually got themselves into fights in pubs and street corners, but this was a story which perfectly encapsulated the situation they were in. A respectable family man, on an errand of mercy, had been pointlessly attacked and beaten. This was precisely the sort of incident which enraged the migrants and made them willing to encourage retaliation.

'After that incident, they told me that they went out the following week looking to see if they could find Teddy Boys to hit back, but nothing happened. And then, gradually, an incident took place at a pub. And the fighting started.'[12]

It would not have been difficult to get into a confrontation outside the St Ann's Well Inn at closing time on a Saturday night, and on 23 August it duly happened. This time, however, there was a group of black men on the scene, ready and willing to fight. In the first phase dozens of people were injured 'in a matter of seconds' but before the police arrived, the black men had vanished into the nearby alleyways.[13] Eight whites were hospitalised, including a policeman who was run down by a car. To many of the migrants it seemed like a legitimate return for the treatment to which they had become accustomed.

[11] Edward Scobie, *Tribune*, 5 September 1958.
[12] Interview with Eric Irons.
[13] *The Times*, 24 August 1958.

'The chap who drove his car through the crowd, a West Indian chap, he told me what happened. He was at a party and, as soon as they heard that there was these disturbances at a pub nearby, the Robin Hood Chase, they all decided, Well, we must get there. And he got in his car with a few others and went there, and there was this milling crowd, and he felt the best way, Well, I had better drive through this, and he went through it at full tilt, as quickly as he could. I think a policeman must get bumped on the backside or something like that. And I remember when Roy was telling me, I said, "But, look, man, that was dangerous." He said, "I reckon you're too damned nice, man. It give me satisfaction, at least we can fight back, you know, at least we fight back, and people will realise we're not prepared to sit and take this sort of thing any more. If they want to be nasty, we can be nasty as well." '[14]

News of the fight spread like wildfire through the area and, in a short time, a mostly white crowd estimated at about 1,500 had gathered and started attacking black people at random. By the time the police restored order another eight people had been injured. In the following weeks, the St Ann's Well Road affray was widely reported as an eruption which symbolised the racial anger simmering beneath the surface of English life. Oddly enough, this was the last large scale conflict of its type between the races in Nottingham. On the next Saturday night an equally large crowd gathered in the district anticipating another 'race riot', but no black people turned up, so they began to fight each other.

'The following weekend there was another uprising, and that was even apparently more violent than the first one, but the interesting thing, it was only one black person was in the area at that time. And he walked through the crowd of fighting people and nobody noticed him, and had a good laugh.'[15]

At the time, nearly all the commentators, focused as they were on race, missed the point, which was that if there were no black people available on whom to focus their rage, the crowds were equally willing to fight each other. In that sense it was apparent that the riots were as much about the feelings of exclusion and deprivation experienced by a wide swath of the

[14] Interview with Eric Irons.
[15] Interview with Eric Irons.

English population as they were about the presence of black migrants. The attention that the disturbances claimed for the conditions in which the people lived was, in itself, a factor in calming their rage. The liberal press fulminated about the 'shame' of the city but, within the region, although individuals frequently expressed their regret, there was no widespread sense of guilt or sympathy for the migrants. On the contrary, Nottingham's riots put the city on the map and, a fortnight later, the police were obliged to clamp down on bus companies from as far afield as Leicester which were offering coach trips to 'the terror spots of Nottingham'.[16]

In comparison with what came later in London the riot in Nottingham was not very serious. On Sunday morning when the news began filtering through to the rest of the country, groups of Teds in London set out looking for black victims, embarrassed by the fact that a bunch of provincial Teds in a distant town somewhere up North were hogging the sort of headlines no Ted had seen since they had trashed the cinemas during the first showings of *Rock Around the Clock*. Fortunately, it was still a rest day. Most of the young men arrested for street offences during this period had casual, manual jobs – kitchen porter, labourer, fitter's mate. With no work to go to there was time to tour the streets, particularly in west London.

The area between Hammersmith and Notting Hill was, at the best of times, a violent playground for gangs. Leaving aside the local warriors, it was handy for Teds from Fulham, Battersea and Elephant and Castle in the south-east who would come over for a skirmish. Violence between the various factions, the police and any unfortunate bystanders was endemic. In the week before the Nottingham affray several policemen were injured in Hammersmith when they went to deal with a crowd of youths who were creating a public nuisance in Fulham Palace Road.

A man lay unconscious on the pavement. Arrested for insulting behaviour, Smythe said, 'You try it,' while O'Leary added: 'I think you are too fucking small.' They were put in the police van with others. P.C. West added that he saw P.C. Cullen knocked to the ground and all the prisoners started to get out of the back of the van. O'Leary, Smythe and Dorsett attacked him and he drew his truncheon to protect himself. He hit the men, but it was impossible to restrain them and he was finally kicked to the ground. 'They continued to kick me from my shoulders to my feet,' alleged P.C. West. 'I collapsed, whereupon they left me and started to run away.'

This was normal action for a Saturday night in west London. At the trial the magistrate halted the proceedings to reproach the police solicitors for only bringing

16   *The Times*, 15 September 1958.

a minor charge against the men. 'Why aren't these things taken seriously?' he asked.[17] The answer might have been that these things were routine for the time and place; and young black men were not immune from adopting the methods of the Teds around them. The weekend before the Nottingham riot a crowd of black teenagers in Shepherd's Bush attacked a man who was walking home.

They pointed at him and he heard someone say: 'There's one of them.' When they rushed towards him he ran away. The men ran towards him and one of them stabbed him.[18]

On the morning of Sunday 24 August the police began stopping groups of young white men in cars touring west London with aggressive intent. They arrested a group of nine youths in one car, who were armed with iron bars, table legs, starting handles and at least one knife, after they'd assaulted several black people in Ladbroke Grove and Shepherd's Bush. But even then it was not obvious that this was the build-up to something more serious than the usual Saturday night mayhem. In any case, the media focus on race war was actually confusing because assaults of this kind were taking place all over London, and if the presence of blacks was the determining factor, trouble could break out in a dozen spots. On the Friday after the Nottingham headlines the *Kensington News* warned:

Nottingham must be a warning to North Kensington, to Paddington, to Brixton, wherever coloured people in large numbers are living and working side by side with long-established Londoners.[19]

Notting Dale differed considerably from Brixton or Paddington, and it might have been tailormade for the main event. Notting Dale had everything St Ann's Well Road had, and more, in much larger quantities. It had multi-occupied houses with families of different races on each floor. It had a large population of internal migrants, gypsies and Irish, many of them transient single men, packed into a honeycomb of rooms with communal kitchens, toilets and no bathrooms. It had depressed English families who had lived through the war years then watched the rush to the suburbs pass them by while they were trapped in low income jobs and rotten housing. It had a raft of dodgy pubs and poor street lighting. It had gang fighting, illegal drinking clubs, gambling and prostitution. It had a large proportion of frightened and resentful residents. A fortnight before the riots broke out

[17] *Kensington News and West London Times*, 29 August 1958.
[18] ibid.
[19] ibid.

there was a 'pitched battle' in Cambridge Gardens, off Ladbroke Grove, between rival gangs, and the residents of several streets got together to present a petition to the London County Council asking for something to be done about the rowdy parties, the mushroom clubs and the violence.[20]

Notting Dale also had a clutch of racist activists, operating at the street corners and in the pubs. Parties like Sir Oswald Mosley's Union Movement actually had very few members, but in the atmosphere of hostility and uncertainty which had begun to surround the migrants they provided the country with an idiom, a vocabulary and a programme of action which shaped the resentments of inarticulate and disgruntled people at various levels of society. In the week before the Notting Hill riots broke out a drunken fifteen year old approached a black man in a railway carriage at Liverpool Street station and was reported as shouting, 'Here's one of them – you black knave. We have complained to our government about you people. You come here, you take our women and do all sorts of things free of charge. They won't hang you so we will have to do it.'[21]

Leaving aside the peculiarity of the boy's language after it had been filtered through various official reports, the style and content echoes precisely the rhetoric being peddled by such right wing activists as Mosley, John Bean and Colin Jordan.

'I remember going to listen to some of the speeches that Mosley would make, you know. I was too young to really take on board what it meant when you talk about the Third Reich and all that sort of thing. And Britain is a white country and it's for white people, and that sort of thing. That was the gist of the discussion that he would have on this little soap box. And there were a lot of people, who are very respectable now, who used to be supporters of Mosley. I could put my finger on them. I know who they are. Very massive crowds, big crowds used to come, you know. A lot of people would follow him. I mean, he used to have his gatherings on one of the side streets off Westbourne Park Road. And there were people who would really come from everywhere and listen to Mosley, you know. And it was crazy. But that happened. He was a very convincing speaker. And he spoke without a breath, he didn't take much. He would speak and things would roll out of his mouth, so that he was very impressive. When I remember some of the things that were

20 *Kensington News and West London Times*, 22 August 1958.
21 *The Times*, 1 September 1958.

being said. It's very impressive. And he said, and perhaps that is true, he used to say, "Many of the people who are in high places, who are politicians, would love to say what I am saying now." I remember those words. But they are too scared to say it because of the likelihood of jeopardising their wonderful, tidy positions. And, of course, that was borne out by Duncan Sandys, who talked about "polka dot grandchildren". And Gerald Nabarro, who couldn't even drive on a main street without driving up the wrong way. Yet he got away with it, his racism. He was very blatant about his racist behaviour.'[22]

In the last week of August 1958, this was the way the Mosleyites and their colleagues wove together gossip, rumour and complaint about migrants into a political programme, which, following Nottingham, they could represent as a national consensus. For the organised racists one big bonus was the fact that, among the sober Caribbean working men employed by Great Western Railway, Notting Dale contained a higher proportion than any other district of bold, reckless young black men who lived their lives out in public and would not cross the road for anyone.

There were dozens of incidents occurring in the last weekend of August that year which could have started the chain of events.

'I can remember, I was standing at Tavistock and Portobello Road, and this black woman – we didn't have nurseries like what you have today, child-minders, so when Mum going to work she got to carry her kid to child-minder. Push chair wasn't as modern as it is today, so she was going up Portobello Road, just have her hand rest on the chair, pushing it, and two white blokes was coming down the road, and one of them just put his foot on it and kick it away. She didn't hold this firm, so the boy gone right up in the air and drop on his head. Now, like that we stand up there, now we had us to do something about that.'[23]

After a week of excited reporting about racial conflict in Nottingham, all the elements were in place. Television, a relatively new medium, had projected the events and personalities in Nottingham in a way that enlarged them, focused exclusive attention on race and race hatred, and presented

---

[22] Interview with Rudy Braithwaite.
[23] Interview with Alfred Harvey.

models for emulation and competition. By Saturday night all the Teds in west London knew that the action would be in Notting Dale, and began converging on the area. Even so, Saturday night was tentative, an extended version of 'normal' street skirmishes in which gangs of youths pursued black men and broke the windows of houses where black men were known to be conducting business, or where white women lived with black men.

'One of my friends got his teeth knocked in. He used to live in Slough and, on Saturdays, he would come down and visit me. And, of course, there were swarms of people running up and down, and he saw mostly black people running about the streets, so, naturally, he went to see what was happening. And he was attacked by some Teddy Boys, and punched his mouth and he lost a tooth. And he then came to us, and, when we asked what had happened, he said, "Well, I came here, to visit you, and I just stopped to look, and some men came up to me and punched me in the mouth and start hitting me, you know, and I had to run for my life." But that was happening. And I remember very well the Teddy Boys in those days. I mean, taking their chains and swivelling them at night, and smacking them on the ground. It was a terrible sound. You'd hear these chains, they used to travel with chains and you would hear them. And there was silly laughter. And they would swing these chains around, swivel them around and then smack them on the ground, you know. I mean, they were dreadful looking people, at that time, for any new and young West Indian, because it seemed the focus was more on West Indians than anything else.'[24]

On the following Sunday, emboldened by the atmosphere, the locals focused on the mushroom parties which featured in all their previous complaints.

'Sunday night, and I was having this dance in Blechynden Street. While we were there – we're enjoying ourselves – eventually it's like we heard a swarm of bees coming. Although the music were playing loud, we could hear the noise from outside. So, I went to the top door and look out and I saw this mass of people, lot of people coming, with a police van in front, a dog handler in front of the van. And when they reach where the music were playing they just stop. And there was so much people they couldn't control them. They

[24] Interview with Rudy Braithwaite.

started to fling bricks and thing like that at the building. Eventually the police came in and they asked us to stop playing the music and go somewhere else if we can find somewhere else. So eventually we find a place up Lancaster Road, and we went up there, and that's where the party finish.'[25]

According to police reports the crowd at Blechynden Street only numbered about 200. Later on, petrol-bombs began to be thrown at other houses where there were clubs or where parties were known to take place. By the next day everyone in the district knew just how far they could go and what to expect. By the afternoon the Teds were returning and the crowds gathered again. When darkness fell they had reached critical mass. By now a pattern had been established. The Teds were increasingly drawn in to the district as news of the fighting spread. The excited residents spilled out of their houses to identify the targets of their resentment or simply to watch the fun. In the pubs, the street corner politicians were on hand to lend a gloss to the violence and maintain the emotional temperature.

In one street where some of the ugliest fighting has taken place your Correspondent found a group of men in a public house singing 'Old Man River' and 'Bye Bye Blackbird' and punctuating the songs with vicious anti-Negro slogans. The men said that their motto was 'Keep Britain White', and they made all sorts of wild charges against their coloured neighbours. Incidentally, they were very bitter against the Labour Party for 'letting them in'.[26]

On Monday night the fighting took on a different quality.

'There was a battle, a pitched battle, in Powis Terrace where I lived. I looked through the fifth floor window where I was, and there was a battle between black men, policemen, white yobbos and Teddy Boys. I mean, the street was alight, except for fires and that – Molotov cocktails and so on. And blood was everywhere and it was awful. And by that time, the situation had become so bad that black men used to come from surrounding areas, like Paddington and Brixton and Shepherd's Bush, knowing they're going to hit this particular street, knowing the whites were going to hit this particular street, this particular night. They would come in solidarity, to fight. In other words, many black people felt, In for a penny, in for a pound. If

[25] Interview with Alfred Harvey.
[26] The Times, 2 September 1958.

they're going to kill us, well, you know, we're not going to be passive any more, let's fight back. And if they get killed, well, so be it. So that was the kind of battle that I saw, and it was horrendous. The next morning it was like a battlefield, burned out cars and all the rest of it. I will say, however, that sometime afterwards, not long afterwards, the police having brought in reinforcements, this became national news now, you know, and all cameras and all radio microphones and every reporter was focused in the area, some stirring up trouble, very few taking an objective view.'[27]

Rioting on this scale went on for three days. A local reporter walking through the district on Monday night caught the precise flavour of street corner agitation, incredible rumour, sexual hysteria, random violence and holiday anarchy.

As I turned into Bramley Road I saw a mob of over 700 men, women and children stretching 200 yards along the road. Young children of ten were treating the whole affair as a great joke and shouting, 'Come on, let's get the blacks and the coppers. Let's get on with it.' In the middle of the screaming, jeering youths and adults, a speaker from the Union Movement was urging his excited audience to 'get rid of them' (the coloured people). Groups of policemen stood at strategic points carefully watching the 'meeting', while police cars and Black Marias waited round the corner. Suddenly, hundreds of leaflets were thrown over the crowd, a fierce cry rent the air and the mob rushed off in the direction of Latimer Road, shouting, 'Kill the niggers!' Women grabbed their small children and chased after their menfolk. Dogs ran in among the crowds barking. Everywhere there was riotous confusion. Police cars and vans wheeled out to cut off the mob. Meanwhile other police cars and vans in the area stood by to deal with the impending wave of violence.

Within half an hour the mob which had by now swelled to uncontrollable numbers had broken scores of windows and set upon two negroes who were lucky to escape with cuts and bruises. Women from the top floor windows laughed as they called down to the thousand strong crowd, 'Go on boys, get yourself some blacks.' As the crowd swung into Blenheim Crescent milk bottles rained down from tenement roofs where coloured men were sheltering. Accompanied by a dozen bottles, down came a petrol-bomb in the middle of the mob. One eighteen-year-old youth was led away with blood streaming from a head wound. Unable to get at their attackers, the inflamed rioters moved off to vent their wrath on other coloured men. Whilst the mob was active in another street, a young boy of five was dragged off his bicycle in Westbourne Park Road,

[27] Interview with Ivan Weekes.

and beaten up by coloured men. The news spread like wildfire through the streets until it reached the ears of the rioters. Screaming for revenge they broke off from their window smashing. The mob was now moving towards Ladbroke Grove. Cars and lorries were halted as the inflamed rioters poured across the main road into Westbourne Park Road. One youth at the head of the mob ran straight into a passing car in his enthusiasm for window smashing and blood. He was taken to hospital with a suspected broken leg. Once in Westbourne Park Road the rioters, hundreds strong, swore and shouted at a house where West Indians lived. Scores of milk bottles were hurled through the air, smashing the windows where coloured men had appeared. Broken glass and bricks were strewn across the road. The rioters left to continue their rampage through the streets.

Apart from the mob itself, smaller groups of fifteen to twenty were moving around the district independently. All through the evening, gangs of hooligans from all over London came to join in. They came on foot, by train, bus, motorbike, car and lorry, shouting, 'Alright boys, we're here.' Those on motorbikes and in cars toured the district looking for coloured people. When they found them they went back to tell their friends. In this way I saw many coloured people suddenly pounced on . . . Stopping in Talbot Grove I talked to a group of cheerful house-wives and their husbands. I was told that they were expecting a gang of negroes, led by a female brothel-keeper, to come down and set on them. As we chatted amicably on the doorstep, a woman shouted, 'Here comes Madame.' Men, and women alike pulled out railings and iron bars. Some grabbed milk bottles. A solitary coloured man ran down the street being pelted with bottles. When the excitement had subsided, one woman breathed a sigh of relief and said, 'Wrong ones.'[28]

The violence subsided after Tuesday. By then the local whites were beginning to be disturbed by its aimlessness.

Their ardour was being dampened by the indiscriminate vandalism and merciless attacks which were being inflicted on coloured people and their properties by hooligans who were only out to cause trouble. 'In too many cases innocent blacks are getting beaten when it's the rotten ones that's still running about,' said one man in Talbot Road.[29]

It was a judicious use of the word 'innocent'. In fact the blacks who ran and frequented the party houses were hardly inconvenienced by the mayhem, and they knew exactly how to take care of themselves.

[28] Colin Eales, *Kensington News and West London Times*, 5 September 1958.
[29] ibid.

'Well, we had a headquarters, number 9 Blenheim Crescent, where we'd congregate in the days. We'd eat, drink, gamble, we do everything there. We had a few white friends that would come amongst us. One – we call him Peanut – well he was the one who teaches us to make Molotov Cocktail. So we had us to prepare ourselves because, otherwise with Mosley and his black jacket, they worrying us. So, we had a petrol station along Kensington Park Road, and we buy out the petrol. They couldn't understand why petrol can, coming to buy petrol and thing like that. And we had a hardware shop along Portobello Road, Carpenters. Anything that could cut, we'd buy it. So. We did arm ourselves, just like they did. I think that helped to stop it. Yeah, we fling a few, when we see them coming, to stop them. The petrol and the sand, the sand blaze when it break, 'cos you got to light it. So we fling a few of them to stop it. We were on top of number 9. Was owned by Totobag. So, that was the headquarters.

'Another night a birth-night party for a friend, which is a white man, and we wanted some drink and they had an African bloke, we call him Mabuto, he say he'll go an' buy the drink. While we were there he came back in and he says we all sit down here and Teddy boys beat him up outside. Now, they were in front of the gate. When we open the door and look out we saw them. Well, we went out, and they run, and turn into Chippenham Mews. Well, in Chippenham Mews you had a café with some pinball machine in there, so they used to congregate there a lot. So they run and they leave us. The smallest one in the crowd, they left him to taunt us. So, when he taunting us, we're going to him and he's going away from us. When we reach Chippenham Mews we didn't look into the Mews itself, we just go across the Mews, and that's what they wanted, right in the ambush. So they came from behind us from in the Mews and by the time we at Harrow Road, they were on us like bees – bicycle chain, ratchet knife, all kind of implement.

'Well, milk shops used to have the milk bottles in the crate, and you had a milk shop across the road. I went over there, and I grab a few bottles. When I look over I saw on the wall, they were kicking like they're kicking football or something. So when I look it was black man. So, all these things you got to know how to do it, you know. I fling one bottle on top of the wall, splinter; fling one down in the sidewalk, on the pavement, splinter; and the third one I hit somebody. I'm just flinging a bottle like that and I saw they happens to run, leave him. He had about thirty-odd stitches at Paddington

General Hospital just across the road. So we all went there. Well, I get a bicycle chain in the face, which were hot but then I didn't know. When I feel like somebody throw water on me, I went, Oh, wiped my forehead I see pure blood, so I know that I got an injury. And that was the only attack physically that ever happens to me. When we went to the hospital and the police came, they told us the only way we can avoid these things happening to us is to go back where we come from.'[30]

Part of the reason for the scale and intensity of the riots had been inept policing, and the failure to recognise that anything out of the ordinary was happening as the Saturday night skirmishes escalated. Another was the sense that there was a widespread consensus in the country which would tolerate direct action against the blacks. But the importing of police reinforcements, the increasing number of arrests, and the draconian sentences handed out to some of the rioters, had their effect. On the other hand, when the violence subsided, not much had changed. But one of the peculiar side effects of the fighting had been that, far from intimidating the migrants, it actually gave them a renewed sense of confidence. They had taken the worst that the country could throw at them and survived. Almost overnight the Trinidadians, Jamaicans, Africans and Guyanese who lived in London had become a community, bound together by a common defensiveness.

'Well, we never come here to fight anyone. We just come to share life with them. So when it cease, it just cease, you know. They stop and we stop. But the idea was to show them that we can fight them as well. During that time, if one black man is walking down the street, and you see two white blokes, they wouldn't attack you because they feel you one could beat the both of them. But let it be four or so and they see, they murder you. They used to wear some shoe, winklepickers. When they get you down there they kick you senseless and so it's steel in the point of the shoes, you must get caught. Well, we show them that we weren't afraid of them.'[31]

[30] Interview with Alfred Harvey.
[31] Interview with Alfred Harvey.

Within the district of Notting Dale itself a new understanding seemed to emerge almost overnight between the different factions, a new ability to negotiate with each other.

'I was walking up Lancaster Road one night and I saw about four boys. I heard the footstep behind me, look around, stop. They came up to me. One says, "Look what you done to my brother." His brother was bleeding. I turned to him, the one who was talking to me, says, "No, the person who has done that to your brother, it's a war monger, and I'm far away from that. I'm no war monger." I had to was submit no way, 'cos if I run I'd get it. Everybody has got bottle in their hand. If I try to be a bully, they would do what they want to do with me. So I had to play it that way. At the same time, I had a little knife on me. Didn't show it to no one, but in case I was being attacked physically I could use it. But I talked myself out. Don't know how I did it, but I did. That when we finished talk, one of them asked me to give him a light. Now I was afraid, right? But eventually I gave the light and we went our way. So we didn't fight or anything. I walked out.'[32]

Notting Dale placed race and immigration in the forefront of public consciousness. It had been a sounding board for popular discontent, and over the following months the media speculated endlessly about whether the riots would spread to other areas of the country. That they didn't was a demonstration of the paradox that, while the riots were triggered by race, they were not exclusively about skin colour or about the number of migrants in Britain. The disturbances were equally about the conditions of white working-class lives and their desperate sense of exclusion. But for the next decade political debate about the social problems of urban life in Britain was to be distracted and dominated by race, a trend which culminated in the phenomenon of Powellism. In the meantime the miseries which had surfaced in the riots remained unexamined until they re-emerged in the industrial struggles of the early seventies.

[32] Interview with Alfred Harvey.

13

'They say, "Your cousin is Kelso, isn't it?" I say, "Yes, my cousin is Kelso. What happened to him?" He said, "The Teddy Boys stab him in his chest and he's in the hospital." He died on his way to the hospital. They questioned him and he asked them to come to me, and so they came. When they said that, I said, "Who stab him? One of you?" That's what I said to the policemen. "One of you?" They said, "The Teddy Boys stabbed him." That's what they tell me that day, if I want to come with them, get dressed and come, 'cos they met me in my pyjamas and everything. So I got dressed, I went straight off with them. In my lifetime, I never smoke a cigarette. I used to see my school friends and young little boys, they used to roll the papers and light the paper, smoke the paper. So each time I used to go and bash it out of some little mate's mouth, all these things I never practise. And that morning, when I having to wait in the police car, I asked them to stop at a paper shop and I buy two packs of cigarettes, with some kind of expectation, as I see, people smoke and drink and say that relieves the pain. And I start smoking, one light the other, one light the other. I see no good, so I asked the police if he want, and just pass the cigarette to the police. That's the first time a cigarette going in my mouth in my lifetime. But, all of it, as far as it reach, and how we see it, he was already dead, so what could we do about it?'[1]

---

[1] Interview with James Christian. James Christian was Kelso Cochrane's cousin. He came to Britain in 1957 and returned to Antigua after thirty-three years.

Aftermath:
The Death Of Kelso Cochrane

Most people who remember the event associate the murder of Kelso Cochrane with the Notting Hill riots. Some say it was before that time, but most think it was during. In fact it took place nine months afterwards in the late spring of 1959. It was a sort of postscript to the riots, and it closed the era which had ushered in a period of unprecedented change in the nature of British society.

The riot had been a very British affair. During the fiercest hostilities there were white people going out of their way to reassure black people of their friendliness.

> Your Correspondent frequently saw white and coloured children playing together. Just after a violent incident in which a coloured man was chased down the street by white youths shouting racial slogans, he saw a white man deliberately cross the street to shake hands with a coloured fruit vendor who was terrified.[2]

Even the asaults and attacks on property had a random quality about them, in the middle of which there were black people going about their business as usual. No one was killed and no one was recorded as suffering any serious or long-term injury.

In the aftermath, clergymen, social workers, reporters, government experts, politicians, Trotskyists, trade unionists, and well-wishers of every kind descended on the district. Left wing activists like Stuart Hall set up shop in the area and began escorting women home from work. Youth leaders held solemn debates. The police presence increased in size and watchfulness, scattering the prostitutes and raiding the illegal clubs. The momentary coalition of locals with visiting Teds broke down, and a Saturday night tour of Notting Dale became a risky business which involved running the gauntlet of police searches, local Teds and angry black men. The 'Keep Britain White' street corner activists like John Bean, Andrew Fountaine and Colin Jordan continued to hold their meetings, but they were increasingly heckled.

Within the district, as a whole, attitudes to the black migrants had not

---

[2] *The Times*, 2 September 1958.

changed substantially, but there was a general sense of alarm at the moral abyss which had yawned open during the time of the riots.

'Well, I was a Teddy Boy. I mean, there were quite a few Teddy Boys supporting Mosley, but most of the youth in that period you could roughly describe as Teddy Boys in that area: young working-class youths. We had drainpipe trousers and suede collars, et cetera, and four button suits and things like that. I mean, there was obviously Teddy Boys that supported Mosley, but then there was a lot that didn't. And in my group, which were mainly from an Irish background, second generation Irish families, et cetera, most of my friends, I'm glad to say, didn't. Some were actively opposed to him, others were just neutral, didn't do anything. They're described as Teddy Boys supporting Mosley. But his supporters were also the old pre-war Fascist members of his organisation that were there, mainly orchestrating what was going on, as I could see it. And his son was one of the main actors in it as well.

'I heckled him, I used to heckle him. He was a very theatrical speaker, a bit 1930s, a bit old fashioned for that time. And he used to speak from the back of a lorry and they would have arc lights on him, and he would sort of say something and pause theatrically, I suppose for applause and things like that. They said he was a good speaker, I didn't reckon him very much as a speaker. I think he was a man past his time really, but the trouble was that if you were opposed to him, you'd be chased up the road by some of his supporters, so you had to be very careful. Well, being honest, when the troubles first started, I was naive, I wasn't aware of what was going on. But it was a time to make one's mind up, and I made my mind up quickly that I was opposed to him. And I was on my own. Eventually I got together with other people, but I heckled him 'cos I disagreed with him and I thought it was a lot of nonsense what he was saying at the time. And I think quite a few people at that time made their mind up, one way or the other, that I would support him or go against him. It was a time of political change.'[3]

[3] Interview with Eddie Adams.

In the new atmosphere around the Dale there was little or no prospect of the riots recurring, so the news of Kelso Cochrane's murder in the early hours of Sunday 17 May 1959 struck like a bombshell.

Kelso Cochrane was a carpenter from Antigua, and he had been in Britain for five years. He was thirty-two years old, an amateur boxer and saving up to get married in June. He had had an accident at work the previous week and broken his left thumb, which was in plaster. Late the night of Saturday 16 May he left his girlfriend's flat in Bevington Road and headed for Paddington General Hospital because he was in pain. On his way back he was accosted at the corner of Southam Street and Golborne Road by six white youths who stabbed him to death.

Cochrane's murder was headline news, largely because it had taken place in Notting Dale, and because it seemed to signal a return to the violence of the previous year. But in hindsight, what the sequel to the murder revealed was the extent to which things had changed in less than a year. In contrast with the lawless days before the riots when no one had been expecting a general affray, this time everyone was on the lookout for any sign of trouble. Social workers toured the streets and clubs advising young black men to stay indoors and avoid provoking a clash. Policemen and youth workers shadowed the local youths relentlessly. The Duke of Edinburgh visited boys' clubs in Shepherd's Bush and Notting Hill. The newspapers appealed for calm. For a few days the Dale was as quiet as a cemetery.

For once, in this overcrowded area, you can *hear* the steady reassuring gait of patrolling policemen — always two together. I walked in the gathering dusk of Tuesday evening into the troubled area via Portobello Road. The nearer I got to Golborne Road — where *it* happened on Whit Sunday — the more I became aware of the emptied streets and an atmosphere made more tense by people watching the streets below from open windows, or, more cautiously, from behind curtains. Near the top end of Golborne Road, a white man in shirt sleves bent over his motorcycle. He dropped a spanner on to the pavement; the noise it made was almost hideous on this night. On the other side of the road a hoarding advertisement (out-dated) announced: 'Mosley is coming to Trafagar Square.' The Union Movement's leader's picture was daubed with bright red paint. A police car nosed its way into the Portobello Road from a side street. The blue capped occupants looked me over and drove on into the night. Two West Indian men passed me in utter silence. In Kensal Road, with its long line of humble terraced houses, I heard the staccato clip-clop of high heels. A teenage girl ran across the road to a shop, bought some cigarettes and fled back to the house she had left. Outside a pub in Ladbroke Grove a group of four or five youths, hands stuck in trouser pockets, just stood and stared. On a corner opposite them two policemen kept a wary eye on the group. The boys remained silent, hardly moving. Back at

Notting Hill Gate the neon lights and the busy traffic were never more welcome after the deathly hush of North Kensington.[4]

Cochrane's killers were never identified, but the circumstances made his death a martyrdom which would be remembered for a long time. The riots had decisively altered the political status of the black migrants from a minor irritant to a burning issue of popular debate, and politicians were, with increasing boldness, discussing the possibility of unilaterally restricting black and Asian immigration from the Commonwealth. Within the migrant communities, the mood of solidarity which had been created by the riots had been intensified and was now accompanied by a hardened edge of stubborn defiance.

> 'It was the West Indians that the whole focus was on, because they were more volatile in respect of attack, you know. If they were attacked, they fought back. And so they were labelled as loud, boisterous and very, very, very volatile. But it wasn't so. It was simply the fact that people were not going to take being pushed around, sitting down, laying down, or whatever. I mean, it was better to be dead.'[5]

At the same time a loose coalition of left wing politicians, religious groups and Caribbean organisations had begun to be knitted together in response to the racist propaganda being disseminated by the right wing parties. When the White Defence League held a meeting in Trafalgar Square the Sunday after Cochrane's murder the speakers were mocked with Nazi salutes and shouts of 'Sieg Heil',[6] and students chanted 'No Colour Bar in Britain' and 'Who killed Kelso Cochrane?'[7]

All these new anti-racist tendencies were on show when they buried Kelso Cochrane. Appropriately the funeral was arranged by the Interracial Friendship Co-ordinating Council. It was a warm day, and the sun was shining out of a sparkling blue sky. A lot of people noticed the good weather and it seemed significant, because this was a unique Caribbean occasion, one of the biggest funerals ever seen in North Kensington. About 1,200 people in the district were walking in the procession, and more of them were lining the streets on the way to Kensal Green cemetery. The man they were burying was not someone that most of them knew or cared about

---

[4] *Kensington News and West London Times*, 29 May 1959.
[5] Interview with Rudy Braithwaite.
[6] *Kensington News and West London Times*, 29 May 1959.
[7] *The Times*, 25 May 1959.

when he was alive. But in between the night of his bleeding to death on the pavement and the morning of the service, 9.15 a.m. sharp, at St Michael and All Angels in Ladbroke Grove, he had become a martyr. The West Indians and their supporters made the ceremony a State funeral, a demonstration which would leave an indelible mark on the area and its people and speak to everyone who saw it about their identity and their determination to stay in Britain.

The male chief mourners wore tuxedos, and the women were in brightly coloured summer dresses, with black armbands or patches. As they walked through the police cordon holding back the jostling crowds outside the church, they carried themselves with the conscious dignity of people who knew they were playing on an important stage. As each car load of mourners went into the church, the pile of wreaths covering the back of the nave grew higher and higher. There were wreaths from all over. From 'Some West Indian Sympathisers, Paddington Post Office'; from 'The Edinburgh West Indian Association'; from 'The Association for the Advancement of Coloured Peoples'; from 'The Coloured Peoples' Progressive Association'; from the West Indies High Commisioner; from individuals; and, in big, bold red letters a wreath 'From the Martyrs and Victims of Oppression – Nyasaland'. Five hundred people squeezed their way into the building, including Sir Grantley Adams, then Prime Minister of the short lived Federation of the West Indies. Kelso's fiancée, a nurse named Olivia, stood in the front pew with her relatives, weeping. At the front the Bishop of Kensington did the honours, assisted by the local vicar and by Canon John Collins of St Paul's Cathedral. Everyone had already heard the lesson many, many times before, but the Bishop's words seemed peculiarly appropriate, even prophetic, especially to the migrants: 'O death, where is thy sting? O grave, where is thy victory?'

As the procession walked in silence to Kensal Green, the crowds swelled and the traffic on both sides began to back up all the way along the Harrow Road. Black and white people lined the route or stood watching at open doors and windows. Once in the cemetery, the black chaplain, Father Campbell, conducted a short service and when the mourners began to sing 'Abide With Me' hundreds of men and women sobbed uncontrollably. There was only a slight break in the decorum imposed by the organisers and supervised by the police. The irrepressible photographers scrabbled like rats among the tombstones, and Sheriff arrived wearing flowing white robes and a white skull cap, to begin distributing leaflets calling for attendance at a demo in Trafalgar Square against racism the following day. He was promptly arrested and led away to the lodge at the cemetery gates.

'I was walking with the crowds, and then after the thing broke out, it was like Carnival. Everybody was assembled in the street, talking and chatting about this and carrying on and discussing it, and whites were talking to blacks, and that kind of thing, and it was the talk of the place. And then people were more friendly to you when you got on the bus. Normally, in the early days, you know, whenever something appeared in the papers, you could always test the temperature by going on the bus. People would be very hostile. And in this instance, after that funeral, there was a turning point. You could sense a change. People were more friendly. People were beginning to react and respond in a different way.'[8]

'It was a mass funeral. People were crying all over the place. There were white folks who, from their windows, were hailing the processions when they passed. Some of the English people from around here considered Kelso Cochrane as one of theirs. It's rather interesting in that those people had no bitterness, no racist overtones. Of course, if you are in a society that is steeped with racism, you must be touched by it in some way or the other. But, at the same time, those people were good people, and so they were moved. Many of them were quite angry during the funeral, and they accusing Mosley for it, they were openly shouting that this was a Mosley thing. And had not for Mosley, there wouldn't be Teddy Boys and all that kind of thing was going on.'[9]

The death of Kelso Cochrane – an obscure carpenter from Antigua – and the mourning which followed it was a revelation which helped create popular revulsion against the street violence and harassment the migrants had experienced during the fifties. It also helped to move the argument about their presence on to a new plane. Political interest in the conditions which characterised Notting Dale had increased and become the subject of fierce debate. A week after the funeral Henry Brooke, then Minister for Housing and Local Government, visited the district 'to see for himself what progress is being made in slum clearance and re-housing'.[10] This was a hint that political concern about the migrants had moved beyond such zealots as Sir Cyril

[8] Interview with Randolph Beresford. Randolph Beresford came from Guyana in 1953 at the age of thirty-nine. He was a carpenter by trade and became an active trade unionist. He went into local politics after the Notting Hill riots and was elected councillor for the London Borough of Hammersmith and Fulham 1974–5 and Mayor in 1975–6. He organised a fund for the Kelso Cochrane memorial in Kensal Green cemetery. He is now retired and lives in London.

[9] Interview with Rudy Braithwaite.

[10] *Kensington Post*, 15 June 1959.

Osbourne, and that the politicians in senior levels of government were beginning to plan a strategy. The results were soon to be apparent. Cochrane's martyrdom had turned out to be a great event which, for the migrants, signalled the end of an era which had begun with the victory over England at Lords. The same event also stood as a gateway to the sixties: a decade which featured international scandals, Rachmanism, Black Power, Powellism and the ratchet-like progress of legislation which ended the flow of Caribbean immigration.

Postscript

'I saw this article stating that it's a year since he died, and they said he would never be forgotten. And there is not a headstone or a memorial to say who was there. They went as far as to put the cost of it. They said £16, I remember, would give him a headstone, and £32 would give him a memorial. And that same year I made two tailored suits from Burton's, £16, tailor-made suit from Burton's, and it really struck me. In those days, they called us "immigrants". Now, you got "black" and "ethnic" and "Afro-Caribbean", all different labels; but in those days we were "immigrants". We had something in common. We were tradesmen together. And I told my wife, I said, "Look, I'm going to start a memorial fund for this young man." And my wife said, "What! After so many people make collections, what people are going to think of you, now?" I said, "Don't you worry." And one Sunday morning, I went out to my colleagues. I went to some of my friends who lived in a house and collected £7. It was a lot of money in those days. And I rang the editor of the newspaper, told them that I'm going to start a memorial fund for this young man and, if anyone is interested, they can make a donation through the paper. And that was it. Anyway, one of my colleagues, who was Irish, a trade union colleague on the Trades Council, lived in Ladbroke Grove, saw the article. And when we met at the next meeting, he compliment me for starting the fund. And, there and then, he moved that the trade union should take over that fund. And it was passed. All the unions affiliated to the local Trades Council. And they wrote them asking them for donations, and that is how the memorial was funded and came about. The words on the memorial is donated by the trade union and West Indian friends. It's right in Kensal Green cemetery.'[11]

---

[11] Interview with Randolph Beresford.

14

————♦————

'Well, that was one of those tragic meetings. I was living over in Battersea at the time and it was summertime, and I was going to Linden Gardens in Notting Hill Gate to score some dope. So I got a taxi from Battersea and it was such a nice day that when the cab got to Hyde Park I just couldn't sit down and miss all these nice chicks, 'cos in those days the summertime was really good and then Hyde Park was a main place, was a source, get lots of the black guys who didn't have a chick in the summertime. I started walking along Bayswater Road and I light up a spliff, and in a little while I forget all about the chicks and all that. And I was just sort of minding my own business and going down the road and when I get to Earls Court I thought I heard someone call my name, and then they called my name again. And then I looked and followed the sound and then there was this black cab. And I started crossing the road and he opened the door and there was a chick I knew, and Christine was sort of like squashed down in the cab as if she didn't want anyone to see her. And for me this was bad vibes and I closed the door and the taxi drive off and I knew right away then that this wasn't a good situation for me. I promised that I was gonna come back to the spot and paint it red 'cos I knew I was heading for trouble.'[1]

Scandal! The Profumo Affair

At the beginning of 1960 it was obvious that immigration controls would soon be applied and, during the next couple of years, the number of migrants multiplied; from 50,000 in 1960, to over 60,000 in 1961.

'The effect of government legislation in fact was very much the opposite of what was intended. Effectively the Commonwealth

---

[1] Interview with Johnny Edgecombe.

Immigrants Act was intended to control, i.e. stop, Commonwealth
immigration. But of course it had exactly the opposite effect. What
it did was to promote immigration and what you got was a large
rush to beat the ban when it came into effect in July '62. Now you
can demonstrate this very, very easily because if you correlate
unemployment with net immigration from the Caribbean there's a
very, very tight relationship. That correlation breaks down in about
1960, '61 and '62. And those are the years in which immigration was
projected and then passing through Parliament. Immediately after
that the economic controls over migration resume their previous
situation. And so what you can see is that the moment where this
very close relationship between British economic cycles and
immigration from the Caribbean breaks down is precisely the period
in which the immigration legislation was going through, and you can
actually measure the amount of people who are coming in to beat
the ban.'[2]

During the sixties the bulk of legislation about race and immigration was
set in place, deciding the permanent legal status of the migrants in Britain.
The Immigration Bill was published in November 1961 and passed the
following February. It introduced a quota system for ordinary immigrants
and a system of vouchers for those with special skills or jobs waiting for
them. The Bill had widespread approval in the country. A poll soon after
showed that it had ninety per cent support. But it was not enough. The
events of 1958 and '59 had put the issue of race and immigration at the
top of the political agenda. For the next two decades events on the ground
drove legislation. The increase in the migrant population had made them
even more visible to the country as a whole, and even after the Immigration
Bill was passed it was apparent that the immigrant presence would have
unpredictable repercussions.

A major problem still was housing. The Rent Act of 1957 had been
intended to halt the decay of private property, but it became a charter for
the exploitation of poor tenants in areas like North Kensington. The Act
decontrolled the most expensive properties, decontrolled cheaper houses
when the sitting tenant left, and doubled the rent a landlord could charge
to twice the rateable value. Following the Act, stories began to appear in
the press about the intimidation of sitting tenants, ruthless evictions and
homelessness. Peter Rachman was the west London landlord associated by

[2]   Interview with Professor Ceri Peach.

the newspapers with these practices, and his name entered the language as a synonym for them.

'I didn't know there was anybody called Rachmann at all, because I used to rent from a Nigerian man who turned out to be a middle man of Rachmann. Rachmann had a whole army of middle men, to whom he would give several houses for X number of pounds a week. These middle men would then re-rent to people like us for X per week, per room. So I didn't see or hear about Rachmann for about four years. But then, after you lived here for some time, and you become fairly streetwise and common sensical, one heard that the bosses were not these middle men, the boss was somebody called Peter Rachmann. And then Peter Rachmann used to come up in Notting Hill and the Colville area, which is where I lived, with his Rolls Royce and handmade shoes and silk ties and all the rest of it, a big fat chap, very affluent, with a posse of young women, but he never talked to us. You would see him walking along and somebody said, "That is Rachmann." You didn't say anything loud, because, I mean, you take your housing life in your hands if you said anything, so these middle men used to charge us exorbitant rents, not per room, but I used to pay for a space in a room. There were three of us living in a room at the time when we paid a guinea each, twenty-one shillings in those days, for one room. So it was three guineas for a room, and I had a bed in one corner and the other chaps had a double bed in the other corner. But we were grateful for that. We were grateful for it. Even though it was paying over the top, we were grateful, because you can't stay in the smog and the fog, in those days, on the streets. And that kind of thing got up ordinary local people's noses. We didn't get any privileges, it was just that we wanted somewhere to live.

'While, on the one hand, Rachmann provided housing through his middle men and we were grateful, Rachmann and his middle men were also terrorisers. So that if you didn't pay your rent for a week or two, nobody would socially come around and ask you what was the problem, if you were sick or whatever. You didn't pay your rent, out, by mutual consent. But if you didn't get out by mutual consent, he had a whole gang of bully boys with alsatian dogs who used to set on us. He had an office in Hatherley Grove, in Westbourne Grove. On the other hand, if ordinary indigenous English people were living in a house or a flat, and Rachmann had bought that house, he wanted to get rid of them, so as to maximise the kind of income he was making and build the empire that he was building with us. So, it was in his interests to get rid of local English people. And he used to use the alsatian dog bully boy technique with them as well, but not as much as the other method that he used to use to get them out, that is to move a black family next door. And white people didn't want that, and they said, "Oh God, the blacks are moving in, and we get out." And that was easy. So there was a sense in which it was a double edged kind of thing. Thirdly, while Rachmann was bad, he was the only person that would provide housing for us. You can take that whatever way you want to take it. But it was through him that we got somewhere to stay. So, you pay your money and you take your choice really. And then there were an argument that Peter Rachmann himself was fairly reasonable with his charges, but the middle men would bump the charges up by 300 per cent, make a killing for themselves, pay Rachmann perhaps a third of that, that's what he charged them for the places. So the middle men really made a killing. And that led to all sorts of other complications and difficulties.

'We didn't know the score, we didn't know what the values were in this country, many of us had just come here a matter of weeks. And in the West Indies, in the Caribbean, one of the important things about life there is that how ever poor you are, you had to have somewhere to live. So, somewhere to live, us coming here, was absolutely crucial. And we knew we were being charged an awful lot, but you had to pit that against walking the streets and probably getting picked up for all sorts of reasons. But many of us soon got wise, in a matter of months, we soon got wise as to the ride that were taking of us. But everybody didn't, most people just were passive and decided, well, take an easy life.

'The West London Rent Tribunal Service used to sit and adjudicate about the kind of accommodation people had, not only blacks, the whites as well, and how much they were paying. And the idea was to discover whether tenants were exploited under the law, if the law was broken or not. And, as I just said, a number of us became wise as to the exorbitant nature of the rents we were paying. And with the help of several people, and with great timidity, because you never knew if you took a move like that, to represent yourself, you might be kicked out, all sorts of things might happen to you. Nevertheless, some of us took the plunge with other English people, went to the tribunal and got several victories, reduction of rent and so on. But you had to then live a kind of low life. By that

I mean didn't push your head above the parapet. Because
Rachmann's middle men didn't like that. It put the spotlight on them,
as well as it opened a whole can of worms. So you had to lay low
to some extent. But there was an awful lot of intimidation. I've never
seen or discovered so many anonymous people in my life as in those
days. Your windows would be broken, nobody's seen, nobody's
heard, and whoever did it went off.'[3]

Rachman did most of his business in the late fifties, and died in 1962, hotly
pursued by the police for dealing in prostitution, the Inland Revenue for
tax evasion, and by the public health authorities about the state of his
properties. But, at the time, his activities were regarded as a local matter,
and it was only in the wake of the Profumo affair that Rachmanism became
a national scandal. The Profumo affair of 1963 was the first stage in the
series of events which brought down the Conservative government. John
Profumo was Secretary for Defence. In June 1963 it became known that he
had earlier lied to the House of Commons when he denied a sexual relationship with Christine Keeler, a young hustler who shared a flat in Notting Dale
with Rachman's girlfriend, Mandy Rice-Davies. Keeler had also been intimate with Captain Ivanov, a naval attaché of the Soviet Embassy in London,
who was said to be a secret agent. Profumo was disgraced and forced to
resign from the government and the House of Commons. The secret service
was accused of incompetence in failing to inform the Prime Minister, Harold
Macmillan, of a potential security risk. Macmillan was attacked in the press
for trying to protect Profumo and other colleagues. An official investigation
by Judge Alfred T. Denning – later Lord Denning – cleared the other ministers of misconduct, but revealed that many prominent persons were deeply
involved in illicit sex, pornography and drugs.

The entire affair had been set off by the triangular relationship between
Christine and two West Indians, Johnny Edgecombe and Lucky Gordon,
and after Edgecombe had been arrested and convicted for shooting at Keeler,
a trail of innuendo led to questions in the House and the impeachment of
Profumo. The story had all the elements which would put it on the front
pages and keep it there. It linked the low life and degeneracy for which the
racist activists blamed the immigrants with the highest levels of government,
and it suggested that the immigrants had made the country more vulnerable
to foreign intrigues. It had as its figurehead a woman with the most glamorous and dangerous aura since Mrs Simpson, and it focused attention, once

[3] Interview with Ivan Weekes.

again, on the sexual potential of the migrants. To add icing to the cake, Dr Stephen Ward, Keeler's friend and patron – a gay osteopath who was a friend of the rich and famous – was later discovered to have regularly promoted upper-class sex orgies. In the relatively drab atmosphere of the early sixties the entire country was riveted. For the man at the heart of the storm, Johnny Edgecombe, the whole affair was simply another accident in the crowded life of a hustler, but the details of the milieu he shared with the government Minister made for juicy reading.

'There used to be a South African chick who was living there in the flat below and Christine always thought that there was something going on between us. The chick killed a guy in South Africa, and she was drunk whilst she was driving the car and they fine her £5 for being like drunk and driving. Nothing about killing the guy, and then this is why she had a drinking problem, like she was human, she was people, so we get on good together. Christine misconstrued this for, like, we were having a scene. And, next thing, she was on the phone. This time, like, we separated, and she was phoning this chick and saying "Hey, you fucking with my old man", and all that, and, "I'm gonna tell the police that he cut Lucky Gordon", and this and that, and that's what pissed me off. This is why I went round to Stephen's place, 'cos I phoned up there and that's where she was phoning from. And I was walking with a gun, not to Christine, 'cos Lucky got the police looking for me. When I go to a place in the West End they say, "Hey, you just missed Lucky and he's got a big knife", and all this, and they all said Lucky and his brothers are looking for me, so that's why I was walking with a gun. It was nothing to do with no intent to Christine.

'Well, when I get to Stephen's place and I knock on the door and Mandy Rice she came to the window, and she says Christine is not there. So I say, "Don't give me that bullshit. Just talked to her, I know she's there, right?" So then, in the end, Christine come to the window and I said, "Look, come on downstairs, let me talk to you." And she's saying, "Look, I don't want to come down, I don't want to talk to you." I said, "Well, come on, let's sort this shit out", and all this kind of thing, and she just wouldn't come. I say, "Look, I got a taxi waiting", and she threw a pound out the window. And that really pissed me off, so I tried to break down the door, how you sort of break it down, and it wouldn't work. So then I pull out the gun and I start shooting at the door and I tried again and it still wouldn't work. So then Christine came back to the window and says, "Look,

Johnny, don't be silly, man." I had the gun in my hand and I said, "Bitch, this is all your fault", like I was pointing the gun in my hand accusingly, nothing to fucking shoot her. I said, "Bitch, it is all your fault", and she duck, natural reaction. But then, she told the court that I pointed the gun at her and she saw the bullet coming and she ducked. There was no forensic, no bullet in her. All the bullet was inside the door.

'Well, what happened is now after I shot down the front door, I begin to come back, like preservation time. I was beginning to, "Hey you've been really stupid", so tidying up now and I went round the back and stashed the gun. In the meantime they think I was trying to get in, but I wasn't trying to get in, I was trying to get out. So, anyway, I stashed the gun and I get back, the cab wait for me and I tell him, "Look, take me back to Brentford, but don't stop at any cop shop on the way", you know. And he's thought I still have the gun and everything and he's saying, "No, man, I got like wife and kids", and all this sort of shit, like, "I wouldn't do anything like that." And he had radio and things and they phone up and say, "You got this guy and he's dangerous and don't try to apprehend him", and all this bullshit. So, anyway, we got back to Brentford where we're staying and I had a speed clip for the gun, and I try to get rid of it. So I went in the house and this time the taxi was waiting for me 'cos I hadn't paid him yet. So while I got the clip and I came out of my room, then I saw my friend's mother, right, and I said to her, "Look, I just done something silly up town and the police, you know, probably be coming here." So, like, while I'm telling her this now, there is a knock on the door, and there's cops. So I went in the first room which was close to me that led out to the back where you had the back window, but I look out the window and there is all these helmets out there as well and I thought, Shit, I'm trapped.

'In my trial I was sort of pleading crime passionel, but, like, there was no sort of love affair going on between us. But it's more or less like an arrangement. So, like, things when she was telling me about Profumo and other sugar daddies and all that, was just to impress me that she wasn't just a toe rag that there was other things going on with her. And Mandy, I knew Mandy when she was about eighteen. She and Christine used to have this rivalry with men. I mean, Rachman was one of her sugar daddies, and she said to me, in Christine's place, "Look, I fancy you, but I wouldn't screw you because you couldn't get me a part in a movie or buy me a little car for my birthday." And she said, "Look," she says, "you see those flats out there?" She says, "When I'm twenty-one I want to own one of those." So there's a chick who knew what she want, and she knew how to go about getting it. But Christine, she was totally different. She could have been a great model, you know, but, if she had an appointment and she met someone she fancied on the way, then that would be end of story. She was telling me one night she felt randy and she went on the road to try and find a man. And she heard this sounds coming from the party and she followed the sound and she blagged this really handsome black guy, you know. Took him back to her place only to discover he was a poof. So a great disappointment. That's the sort of chick she was.

'I never seen her, like the only communication, someone brought me a *Daily Mirror* and showed me a picture of Christine Keeler sitting down on the desk and it says, "Christine Keeler writes to her lover", or ex-lover, or whatever. And the next day I got the letter. The letter just said "I'm sorry". I'd never placed eyes on her since that day. She didn't appear at my trial at all and they still tried me for attempted murder and gave me seven years for possessing a firearm with intent to endanger lives. Gave me seven years. And the newspaper and everybody just think, Well, you know. So I think it was total conspiracy, like naturally the establishment, the media and everything agree, "Yeah, let's put this motherfucker away" 'cos of trying to save the reputation. If Profumo got away with the lie, right, then there would not have been no problems.

'I had people used to come and show me all this thing. I knew I was a victim, I knew that. And I was scared for my life because, like, my solicitor, he was more interested in finding out what I knew about spying than anything that was more relevant to my case, right. So I was beginning to get frightened for my life, like in case he gave me an injection or some shit. And I said to the guy, "Look, I don't know anything about spying like I told Denning, like when I went to see Denning." I said to him, I says, "I don't know anything about spying. I just come to see because of injustices of my case." And he says, "I'm glad you don't know anything about spying, but I'm not here to investigate your case." '[4]

---

[4] Interview with Johnny Edgecombe.

Under the headline 'The Two Worlds of Christine Keeler' the *News of the World* quoted Keeler's patron Dr Stephen Ward in a mood of outrageous hypocrisy. 'She was utterly oblivious to my warnings that she could not trifle with the affections of engaging but primitive people.' Christine herself echoed the same tone. 'I like and am interested in these people. I want to be kind to them. That was the trouble with Johnny Edgecombe. I was too kind.'[5]

As the scandal unwound, its repercussions spread. The Russian diplomat was expelled. Dr Stephen Ward committed suicide before he could be tried under the Sexual Offences Act. Rachman's role had only been marginal, but his activities were soon exhumed in the light of his relationship with Mandy Rice-Davies. And in the resulting publicity he became a symbol of the housing rackets which had flourished over the previous years. In Fleet Street there were rumours that he had faked his death and was now operating under another name.

In the circumstances the scandals put the government under considerable extra pressure. Economic growth had slowed down from the heady days at the beginning of the decade when Prime Minister Harold Macmillan announced, 'You never had it so good.' Industry had begun a slow decline in productivity. Taxes had risen and a major balance of payments crisis was looming. Teddy Boys had faded away, but public disorder threatened every Bank Holiday, when Mods and Rockers engaged in huge running battles through the seaside towns. Decolonisation in East and Central Africa had proved more difficult and controversial than in West Africa. And white propaganda, passionately supported by domestic politicians, beefed up from outside by Empire Loyalists had been troublesome. There were developing splits over Britain's role East of Suez, and when Macmillan tried to blag his way into the European Economic Community, France's General de Gaulle looked down his long nose and said No. British humiliation was compounded by the sense that they had saved his career and his country only a few short years previously.

The Profumo scandal had made a laughing stock of the government and its Ministers. In the week of the Ward case Lord Hailsham found himself denying 'the most extraordinary rumours'. 'I am not the man without a head, the man in the iron mask, the man who apparently goes about clad only in a masonic apron or a visitor to unnamed orgies', he told Young Conservatives at Melton Mowbray.[6] On top of all this, the scandal of

---

[5] *Daily Express*, 17 March 1963.
[6] *Daily Express*, 30 June 1963.

Rachmanism was more or less the last straw. The Conservatives hurried through a new Housing Act in the spring of 1964, but it was too late. The election in the autumn saw a Labour victory, fuelled by general disillusionment with the Conservatives.

But there was one revealing element in the '64 election which was a sign of things to come. While the scandals were going on in London attitudes had hardened in other parts of the country, especially in the Midlands.

'At that period, I felt Birmingham and the West Midlands generally, and the Black Country, was a very mean spirited place. It had something to do with its sort of isolation, it was as if it wasn't true that Birmingham was an immigrant city, actually, because of the motor industry, a lot of white workers had come there, as well as black workers, so, there was movement in and out. But it was a place which wanted to protect or defend itself, set up barriers around itself. And, so, I wasn't surprised that Birmingham and the West Midlands found it extremely difficult to deal with the influx of substantial numbers of black people. I remember, when I first moved there in 1964, I was just married and looking for a house. And I can honestly say, this is the first time that I personally encountered people who said, "We don't take any blacks here." I had been insulated from that. I'd been a student, living in college or living in student housing. I hadn't encountered that, personally. I knew it was going on, but this was absolutely straight, "No blacks here", "We don't take any blacks", et cetera. And people shouted at us in the street when we were going around trying to find places, you see, myself and my white wife. You can imagine. She was the particular object of vile remarks about mixed race couples, and so on. So, I had a very bad introduction to the West Midlands, I must say. And I have always thought, it may be wrong, but I've always thought that I could understand that Powellism would have come out of the West Midlands. I thought one could hear a particular kind of resentment, deep resentment, almost as if we'd been left behind by England and now we were going to be left behind in relation to race, you know, permanently left behind. And that's a historical resentment, latched on to race, the symbol signifying its isolation. So, that was a very troubling experience.'[7]

[7] Interview with Stuart Hall.

Smethwick, in particular, was the site of intense resentment. It had a population of 65,000 of which about a tenth were black migrants, and it was racked with rumours and allegations about their activities. During the spring of 1963, a Tory councillor, Donald Finney, had begun leading vigilante patrols around the streets at night, looking for 'immorality involving black men and white girls'. This was the thin end of the wedge. When the '64 election was announced Smethwick was ripe for a racist campaign. In the run-up to the poll, headlines in the *Birmingham Post* asked the question: IMMIGRATION: CONTROL, CONFLAGRATION OR BETTER HOUSING? Patrick Gordon Walker, a former Labour Minister and one of the most senior Opposition spokesmen, was up against the Conservative Peter Griffiths, the right wing headmaster at Hall Green Road Junior school. Gordon Walker had a 3,500 majority and, given the swing to Labour, could have been expected to win comfortably. But in the 1963 municipal elections the slogan: 'If you want a nigger neighbour, vote Labour', had been an effective weapon. Griffiths wanted to toughen the Immigration Bill, and was quoted as saying, 'The word integration is not one we want to find in the town.'

Gordon Walker was duly defeated, sending a shock wave through the political culture. Harold Wilson had been endlessly heckled about immigration at the hustings, and many experts blamed the issue of race for the low turnout by Labour's traditional supporters. Wilson denounced Peter Griffiths as a 'Parliamentary leper', but the lesson had not been lost. A few months later, in February 1965, the Labour government tightened immigration restrictions. This was the first part of a two pronged piece of legislation, but the political pressure was such that the government hurried to put the restrictions in place. On the other side of the coin, the Race Relations Bill, which banned racial discrimination in public places and introduced penalties against incitement to racial hatred, had to wait until April. But no one had missed the point. Race and immigration was a central political issue and the stage was set for the emergence of Powellism.

15

———— ·❖· ————

'I think the conflicts that I saw in my own life in the late fifties were conflicts that I think that many other young black people were not prepared to take on – a different regime at home, in the school, on the streets, in the playground – and those were enormous conflicts to deal with because you're getting one pressure in the home, another one on the streets, seeing things happening around you, another pressure in the school and the playground. I think you started to see the emergence of a bit of rebelliousness. And then you had bodies like the police, you had social work interventionists, you had some parents who were finding it difficult to cope. And very often the threat, the very common threat to a lot of black kids was, you know, If you don't behave yourself I'll put you in a home. And a lot of black kids did end up voluntarily being placed in local authority care – in institutionalised care. So there was a pattern emerging in which there was a rejection of jobs that might be available that black young people didn't feel they were going to take. And that was, I think, the start of the difficulties for some young black people coming out of school.'[1]

'Educationally, it was fine. I was very academic, I absolutely loved school, I loved books. And I was the first black girl to go to the grammar school that I went to, a very supportive environment, and I think that that's because I was a first and I was unique. I'm not sure my school experience would necessarily have been the same if I were in inner London, for example, and there were a lot of black kids, because I think the perceptions at that time, in terms of teachers not being able to deal with the experience of black children when they were in groups, was very different. But my school experience was very positive. And I think part of that was about the support of my parents, part of it was about the support of my teachers, who recognised that I had this thirst for learning; and some of it was about me. I enjoyed what I did at school. It was a good experience for me.'[2]

[1] Interview with Sir Herman Ouseley.

[2] Interview with Baroness Amos. Valerie Amos came from Guyana at the age of nine and went to school in Kent. Later, she was part of an influential group of young black British academics whose

School Daze: 1960–70

In 1960, or thereabouts, children began arriving with their migrant parents or with friends and relatives to join their parents. People travelled by air, no longer having to endure a long boat trip. During the run-up to the Immigration Bill in 1961, and immediately afterwards, most of the migrants who had families waiting in the Caribbean made the decision to send for them, whatever their circumstances were. They could not be certain of leaving in a reasonable space of time, and no one could envisage going back and forth between two countries, so sending for the children became the only thing to do. This movement also brought in more women, and the bulk of the migrant population began to separate itself from the lifestyle of the itinerant single men.

The new influx made a fundamental alteration to the tone of life for the majority of immigrants. For one thing it sharpened the pressure to own property, and the Caribbean migrants began moving out of the centres where they had originally settled. Few migrants qualified for council housing and private ownership became the overwhelming pattern. The immediate result was to privilege the habits and institutions which would help in this process. Caribbeans had been fervent churchgoers and accustomed to using the church as a gathering place and a community centre. In Britain the official denominations were cold and unwelcoming, especially the Church of England, to which many of the immigrants, ironically, already belonged. Pentecostal churches, created and run by immigrant groups and individuals in their own houses, sprang up to fill the gap.

'Heaven in my view begins right here. So it's not just about preaching and speaking to people how to get to heaven, but it's how to get on with themselves, how to handle themselves and to get on with their neighbours right here. And whatever that means, then we would be there. And whether it was marriage, whether it was a separation, whether it was a lack of understanding of the system, whether it was how to penetrate the areas of misunderstanding, that people could access some of our services that are there, the church soon take that on hand, to offer advice, very positive advice, apart from the

---

best known work, *The Empire Strikes Back*, was a polemic which called attention to the views of the generation which had grown up in the sixties. In the mid-eighties she became head of the Equal Opportunites Commission. She became a Labour Peer, Baroness Amos, in 1997.

financial support. We didn't have money to dish out to people, but by pooling our resources together we were able to support one another in sending for relatives back home, pooling our moneys together to buy houses in partnership so that we could house our people. Here it was a very significant area, and when we purchased those homes in partnership, when one was able to buy oneself out of that property, then we move on to buy independent properties, and then offering people, you know, that independence that they need. So the church has been very, very active in dealing with the social and personal issues of our people, not least our constituents, people who have no connections with the church but come to us, then and now.'[3]

At the other end of the scale from this fiercely protective environment the migrant children had to go into an educational community which contained many of the obstacles with which their parents struggled. For many Caribbeans education had an immense value. In the rural districts from which many came, the teacher was part of a hierarchy which wielded a benevolent and unquestioned authority. Most Caribbean parents, pre-occupied with working long, hard hours, assumed the same attitudes towards education in Britain, and it was a number of years before they began to understand the differences in the role and style of the system.

'I think what happened was that we come from the West Indies, where working-class people had middle-class ambitions. The whole society's motivated. Exam results are carried in the newspapers, as Oxford and Cambridge are carried in *The Times* here. You work your nails and your knuckles off to send your children to school and that was the only way that you can move up socially and economically. So when we came here, the white working class, on the other hand, have accepted, more or less, their role in the society. We came with ambitions and that was the main conflict with the education department. So we would go to school – it still happens now – we would go to the schools and our children will tell the careers officer, "I want to be a doctor", "I want to be a lawyer", "I want to be an architect." And they look at you in amazement, because when they look at your family background – your father's a bus driver or a carpenter or a whatever – and, as far as they're

---

[3] Interview with Carmel Jones.

concerned, no way. So that was one of the main clashes. And you will find that most of the positive changes and the struggles for a better education system took place in the sixties and seventies. We were the motivators. We were the pioneers, because the middle class have always been alright, except now, except now. But the working class have never really looked towards education as a means of social mobility. We, on the other hand, did. And that was the tremendous clash.'[4]

For many of the migrant children school was a trauma, trapped as they were between contradictory expectations. Invariably it was the boys who were most frustrated and the girls who benefited. Where you went to school also mattered a great deal, then as now. On the other hand, the entire generation of migrant schoolchildren in the sixties emerged with distinct attitudes in common. It was this generation who, in the later decades, began recreating the identity of the migrants as part of the British population. However difficult the relationship may have been, they had, unlike their parents, shared a major part of their childhood and upbringing with their neighbours; and their dreams of the future would come to merge with those of their compatriots. In the short term the experience opened up a gap between the generations which was all the more disturbing because it was unfamiliar within the cultures from which the migrants came, but this was the experience which was to define the future shape of the Caribbean migrant community.

'Yes, there was a gulf, a very wide gulf. That gap is closing now, because whereas parents were turning their back on youngsters and saying to the authorities, "Do as you like with them, this is not our star", people realised that was a mistake. And they are now giving the proper support that the youngsters need and are actively involved themselves in schools and local associations in providing a better support for the youngsters in the community. The alienation, I am not saying it's eliminated – there's always been conflict between parents and youngsters, young and old, in every generation – but the gap that existed then between youngsters then and now is closed tremendously.'[5]

4   Interview with Eric Huntley.
5   Interview with Carmel Jones.

'I arrived in England when I was about twelve or thirteen, so I'd experienced primary school education in the Caribbean, and was brought specifically to Britain "to be educated", as it was put by my family. So I anticipated being able to attend secondary school and spend a lot of time being able to learn and develop skills that would enable me to make a way of life. I was also interested in thinking of long term careers, because this is always your goal as you grow up in the Caribbean, you either go into religion and the ministry, or you would become a lawyer, or a doctor, or something of that sort. And so I was very focused on the idea of making a career for myself when I arrived.

'The school experience was confusing, because on the one level, most people in senior positions wanted to be helpful, but I don't think they really understood the emotions I was experiencing, having to come to terms with the racial issue, having to come to terms with an education system that was quite different from the one I'd experienced in the Caribbean, where we were a lot more formal and a lot more structured and set in relation to work that we had to do by certain times. A number of black kids just got lost in the system 'cos they couldn't see ways into it. I was lucky, I had one or two school masters who I was able to relate to and find things that I could actually get my head stuck into. And also I had a lot of family support to enable me to really dedicate a lot of time to working and making something of my life.

'My mother hadn't gone through education in Britain, and so I don't think she fully appreciated the way the system worked. And I remember having lots of discussions about "Where's the homework? Why aren't you doing homework? Why aren't you sat down with the books? Where's the books?" These types of discussions. But, in fact, there was no homework. The pressure was not on in the way that I think Caribbean families expected pressure to be on teenagers, to structure their lives so that they devote as much time as possible to study as opposed to leisure and pleasure. And, of course, as a young person growing up in sixties Britain, there was a higher priority on getting stuck into the leisure and pleasure side of life and, naturally, I wanted to experience that. So we did have some difficulties trying to make sense of what was happening at the time. There's no one that one can turn to, at that stage, to provide any advice and support, to make your way through the world, either. That was the difficulty. Well, it was a failing of the system because it was not the case that the kids were thick, that the kids were not able to deliver the goods.

But, at the end of the day, a lot of people fell out of the system, and you've got to put that down to an indifference within the system about the facts of race and racism in our society. And I would imagine that would be typical of a lot of British institutions at the time. And so all of the early marks that would later become a pattern were being made in those early sixties where institutions in Britain failed to appreciate what was really happening and respond positively.'[6]

'My parents came from Guyana. In fact, my father came first, he came over to do a degree and he was here for a couple of years. And then suggested that the family come and join him, which we did. We came over in 1963. I was nine, and I have this memory of the drive from London Airport through to south London, which is where we lived, we lived just into Kent, and of it being very kind of grey, and I think it was raining as well. I mean, that might be my imagination but that's what I remember. I don't recall having any real expectations about what it would be like. It was going to be exciting, we were going to see our father again.

'When I went to school, that was a bit of a shock, because I wasn't tested before I was put into a class, and I was put into the bottom class, and I found everybody was kind of way behind what I'd been used to. But my parents were very assertive about that and went up to school and ensured that I was given a test, and I was moved. I think the other thing that I found difficulty in dealing with was the environment, and the fact that it felt like a much less disciplined society. This is looking back, I mean, this is not how it would have felt to me at the time. And I was also quite shocked at the way that I was treated. I was in the school choir, we would go and sing in what were then called old people's homes, at Christmas. And they would all touch my skin and touch my hair, and I was the first black person they'd ever seen. And I was really shocked and surprised at that, because, of course, it was very different to what I was used to.

'Well, I suppose the school experience was that, for example, my sister, when she did a geography class very soon after she went into her school – she was six at the time – they did this whole lesson

---

[6] Interview with Russell Profitt. Russell Profitt came to England early in the sixties to join his family. He went to school in north London, and became a primary school teacher. As deputy head of Deptford Primary School he became a local Councillor in Lewisham, and in the seventies stood as a Labour candidate for the City of London and Westminster South.

about what it was like where she came from, and, of course, they got
the continents wrong, for starters. I mean, they were talking about
Africa rather than South America, and they started to show the kinds
of houses that they thought people like us lived in, and it was all
wrong. And she was absolutely furious and came home, and my
parents gave her stacks of photographs and told her the kinds of
things that she should talk about. And it was that kind of support
that they were very good at giving us. I mean, they gave us
permission, in a way, to challenge and actually to stand up for
ourselves. And I think that that has stood with us through all our
lives. I mean, I think it's helped me to be much more assertive about
who I am and what I'm about.

'My mother was a very glamorous woman, that's what I
remember in Guyana. And what I remember here is the fact that my
parents were having to work such very long hours, and somehow
the glamour was rubbing off. It was very different. And my parents
put in incredibly long hours. My mother was working in London,
my father was working in Kent. And she would do a full-time job,
come home, cook for the family, then help us with homework, and
then be up very early in the morning. And those kind of long hours
and the kind of hardships that they went through have really stuck
with me, because my memory of our life in Guyana was one that was
much more open, much more social. That's not to say that my
parents didn't have friends, they did. But it was a huge effort to move
from Kent to go into central London to see people. And, of course,
it was important for them that they brought us up in the way that
they wanted to, that we recognised our cultural heritage, that we
understood those traditions.

'I think that they spent a lot of time guarding us from the overt
kind of racism which I don't really remember as being a real part of
my childhood. I think that my parents had a lot to do with that,
and quite a lot to do with the fact that I was so much into social
justice issues from a very early age, because growing up in a part
of Kent where there weren't many black people in the sixties, it's
quite hard to think about where that came from. And I think it
came from the fact that I grew up in a family that's very interested
in politics, that's very interested in social issues. We were always
encouraged to debate and discuss. And, from a very early age, I was
very conscious of being black in Britain, but not in a sense that was
overemphasised, or that took anything away from my confidence or
the way in which I was able to operate in white society. It was very

much about my parents helping to build my confidence, to help me to deal with being black in a white society. I was around for the "Rivers of Blood" speech, and it impacted on me in the sense of making me always want to think and work around race and gender and social justice type issues, and that has been with me throughout my life and career.'[7]

'My parents went to Dudley in the West Midlands in the mid-fifties. My mum came over first because my uncle Clifton wrote to her and told her that you could earn something like sixteen shillings a week. There were many factories there that would give you good work and if you come over you could earn money and send for the rest of the children, and send for Winston, that was my dad. And so Mum came over first and I think she was a catering lady first, and she did a bit of nannying. And then she got a job in a factory and started to earn quite good money, and it was a huge surprise. She'd sold vegetables, she was a higgler. She used to, you know, grow vegetables on a plot of land and then take it into town and flog it, back in Jamaica. So to earn this amount of money for sort of pressing a button on a machine, or for doing sheet metal working – it just seemed inconceivable.

'So, Dudley was this industrial town with factories, and it was called the Black Country because everything was covered in this black soot from the factory chimneys. And there were nail makers and there were car manufacturers nearby and piece work and, you know, making metal components and working on these lathes and stuff, so it was a very industrial based city. And even when I was leaving school, you know, I got a job within two weeks. This was a place where industry was important. We used to say, Well, you know, if you don't work hard and get your exams you will end up in a factory, but you knew the factories were there to be a safety net for you.

'But in the fifties, this was the new industry, this is what was going on now. My mum was part of that new workforce. And when my dad came over he became part of that workforce too. He was a foundryman. And the two of them worked very, very hard and sent for the rest of the family, and, I think, Mum got us a big room in an Asian housing project. We were in a big house with lots of rooms,

and we were in one room and there'd be other families in another
room. And then, as she earned more money, she put more money
down on buying a small house. And then, you know, it was always
the thing, we were always going to, bit by bit, get money to get our
own house. And eventually we did. So I think it was very, very hard
for her coming here on her own. She experienced people following
her down the street and asking her where her tail was, and asking
her what part of Africa she was from. And Mum arrived, having
studied, you know, vaguely the English educational system,
thinking that she was going to get a welcome in the mother country.
And, like millions of others, she came and was surprised at people's
ignorance of the West Indies and what they meant, and who they
were. She thought she'd be welcomed with open arms and she was
really pulled up short by it when she arrived.

'I can't remember the first place that we lived in, I can remember
this place called Victoria Terrace, which was this big old house that
was our first proper home. Huge old Victorian terraced house with
a back yard, not a back garden. We had an outside toilet that
eventually got built into a sort of corridor walkway, but you'd walk
to the toilet, freezing cold. I remember falling over in the snow once,
when I was about four or five and cutting my hand on broken glass
in the back yard. I remember the kid next door, William, who was
my best friend – you always had a best friend – but he always had
loads and loads of toys. This white guy befriended me, but would
just turn off the friendship and, you know, I'd go and call for him
and I'd shout, then he'd spit through the letterbox at me. Things like
that, you know. And it would be on a whim. You know, one day
I'd be his best friend, the next day I'd be that blackie who lives next
door. So I had one of those strange relationships, but, generally, in
that house, we had very, very good times. Mum and Dad worked
very, very hard to make sure there was food on the table, and all
that. I remember we had a line of credit at the corner shop with the
woman, Rita, who was astounding, when I think of it now. This
woman allowed my mum to extend a line of credit from here to, oh,
Sweden. Rita was the most patient person, and my mum would pay
her what she could. But it was clear that she was doing big favours
for quite a lot of people in the community. This was how we
survived. There were no easy answers to anything. We survived, we
had credit, we got things on tick, we did what everybody else did.

'My mum had a big religious childhood in Jamaica, and then
when she came to England it felt like the work was so hard and the

environment was so demanding that she had to sort of put church to one side and get food on the table and get a roof over our heads and make sure that my dad was all right, and make sure that the family was okay before she could even think about church. And it wasn't until, I would say, about fifteen years ago that Mum became born again. But although she wasn't in the church, we had to go to Sunday school. Every Sunday morning a van would arrive at our house, whether we wanted it to or not. And we would all have our Sunday school clothes on and for most of the day we'd be at Sunday school. And even though Mum wasn't practising at the time, it was an important thing. My dad just didn't go, but it was important for the children to go through this experience. What was very funny was that I went to a Church of England school, great school – Bluecoat Secondary Modern – and our church was called 'top church' because it was the highest point of the town. But we didn't go there, and I think there was a place round the corner called St Thomas's Parish Hall. And that's where we had the Pentecostal Church meetings. So that's where Sunday school was and that's where our church was. And a guy called Brother Shepherd ran the church. Off his own back, sorted it out, got it interlinked with other Pentecostal churches in the area. Every time the season came around we would go to a convention, either in Wolverhampton or in Birmingham, or wherever, but imagine the foresight of these people – we'll just have our own church then. It was almost like we weren't acceptable – or accepted – in the Church of England, or whatever, so we'd have our own church. And that's what we did, that's where we went to church. I remember it being quite joyous and quite happy. We had Bible class – I found it a bit boring – but the singing and the spirited preaching of people like Brother Shepherd, you sort of got swept along with it and it was exciting. And I did it from the time I was seven years old till the time I was fourteen, or something. Every Sunday.

'There would be some people from school at church but, even though I enjoyed it, my main friends were people that I'd met at school or at the park. We had a huge park over the road from our house, so quite a lot of my friends were sort of made there, really. Church was this thing that you had to do, but you sort of grudgingly enjoyed. And there's a big network in Britain now, but I get a sense that in America there's a much stronger underpinning of church in the black community. It just felt like it was something that I was going to do for a while and then move away from eventually.

Maybe that's more to do with me than it is to do with the church itself.

'I went to St James' Infants School, where I was one of two black children in the whole school, at one point. And that felt completely normal to me, and, apart from odd problems that I had with some of the lessons, it was very normal, play was normal. I remember my mum and dad couldn't come to the school to see me during class because they had to work – the motif throughout my childhood. Childhood was Mum and Dad work really hard. And you've just got to run with that. And I just remember my brother, Hilton, coming to see me on a school open day. This huge, tall black guy walking into the school and me going, "That's my brother, that is," and he was a big, grown-up man, coming and being interested in my lessons, and sort of looking at my work and nodding his head and saying, "Yes, that's good." And I just remember thinking, "Wow, this is great. Hilton's come to see me", and by this time he had his own wife and family. He didn't have to do that. So he'd had a day off work.

'Then I moved to Jessoms Junior School and I really enjoyed that and, once again, I was one of, I'd say, four black children in the school. But we moved house then, from Victoria Terrace up to Douglas Road. And I moved to St John's School. And it was very clear that this was a different kind of junior school, there were many more black children in this school. And it was of similar teaching standard to Jessoms, but it was a tougher school, it was just tougher. There were Asian kids there, there were black kids there and they'd been there a while. And there was swearing in the playground and there was fighting, and stuff like that. And it was much more grown up and I had to assimilate really fast and I think that school had a lot to do with my growing up and expanding my personality to fit, if you like. I'd be in a class and there'd be like twenty-eight or thirty kids – but it would be me and three other black kids and a couple of Asian kids. And it was hard to sort of get with it in this new school. But I did eventually. It was just socially hard. Jessoms was an easier school for me to fit into because my sister had gone there. But we all had to move to this new place and we were all finding our feet, and I guess I'd been used to being sort of special 'cos I was like one of three black kids in the whole school. And then, suddenly, moving to St John's School, and there were three or four of us in the class, it suddenly became more of a challenge to maintain one's social standing, if you like. You had to sort of fight for your place.

There was already a funny black guy in the school, what do we need another one for?"[8]

'My family are from Jamaica, and Jamaicans are really quite clannish. And every weekend we would go and visit relatives and friends and family. We moved to Harrow when I was about three, and everyone said to my father, "Why you go live ah bush?" Why had he left the kind of clannish, cohesive communities of Notting Hill, and so on, to live out in Harrow which, at that time, was an all-white area. And so every Saturday we left Harrow and drove from Harrow, through Neasden, back to Paddington and Notting Hill to see friends and family. So I was always aware of coming from a very tightly knit family background. In fact, until I became a grown woman, I didn't realise there were so many black people in London who weren't Jamaican, 'cos, as a child, the only people I met were other Jamaicans. My mother, in particular, felt a very strong attachment to her family and to Jamaica and she took me to Jamaica for the first time when I was about twenty-one and I've gone back to Jamaica regularly ever since. In the past ten years I've been back to Jamaica every year. And they combined, as a lot of people do, a very strong cultural attachment to Jamaica and the Caribbean. But with a sense that they were British, and they were entitled to be here and live their lives here. As an adolescent and in my twenties I kind of rebelled against that. But as I've become older I've been drawn back to that stability and that safety of a network of extended family and friends. In the end, blood is thicker than water. I thought it was pretty tedious, just one of those tedious things your parents make you do. It's with time and with perspective that I've realised the importance of family.

'I think all of that generation, the West Indian immigrants, came to get a better life. They came thinking they were going to go home. I mean, all their lives – both my parents are dead now – but, all their lives, they talked about going home. They came, they thought, for a short or a medium period of time, to make a better life, to make some money and to go home. I think for that generation – most of them die thinking they're going to go home the next year or the year after.

'I think that generation had a very strong sense of being British.

---

8 Interview with Lenny Henry.

That's what they got at school, that's what they were. There was this
strong sense of the Empire, and you were all British. So it did come
as a shock, I think, to my parents' generation to find they weren't
really British. They were black. That came as a little bit of a shock
to them.

'My parents never talked in abstract terms about being black in
British society. But you could see it. I always remember when we
used to have a parents' day – my father always used to go to parents
day – he always used to carry a brief case. The brief case was
completely empty but, somehow, the brief case was his armour
against the white world. A lot of the things about my parents and
how they related to the racism that they found I can only understand,
years later, now they're both dead. And I'm an adult too and can see
what their behaviour was about.

'I went to a very respectable, middle-class State grammar school
in the London suburb of Harrow. And for the whole time that I was
there, I was the only black girl in the girls' school. And my brother,
who was at the boys' school, was the only black boy in the boys'
school. It's hard for me to say how it was, because I never
experienced anything different. I was fortunate. I had one or two
teachers who were very supportive, who could see I was bright, and
encouraged me. And, I was too young then to understand that the
sense of isolation I had stemmed from the fact that I was the only
black child in the school. When you're that age you think it's about
you. You don't have the context to put it in. If you were going to
be part of the group, you had to fit a sort of stereotype, be the class
joker, that type of thing. I've never been one for being a class joker.
I remember at school, for instance, there was a girl, very nice girl,
and she and I were absolutely best friends. Completely inseparable.
But I was puzzled and baffled to realise that every year, when she
had a birthday party, I was never invited. And she invited girls who
she hardly spent any time with at school. And it's only with the
perspective of years I realised that her mother just wasn't having a
black girl in her house. But when you're a school child in particular,
you don't understand. Because when you're a child, there is so much
that is baffling about the world that racism, as it manifests itself to
you, is just another baffling thing you can't comprehend. You can't
give it a name.

'I was always seen as difficult, as a trouble maker, as lazy, as all
types of things. And to an extent it was all true. What I was, though,
at that age was very clever indeed. And that saw me through.

'They wanted me to be a success, marry a very respectable Jamaican man, hopefully from the same parish as them, and just go on to achieve, to be successful. And in a small way I've lived out some of my parents' dreams. I mean, I didn't find the very respectable Jamaican man from the same parish. But when I was a new MP, people were always asking me, "Ooh, why are you different from other black people?" I always had to keep telling them that somebody like me, someone's that gone on and done well in their chosen career is exactly what that generation of black people came to this country to see.'[9]

---

[9] Interview with Diane Abbott MP. Diane Abbott was born and brought up in London. After a degree at Cambridge University she entered the Civil Service, then worked for the National Council for Civil Liberties before becoming a reporter and television researcher. Later she worked for the broadcasting union, the ACCT, and became a prominent member of the Labour Party, and one of the leaders of the campaign for black sections in the Party. She was elected MP for Hackney in 1987.

16

---•◆•---

'I said, "Well, let me put it this way. First, I am not surprised that you don't find blacks in WEA[1] classes, I don't know what WEA is, and I am sure many others don't know what it is. And the second thing about it is, most of us coming from a colonial background, you don't socialise with white people, you work for them. And all of these are obstacles that must be overcome, and understand on both sides." And we went along, and we discussed various aspects, and I said, "Unless a special effort is made to encourage black people to participate in this sort of thing, you won't get them." The vast majority expect to be here for three, four or five years, work enough money to go back home, and settle down. They didn't see their coming here as a permanent situation. And then he asked me if I would be interested in such a programme, I said, "Oh, I certainly would." And then, later on, I find myself becoming involved, you know. They advertised for a post for someone to develop education activities among the immigrant coloured people, as they called in those days, and I was a successful applicant. And, of course, from there, one was able to encourage various things. I think, in those years, one would see it more as a PR operation, rather than anything else. People have to recognise the fact that the likes of me are here, and there is no question of saying when we go back home. We were part and parcel of the scenery, and that had to be established.'[2]

'What was important about America was the example. You could get somewhere, you could push white legislators to open up schools, you could break a boycott, you could push the consensus in a liberal direction. And that was very important in the sixties because, otherwise, it was a very pessimistic moment, deeply pessimistic moment. I mean, this is the beginning of the second generation, the first generation knew what they were coming to, came in the middle of their lives. But we're now into the beginning of the second

---

[1] Workers Educational Association.
[2] Interview with Eric Irons.

generation, of kids either brought here when they were fourteen or fifteen or twelve, or sometimes younger than that, or some of them beginning to be born here. They're not West Indians. They've never seen the West Indies. At that stage, there were many fewer people going back and forwards between Britain and the Caribbean than there are now, and if Britain wasn't going to accept them, where were they to stand up? How were they going to survive? So any example that black people could survive, that you could be proud of being a black person, was a matter of survival. It wasn't a matter of let's do this because it feels good, it was a matter of survival. You either were black in one of these sorts of ways, or you were going under. That's what the sixties were like.'[3]

England, My England

A letter from Mike Phillips to Kwesi Phillips: From the past, to the present

I distinctly remember the moment when it struck me that something fundamental had changed about who I was. This was just before the start of the decade of the sixties, and it was after my first trip abroad, out of Britain. I was doing French for one of my A-Levels, and when some of my classmates suggested spending the summer picking grapes in the South of France, I agreed without hesitation. It was going to be great. There was a whole bunch of us planning to go, but the closer the day came, the more boys dropped out, until it was just down to me and two others, who I shall call Smith and Jones, which weren't their names, but it seems petty to tell the world what gits I thought they were after forty years. These were two white boys, of course, since there was only one other West Indian boy in my class and we weren't doing the same subjects. I didn't think it was going to be a problem because I got on well enough with them, but we'd hardly got off the plane before I realised that they were really and truly getting on my nerves. It wasn't anything directly to do with race, because they were well mannered and very polite for

[3] Interview with Stuart Hall.

our school at that time. It was something else, which I was never
quite clear about, but which I put down to their Englishness. The
first thing was that they wouldn't speak to anyone we met. That is,
they turned their noses up at the other young men who were
travelling on the plane. I can't remember why, but I remember Smith
making a dubious face when I sat chatting with another couple of
boys from London, and when we got on the train, they were the
same, like young women clutching their skirts round them and
shrinking from being touched.

I was feeling, on the other hand, liberated, full of delight at being
away from London. I had heard, as we all had, that the French were
more friendly, less inclined to be stand-offish to blacks, and I was
looking forward to the experience, practically hugging myself with
joy. Smith and Jones seemed dour and miserable. The penultimate
straw, if there's such a thing, came that same evening. We had
travelled to Auxerre and walked to the youth hostel outside the
town. To be frank, I didn't like walking and I still don't. When I
was growing up in Guyana I used to walk a couple of miles to
school every day and it always felt like a kind of punishment. Smith
and Jones loved it, of course, shouldering their rucksacks manfully
and striding out, while I limped along behind. Once we were settled
in they insisted on a long discussion about budgeting our money
and about how much we should spend each day, allocating some of
it to travel and some to food, and so on like that. The hostel was
in a rural spot, and I remember sitting with them on a bench under
the trees outside the building having this discussion and thinking
that it was the most boring time I'd had in my life. To make matters
worse they'd both changed into shorts in which they looked
ridiculous, like scrawny overgrown boy scouts.

On the other side of the building a group of boys and girls from
various places like Germany, Italy and Holland were sitting around,
playing a guitar, singing, shouting and laughing. In comparison with
my companions they looked tanned, grown up and cool, and I felt
increasingly embarrassed to be tied up with these two gauche
palefaces. I was getting curious looks and friendly smiles from the
other kids, and instinctively I knew that, in that time and place, it
was cool to be young and black, whereas no one seemed at all
interested in the two gawky English kids with me. To make matters
worse, two of the girls had strolled over and asked us if we wanted
to join them, but before I could reply, Jones said No with a curtness
which I understood later was due to his shyness, but which seemed

at the time simply rude. That was the last straw, but I had the sense that my friends would have taken it as a kind of disloyalty if I'd got up and gone over to chat up the German girls. While they drew up a detailed budget and carefully counted their money, I sat fuming with rage, and by the time they'd finished the party in the garden had run out of steam, so there was nothing for it but to go to bed. In the morning I woke up still fuming, and told Smith and Jones that I wasn't coming with them. 'I came for a bit of fun,' I told their disapproving faces, 'and being with you is no fun at all.' After I watched their rucksacks swinging off down the road I walked to the railway station and took the train to Paris.

On the train I made the mistake of hitching up with another pair of British boys. They were Scottish this time, and they knew about a cheap campsite in Paris. I had just enough money to manage it if I avoided eating, so I went with them. On the way, walking through the Paris streets we kept seeing prostitutes lining the side of the road, and the Scots boys started tut-tutting. 'This is terrible,' one of them said. I was used to seeing women hanging around the streets in London so it didn't seem surprising to me and I made some remark to that effect. 'Well, you wouldn't exactly call it a pleasurable past time now, would you?' the Scots kid came back, and I laughed and laughed until I could hardly stand up. After that he didn't speak to me again. But I had a whale of a time in Paris. It was the first time I'd been around another bunch of teenagers where I wasn't the enemy, mostly, I suppose, because we were on holiday and away from home, and full of youth and the excitement of it all. The only fly in the ointment was that I had to keep explaining to everyone I met that I wasn't from Africa or the United States, and that I couldn't sing the blues. 'I'm from London', I kept on telling them. But that wasn't too bad because I met up then with some girls from Lancashire who started teasing me about talking like a Cockney, and that was a great way of getting to be pals.

So when I got back to London I felt as if I'd had a good time and I was glad to be home. The strangest thing that happened then, was that I got off the tube at Tottenham Court Road because I was dying to go to the loo and I knew there was a gents' there. I went in and, all of a sudden, I knew I was in a place which I found familiar, which I trusted, and the difference was all about the fact that for the last three weeks I'd been dreading it every time I had to go. The problem was that, in those days, in the poorer parts of Paris which is where I'd been, you couldn't find a decent loo that you could sit

*on. Mostly they were like holes in the ground, and most of the toilets
I'd been in stank. The pissoirs in the street felt open and exposed
because they were a metal screen behind which people could see half
of you while you peed. I'd never got used to it, and when I walked
into that toilet at Tottenham Court Road it struck me that it smelt
disinfected and clean, the floors were scrubbed and the metal pipes
were polished to a gleaming shine. At that moment, I knew that I
was really in England, and I looked round and I felt a surge of
sheer relief and I thought – Thank God, I'm back home. That's when
I realised that whatever it was I was becoming, England had already
become part of me.*

One reason why the issue of race and immigration occupied a central position in the political culture throughout the sixties was the fact that the
Macmillan/Home government had run out of steam and had been under
enormous pressure during most of its life. The Labour Party won the election
in 1964, but its majority was small, at one point down to a single vote. It
only lasted for eighteen months; and although the 1966 election returned
Harold Wilson with a comfortable working majority, there seemed to be
no clear mandate from the electorate, and every politician came to fear its
volatility. In the circumstances, Smethwick continued to cast a giant
shadow. Patrick Gordon Walker was found a safe seat in London at the
beginning of 1965, but, haunted and taunted by anti-immigrant activists
promptly lost the Leyton by-election. The government was, in any case,
increasingly unpopular throughout the decade. The '64 election was the
start of a long struggle to tame the balance of payments problem, provoking
a 'boom and bust' economic cycle. Substantial pockets of poverty and
deprivation remained, while some wages were so low that in 1965 government estimates said that up to a quarter of a million families were living
below the National Assistance level, even though the father was employed.
A gap yawned between the government and its traditional supporters in
the trade union leadership over the issue of incomes policy and differentials.
In July 1966 the government tried to balance its debts with the most vicious
cuts yet, decreasing bank lending, imposing restrictions on hire purchase
and building, cutting services and instituting a £50 foreign travel allowance.

Matters were not much healthier in foreign affairs. The controversy over
Britain's role East of Suez continued to rumble on. Wilson forced the issue
with defence cuts at the end of 1967 which took the British army out of
its bases in the Gulf. But a substantial bloc of right wing opinion saw
this as treachery, and intensified the personal harassment to which he was
subjected by elements in the military and intelligence community. A long

period of stubborn negotiation with the Rhodesian settlers ended with their unilateral declaration of independence and the introduction of a controversial boycott against the country. In 1967 civil war broke out in Nigeria, into which Britain was reluctantly drawn, largely for the fear that the Russians would steal a march on them by supporting the Federal government.

During the same period Asian holders of British passports began coming to Britain, and their arrival was a shot in the arm for the 'Keep Britain White' activists, reminding the country that, while Labour had imposed a number of restrictions, they hadn't completely shut the door on black and Asian immigrants.

Political passions over the immigration issue had been lulled by the feeling that the Labour government was sympathetic to the anti-immigrant undertones of popular opinion. Presenting the hastily drafted White Paper of 1965 to the Party conference that year shortly after Gordon Walker's defeat at Leyton, Bob Mellish asked the rhetorical question: 'Am I, as Parliamentary Secretary, to go to Lambeth, which has a waiting list of 10,000 of its own people, and ask them to give preference to the coloured people who have come in? If you ask me to do that and say this is a socialist approach, I say to you frankly and fairly I shall be asking Lambeth to create the most grievous racial disturbance we have ever seen in London.'

Few black or Asian people were likely to get preference on housing lists in any case, but statements like these, harking back to the Notting Hill riots, were as good as a nod and a wink to a wider audience. Clearly, the government did not intend to risk any further unpopularity by being seen to be in favour of the immigrants, or even neutral about the issue. The immigrants themselves had little or nothing to say about the matter. There was no organised political group or recognised spokespersons on the American model who might have ventured an opinion, and most of the migrants had no interest in creating such a thing. Most of them literally had no time to spare.

'The thing about me is that because I worked, and because I have my housework and things to do, in those days you didn't have much time to fraternise a lot, and talk a lot and gossip a lot, so, I didn't know that much about it. And then those days, as a man, you'd know more, because you might go to the pub and you meet people at the pub and tell you. But in those days, I didn't go to the pub, so I didn't sort of mix with people to bring me up to date with intricacies, or whatever, or such a movement. And my husband is not a political man anyway, so I wouldn't be getting anything from him.

Personally, me and my husband, we weren't really that political. So, if I'm very honest with you, I can't say that I knew much about it, but I know the people who knew about it, they were in it, hot, hot, hot. But then, you see, I had my housework to do, I had to go and do a full day, come home, wash, cook, clean, look after my baby, I don't have no time to go to meetings and things like that, like I have now. You get a sense of it in newspapers, but you as an individual was not involved. There was a lot of political activity and a lot of meetings were held, mostly in people's homes, and, you know, the men meet and they have the drink and the cigarette and they play the dominoes or whatever, but they met in people's homes, they wouldn't go to a public place, 'cos they wouldn't want anybody to know what's happening. But where we women were concerned, not that we weren't interested, but we were too busy. The rents were so high, so much of us had to work, and most of us had one, two, three children, had the children to look after, there was food to be cooked. There's the men to be fed. Ironing, washing, laundry, everything. So we more or less kept the home side going. Not that we weren't interested, but we didn't have the time.'[4]

'I think most Afro-Caribbeans just wanted to come, settle down, get their money, go home, and what have you. They didn't want to come into a confrontation. This was the mother country. Everything they'd been taught about this was as a civilised mother country. They weren't taught about racism. I went on from America, on to Jamaica and spoke about racism. They didn't quite understand what I was talking about. Didn't have any meaning or relevance to them.'[5]

The political habits that the migrants had brought with them were not useful at all, partly because they traditionally belonged to a group which, while they shared the experiences of the migrants in England, actually came from a different background and had different pre-occupations. Most of them would spend the next decade criss-crossing the Atlantic, and, their interests impelled them outwards, back towards the Caribbean, or towards the USA and Africa. In contrast to the migrants now engrained in working-class English life, their perspective was global and abstract, and while they were usually knowledgeable about events in Harare or Nashville or Port

4   Interview with Connie Mark.
5   Interview with Paul Stephenson.

of Spain, the routines of housing or working practices in Nottingham or Tottenham hardly interested them.

'I think that what we need to remember is that in the fifties, a lot of the students who were here, some of them who were fairly well off and whose fees were being paid by their parents, there's a lot of students here, and they were very active, culturally and politically. And then all the writers were here in – in the fifties, Naipaul, Lamming, Selvon, they were all here. So there's an exodus of, not only the mass exodus which took place in '62, but a mass exodus of intellectuals and activists, political activists and cultural activists. So that we had a new population of West Indians here who were capable of doing exactly what they were doing at home, organising. But the organisation, the structure of organising, was very much along island lines, so each island had their own island organisation. And when CARD [Campaign Against Racial Discrimination] came, that embraced a broader spectrum. And, of course, later you got the West Indian Standing Conference which would embrace a broader cross section of West Indians. But in the early days, it was very much an island thing.'[6]

The political groupings which represented immigrants on the ground were a mixed bunch of individuals and organisations, which had little in common. They were led by the bodies which the government had set up as part of the successive stages of immigration and race relations legislation: the Commonwealth Immigrants Advisory Council in 1962, and in 1965 the Race Relations Board and the National Committee for Commonwealth Immigrants. They were largely staffed and supported by people and individuals already engaged in welfare and charitable activities, notably church groups, liberal academics and voluntary organisations whose work was expanding in the urban areas. 'Social' and 'friendship' and 'welfare' councils proliferated in the cities where immigrants lived, and their first priority was policing the minutiae of the Housing Act.

'Well, once the Church and the local community woke up, it became very effective. The reason was that a number of us banded together to form an organisation called the Notting Hill Social Council, and this brought together the clergy, the Citizens Advice Bureau, the

[6] Interview with Eric Huntley.

school teacher, the family welfare, all the usual voluntary organisations. And when you actually look at a group like that, it's quite a gathering of talent and strength. And we met monthly and we just took head-on housing conditions. We organised a mammoth petition to Kensington Town Hall demanding that something be done to make better use of the rent tribunal, for example, and the Town Hall cooperate with the local organisations. The Town Hall sat on the petition for a few months. The local newspaper began to say, "What's happening to it?"

'People were frightened to go to the Rent Tribunal because they believed that even if the Tribunal fixed a fair rent, sooner or later the landlord would put it up again. And, second, they argued that when they moved and perhaps asked a friend to take over their flat, he would automatically put it up again. We responded that there was actually a Rent Register which was publicly available and we guaranteed – "we" being the Notting Hill Social Council – we guaranteed that we would scrutinise the Rent Register regularly, and if a landlord did illegally increase the rent, we would immediately inform the Town Hall so that he was forced to put it back to where it was. So it was a very effective weapon for helping poor families pay a reasonable sum for their accommodation. It was still too high, but nonetheless it was not impossible, and it was a major weapon to be used by and on behalf of the West Indian community, and it worked. It really did work and, of course, increasingly the rent legislation was toughened up, so once one had this foundation that I've been describing it became even more effective as you had incoming Labour governments in the mid-1960s who made the rent legislation even tougher. So by 1970 the power of the slum landlord had been effectively smashed. And again we, the Notting Hill Social Council, started projects for people drifting in to London; people coming and expect to find work and didn't; expect to find somewhere to live and they didn't. They were caught up in prostitution, the lot. All this began from this rather loose federation of local people that called itself a Social Council. So, after a year or two, the community as a whole, the institutions as a whole, did make a good response. But, to be fair, we had a lot of people to help us. I mean, George Clark of CND threw his weight behind us. Donald Chesworth[7] was a tower of strength. Donald Soper was there in the background.

---

[7] Donald Chesworth was a Labour Councillor in North Kensington.

There was all sorts of people ready to be mobilised. And to know we had those father-figures, if you like, was a great encouragement to the people actually on the spot at the time.'[8]

The work of the voluntary groups at this level had the side effect of politicising a number of black individuals and sucking them into local politics and local government. West Indians had been notoriously unwilling to join up for anything not directly associated with the welfare of their own families,[9] and, in any case, were also notably reluctant to commit themselves to any formal association with West Indians from other islands. So this trickle of West Indians into local government went unremarked at the time, and in many quarters was seen as a kind of aberration from 'normal' migrant behaviour. The best known was Dr David Pitt, later Lord Pitt, but most of them were middle-aged Caribbeans who had arrived on the *Windrush*, or ex-servicemen, and settled into the life of the skilled or semi-skilled working-class trade unions. In an age dominated by the more romantic American images of Civil Rights and Black Power, their activities were treated as insignificant or futile, even by the race relations organisations. In the same period the media tended to focus on the dark glasses and leather jackets of the short-lived but highly publicised 'Black Power' groups strutting around London. In fact, it turned out to be the migrant councillors who established a tradition which was based on the unions or on local elections, and which led the next generation of black politicians to their most authentic and effective entry into British politics.

'I was ten years on the council the year that I was nominated and elected as mayor, because it's been done democratically. There were four candidates, and I was the only black. In fact, I was the only black councillor on a council of fifty; fifty of us, male and female, and I was the only black councillor. In fact, the first thing to mention, is that my first involvement with the Labour Party was as a delegate from my union to the Labour Party hierarchy. I was not politically motivated, I was elected as a delegate to the party, representing my union, all these bodies. And from there, naturally, I mean, I take

[8] Interview with David Mason OBE. David Mason is a Methodist Minister who set up home in Notting Hill after the '58 riots and started a race relations project, supported by Donald Soper, the leader of community welfare tendencies in the Methodist Church.

[9] A fact which various academics chewed over for several decades. See David G. Pearson, 'Race, Class and Political Activism: A Study of West Indians in Britain' (Gower Publishing Company, 1981), p. 37.

part, I take a lot of interest. I've done lots of preparatory courses, from Ruskin College, TUC training college, so I was prepared, did a lot of work, of myself, when I was elected on the council. I did one of the things that – if you find another councillor did it, then I'm wrong – I took one year, when I was elected, I took a year in English local government, to know what it's all about. So, when I sat there, I sat with all the confidence in the world. I knew what I was into. So, when the time came to elect or nominate me for the mayor, well, it was just my turn come, 'cos, as I said, there were four of us. Three white folks, members of the council, and myself. But I had the longest serving time there. And 'cos I was Deputy Whip, so I was senior. No mayors went on the council in opposition, through opposition, and got control. You had to select offices for everybody, and there were mayors, deputy-mayor elected, the second year they were mayor. Whereas I was ten years on the council chair of all different committees, in opposition, in control, in opposition, in control.

'And then, in ten years, I was elected mayor in 1975–76. So, it came in a time when I was prepared and ready for it. Naturally, a young fellow from Hammersmith said in the press that they should never accept me as mayor, they should elect their own mayor. And one of my trade union colleagues, an Englishman, wrote in answering him, saying that the work that I have done for the borough, at which time he was in his nappies. I haven't had to answer to him, and it was said on record, I was one of the best mayors, because everybody wanted me. I was like a novelty, everybody wanted me. 'Cos one of the things that I learned is human relationships, to get on with people, to fit in with everyone. So I get on with people, never suffer. Eighteen years, when I said enough is enough, never lost an election, fought election after election. Many of my colleagues, English and other nationalities, lose, come and said, "Randy, how did you do it? You know, I mean, here's us, after the election, with tears." They've lost their seat. They say, "How did you do it?" In fact, in '64, when I was elected, there's about fifty majority, and five years after, we went down to five councillors and six aldermen – in those days, we had aldermen. And I was the only councillor with the postal address W12.[10] All my colleagues was not elected. So

---

[10]   Shepherd's Bush. Then a working-class and undesirable district in which to live.

it came at a time when I was prepared for it and accepted it, and did a good job.'[11]

'I should mention the organisation that was formed at my home. We called it the Cosmopolitan Social and Sports Club, and that was the first non-white organisation to be formed in this city. And it is through that committee that I then began to do much more extensive work as the only white collar worker in the whole area. I was the only person that had access to a telephone during the day, and if there's anyone want to make contact, they would come through to me or to the Consultative Committee, which we'll mention later. And it was that committee first, that Ivor[12] come and talk to about the setting up of a consultative committee. Now, after we discussed it, Ivor take the matter to the Consultative Committee, which the Archdeacon of Birmingham set up to bring industrialists and various other people together to discuss the situation relating to the presence of, in those days, it was mainly West Indians, in the community. And Ivor saw that and came and talked to us with it.

'Before that, after we formed our organisation in '62, I was introduced to the Secretary of the Council of Social Service, a lady by the name of Dorothy Wood. Dorothy Wood came from an area of Stafford known as Croxton, and when I met her, I was fascinated by the lady, because she was the first white person that openly admitted to me that she could not empathise on the issue, as far as it is concerned. I remember, she said, "Look, I can sympathise with you, but I cannot empathise with you on those issues. If we are to do anything, it's about you, and people like you. I am powerless to do anything," et cetera. And that was, to me, the remarkable thing about her and that committee, it is known today as the Nottingham and District Equal Opportunities Committee, whatever the title may be. From that committee, and through it, we set up a housing association and, eventually, it was through Dorothy Wood – Dolly to her friends – she persuaded the great Nottingham Co-operative Society to give us premises on Anfield Street Central, where our club could meet. And that gave us perhaps the first stable address from which we could work. And the Co-op even take it further, for us to get a licence for the premises and various things like that.

[11] Interview with Randolph Beresford.
[12] Reference to Ivor Da Souza, another prominent Jamaican in Nottingham, who was well known for his organising and welfare work in the Jamaican community.

'I wasn't appointed until 1962, when I was appointed as a magistrate, which was some four years after the riot. I was at the right place at the right time and in the right position. I don't know who nominated me, I was only told that my name has been put forward and if I would be interested I should respond, which I did. I was duly appointed. It had its problem, of course, because when the appointment, I received several letters of congratulation from all over the world, including a few nasty ones, including one from the Ku Klux Klan and people like those. But I always operated on the idea that if I am not prepared to do it, how dare me ask anybody else to become involved.'[13]

Before the Race Relations legislation in 1965, there was no legal redress for blacks who faced discrimination in employment. Recruitment was often subject to informal and unwritten agreements between unions and the employers and, in a number of districts, especially outside of London, it was understood that the major employers would keep blacks out. This applied equally to employment in both the public and the private spheres. Ironically, given the extent of black recruitment to the London Transport network, transport companies in the major provincial cities were among the most stubborn. In Nottingham, Eric Irons had to mobilise support to negotiate with the City Transport company before black workers were employed. In Bristol desegregating the bus company took a major campaign, which was led by Paul Stephenson, who was not a West Indian, but came from an English, mixed race family.

'Well, I was teaching in Bristol, in the St Paul's secondary school, and I was doing youth and community development work, and I was also meeting up with people, parents who had just brought their children in. I was helping with extra classes in the evenings for those that wanted it, and there was an enormous appetite for education by the youngsters who were coming in. I then began moving with some of the people I'd considered community leaders who were there before I was there, and all said, "You know, one thing we feel really shocked about and we don't feel we can do much about is the Bristol Bus Company." There are people, they were saying to me, who're coming from London, who'd been recruited from London Transport and been trained on buses in London, who were moving

[13] Interview with Eric Irons.

down to Bristol but couldn't get the jobs in Bristol, same as in Birmingham. I said to one of my pupils, Guy Bailey, "Would you like to get a job as a driver, or a conductor, on the buses, and be trained?" He said, Yes, he would. I said, "You know they don't take black people?" He said, "Yes, I know." I said, "Would you like me to fight for this and take up a major campaign, and would you support it?" He said, Yes, he would. And that's very good, because he'd only just recently arrived in England, he was a Boys' Brigade officer in Jamaica, he was quite prepared to get involved, and I was heartened by that.

'Then I wanted to know how best I could bring this dramatically before the public, in a way that would capture the imagination, not only of the black community in Bristol but far wider. And I went on the downs thinking and in one sense praying about how one does it, and then the idea came. A boycott. Luther King had boycotted the buses in Alabama over black people being forced to stay at the back of buses, so I thought I'd do the same tactic but this time over employment. So I called a press conference and said we're going to set up this group called Bristol West Indian Development Council. I said, we are now going to confront racism head-on, and we're going to call a boycott of the buses, because I'd already spoken to the director of the bus company over whether they would employ Guy, and when they realised he was black they said, "No, it's not the company policy to employ black people." And I said, "Well, I'm going to oppose you, and I'm going to campaign against it." He said, "Well, you can go out and campaign, but you're not getting anywhere with it because this is company policy, we are not having them." Must remember, there were no laws, no laws protecting black people against discrimination, nothing at all. So I called the boycott, not just for the black people. I said, anyone in Bristol who feels that this policy is wrong, don't use the buses. And it did do what I hoped it would do, it caught the imagination, first of all of the local press, who blazoned it in headlines, and it also caught the imagination then of the national press, and it became known as the Bristol bus dispute.

'I then decided to get hold of as many people as I could, not only from the black community but also from the white community to support me, and I knew the Bishop of Bristol quite well, Oliver Tompkins then, and Tony Benn, who was then at Bristol, and launched this boycott. Now, at first, it really did catch the imagination and people, most people saying it's wrong. Ian Painty,

who was then the director of the bus company, came out publicly
and defended the policy. He said, "White people won't work with
black people on the buses and, moreover, it could be that we'd lose
even more customers if we had black drivers and black conductors
on the buses." The unions were ambivalent and didn't want to push
it because the racists within the union – drivers and conductors, who
were white – peddled the line that having black people on would
lower their wages. Having black people on would frighten white
women off from becoming conductresses, and having black people
on would probably cause a lot of violence between passengers and
the crews. And one woman actually was heard to say it would be
wrong, morally wrong, to be seen on the bus after nine o'clock with
a bus driver who's black. So that was peddled, and the union, at
that time under its regional director, wasn't, as far as I was concerned,
pushing the issue as it could.

'It opened up a Pandora's box, because Bristol was well known
as a slave trader, and most of Bristol's wealth came from slavery.
This was April 1963. Jamaica, Trinidad had just become
independent countries, so their High Commissions wanted to get
involved. So I had the High Commissioner for Jamaica and Learie
Constantine, then High Commissioner for Trinidad, supporting me.
And the press, the Church, and all the establishment in Bristol
decided to turn on me. I was forced then to issue writs for libel and
slander, and I did. I issued it to newspapers and to the Transport
and General Workers Union, at the time, and pursued it till I got
apology in the court and damages. I was pleased when I read when
Tony Benn in his *Wilderness Years* diary mentions quite at length
how he saw that situation, and how he brought Harold Wilson into
it. I always remember Harold Wilson's telegram to me, in supporting
it, when he was Leader of the Opposition in those days in '63, and
I was told by Tony then that, if Labour comes to power, one of the
first things they will introduce will be a law against racial
discrimination. And I was a bit sceptical, as many black people were,
because we could see that perhaps the government wanted to take
the sting out of this racial protest that we had started. Black leadership
would have come from the streets, as it had come in many ways
from the churches and the streets in America, and dictate the agenda
of how race relations would be developed in Britain. But by
introducing a law as early as they did they took on the agenda, and
we had a whole lot of community liaison committees, and so on
and so forth.

'It took us six months, nevertheless, to get the first black person on, and it happened to be a Punjabi, so I was very pleased. I didn't say No. Guy didn't say No. We'd fought the battle, it was a moral battle, it wasn't a political one. And it was the first black-led protest, national protest against racial discrimination and the promotion of equal opportunities that this country had seen. I got attacked by racists and threatened, threatened with my life and all the usual things that one would expect. There was confusion within the black community, some thought I'd gone too far, I was making it more difficult for them. I've upset the white man, that's not your job, and all that attitude was coming through. But there were equally those who came on my marches, the University of Bristol brought the city to a standstill, marched down Park Street for the first time ever on an issue of race, so it was a very educating and healing issue.

'After the boycott I took a taxi from the station, and the taxi driver said to me, "Oh, I recognise your face," he said, "You're Paul Stephenson." I said, "Yes." He said, "Oh, that boycott you had was great." I said, "Oh, thank you." He says, "Oh, we did more business at that time than we've ever done." '[14]

Although Stephenson received a significant amount of support and encouragement from senior Labour Party members, the potential dangers of a struggle over widespread discrimination in employment were obvious to the government, and unemployment was not yet the political bogeyman it came to be later on. So the Race Relations legislation of 1965 included measures against discrimination, but, instead of imposing penalties, set in place a complex system of conciliation. On the other hand, the Bristol bus boycott set up a standard which the law had underpinned. The boycott hadn't been a simple plea for shelter, in the sense that it was possible to read the argument over discrimination in housing. It was a bold step into the territory which had traditionally been the exclusive property of white workers. It also demonstrated that concerted action could change established customs, and it represented a significant advance in the scope of the demands that the immigrants might be prepared to make. This had its effects on both sides of the racial divide and, as the sixties wore on, the migrants became more and more assertive about discrimination, while the political Right, inside and outside of Parliament, seized on the law as one more example of how the white British were being disinherited.

[14] Interview with Paul Stephenson.

17

———•———

'I think what most impressed us was by the time we saw Malcolm X, he had transformed himself, and it was that image of a self transformed person, who had come from one kind of life and made himself into another sort of person, that was the most impressive thing, really. I certainly was more impressed by that than, literally, his politics, because I didn't understand, really, his connection with Islam and all that sort of a different world from the world which we were inhabiting. We were thinking about what would it be like to have a kind of organisation like this in Britain, with the image of the capacity of a young man like this to make himself into a leader, and with the kind of quiet confidence that he had, and that kind of grounded sense of his own blackness, of his own black identity, that was a very powerful image.'[1]

'Now, I've been brought up in a society all my life where we were looked on as black people not having beauty. It was all blonde and white where real beauty was. When I got to the States, that was to have quite a psychological effect, that we are a proud and beautiful people. As I was going all around America I just wanted to be around with black people, 'cos I could appreciate beauty in a way I'd never met and seen before, and that was quite profound at that time. And then they were moving into Afros at that time, and I saw little children with Afros, and I always used to say, when I have my own children, my little boy's going to have an Afro. Great psychological barrier to go through.'[2]

'When Malcolm X came here, he found Islam and called himself Michael X. And the press was always looking for a line, so Malcolm and Michael, and he became a black Muslim in the twinkling of an eye, from a Roman Catholic. His mother was a staunch Roman

[1] Interview with Stuart Hall.
[2] Interview with Paul Stephenson.

The Bouillabaisse in New Compton Street, one of the war-time haunts where African American and Caribbean servicemen mingled with their white colleagues.

Sir Oswald Mosley addressing a meeting of his Fascist Union movement in Dalston, Hackney, May 1948.

Aldwyn Roberts, Lord Kitchener, in 1950. One of the best known and most popular of Caribbean calpysonians. He was the *Windrush* passenger who for a few years became the voice of Caribbean culture in Britain.

Clement Attlee, Prime Minister, in 1948. 'I think it would be a great mistake to take this party of Jamaicans immigrating to the UK too seriously.'

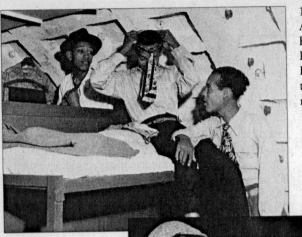

1948 in the Clapham
Air Raid Shelter.
Kenneth Murray, Eric
Drysdale and Aston
Robinson adjust their
ties getting ready for a
night out on the town.

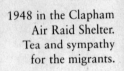

1948 in the Clapham
Air Raid Shelter.
Tea and sympathy
for the migrants.

1948 outside the
Clapham Air Raid
Shelter. 'The boys
used to go and stand
up by the common
there.' (Oswald
'Columbus'
Denniston)

Notting Hill in 1954. The two local lads in the foreground are dressed in the style which identifies them as 'spivs'.

Teddy Boys on the quayside at Lowestoft, 1956.

June 1956, Victoria Station. The Sally Army to the rescue.

October 1959. Dr David Pitt, Labour candidate for Hampstead, on the steps of Hampstead Town Hall, addressing Ban the Bomb marchers.

Peter Rachman, the most notorious west London landlord of the century in 1960.

Michael de Freitas, also known as Michael X. The prominent poster in the background pictures Malcolm X from whom he got his name.

Enoch Powell in 1985.

Darcus Howe (centre). A leading member of the Mangrove Nine, organiser of the mass protest which followed the New Cross Fire, journalist, columnist and TV star.

Diane Abbott, Britain's first black woman MP, with Ken Livingstone, MP for Brent South and former leader of the GLC.

Catholic, and she had him from a Portuguese shop keeper, so he was a nice brown skin Roman Catholic boy, and he turned bad in England, and Malcolm X came, and he got like Sir Malcolm. That's all. They say, "Who are you?" He says, "Michael X. I am Michael X". So they saw a guy called Franky next to him, and they say, "Who are you?" He say, "Why?", and they call him Franky Y. It is this way. I'm not cracking a joke. He asking the reporter, "You want to know who I am?" So the next thing it appears in the Press: "Malcolm X, Michael X and Franky Y." [3]

X, X and Y

When I heard that President Kennedy had been shot I was on the top of a bus going down Green Lane, and we'd just passed the old Haringey Stadium. It was about half-past eight at night. A woman had just got on the bus, and she started telling this story to another woman on the other side of the aisle. It was such extraordinary news that the half dozen white people on top with me all reacted in a most untypical way, turning round and asking the woman to repeat what she'd said, and asking for the details of what she'd heard on the news. One man asked her who had done it. She hesitated for a moment, and, oddly, she glanced round at me before speaking. "They've arrested a white man," she said, emphasising the "white" as if to reassure me. When I got home a few minutes later, it was all on TV. This was how I remember experiencing the world in the sixties. First there were hints, vibes shivering through the air, and then you'd be zapped by the whole thing in sight and sound in your sitting room.

Years later I was in Harlem watching the Last Poets perform on the back of a truck in a housing estate, and they yelled that the revolution would not be on TV, and I had to laugh, because if there

---

[3] Interview with Darcus Howe. Darcus Howe came to Britain from Trinidad in 1961. He worked in Notting Hill at the Mangrove Restaurant and was famously one of the nine victims of a police raid which gave rise to a series of trials at the end of the sixties, a cause célèbre in its day. Later he was editor of *Race Today*, and organiser of the New Cross March in protest about the circumstances surrounding a fire at New Cross in 1981 when several black children died. Recently presenter of The Devil's Advocate, a talk show on Channel 4, a columnist for *The New Statesman*, and independent television producer.

was one thing certain, it was that such a big event would have to be up on the screen in living colour. That is how it was, and what happened in the world became part of your domestic space. You have to remember this in order to understand some of the things that happened to migrants in the sixties.

It's often said that the Vietnam War was the first major conflict to be played out nightly on TV. It wasn't so for us. For us, it was the Civil Rights struggle and the subsequent battle between the Black Power activists and the American Government. During those years we got to know their names and faces better than the next door neighbours'. There was Martin Luther King, of course, and Stokeley Carmichael and Rap Brown and Angela Davis and Julian Bond and Malcolm and Cassius Clay and Eldridge Cleaver and Huey P. Newton, sitting up in that chair with the guns and the spear, looking twice as heroic as Che Guevara and several times more sexy. In our eyes it was a serial more potent and full of drama than anything before or since. On one night Martin Luther King would be trapped in a church, with the President hesitating about attempting a rescue, while a white mob bellowed hatred, boiling round the building like raging surf; and that would be the first instalment, so that you went off to bed wondering what his fate would be when you switched on the news next day. Or Stokeley would be sitting on a bus surrounded by students, on his way to a confrontation with a clutch of angry white sheriffs armed with guns and electric cattle prods, his eyes glittering, his black skin so smooth and glowing that you wanted to reach out and touch it. Behind it all was a soundtrack of deep voices throbbing with emotion, screaming with passion, and always singing beautifully, then sweet gospel and soul music: Ray Charles, Wilson Pickett, James Brown. These were great days, when we could watch black giants walking the earth.

Talking to various black people who lived through those days when the magic of television brought us these images, one of the things you hear over and over again is that this was the time in which they became black. That way of describing what happened to them makes sense when you consider the various different processes which were working on us from the moment we landed in Britain. Leaving Trinidad or Jamaica or Grenada, getting off the boat or the plane and stepping on English soil was not only a beginning, it also closed a door behind you. Whatever backgrounds we came from, it was increasingly that moment of arrival which began to be the most significant event in our lives: and however hard you tried to preserve *an unaltered sense of who you were, as a Caribbean, it was impossible to stop the routines and circumstances of your everyday life re-defining your identity. In the end, the fact that you went out to work every day or caught the train in a certain place or a hundred other crucial things began to matter more than your memories, and, of course, the longer you stayed the more your life filled up with new and different souvenirs and remembrances. The children, those who had arrived before adulthood had shaped them, were further along this road, but all the influences which acted on migrants created the same inexorable pressure. We were no longer Caribbean, but our new environment offered no alternative sense of belonging. The concept of citizenship within the British Isles was still unwritten and, as most people understood the idea, it was an informal and traditional code whose main thrust was to exclude dark skinned people from abroad. So all the responses around us, both hostile and friendly, referred somehow to the colour of our skins.*

At the same time, blackness, being black, suddenly began to be an idea which could define us all, reconnecting us to our former roots wherever we lived or where we were born. And the experience of the Americans gave the idea a shape, turned it into a programme of action which energised the migrants everywhere, no matter how passive or isolated they were. When figures like King, Stokeley Carmichael and Malcolm eventually visited Britain their presence had an enormous impact. After King's tour a number of Caribbeans, many of whom were showbusiness personalities or already involved in race relations work, together with a group of white liberals and clergy, created the Campaign Against Racial Discrimination. It had no roots in any community, however, and it rapidly collapsed without achieving any of its aims. On the other hand, the ideas disseminated by the Americans' influence had different, less predictable effects.

'I don't know whether ordinary families working in a foundry in Birmingham, or working on the buses in Oxford, or something like that, I don't know whether they would have been aware, and at what level they were aware, of what was happening in the States in the Civil Rights movement. Where I think their impact is obvious is in the more politicised elements, people who are trying to make a political response, who are trying to organise the black community as a political force to counter racism, both at the local level and in national politics. And, for them, obviously, the example of Civil Rights is very, very important. Black people can get into a struggle, they can change legislation, racism can be outlawed. There's a long debate in the sixties about whether to go down the American road of legally outlawing racial language, for example, or whether one should do it in a more British way by, you know, not having a law, et cetera. And the American example was very important in persuading people to fight for legislation, for actual legislation that would make it illegal to say, or, you know, to stimulate racist attacks and violence against black people. So there's a very important effect, and the visit of Malcolm X was extremely important. I don't think King's strategy appealed to people as much, because there wasn't a tradition of philosophically driven, non-violent work as there had been in the Southern churches, and so on. I think it's a broader impact. Blacks in the States have got themselves politically organised, they're not taking it. There is, in addition to that, a cultural movement, the Black Power movement, which is, you know, "Black is Beautiful". We are Black people, we have African roots, we can affirm ourselves, we can do things; which was an extremely important element of the whole influence from the States. And this is shaping the sort of political – lower-case "p" – broad black political response to everything that has happened, from '58 onwards, in terms of growing racism in society.'[4]

'We were very much part of what was taking place in America. So that, in that period of Black Power, you had the Black Consciousness period, where our roots for Africa, and everything around us, we felt, had to be like that. Stokely came, and the West Indian Student Centre was a very active place. It wasn't just for students, it was workers as well who were there, and the entire Caribbean. And prior to that, Africa House was the next building to the student centre. So Africa House was where we congregated, and then, of course, the West Indian Student Centre became the hot bed for Caribbean politics. So Stokely and Malcolm, they all came to the West Indian Student Centre. It was just a re-defining, re-asserting of one's self.'[5]

'In the sixties there were all these books coming out and there were people like Malcolm X, Eldridge Cleaver and all these guys, all

---

[4]   Interview with Stuart Hall.
[5]   Interview with Jessica Huntley.

these wonderful people who were so articulate, and they highlighted the problems facing black Americans. And to us, because we didn't have that type of mobilisation over here, they became very, very important. And it's also to realise that most of these black guys who were doing this in America were guys with West Indian backgrounds. You know, they had either West Indian mother or West Indian father, or that type of background. Like Malcolm X. Like Kwame Touré. Kwame Touré was born in Trinidad. And so we were listening attentively to what they say.'[6]

'I can't say much about Martin Luther King other than that I remember, when he was shot, I was staying in Tedworth Square, at 36 Tedworth Square. I was going out then with James Baldwin's sister. And Jimmy called from New York, and his words were, "They've shot one of their own." That's what he said, those were his words. It is ominous really that I was at the same 36 Tedworth Square when Malcolm was shot as well, and the same James Baldwin called and said, "Malcolm is shot." It happened like that.'[7]

The influence of the Americans, along with the media attention commanded by Black Power also had unhappy consequences. Since the '58 riots the media had linked migrant life with Notting Hill. Its dissident social life, the basement clubs and all-night parties, the gambling, the poncing and prostitution, had continued to draw in the rich and famous who wanted to taste the life of the slums. But after the Christine Keeler affair the social elite had withdrawn, to be replaced by a more raffish crew of artists, writers, showbusiness or media people; and the local activity around the issues of housing, street violence and police harassment, gave their presence a fashionable veneer of social concern.

The prominent Civil Rights and Black Power activists who trickled through London raised the consciousness of the community as a whole, but they also left in their wake a scattering of individuals who took from them invaluable lessons in style and public relations. The best known of these was a Trinidadian 'hustler' named Michael de Freitas, who claimed to have been one of Peter Rachman's strong arm men. This might have been part of the legend Michael built around himself, since other witnesses maintain that at the time he was telling this story to worthies like Stuart Hall and

---

[6] Interview with Ben Bousquet.
[7] Interview with Rudy Braithwaite.

Donald Chesworth as evidence of his 'conversion', he had only actually met Rachman once. Michael had come from Trinidad and as the fashion for political radicalism crept in, he converted his image from small-time hustler to Black Power activist. The story of how he came to be dubbed 'X' is typical of the comical confusion surrounding the black activists at the time. He was in the process of checking into a hotel together with Malcolm X and, pointing to his companion, Malcolm said, 'And my brother, Michael.' The receptionist, unfamiliar with the idiom, solemnly wrote down X after Michael's name. This was a useful accident for Michael and he took to calling himself X, and rewriting his career as a parallel to Malcolm's.

The newspapers loved him. He could always be relied on to issue a provocative quote and his style and manner fitted precisely with media stereotypes about the violence and arrogance of American Black Power activists. The publicity won him several patrons among the showbusiness crowd drawn to the radical chic of Notting Hill, including John Lennon and Sammy Davis Jr, but his only evidence of political activity was the announcement that he had formed an organisation entitled the Racial Adjustment Action Society. Typically of Michael, the acronym spelled out a Jamaican obscenity. The organisation had few members and never did anything, but he used at least some of the money he assembled to buy a building in Holloway which he called The Black House. It all fell apart when a white man claimed to have been held prisoner and tortured in The Black House. Michael fled to Trinidad before the trial could come up. At his house there, an English woman and another Trinidadian, both of them his friends and supporters, were horribly murdered in a peculiar ritual. Michael fled again, to the jungle in Guyana this time, but was eventually captured, brought back to Trinidad and hanged.

He was a Trinidadian boy who came to England and became the corrupt and vicious man he was in the hothouse atmosphere of Notting Hill. The Trinidadians who knew him treated him warily, or with a tolerant contempt. Others, unfamiliar with the culture of 'grand charge'[8] were naively impressed by his antics. In the end, the most notable effect of his activities was that the publicity given to his off-the-cuff 'statements' discredited black politics and politicians in Britain for a number of years, especially within the black community.

'Well, in 1967 we had the Notting Hill Summer Project, involving

---

[8] A Trinidadian phrase denoting an aggressive and pretentious pose designed to create a big impression.

300 students, to really help us with the Housing Register and neighbourhood care centres, and so on, and they had public meetings. And Michael de Freitas was invaluable in getting the radical black community to come, and, indeed made a magnificent contribution. He said the greatest step forward for race relations is to be a little black bastard. That brought the whole house down, and then he combined with another black leader in saying that the enemy were the slum landlords, not the whites, and that the black and the white poor fight together for justice. And that was a magnificent contribution. But he wasn't really interested. But I liked him. I mean, he was a loveable rogue, but a very able person, enormous ability, and it's just one of those things that Rachman met him before some others met him, and he never quite got away from the grip of that crowd.'[9]

'Michael wanted me to join with him. Michael is an amazing person, in that the people who Michael had around him amaze me. Very bright, sensible people. I can see the smoke on Michael's face and in his voice I can say Michael is up to no good, that's the impression I get. I'm surprised that the people who he had around him took him serious. I could see the smoke and he didn't have no good intentions as far as I'm concerned. So I kept away. I didn't sort of try to tell other people that he's up to no good, but I just didn't want to know. Well, for instance, when we had a big demonstration I remember what Mike did. It was after the Mangrove Nine demonstration, he was on television and Mike had nothing to do with the demonstration and he didn't take part in it at all. But the television shot was that he said he went to get help from Canada to deliver the situation and things. But that's nothing to do with him at all. He exploit the situation.'[10]

'Michael de Freitas in the beginning, well, my impressions of him were good impressions. All the things that they say about him and that I read about him, I have never experienced. I found him a very

[9]   Interview with David Mason OBE.

[10]   Interview with Frank Critchlow. Frank Critchlow came from Trinidad in 1953 at the age of twenty. He worked on the railways before opening the Rio Coffee Bar in Notting Dale in 1959. In 1969 he closed the Rio and opened the Mangrove Restaurant in All Saints Road. As a result of frequent police raids he went through a succession of court trials – the Mangrove trials of the sixties and seventies. He still lives in Notting Hill.

gentle person. He may have had all his bad sides, or the dark side of
him, but my impression of him was a gentle man; a father who
really cared for his children, you know. And a man who was very
concerned about his wife, Desiree. I met him with Stokely
Carmichael. Stokely Carmichael was at his house, and Michael was
talking – he was sort of being dubbed, slowly, as Michael X. He
had a beautiful mohair suit, with a diamond medallion around his
neck, and he invited me to the Round House, and they had this big
gathering. Stokely Carmichael was on the platform and Stokely talked
for hours and hours, really, and then everybody returned to
Michael's place, and there was a number of people, people like
Stephen Khalifa, Horace Ove, Eddie Braithwaite,[11] all of those were
there to talk to Stokely. Later on, one of the last times I saw him, he
reached a stage where he became philosophical and prophetic
and all this sort of thing, and he was walking down Camden Hill
Road, barefooted, and by then, he had changed from Michael de
Freitas to Michael X. He had grown a massive afro. And I saw this
person walking, and he was wearing a sort of jumper, and he was
walking down the street barefooted, and these dark trousers and a
white sort of caftan like thing. And I had a little Austin car then, and
I shouted to him, "Michael, is that you?" And he came across to
me. "Can you give me a lift?" And I gave him a lift. And whilst
driving in the car, he was talking about himself, and he was saying,
"You know, Rudi, I think they're going to kill me, you know." He
says, "They killed Malcolm and they want to go for me." Or words
to that effect. And I said, "Well, Michael, you needn't fear. I mean,
you know, they wouldn't kill you." And he says, "Yeah, they're
going to kill me, man, I can feel it in my bones. They're going to kill
me, you know." I found that obsession with the fact that the system
is going to murder him in some way, very, very potent, I mean, coming
from him. I did not, when I was in his presence, get a feeling of
fear or that he was insincere or any such thing, I didn't get that
impression at all.'[12]

'Michael de Freitas was made by the media. Michael professes
to belong to the Black Power movement, he professes to be a man

---

[11] Both Trinidadians, Stephen Khalifa is an actor and Horace Ove a film director. 'Eddie' refers to
E. R. Braithwaite, the Guyanese novelist.
[12] Interview with Rudy Braithwaite.

concerned about blacks. First of all, he was not political. He was not concerned about blacks. It was the media who follow him all over the place. Now I saw Black Power as something to show the blacks as being men and being responsible. Not to kill people or destroy people as it was portrayed to be by the media itself.

'They see that they could destroy the Black Power movement in this country by building up Michael de Freitas and that's exactly what they did. Everywhere they go they present Michael as the leader of the Black Power movement. He never was. I can remember the first time when he made some statement, he was arrested. I went to see him. I belonged to an organisation then and we decided that we'll get him a lawyer. He said he did not want a lawyer, he would defend himself. He defended himself, but he did it so poorly that he got two years in prison. And this is the proof that he had no following, although the media portrayed that he had a following, he had no following at all. The media portray him to be a leader of the Black Power movement. He was not. The media portrayed him as being fighting for black people. He was not.'[13]

'Michael X is a really interesting phenomenon. I had met Michael around 1958. He walked into the New Left offices, and he said he was a hustler, he was a criminal, he took drugs, he ran prostitutes, he loved jazz, he went to Stockholm every three months to listen to American jazz. I mean, he was an extraordinary character. He sort of came in to make a confession. We had been active in Notting Hill and he'd seen us moving around, trying to organise tenants. And he came to say, actually, he was one of the people who hustled tenants out of their accommodation when they couldn't pay their rent ... He was a street boy, a street hustler, and what he said to us was, "I don't want to do this, you know. I don't want my people to suffer, but I don't know any other way of living. Are you going to do something in Notting Hill? Can I be part of it?" From then on, Michael began to really try to help tenants and try to be on their side. And he associated himself with other people who were doing

---

[13] Interview with Rene Webb. Rene Webb came from Jamaica, having joined the RAF at the age of twenty-two. He was stationed at Biggin Hill and settled in west London before moving to Brixton. He was an ILEA youth worker, and was awarded the Jamaican Badge of Honour by the Jamaican Government for his services to the black community in Britain. In the seventies he started the Melting Pot Foundation in Brixton, one of the earliest 'Self Help' projects, and became chairman of the Lambeth Community Relations Council. He is retired and lives in Brixton.

community action there, and I think that was sort of the beginning of a big transition from his point of view.

'Well, then he was very influenced by the presence of Malcolm X. He went to the meetings, he met Malcolm in private discussion, and by then what was beginning to happen was that the British media wanted an articulate political voice to tell them what the black community was thinking, 'cos there was no political organisation. And Michael X was very articulate, had the gift of the gab, and he could see that there was a role of local leadership combined with media visibility for him, and he took that and set up this organisation, called R.A.A.S., which has interesting Caribbean connotations. I remember he sent me a card saying, "I think I'll make you Foreign Secretary of the R.A.A.S. organisation." You couldn't tell in those days whether he was serious about what was going on or not serious. But, actually, he did have a lot of local influence, and he did set about sort of giving voice in the media, and the media did attend to what he was saying, because there was so few spokespersons who were able to command the media in an articulate way. He did have an impact on what was happening on the ground. But he was also somebody who got very carried away in terms of his own charisma. He was a powerful person, but he knew his influence, and he was manipulative about it.

'I think it's a kind of tragedy, 'cos I think it's a story very much like Malcolm X's story, except that Malcolm did really re-make himself, and Michael half re-made himself. And if he had fully re-made himself, he could have been, you know, possibly the sort of person in a Malcolm X role in relation to British black politics. But he was too much a bit of a clown, too much a bit playing around, and very, very caught up with his own capacity to dominate people. He went back to Trinidad to kind of move his base from England to Trinidad, and I think that, in itself, was a sign of defeat. It meant that he hadn't had the influence in Britain. He hadn't really won a leading position outside of London, outside of rather small communities. He never had the support of ordinary, respectable, black working people.'[14]

'Well, he was hustling. I mean Michael's response is that any publicity is good publicity. "Yes," he would say, "I was hustling, and

---

[14]   Interview with Stuart Hall.

yes, I was making money. So when Rachman wants to make money, I was making it." He didn't have much conscience about it. I mean, you couldn't make him feel guilty about anything. His slogan was, Whatever you do, you well do, you've done it already. The press made him the militant activist he was. Michael never organised any large numbers of people in pursuit of any right, civil or human. Michael was a commune always, and I was the Prime Minister of his commune at one time, and he had a remarkable capacity to raise money from the likes of John Lennon and Sammy Davis, and he had a group of people round him who he'd look after. Big men. Give you £40 a week, or whatever, and if he tells you to chop his head off, then you do it. I wasn't around it long time because I had a wife and children and I wanted to live with my wife. I was homeless at one time, so he put me up for a few days, well, a few weeks really. I was always very grateful to him for that. But I used to tease him mercilessly, and once he came with some guys to kill me, he said. But what I had in my pocket he didn't want to know at the time, 'cos, you know, you always try to defend yourself. But he was a great person for inciting mayhem against his enemies. I wasn't afraid of him, but I was careful.

'The commune of all communes was The Black House. My sister used to be in there, my brother used to be in there, and he had a whole thing going. I didn't quite know what was going, it was going to be a complex, have a supermarket and stuff, and this and that. And then, suddenly, I heard somebody had shot at him in Holloway Road or somewhere, and then the next thing I heard The Black House was closed down. And it was all part of a Walter Mitty fantasy, a lot of disgruntled people, and he went off to Trinidad, whereupon he was charged with murder of a friend of mine, both of them friends of mine, and they popped his neck. It was just plain tragedy. What I always found difficult was how a man of that age and therefore wisdom could find himself doing something like that. But Michael was reckless, careless, and I never knew what he believed. He was part of the confusion of his time.'[15]

[15] Interview with Darcus Howe.

18

---◆---

'Well, he was worried about the uncontrolled immigration, and, of course, it clearly was a period when he was in favour of some sort of repatriation. It wasn't a concern of his for racist reasons, as such. But a concern just that the whole culture was changing. But, I mean, on one occasion, and this was before he made his 'Rivers of Blood' speech, I remember him saying, whether he was – not that he joked very much – but whether he was intending it as a joke or not. We were just sort of talking casually, and he said, "Do you know, Clem, there'll never be real peace and satisfaction in this country or anywhere in Europe until we're all coffee coloured." Well, I actually think he meant it quite genuinely. It was the only time he said that, but it was an odd remark.'[1]

'I'm sure there were a lot of British MPs at that stage who were beginning to see race as one of the possible populist themes that they could improve their popularity with. So I'm not surprised that he took it up. There were other people who were willing to take it up, too. But there's a particular venom about the images which Powell used, 'Piccaninnies' and of excrement through the letterboxes, and he found a language which was deeply repugnant, really, and which was full of these physical images which I thought was a particular sort of pitch. It was pitched at a particularly deep level, really. So, it's a specific populist appeal, to go over the heads of the liberal intellectuals and to speak to the people very direct. His imagery is adapted to that base level appeal, it's not intended to be thought about rationally or intellectually.'[2]

'I believe in plain talking, and Enoch Powell, without any question, said what he was thinking, that he was speaking for

[1] Interview with Clem Jones CBE. Clem Jones was editor of the *Wolverhampton Express* and *Star* during the time of Enoch Powell's 'Rivers of Blood' speech. He was also a friend of Powell's from the time of his arrival in Wolverhampton in 1959, sharing an interest in literary figures like A. E. Housman and George Borrow.

[2] Interview with Stuart Hall.

thousands of Englishmen. He was speaking for them, and if things like this come out where he said, "I don't like you because you are black", we know where we are. But don't mollycoddle me when you know exactly that you're thinking differently. And out of his speech, without any question, there were a lot of black people who came to the conclusion, say for us to live together in a multi-racial society, we ourselves must make a contribution. We have this contribution to make. You cannot expect to live in a community or in a society where you make no contribution at all, and I think at that time people begin to say, "Well, we are living here." I came to that conclusion a long time ago because I have stayed here a lot of years now. So, if we are living here, you have your contribution to make, and if you make the contribution towards that society, eventually, they will be compelled to accept.'[3]

Powellism And The Politics Of The Seventies

In 1965 the government brought in new legislation further restricting immigration, followed by legislation against discrimination in public places and the establishment of a Race Relations Board to police the 'conciliation' procedures it outlined. In the following year the spring election returned Labour with an increased majority. Smethwick was recaptured from the Conservatives, by the flamboyant former actor Andrew Faulds, who attacked the right wing's racist polemic head on, and after the election, declared, 'We've buried the race issue.' For a time, it seemed that Labour had driven a stake through the heart of the beast which had briefly stalked the corridors of Westminster. The then Home Secretary, Roy Jenkins, in the years following, tried to consolidate the emerging consensus by separating the issue of immigration from race relations. He started by floating the idea of extending the Race Relations Act to cover employment and housing, spelling out his ideal of a society based on 'mutual tolerance'. Reaction in the country was unenthusiastic. The CBI and the TUC got together at the beginning of 1967 to present Jenkins with a joint statement opposing any

[3] Interview with Rene Webb.

extension of the Act into employment. On the other hand, the public focus on the migrants had wavered. Suddenly there was a series of burning issues, all of which were to be argued out in Parliament, but which inspired an explosion of public interest and excitement. Many of them ended up in the law courts, becoming the subject of long-running debates in the media and on the streets.

The decade began with the trial of the publishers of D. H. Lawrence's novel *Lady Chatterley's Lover* for lewdness and obscenity, and ended with the trial under the same Act of the publishers of *Oz* magazine for the same offence. Another struggle was taking place over issues like abortion and the reform of the homosexuality laws. The agonising row over nuclear disarmament which had wracked the Labour Party only a few years previously was still rumbling on. The media were full of the amazing doings of the new pop stars, like the Beatles and the Rolling Stones. The creation of new universities had vastly expanded the number of students. Some of the large unions were increasingly out of touch with their rank and file, so localised disputes and wildcat strikes proliferated through the decade. Everywhere you looked the ground was shifting and, by this time, the presence of the migrants was relatively unremarkable. The consensus masterminded by Roy Jenkins had even succeeded in further marginalising the grassroots propaganda of the 'Keep Britain White' parties, along with their allies in Parliament, like Sir Gerald Nabarro and Duncan Sandys.

The event which broke the consensus was to do with the fact that a number of Kenyan Asians who held British passports were exempt from the provisions of the '65 Act, and were therefore entitled to enter Britain on a permanent basis. Early in 1967 the Wolverhampton MP, Enoch Powell, had begun writing to the newspapers protesting about the possibility that an unknown number of Kenyan Asians might decide to come to Britain. He had been a major contender for the leadership of the Conservatives against Edward Heath, and he was widely respected for his anti-European and free market attitudes, so his views were noted by the politicians and media. In February, Powell stepped up his efforts in a speech which accused the entire political culture of being remote from the concerns of ordinary people. 'You and I might as well be living in Central Africa for all they know about our circumstances,' he declared.[4]

The new Home Secretary, James Callaghan, apparently worried that the issue of the Kenyan Asians might disturb the political consensus on

---

[4] Speech given in Walsall, 9 February 1967. Cited in Nicholas Deakin, *Colour Citizenship and British Society* (Panther Books, 1970), p. 130.

immigration and race, introduced new legislation with embarrassing speed. The new Commonwealth Immigrants Act withdrew the right of entry of remaining Kenyan Asian holders of British passports; and, for the first time, distinguished between British citizens who were 'patrials', i.e. possessed identifiable ancestors within the British Isles, and those who were not. The Act was hotly contested in Parliament, since it was clear that patrials would be almost exclusively white, but it seemed to settle the issue, clearing the way for the introduction of a new Race Relations Bill which extended the scope of anti-discrimination law to the fields of employment and housing. The Bill was published in April, and in the same month Enoch Powell made his famous 'Rivers of Blood' speech, which drove a train through the difficult peace.

Powell listed a series of alleged complaints from his constituents, using case histories and letters which were actually part of a black propaganda campaign by the National Front. He talked about 'grinning piccaninnies', and climaxed his rhetorical flourishes with a quote from Ovid: 'Like the Romans, I seem to see "the River Tiber foaming with much blood."' In a popular culture still haunted by the memories of the Nottingham and Notting Hill riots his words were electric. In the ensuing uproar Edward Heath sacked Powell from the Opposition Front Bench. The next day a group of London dockers marched on Parliament in his support, followed by a number of similar marches throughout the Midlands and other provincial centres. The Race Relations Act was not passed until October but, by then, race and immigration were once again firmly tied together in the public mind. At the beginning of 1969, Edward Heath, who had until then attempted to preserve an all party consensus on the subject, began urging the government to halt all immigration. In the same year Powell's speeches became more demanding, winding up with the proposal of a Ministry for Repatriation, a step that no senior politician had, until then, even considered.

'When I first knew him, he was a young bachelor, more or less straight from the Army, though, of course, he'd been an academic and a professor and all the rest of it, but he had decided to go into politics, and he had been a researcher, until he got selected for a seat. After he was elected, he held a regular surgery in Wolverhampton on a Friday and Saturday. He always came up after Parliament had finished, midday, and he and I had a social meeting, if you like, over a cup of tea, in his offices, on the Friday afternoon. I went to sort of pick up on any parliamentary news, but a lot of time we spent discussing things like – he was interested in Borrow's connections with North Wales, because I'd lived in that part of the world, I was interested in Borrow's connection with mid-Wales, and had picked up on his connection in the Midlands.

'Another of our joint interests were the poems of A. E. Housman. Enoch was very, very much a Housman man, and his poems were very much modelled on A. E. Housman. He didn't know much about Housman's 'Shropshire Lad', he knew the poems, but he didn't necessarily know the places. Well, oddly enough, Housman wrote all his 'Shropshire Lad' poems before actually setting foot in Shropshire, from Worcester. And all the names he chose because they were nicely alliterative and fitted in to his poems. Well, Enoch and I used to go through these poems and identify the places concerned and, after a period, actually, we used to go out on picnics and pick them up. I got to know him very well indeed. I think I was probably the first person in Wolverhampton to whom he introduced Pam, whom he subsequently married. I mean, it was that kind of friendship. Subsequently, my wife and I and my children and their children got to know each other, as two normal families, very normal families.

'He was a very human man. He was always slightly stiff. He'd got his principles, he was deeply Christian and fairly High Church at that. I mean, for instance, he absolutely strictly obeyed Lent, he never touched any alcohol during Lent. And I think his first drink after Lent was usually a glass of sherry in my house, that sort of thing. But he went to communion, I would think, practically every Sunday of his life. He was that sort of person. He didn't exactly gel with a lot of his constituents, a lot of his upper constituents, they found him a little bit stiff, a little bit awkward. I don't think they made an effort to get to know him, certainly not in the way I got to know him. But he did have a great deal of respect. He was a brilliant constituency MP. In my profession, of course, I met a fair number of Members of Parliament, and there was not a single Member of Parliament I knew, of any Party, who was as conscientious a constituency MP as he was. And every either Easter or Whitsun, during the parliamentary recess, until he ceased to be a member for Wolverhampton, he used to come up to Wolverhampton and he'd get out the electoral roll, and during that year, he would knock on every constituent's door in the constituency. Mind you, it was a compact constituency. But he would say who he was, ask them if they'd got anything they wanted to say to him, good, bad or indifferent. But, he made a point of calling at the door of every constituent in the constituency, and he ran a brilliant surgery, and he really did watch the total interest of his constituents, I mean, much more than you could say for a lot of Members of Parliament.

'He had strong opinions on monetary policy. I mean, forget the one thing for which he does go down in history, he had a very considerable following at one stage. Lots of people felt that he had got his finger on the economic front. But he was very single minded on that. Well, he was single minded on everything. But he had a very humane side as well. And when he was Minister of Health, he was particularly kind towards people with mental disorders. And he did an awful lot of work and an awful lot of quiet reform on the mental side, which I don't think anybody hardly now recognises or gives him credit for. There are all sorts of things like that which unfortunately, I think, are buried in the mists of time.

'Inevitably, because of his close concern with his constituency, he knew exactly what was happening, right from the very start. And he had seen a whole number of his more elderly and less well off white constituents being very, very concerned about the way streets were turning one way, ethnic, and, in the end, he decided that he must make some sort of reference to it. His first public reference was when he made a speech in Walsall, in which he said, "And I have a constituent who's worried because his little daughter, in her primary school, is the only white child in the class." Well now, we tried, as the newspaper, to find that class and that child. Whether it was ethical or not, I don't know, but we checked on virtually every school in his constituency and we did not run that child to earth. And, at that particular time, the National Front were very, very strong, and they were running a myth factory in the area. They were inundating me with anonymous letters of one sort or another, abusive and that kind of thing, they were taking part in various things. I quizzed him afterwards about it and he would never admit to it, but I'm quite sure that one white child in the class business came from a letter to him from the National Front. I learned very, very early on not to fall for them. But he didn't.

'Anyway, he made that speech. It was reported by me, by our paper, I think the *Birmingham Mail* reported it, but it didn't have any sort of impact outside the area. But, as a result of that speech, he had bags and bags of supportive mail. And, he more or less indicated to me, that started his train of thinking, which led up, in about three weeks or a month, to the subsequent speech. I date that kind of realisation, something must be done, as far as he was concerned, to the reaction that he had from making that speech.

'I knew what was happening quite a long time before. Largely because of reader reaction. Largely, also, because of the National Front, either directly or National Front supporters, racist activity, which was very, very strong. There were little cells which used to meet regularly, usually in some of the working men's clubs, which were hotbeds of racism in those days, but there were so many, what one might call social factors. At that particular stage, local authority housing hadn't taken off very much. There were a few council house estates, but they hadn't yet got round to building tower blocks and that sort of thing. And the people who had worked, and they had worked hard, long hours during the war, running the iron and steel industry, and they'd made enough to buy their little one up, two down, one up, sort of houses, very few of them had bathrooms or any sort of indoor sanitation, but they bought these houses. And they represented their livelihood, their capital. I mean, taking a typical family – elderly couple, living in one of these houses, and the next door house falls empty, and is bought by somebody, and a whole number of ex-*Windrush* people move in, now, in themselves, they weren't doing anything wrong, but they lived a different type of life, an extrovert type of life, a noisy type of life, and, it upset these people. And they probably couldn't afford to move out. But, then somebody a little lower down the street either died or moved out, and another house went like that. And gradually, property values went to such a degree that none of the older inhabitants could get a reasonable price to move out to better accommodation, and they only moved out when there was enough local authority housing for them to move into. Nobody would buy a house next door to a West Indian family or an Asian family, if they could avoid it, and, indeed, though I'm sure it didn't colour Enoch's own attitude, his own house in the constituency, in what had been a very respectable road leading out of the centre of Wolverhampton, of good, solid, Victorian houses, next door went sort of coloured, and then another house, and he saw the value of his own house go down.

'The silly part about it, he was never a racist. Even after his "Rivers of Blood" speech, I do know that he worked very, very hard as a constituent MP, for any constituent, whatever colour, whatever race, who came to him with a problem. There was no trouble at all. We quite often used to go out for a meal, as a family, to a couple of Indian restaurants, and he was on extremely amiable terms with everybody there, 'cos having been in India, and his wife having been brought up in India, they liked that kind of food. But there was never the slightest suggestion, and I must admit, I was surprised, in that sense, at his speech.

'Two or three days before he made that speech, we were talking together in my dining room, and I think I said, casually, "Well, what have you got coming up, Enoch?" And he said, "I'm going to make a speech at the weekend, and you know how a rocket goes up, breaks up in the air and falls down, well, this speech I'm going to make is going to go up like a rocket, but when it gets up to the top, it's going to stay up." I said, "What's the speech about?" He said, "I'm not telling you. You'll get an advance copy in the fullness of time." Now, I didn't think that that was going to be the subject of his speech. I thought it might be something to do with mental health. But I never, until I actually knew, never for one moment dreamed that was what he was going to do. But, of course, he was very astute.

'It's common knowledge now, but that speech never went through Central Office. The advance copies of the speech were distributed personally to a few people. It was impeccably timed. And this'll show you, in a way, the level of friendship that existed between us. Some months, quite a good time before he made that speech, he said to me, "Look, Clem, I'm not satisfied with the way my speeches are handled by Central Office, how can I maximise my newspaper coverage? Not necessarily with you, but nationally." So we sat down, and I gave him an impromptu lecture on PR – I mean, it's long before spin doctors – on PR business, on how to time, particularly on missing the Saturday afternoon sporting papers, hitting the six o'clock news, then the ten o'clock news, and then being in time for all the Sunday papers and then picking up on the Sunday papers on the Monday morning, all that sort of thing, which he did, and all the necessary points about making contacts, and all that sort of thing. I said to him, because I knew, from having handled a lot of his speeches, I said, "Your speeches are very good, Enoch, but the real gist of them, the real guts to them, are usually buried somewhere in the middle, towards the end. And journalists," I said, "are a lazy lot of so-and-sos, and half of them won't read down there. What you want to do is not only send us the full speech but also to put an aide-mémoire on the front, picking out three or four good points and indicating the pages in the speech in which they come. And you'll find that people will pick up on those. They'll probably ignore the rest of the speech, but you'll get the maximum publicity." And he did that immediately and did get very, very good results. I never charged him a fee or anything like that, I did that as an act of friendship. But he was a very good pupil. He had a wonderful turn of phrase for headline writing, if you could find it. But it really meant sitting down and reading through perhaps ten, fifteen, twenty pages of duplicated matter in order to find the good bits. But he knew which were going to be the good bits and he put the good bits in alright.

'He carefully timed the release, and it was made, I think, about three o'clock in the afternoon and, of course, being the evening paper, we had it perhaps the morning before. So, I didn't know what was going to be in the speech until around about the morning of the day he made it. But it was no use to us, of course, because our evening edition was out before the embargo was broken. But, after that, we had to decide what we were going to do. Then, of course, the Heath dismissal came. Despair, despair. Actually, he and his wife came, having made the speech, to collect their two little girls, and I must admit, I funked going to the door on that occasion. My wife went to the door, but Enoch said to her, "Well, I suppose it's the end of a good friendship now, isn't it?" And she said, "Yes, it is." Handed over the two little girls and that was it.

'The reference to the little old lady being the only person in her street, having excrement put through her letterbox, whenever she went out being surrounded by – this was a phrase which both my wife and I found particularly offensive – being surrounded by grinning piccaninnies who shouted abuse at her. That was just too much. We, my own paper, we got out all the electoral rolls for his constituency, we marked off every street in which it was likely to be, and members of my staff went up and down the streets. We never identified this lady. I know other newspapers did exactly the same, she was never, ever, ever found. Now, you can't tell me that the united efforts of the newspaper industry wouldn't have located her had she been in existence, in a relatively small area, twenty streets, perhaps, at the outside. Just the same way, of course, over the "one white child". We listed all the primary schools in the area, staff went and not only spoke to the head teachers but spoke to other members of the staff to see – and none of them said that this could ever have happened in their school.

'I think there was a certain merit in warning and in drawing attention to the problems. It was, as far as I was concerned, and as far as my paper was concerned, it was basically the language and the manner in which it was done. Because, as far as I was concerned,

I think, unintentionally, he overstepped the boundaries between an objective view of immigration and the problems of immigration and what should be done about it, and the emotive one. And by bringing in the emotive side, he did, for the time being, bring in racism. I don't think necessarily from his heart, but, I mean, he did.

'I discussed with my chairman the way we were going to handle it. Fortunately, we agreed on the line that it was an emotive speech, that wrong language was done and a lot of harm was going to be done as a result of it. Then there was the Heath dismissal. Now, that altered the whole set of circumstances. I don't know quite what he could have done otherwise, but if he hadn't done that, and hadn't thereby made a martyr out of Enoch Powell, I think the whole thing would have simmered and boiled down. But Enoch was made a martyr and, as far as our circulation area was concerned, virtually the whole area was determined to make a saint out of him. He was a martyr, irrespective of the nature of the speech, et cetera. Lots of people who would never have thought about the matter, and who certainly couldn't, under any circumstances, be considered racist, felt so strongly about that, that they came out whole heartedly in support of Enoch. Well, now, from the Tuesday to the end of the week, every day, I had, I suppose, ten, fifteen or twenty mail bags full of readers' letters. And a week or two afterwards, I was talking to the head postmaster, and he said to me, "You know, Clem," he said, "you didn't half get us into trouble." He said, "That week, we had to put so much staff and so much effort into dealing with your mail that we had to delay a lot of the mail to some of the most important business enterprises in Wolverhampton." And he said, "I had no end of complaints from managing directors and chairmen and that sort of thing, that we had delayed their mail." That was it.

'As a newspaper, we even had to take staff off advertising canvassing, which, you can imagine, meant quite a bit, in order to sort that mail. We gave over a couple of pages to readers' letters. I only used letters that I was one hundred per cent sure of where they came from. The proportion was, I suppose, ninety to ninety-five per cent pro-Enoch. We had to scrape, every day, to try and find a few balancing letters, some of the letters that I had were pretty abusive of me, containing excrement and that sort of thing, half a dozen sheets of used toilet paper. I had people ringing me at home, all sorts of hours, and saying, "Oh, is that the bloody nigger lover?" Just like that. But that was inspired sort of stuff. I had a couple of windows broken at home, and a lot of abusive telephone calls. I mean, it was a horrible week as far as I was concerned. I suffered, I think, as much as anybody, but there you are. This, I think, puts it rather in balance. On the Monday following, I went along to the Rotary Club and I was sitting next to a very dear friend of mine, a very, very staunch Christian, non-conformist, a man of very considerable integrity himself. And he said to me, "You know, I never thought about this, but if Enoch has said what he has said, it must be right." Just like that. And that encapsulates what a lot of people in that area did and felt. I can't speak, obviously, about areas outside, and the reaction outside, there are a number of people, of course, who totally agreed, but there were a number of people who felt that he had been wrongly dismissed, and a number of people who felt that here was a man of such considerable integrity and such considerable mental ability, that if he said something like that, it was like gospel, it must be right.

'For a long time, he would never admit it, but he knew it had dished him. I do know that he has half implied to one or two people that he thinks it was a mistake in the way he did it, at the time he did it, but that it had to be done. And I think, if he had his time over again, there were certain aspects of that speech that he wouldn't have made. He would probably have kept the "Rivers of Blood", because, being a classicist, he couldn't resist that. But that went up over the heads of most people anyway. But the rather more emotive stuff, I'm quite sure that he would not have put that in again. It had a blood letting effect at the time. Blood letting's never very pleasant, is it? But, I think it probably brought the problems more to the notice of people. And I think, deep down, it probably led to, ultimately, to the formation of things like the Community Relations Council, and strengthened the Runnymede Trust. And I think it made people realise that here was a social problem, not something that could be brushed under the carpet, but here was an open social problem, which, for better or for worse, had got to be tackled. And, indeed, half heartedly, perhaps, perhaps not half hearted, was tackled, I think, to quite good effect as a result of the speech.

'There was an aspect of Enoch's character which sometimes I found frustrating, sometimes I found endearing. It was that never admit you've made a mistake, never correct yourself, which was followed by, never apologise. But he very firmly would never, ever admit to having been wrong. And there are two particular, very personal occasions when I do know he was wrong but he wouldn't admit to it. On one occasion, we were on a family picnic, going out into Shropshire along the A5, and we crossed over the River Severn at a place called Atcham, on a newish bridge over the Severn. But a little way down river, there was the old pack horse bridge, the old arch bridge. And Enoch said, he was driving, he said, "Doesn't Telford's bridge look lovely in the sun." And it did. There were swans and that sort of thing. And my wife chipped in and said, "Well, look, Enoch, Telford didn't build that bridge." "He did," he said. "No, he didn't." And she named the person who did. He would not accept that. And she said, "Well, look, if you stop the car, and if we walk back, on the other side of the bridge there's a metal medallion which says by whom the bridge was built." He not merely wouldn't stop the car but he pressed down on the accelerator and drove along a good deal faster.

'There was another occasion, again, on a family picnic, we were up on the top of a range of hills on the Shropshire-Montgomeryshire border, called the Britherns, and looking out towards the hills of Wales. And it was a beautifully clear day. And Enoch, again, volunteered the remark and he said, "Doesn't the Caderidis group look lovely?" And I, foolishly – I could have just said, Yes – foolishly said, "That's not the Caderidis group, Enoch, that's the Burwins." "It's not ... it's the Caderidis group." "No, it's not the Caderidis group," I said. "The Caderidis group is so many points to the west." I know the Caderidis group because, as a boy, I climbed those hills, dozens of times actually, and I know the configuration. "No, it's not," he said. I said, "Alright, well, take a bearing, and when we get back, I've got all the one inch maps of the area, and we'll put them out on the floor and I'll show you." And I took a bearing, and when we got back I produced the maps, and I was about to put them on the floor and spread them out, and, "No, don't bother," he said. "Don't bother." And he wouldn't accept that fact. Those are two foibles, if you like, but that was part of his character, refusing to accept correction. Actually, I did discover that, at a later date, next time he was driving to Shropshire past Atcham, he did stop the car and he did walk down the River Severn bank and he did look at the bridge, and he must have read the medallion on the back and saw who had constructed it. I mean, it's a silly business, but there you are.'[5]

⁵ Interview with Clem Jones.

Powell's influence was to have enormous and continuing effects. The Labour Government was defeated in 1970. Although the effect of race and immigration was not sharply discernible as an issue, Powellism had distracted, discredited and intimidated the government to the point where it had lost confidence. Many of its traditional supporters abstained, and in the key Midlands constituencies a significant proportion switched their allegiance to the Conservatives. The new government brought further immigration legislation as Heath had promised during the campaign, including the 1971 Act.

Powellism had brought the sixties to an end in a furore of nationalist feeling, but, paradoxically, the patterns of citizenship which emerged as a result of the process he set in motion were the very opposite of the traditional outline he had tried to restore. Instead, he had been instrumental in clearing the ground for a new and developing definition of what it meant to be a citizen of the British Isles. At the opening of the decade British citizenship still applied to a large part of the globe. Decolonisation had already drawn one set of parameters which narrowed down the definition. Immigration legislation provided another network of boundaries. In the following years, race relations law was to refine the concept further.

Powellism was disturbing, alarming and dangerous for the Caribbean migrants, but it also stimulated us in a way nothing else had done for two decades. After Powell, the different Caribbean communities had been completely racialised and radicalised, welded together into a single black community by the heat of the political passions he ignited. Powellism also brought into being and hardened an anti-racist coalition among liberals and the left of British politics, focusing it around the contention that the black people in Britain were entitled to the full rights of citizenship. From 1968 the consensus among black people began to be that we were in Britain to stay, and that we would respond to the threat he posed by a greater, more positive involvement with the political and social environment.

19

'There were times I felt as though I was in the pits, or trying to get out and as soon as I get my fingers up on the ledge, somebody would trample on them. Yes, it was that kind of feeling. It is never a feeling that your ability, your contribution, and so forth, will always be recognised. You have to be cheeky, you have to put them up front yourself, you have to, if you like, endure all the problems which are going to come your way, otherwise you're finished. There are many of my colleagues who just gave up after a few months in the profession, it's just so bad for them. And sometimes you can't really blame them, because why should they suffer that kind of indignity, neglect, when their other colleagues in the system didn't have to do that? Those black teachers who came into the system and experienced exactly the kind of things which I'm talking about, would say, "Better off driving the buses. I don't have this kind of problem." So a lot of bus drivers in my time, who were people with qualifications equal to mine, found it less stressful, more humane and more self-respecting to put their energy into bus conducting or bus driving in the London area, than to put up with the kind of things that I had to put up with as a black teacher. I would look any black person in the eye and tell him or her that he's lying or she's lying, if they tell me that they have not had to put up, as a teacher, with this racism at its heights. That would be just total falsehood.'[1]

[1] Interview with Carlton Duncan. Carlton Duncan arrived from Jamaica in 1961. He had to repeat his school qualifications while working in the evenings as a dancer before gaining the grades he needed for university entrance. After seven years' experience he was appointed deputy head of a school in Coventry. He was subsequently appointed to the Rampton Committee, later the Swann Committee, which had been commissioned to prepare a report for the Department of Education and Science on the situation of migrant children in the education system. He was appointed to his first headship in Bradford and is now head of a grant maintained school in Birmingham.

Vehicle To Progress
1970–75

Caribbean migrants became black people during the decade of the sixties, and by the end of the seventies we had begun to share the same assumptions about our national status as our white compatriots. That is to say, we became black Britons. This was a fundamental change, driven by the generations who had arrived as children, or had been born in Britain. In later years it became conventional wisdom to describe this as a kind of generation gap, as if the experience had effected a complete separation between older and younger migrants in their understanding of British society and their response to their environment.

This was part of a racialised context in which the history of Caribbean migration increasingly began to be discussed. One formula which was touted with increasing frequency was the notion that the generations of migrants who arrived as adults had somehow 'accepted' their role and status in Britain, in contrast to their children whose behaviour throughout the seventies was symbolic of their 'rebellion'. It was a simple and seductive idea which implied that the black Caribbeans were, by nature, able to adapt without complaint to the treatment they received, in contrast to their children, who had become more like whites and therefore humanised by growing up in Britain. As an explanation of what had been going on it compartmentalised the social and political processes going on in the country, and transformed the external conditions that the migrants faced into a function of their collective personality. In the more liberal atmosphere of the seventies, this account shifted blame to the migrants, and expunged at a stroke the guilt which lingered over the blatant racism of previous years. It also cleared the way for the argument that the problems this generation of migrants faced were not due to the racist framework in which they lived, but were concerned with their own peculiar response to the environment.

This was an argument which had its most crucial consequences within the education system. It was the one experience which Caribbean parents could not share with their British children. Their instinct was to trust the system, and to assume its goodwill. In the circumstances it was a reasonable reaction. Their own education, after all, had been 'British' and, even after the first flush of Powellism, Caribbean migrants had not begun to explain all their relationships in racial terms, and few of us yet appreciated the extent to which the response of all the institutions we encountered were conditioned by skin colour.[2]

On the other hand, it soon became obvious that Caribbean parents' expectations did not match what was happening in the school system. Right from the beginning, for instance, once white teachers became aware of what migrant parents' hopes were for their children, the terms they tended to use were 'unrealistic' or 'over ambitious'. British education had only recently emerged from a long period in which children were rigidly separated into different levels of ability, and, by and large, ability tended to coincide with social class. A group of manual workers who talked grandly about their children becoming white collar professionals induced incredulity and sometimes indignation. The school experience began as a trauma for the majority of black school children and went on to be a rallying point and a radicalising issue for their parents. Throughout the seventies the anxiety of black parents expressed itself in the organisation of such bodies as the Black Parents' Movement and the 'supplementary schools', which operated at weekends and in the evenings. This was the first expression of a political impulse which created a consensus within the black Caribbean community as a whole. The movement planted the seeds of a new mood which, at the end of the decade, would begin to unite the original migrants with their children around a network of new issues and problems.

'And we, coming from the Caribbean, see and saw that education was the vehicle to progress. That's how we thought it was. So, education became very, very focal in our thinking, and, of course, the whole question of ESN[3] children, children being put into dumb houses, dumb schools, you know. And parents thought, at that period, that if their child is going to a Special School, then they're going to a good school, because in the Caribbean, where we say "special", we mean "good". But then we realised it wasn't so. And it was at that period that all that took place – late sixties and very early seventies – when a group of us came together and organised a group called Caribbean Education and Community Workers' Association; CECWA, it was known. It was through CECWA that we brought out the book by Bernard Coard called *How the West Indian Child is Made Educationally Sub-Normal in the British School*

[2] A truism of sociological research in race relations has been that a large proportion of black people, when interviewed about racial discrimination, deny ever having been discriminated against, even where it can be clearly demonstrated that they have been the subject of it.

[3] Educationally Sub-Normal.

System.[4] And the focal issue was that we must start doing what we did at home, that is, teaching the children after school hours. So, many of our homes, including our home, was used to help children after school. 'Cos I had my own children. And then, what we did here in Ealing was to have taken down a group of children to the West Indian Student Centre, as we had a lot of people who were teaching them – they didn't necessarily have to be teachers – but we start talking to them about Caribbean history, about African history, you know. And that is how the whole supplementary school movement was born out of that period. So, a lot of what the Labour Government is doing now with after-school classes, we did it in the sixties. All the basic attitudes to education, going back to basics, we've never left it.'[5]

'And he said, when the teacher asks the question and he puts his hand up, she always ignored him. Now, Chauncy wanted to do medicine, and he's very good in the sciences. He did very well in his science subjects, you know. But every time he put his hand up, she ignored him. So he just couldn't be bothered. And he was encouraged into sports. He was a good footballer. And that's where they were leading him. Even as recent as my third child, Accabre, the girl, going to school here, in Ealing, in the Borough of Ealing. What is surprising is that, by that time, we were doing so much in the borough, so much around the country. You know, we had a book shop, we were publishing, we were activists. We were here, there and everywhere. And we went to all the parents' meetings and talked to the teachers, and they were very friendly and whatever. But they were telling us that Accabre can't do her O-Levels. So you could imagine those parents who were intimidated by teachers, and we had to work on Accabre, too. We had to say, you're going to take your O-Levels, and we were determined about it, even if she had to fail her O-Levels rather than taking the CSE. So we had that experience, and when we held our first summer project in Shepherd's

---

[4] Bernard Coard arrived in the seventies as a post-graduate student from Grenada. His book, *How the West Indian Child is Made Educationally Sub-Normal in the British School System*, was written while he was a teacher at a Special School in Wimbledon. It was part of a programme of research he had undertaken for his doctorate. Subsequently he returned to the Caribbean. He was a leader of the Marxist New Jewel movement, which took over the government in Grenada. He later led a coup which deposed and executed the movement's leader Maurice Bishop. Coard was arrested and sentenced to death after American troops invaded Grenada.

[5] Interview with Eric Huntley.

Bush, most people who were there at that time were not only parents but teachers themselves, who were conscious and aware of what was happening in the State school. So out of that summer project, in the late sixties, the whole supplementary school movement just blossomed.

'I remember going up to Leeds, and I had a school there, and they used to have hundreds of children there on Saturday mornings, and it still goes on today, up and down Britain, because of parents' dissatisfaction with the educational system. Everybody gave. Nobody was spared. It's a different thing now, because local authorities have come in and have more or less taken over a lot of it, and they pay the teachers. But in the early period, it was us.'[6]

The Headmaster's Story

'When you come into the system, and you look at the tools you are using, to take the National Curriculum itself, this is the main business of any school. The stories that you are transmitting to youngsters by this great tool is telling youngsters that everything which is important and of value is white and European, and the negatives which are found in the curriculum for black youngsters are quite appalling, then you begin to appreciate why black youngsters are often turned off in the system. I have youngsters joining the school that I'm head of now, directly out of Jamaica, and trying to place them at the level which was suggested by their age, I find that very nearly always they're far more advanced in their knowledge and capabilities than youngsters round about their same age groups. Not in all cases, but that was my experience, too. There were no problems for me, because I'd done the work, and, in fact, what I was finding was that it was far easier to cope. And that has been the picture, that the levels of education on the National Curriculum at the moment are set at the standards below that required by youngsters in the part of the Caribbean where I came from. But it's hard to be motivated if you're sitting in a room and reading a book which tells you that people from Africa are savages and backward races, and so forth. It's hard for that kind of thing to switch you on. In addition to that reality, born of experience in the classroom, we had, in the sixties and early seventies, a considerable amount of noise being made by

[6] Interview with Jessica Huntley.

the black communities, who were, at that stage, realising that many of their youngsters were in Special Schools, as they were called then, meaning schools for the education of the sub-normal. And parents were making a lot of noise about it, and meetings on the development and the birth of the supplementary schools which were being held in people's homes on a Saturday morning or Sunday mornings, were focusing minds, certainly mine, on the issue, especially since I was now part of that profession which was quite rightly being accused of creating these difficulties and problems for black youngsters.

'In those days they didn't have the GCSE, what they had was CSEs and O-Levels (GCEs) running together. The GCE O-Level at that time was the quality certificate to have, whereas the CSEs, as they were called, were really second-class stuff. Black people found that their children were largely taking CSEs. If they weren't taking CSEs they were overwhelmingly to be found in special needs schools, Special Schools, schools for the educationally sub-normal. And if they weren't in those categories then they were disproportionately being excluded from schools. They were called "suspension" in those days.

'When I applied for my second post I was called for interview and, on arrival at the school, we were asked to come and look at the school in the morning, and the interviews would take place at the Brent Town Hall in the afternoon. And there were five of us. I was the only black one. But I felt hopeful, because the school was essentially a truly multi-racial school, a lot of black faces, unlike Pimlico, where I would have been leaving. And although there weren't any black faces on the staff, certainly the presence of a black school population was a great deal more comforting than what I would have been leaving behind. But the first shock was when we, all five us, gathered in the head teacher's office, just to talk about what the job consisted of. And the head teacher said, "I don't know why you all want to come and work here anyway. Did you notice the school is full of niggers?" The shock. "And they're pure problems, and they're noisy." Comments like that he was making. I don't know whether that is why, when we arrived at the town hall on that afternoon for the interviews, there were only two of us. Three people disappeared. Whether it's the fact that the school is full of niggers, or they were disgusted at the remark made by the head teacher, three of them dropped out on the spot. So only two people were interviewed for that job on that afternoon. During my interview, the head teacher himself asked me a pointed question. "Mr Duncan, what if you were taking a class and a parent turned up and said, 'I didn't want my son to be taught by a nigger', what would you say? What would you do?" "As you know, I've been teaching only two years, Mr Peddler," I said, "but during the course of that two years, I've never come across that experience. But, I'll tell you what, if it happened now, I'd come and find you," I said. And the panel laughed. It wasn't offered to me anyway, 'cos the job was offered to the other chap. But he said he wanted time to think about it and, before I left the building, he had already changed his mind and said he didn't want the job. So they had no option but to offer it to me.

'But racist though Mr Peddler was, in his statements and attitude, he called me into his office and he says, "Whatever becomes of this department, it will be you, 'cos I won't block anything." And he never did. And within two years that department had gone from one and a half staff – meaning myself and half of somebody else – to eleven members of staff. I got my next promotion in that school, because Mr Peddler kept on making all these racist comments and they promoted him upstairs. They took him out of the school and gave him a job in the office as an advisor. The newspapers had got hold of some of his comments and had made quite a splash. This was a particular one a newspaper got: he would go into assembly in the morning and he said he'd received a complaint about somebody who had been smoking behind the school, or something. He wants all the Caucasians to leave, all the Asians should go, all he wants is the niggers to stay behind. And the newspaper got hold of that, it was all over, so they promoted him upstairs. He died within two weeks of going, he had a heart attack. He cried like a baby when he had to leave the school. It was difficult for him.'[7]

'Well, initially I tried, but what I find out – and it was so direct and in your face, I discovered, for some unknown reason – because the whole syllabus was based on the same syllabus, they felt, well, coming from Jamaica, my standard of education was well below theirs. So, you started off with people actually setting you tests that they're showing you how to count, and things like that. So, trying to get into the school system was very, very off-putting, but, tentatively, as far as I'm concerned the whole system then was well below the

[7] Interview with Carlton Duncan.

standard of Jamaica. You know, Jamaica, from where I was, the primary to secondary was far in advance. So, to be honest I was wasting my time because, basically, they weren't prepared to just accept me as a bright boy. They couldn't see me, probably. I don't want to hit this coloured thing too much, but at that time they couldn't see me as a young black kid coming from Jamaica with the standard of education that they feel would require me to be an equal parallel, you know. So, I had major difficulties then and, at fifteen, there wasn't much time left in school. So, in the end, I haven't done any formal education in this country because there were hidden agendas, and I feel that agenda was played on me. As soon as I could I got out, because they didn't expect me to be able to do the things that they were doing here, just coming from Jamaica. Because they are seeing me coming into their school system very, very late, and they have this preconceived idea about, probably, people coming from Jamaica weren't up to scratch as far as their education standard goes. But I honestly do believe that the primary standard of education in Jamaica was far, far ahead of this country. So I didn't spend much time in school because they didn't give me the opportunity to pick it up at the standard that I expected to be at. The stuff that they were giving me was stuff that I did in Jamaica when I was probably eleven. I didn't want to be a part of that, so I move on.'[8]

'I remember, just before I had left school, we'd begun to demand Black Studies, and all that. And, in fact, at my school – Tulse Hill Secondary Comprehensive School – we did start a Black Studies course there. I don't know if it became a big thing nationally, but certainly at Tulse Hill School there was a strong feeling that the educational system were failing a lot of young blacks; that teachers in some inner city areas didn't see their role as a challenge to educate a group of black people, but of disciplining them and keeping them under control. That was their priority. "How am I going to keep this noisy set of black kids under control?" Not, "This is the challenge, how can I get across to them? How can I teach them? How can I educate them? How can I get them to learn something?" And the school system was failing black youths in a very bad way. Another

[8]   Interview with Michael Nesbeth. Michael Nesbeth came from Jamaica at the age of fifteen. A well-known keyboard player, he performed with Matumbi and Dennis Bovell. He is the older brother of the boxer Frank Bruno.

problem was the disproportionate amount of black students who were being suspended from school and expelled from school. It was precisely because of those things why the Black Parents' Movement was formed, to combat that, to fight and agitate against that and to demand, as taxpayers and rate payers, decent education for our children.[9]

'The Black Parents' Movement was an organisation based in north London, of West Indian parents who were concerned about what was happening with blacks in the educational system. We campaigned for parents and pupil power, within the educational system. We said that we were tax payers and rate payers, and demanded to have our voices heard. It was an irony that the Tories decided to promote people power some ten years afterwards, but it wasn't that kind of people power we were talking about.'[10]

[9] The Black Parents' Movement was born out of a racial incident involving a youth called Cliff McDaniel.

[10] Interview with Linton Kwesi Johnson. Linton Kwesi Johnson is the acknowledged poet of the seventies generation of black British youth. His first book of poems, *Dread, Beat and Blood*, became a bestseller in Britain and was widely read internationally. The phrase 'dub poetry' was coined to describe his performances of his work. During the marches and riots of the early eighties it was his voice and his performances which came to represent the style and the emotions of black British youth.

20

'I started work at King's Cross as a clerk in the civil engineers department and joined the transport salaried staff association. Then I started with international telephones which was then the Post Office, and I and three others engineered a strike at the Garrick Telephone Exchange in Judd Street and we led the strike, because the conditions were terrible. As a result of this successful strike I was asked to stay on as the exchange representative for the telephonists. Then I attended union conferences, went to the TUC college, did a number of trade union courses, and from that I progressed and became the chair of the branch and then later a full time official for the National Union of Public Employees. My colour didn't matter at all, a lot of the workers were black, or from various foreign countries, because you spoke a number of languages in the Post Office. So you had French-speaking people from Mauritius and so on, so that it wasn't a problem in the area that I worked. Our General Secretary was very much against racism and we were quite vocal at that time and the union was quite vocal. And one of the reasons for that, of course, was the fact that there were large numbers of black and other minority groups in the ranks of the union of Post Office workers, and in a number of post offices, there were black people who were shop stewards and district officials of one sort or another. There were some branches, notably in Chapel Street in Islington, where the National Front had taken control. We organised against that and, as a result, we were able to help to defeat the National Front, not only within the trade union movement, but in the country as a whole.

'Locally in Haringey we had a campaign against the National Front and against racists generally. We set up an organisation called the Haringey Labour Movement Anti-Racist and Anti-Fascist Committee. It was one of the longest names of any organisation that I have been involved in. We defeated the National Front. They tried to march through Haringey and we organised people in the trade union movement. We organised with the board of deputies, we organised amongst the community, and we drove them out. When that was finished and it was quite clear that the National Front were no longer an electoral threat, then people asked me if I would get involved with the local authority, because the question of institutionalised racism was even more pernicious than the overt racism of the National Front. So there was a job to do, because housing departments were discriminating, people were being discriminated against in the education system, and so on. So the big battle then was against institutionalised racism from the institutions in Britain. So we had to get involved in that and I was fortunate to be elected as a local authority councillor at that time.'[1]

The Politics Of Entry

1970–80

The years which led up the mid-seventies were probably the real end of the post-war period. Throughout those years the country finally gave up its imperialistic pretensions and began to see itself as a middle-sized European state. But the transition was accompanied by the greatest period of turmoil and uncertainty the country had yet encountered. It was marked by a savage battle between government and unions, which started when Ted Heath, the then Prime Minister, brought in an Industrial Relations Bill which set out a new legal framework for the structure of industrial relations. Before the government was forced into an election in February 1974 there was a miners' strike, a war in the Middle East which caused a dramatic rise in oil prices, and a succession of increasingly militant strikes and labour disputes. 'Who rules Britain?' and 'Is Britain governable?' became popular headlines for the political experts and journalists. In Northern Ireland the situation deteriorated and the first British soldier was killed. In 1973, in an attempt to save electricity, the government announced a three-day working week. This was the last straw. The following election returned Labour with the largest number of seats in Parliament, but without an effective majority. Another election was called within a few months, but the poll in October only gave the Labour Government a majority of three seats.

[1] Interview with Bernie Grant. Bernie Grant came to Britain from Guyana. He studied engineering at Heriot Watt University in Edinburgh. Subsequently, he worked for the Post Office and became a full time official of NUPE, the National Union of Public Employees. He was elected as a councillor in Haringey and became the leader of the council. He was elected MP for Haringey in 1987.

The years leading up to the end of the decade were marked by political instability.

Within this period of turmoil what was happening within and around the black community went, more or less, unnoticed. But the breakdown of stable industrial relationships, together with the frequency and intensity of battles in the workplace, created a whirlpool of political activity which pulled in a number of younger black immigrants. On a wider front, the extended period of strife and the repeated election campaigns had thrown up a number of small parties and groupings on the political left of Labour. They were often focused on conditions like housing and poverty. They brought a new militancy to these social issues and, in the new atmosphere after Powell, white activists began to take up the issues which affected black people.

Following Powell, also, the issue of uncontrolled immigration had been wrested away from the National Front by the major parties. The 'Keep Britain White' activists had therefore lost their thin veneer of political rationality and become racist street fighters, their policy reduced to mounting provocative demonstrations and assaulting immigrants and their property. Their activities provided yet another radicalising strand which began to draw black people into a new relationship with the politics of their environment. As the decade wore on the politics of young people and students increasingly focused around 'anti-racism'. At the beginning, this largely consisted of opposing the National Front on the streets, and spawned movements like the Anti Nazi League and Rock Against Racism. These were periodically popular among young people, although, for many, participation in anti-racist demonstrations became a matter of fashion, or an excuse for a punch-up with their opposite numbers in the NF. On the other hand, the battle between the two factions also focused attention on the role and status of the immigrant communities in Britain and, for the first time, engaged the loyalties of young white people.

The great climax of the street fighting years was the anti-racist demonstration against the National Front in 1977, comprising a march through Lewisham, south London. It ended in spectacular and well-photographed violence, became a cause célèbre and resulted in a number of court cases. The press bemoaned the street mayhem which had become a characteristic feature of anti-racist politics but, from that point, it was clear that something fundamental had changed. Whites fought whites viciously in defence of blacks. Families split, and the racists who had ruled the street corners only a decade previously were challenged and harassed everywhere they appeared. Britain was still riddled with racist values, but it was now obvious that the migrants no longer existed on the margins. Instead, black people had become part of the moral and social landscape in which young Britons grew up.

Black involvement in all these matters was inevitable and created a kind of chain reaction. The effect of the political turmoil on the immigrants' prospects can be deduced from the fact that the black people who, later on, became part of the British political landscape, began their careers during this period, through the trade unions, local government or through the new politics of community.

'I was the Liberal candidate for Deptford in both the 1974 elections, with John Silkin and a man called Hugh Cross as the Labour and Conservative candidates, and the three of us fought the February election. But in the October '74 election there was a Nazi. I think it was then called the National Front, but he was a man called Richard Edmonds who's still around, and he was the National Front candidate in October '74. Regrettably, he got something like seventeen hundred votes in that election. So that was rather distressing. And 1966, in Deptford, in the same constituency, there was also a Nazi of some description, a British National Party candidate who got getting on for nineteen hundred votes. So there has always been that element in our borough. All through the seventies there were outbursts of it. Then, of course, in August 1977 we'd heard that there was going to be a National Front march or meeting of some kind in New Cross, so ALCARAF,[2] which was an anti-racist, anti-Fascist body, organised a peaceful march in protest against what was going to happen later on in the afternoon on that Saturday. A lot of people came from other parts of London to join those of us from Lewisham. The march was led by the then Mayor of Lewisham who's now a Birmingham MP, Richard Godsip; a close friend of mine, Peter Hain, who is now an MP and a junior minister came; and Lord Avebury, formerly Eric Lubbock, he was on the march. And so we showed our hostility to the National Front in this major way. We were then stopped by the police just on the other side of the centre of Lewisham because they knew that further up the hill, about a mile away, the National Front were gathering. Many of us dispersed and went home, but I hear later on that there'd been a bit of a battle at Clifton Rise between the police and those more vigorous opponents of these Nazis.'[3]

[2] All Lewisham Campaign Against Racism And Fascism.

[3] Interview with Mike Steele. Mike Steele was Liberal Party candidate in the 1974 General Election. He established the Ladywell Action Centre in Lewisham in 1969. Formerly a member of the Police/

* * *

'I remember the mid-seventies were particularly bad in Eltham,[4] and it may have been due to things like perceived black involvement in street crime, and stuff like that. That may have had a deciding factor, I don't know. It certainly was the seventies, for the first time you started hearing that sort of view expressed all over the place. In fact, it became the predominant subject of conversation. '76, '77, race was the one thing that everyone was arguing about, everywhere you went. Obviously, I was aware, as many people were aware, that the Anti-Nazi League was an umbrella organisation, just as Rock Against Racism was an umbrella organisation for the IS,[5] and its principle purpose was to draw people in and recruit them. When I was in the IS, most of the activity was based around Anti-Nazi League, and stuff like that. I certainly remember going up to Leicester with a docker called Eddie Preverstone, us tearing down a load of NF posters on the wall, not realising that the headquarters was over the road. And, all of a sudden, there was Tyndall[6] and about ten of his honour guard chasing us down the road. Lucky the car started. And obviously there was the Lewisham riots of '77. I was at that. A nice brick on the head I had then. There was a National Front march from Deptford, certainly through Lewisham, and we all assembled to stop them. I remember it was pretty hot. I remember standing there, we're being held back by the police, and they marched past us at one stage – this is before you got into Lewisham properly – and we effectively stopped the march. But I remember the police chased us up Belmont Hill, and all I could hear in my head was The Clash, 'White Riot', that was the soundtrack as it was all happening. It was very bloody. There was a lot of ammonia confiscated off a lot of kids.

'I had relatives by marriage on the other side of the march, as well, so it was a real family at war thing for us. One of my relatives by marriage was an organiser for the Young National Front, and it did make for some very uncomfortable times. I particularly remember

---

Immigrant Sub Committee on the Lewisham Council, he has been a lobby correspondent for several newspapers and still works at the House of Commons.

[4] Eltham, in the south-east, was an overspill area for working-class Londoners. It later became the district where the British National Party (BNP), one of the major 'Keep Britain White' groups, established its headquarters.

[5] International Socialists. One of the left wing parties with its membership roots in youth and student politics, which flourished in the early seventies.

[6] John Tyndall was the chairman of the BNP.

my stag night was marred by constant political arguing, and, at one stage, someone almost going under a tube train. It was pretty heavy. We don't really talk now.'[7]

'Here To Stay, Here To Fight'

In September 1971 I flew back into a London still reeling from the back end of the sixties. You could wear an afro and flares were still acceptable. The city had established itself as the place that swung every which way. On my first night here we mooched down to King's Road and drank in a bar which boasted a go-go dancer; nothing special about that, except that to my eyes, used to the strait-laced Caribbean, a go-go boy in white flares and a translucent floral shirt seemed to belong to a bizarre, foreign world, far from the London I had left just four years previously.

The previous year had brought Edward Heath to government against all the odds. Wilson's government had spent its credit, both political and financial, and the British people had rewarded Labour with the order of the boot. The Heath government had come in with a determination to cut spending everywhere possible and to suppress wages; the three-day week and the miners' strike were yet to come, but students had already christened Margaret Thatcher, the new Education Secretary, 'Margaret Thatcher, Milk Snatcher' for her decision to end the daily ration of milk to children in primary schools. The five years that followed would both disillusion the British people and, more importantly, open their eyes to their new place in the world.

As a student, I lived far away from the majority of black people. If I saw a black face on campus it was almost certain to be an overseas student. But my life was never going to be separate from the thousands of black people whom I did not know. I was, as far as everyone else was concerned, one of that anonymous mass. With the passing of the 1971 Immigration Act, everyone knew that in spite of his political fall Enoch Powell had to some extent triumphed. Within weeks I had immersed myself in student politics. Left wing rhetoric came easily, and amongst students whose only experience

---

[7] Interview with Gary Bushell. Gary Bushell is a hugely popular tabloid columnist and broadcaster, a major figure in popular culture in the nineties.

*of black people was watching Civil Rights protesters on TV, I could
boast a kind of vicarious glamour. I even managed to sport the odd
Black Panther beret from time to time. But there were only three real
issues for us beyond the usual student causes: apartheid, immigration
and the Common Market. All three were rooted in a crucial debate
about the place of post-imperial Britain in the world. To what extent
were we responsible for racism in South Africa? Could we abandon
our historical relationship to our colonies by simply removing rights
of people previously free to come and go, on the grounds, ironically,
that there were too many of 'them' here – ironic, because by this
time Caribbean immigration had nearly halted. And most of all, what
place would we have in the new European club?*

*On the face of it, the major political events of the seventies
suggested a shift towards an insular, isolationist Britain. The oil price
hike of 1973 was economically devastating to the West, and swiftly
gave rise to the popular vision of the 'oil-sheikh', squeezing the life
out of Britain. The premier current affairs programme of the time,
Weekend World, regularly used a piece of film with the image of an
Arab oil worker turning off a supply pipeline as the starting point
for its explanations of the problems of the British economy. The
three-day week which followed, triggered by the miners' strike, also
increased the country's sense of being beleaguered by sinister outside
forces. Even the referendum decision to join the European Economic
Community was won principally on the grounds that Europe needed
to club together to stave off the economic threat from elsewhere on
the globe – the Japanese, the Americans and, of course, the devilish
Arabs. In some senses, the place of black people in British society
seemed marginal set against these momentous questions; and for
many of the Windrush generation that was just how it should have
been – head down, keep quiet, work your way to respectability.
However, amongst young black people, things were changing, and
a series of events which were to scar the next decade were just starting
as I discovered student politics.*

*The controversy which raged for my four years as an
undergraduate, which became known as the 'No Platform For
Fascists' – and for which I was largely responsible – dramatised
these questions. When, in 1972, the government proposed to raise
fees for students from overseas, the National Union of Students
denounced the proposal as an effective cut in funding to higher
education. By 1973, the campaign was in full flow. Though I was
born in London the fact that I had been abroad for three years before*

coming to university meant that I had been obliged to register as an overseas student. Having to pay my way through college meant that every hike in the annual fee was a crushing blow. I joined in the campaign with a vengeance, carrying banners, writing letters, lobbying and sitting-in. I managed to get myself elected to the NUS conference that year and, being one of very few non-whites amongst the 700 or so delegates at the conference, I found myself entrusted with the ticklish job of drafting a resolution that would unite us round the issue.

The night before the debate I huddled with the main representatives of the factions. We nearly had agreement, until one of the far left groups proposed what, in the overheated atmosphere of a student conference seemed a relatively trivial change. They demanded that the 'racist' implications of the fee rise should be recognised, and that as a declaration of our opposition to the growing influence of far-right parties, campuses should effectively declare themselves off-limits to the then growing National Front. Thus the infamous 'No Platform For Racists' clause found its way into the resolution as an afterthought. When I rose to move the whole resolution the following day I didn't even mention it; others did, but it seemed a sideshow. Yet within days it had become the only issue, with banner headlines in newspapers denouncing student 'fascists'.

Worse was to come when small groups of ultra-left students began to harass right wing MPs they declared to be racists. At the London School of Economics, a celebrated American academic was physically bundled off the platform at a lecture, and others were, it was said, intimidated by extremists. Inviting right wing Conservatives – most of all Powell and his associates – was an invitation to the Socialist Workers' Party to organise a high-profile demonstration, frequently ending in a fight. It paved the way for a series of violent conflicts with the far right and the police that were to have tragic results.

In 1978, shortly after I had become President of the National Union of Students, a demonstration organised to stop a National Front rally in London's Red Lion Square erupted into a running battle between students and the police. I was speaking at a separate meeting not far away. In the midst of the discussion there was a commotion at the side of the hall, and one of the students we had detailed to keep tabs on the demonstration burst in, blood pouring from the side of his head. 'You're sitting here while the fascists are beating us up,' he shouted. Even then he did not know the full extent of the disaster. In the mêlée, a young man from Warwick University, Kevin Gately, was struck on the head and died.

Kevin Gately and many like him had probably never met a black person before coming to university. But they had watched the Civil Rights marchers being hosed down and beaten in the US, they had protested against apartheid in South Africa, and they had come to admire black icons like Luther King and Muhammad Ali. The discovery that they themselves lived in a country where discrimination was rife was to some extent shaming; and the sense of shame was adroitly exploited by the left. Whatever the motives, this was probably the first recognition by the majority community that they now lived in a society where black people were going to be part of the fabric for good. This was the first generation that was to grow up with the assumption that Britain would be a multi-racial society.

Of course, most of this was taking place separately from the process in which black people were coming to their own parallel recognition that there would be no going back. The Bristol bus boycott, the start of the Black Parents' Movement, the first stirrings of black involvement with the major parties were all clear indications that from the other end of the process, black people too were coming to recognise that they had to find ways of making their lives here work in the long term.

My election as NUS President was a moment in which the two different streams came together. It was probably an inevitable outcome of my fellow students' determination to signal some concrete recognition that they had rejected the racial attitudes of the previous generation. The Fleet Street headlines picked up a quote from a speech I made at the time – 'Here To Stay', and the Trots turned it into a slogan – 'Here to stay. Here to fight.' All this was an indication, both to me and to a wider public, well beyond the confines of student politics, that there was a new potential for black people within the mainstream life of British society. If it was possible to become the democratically elected figurehead of a mostly white national organisation, many more things were possible than we had ever dreamed of.

21

'The police would be waiting in the Mews. We can see them, all the customers are there, sitting down and eating. And they'll come in and say it's a raid. And they would search people and never found anything. Five raids in the first year. That's how the Mangrove Nine trial came about, you know. Never found anything, what they was doing. But the big question is why the police would want to destroy success with a sort of upmarket restaurant. Small, only seat forty-odd people, forty-two people. And why would you want to destroy that? We have about six people working. We have licence, we've got planning permission. Everything is in order, why do you want to destroy that?'[1]

'Everybody had a standard three charges. So we went to a solicitor's, but when they saw my notes of evidence – which is the transcript the police give you with all their statements – the solicitor told me, "Listen, Darcus, I think you better plead guilty. I brief you, you do five." I just said, "I spend that with your wife, my friend – that five years." And I just took off my file and walked out.'[2]

'Although Carnival is a very contested moment, heavily policed, nobody wants it, really, very much, in the middle of London. Anybody who knows Carnival now, joyous occasion, and its wonderful food and music and people wearing policemen's hats better go back to '76 and '77 and '78 when the negotiation as to whether the Carnival was going to happen at all, has to begin as soon as the last Carnival ends. You set up the Carnival committee and start to negotiate with the local authority and with the police as to whether they're going to allow it to happen. But, nevertheless, right in the middle of the seventies comes this explosion of black creativity. People had never seen the costumes before, had never seen dancing in the street like that. It's kind of re-colonisation. And this re-colonisation is symbolic

---

[1] Interview with Frank Critchlow.
[2] Interview with Darcus Howe.

of a great deal more, because, in the seventies, what is also happening is the shops are being re-colonised, you know. Shops, ordinary shops, are beginning to sell sweet potatoes and okras and avocado pears, you know. Urban British life is just being sort of quietly re-appropriated to certain aspects of black life. So the colonisation that enforced the driving of the black population into their urban redoubts, in a way, moves the other way, as the black population begins to assert its cultural authority and its cultural customs over the narrow spaces in which they live. And this is the beginning of a huge transformation, enormous transformation. It's an enormous time of cultural creative explosion out of the middle of marginalisation.'[3]

Carnival

By the seventies the groups of migrants from various countries in and around the Caribbean had founded a network of black communities distributed throughout most of Britain's industrial centres. All of these were now linked together by a broad consensus, firstly, about how to negotiate their progress within society and, secondly, by a similarly defensive reaction to the political and social eruptions which had marked their presence. The bulk of migrants and their children remained in London and the surrounding area, but from halfway through the decade events in such cities as Birmingham, Bristol, Leeds and Manchester were to have a substantial impact on public opinion across the nation. In London, however, Notting Dale had been the cockpit of conflicts and issues which played a crucial role in outlining the imagery of race and immigration; and Notting Dale still had a final, devastating, trick up its sleeve – the Notting Hill Carnival.

There are a number of different accounts about how the Carnival came into being. One of the most convincing is to do with a local playleader's attempts to invent a local festival for the reassurance and amusement of her charges.

'Mrs Laslett, a charming Polish woman, who used to have a playgroup in Tavistock Crescent, looked after all sorts of kids – black,

---

[3] Interview with Stuart Hall.

white, pink, blue – the lot. Well, she had a little parade, trucks for the kids – that was the first time. We were just doing up the restaurant[4] that's why it sticks in my memory so well, and we saw all these trucks going by and all the kids and thought, that's nice. That was the first time I ever saw anything in Notting Hill and that was about '61 or '62.'[5]

In the gregarious atmosphere of Notting Dale, an event of this sort was bound to attract attention, and for Trinidadians long deprived of the opportunity to 'play mas', a procession of this sort was like a standing invitation to a jump-up. It wasn't long before the parade of children was augmented by a steel band.

'Eventually a steel band got involved and because of the nature of the steel band, walking pan round neck, the trucks went around much faster than the steel band but the steel band had all the Caribbean people behind it. So the trucks just went on their way and all the foot soldiers from the Caribbean followed the sound of the steel band. The police had to divert them on a shorter route – they were supposed to go down to Notting Hill Gate – the route was Tavistock Road down Ledbury Road, Portobello Road and back to Tavistock Road.'[6]

'I have been involved in Carnival from day one. Trinidadians are real carnival people, and it's a lot of angles, but you can't really get the true story. I just think that the time was right, and people were talking about it, and they have a group there do something, and it all come together.'[7]

Within a couple of years the Carnival was an established annual event, and by the end of the sixties it had grown to the point where it involved an increasing number of local people and associations.

The district was going through a transitional period. Since the riots, and

[4] Larry Ford's restaurant Fiesta One, on Ledbury Road, was one of the earliest and most important social venues in the district, frequented among others by Christine Keeler, Stephen Ward, Mandy Rice-Davies and their friends. Larry Ford came from Trinidad and is a furniture maker by trade. He now conducts one of the major steel band troupes involved in the Notting Hill Carnival.

[5] Larry Ford quoted in Mike Phillips and Charlie Phillips, *Notting Hill in the Sixties* (London: Lawrence and Wishart, 1991), p. 106.

[6] ibid.

[7] Interview with Frank Critchlow.

increasingly after the 1965 Rent Act, Notting Dale and Ladbroke Grove had been filling up with social workers, workers from voluntary and religious groups, left wing activists, housing campaigners, middle-class hippies, pop musicians and academic researchers of every kind. All of these embraced the new festival, seeing in it a moment when, for once in a year, racial barriers could be surmounted and everyone could share the invigorating manna of West Indian *joie de vivre*. Westminster and Kensington Councils kicked in with the loan of short life property and small grants, and the local schools and youth clubs began assembling groups of children to join in the music and dressing up. In this sense the early years of the Carnival, while they were about Caribbean self assertion, were equally the product of the liberal coalition which had emerged in the district after the riots and the various housing scandals.

Another factor which was influencing the tone of the area was the local authorities' programme of compulsory purchase and rehousing. The multi-occupied slum houses in streets like Powis Terrace, St Stephen's Gardens and Tavistock Crescent were pulled down and rebuilt, but, in most of these conversions only half the number of families could be accommodated. Westminster City and Kensington Councils vigorously denied that this constituted 'black dispersal', a form of ethnic cleansing, but the fact was that a high proportion of the West Indians who lived there now found themselves, throughout the latter part of the sixties, being moved out to Queen's Park, Harlesden, Neasden and Wembley, well away from Notting Dale. As redevelopment progressed, the social life of the Dale, centred as it was around the black restaurants and clubs, broke down and shrank into islands. By the same token, when the Carnival took over the streets for a couple of days it became a symbol of the West Indians' continuing presence in the spot haunted by so many memories; and from all over west London they came to stage a re-creation of the legends of the Hill, the Dale and the Grove.

Towards the end of the decade the participants in the bands began arranging the festival into a coherent shape. They knew how a carnival should look, having been brought up in a culture dominated by its annual carnival. Another important factor in enlarging the possibilities was the availability of more money, spinning off from the projects funded by various government projects and charities linked together under the 'Urban Programme'.[8] Trinidadian organisers, like Leslie Palmer and Selwyn Baptiste,

---

[8] The Urban Programme was a series of regulations which made funds available to local groups and projects.

brought the whole structure under a single umbrella, and began creating special events like band contests and costume competitions, granting concessions and raising money. At the beginning of the seventies the Notting Hill Carnival was expanding rapidly, and was on the way to its present form. But this was the precise moment that the political culture had begun to express itself in the streets. Vietnam and student protest had provoked a long series of demonstrations. In France, Germany, the USA and Japan a generation of young activists were taking their grievances out into the street in a cloud of tear gas and flying bricks. Across the world, police forces had responded by developing riot control tactics which were themselves provocative, corralling crowds and forcing them into losing confrontations. In those times, every gathering of disaffected young people contained the elements which required only a spark to convert it into a full scale riot. As the Carnival grew it drew in and concentrated the tensions of the period; and there was an issue ready at hand which roused passions in the district, and also provided a link with the mood of restless and anti-authoritarian anger which was sweeping through Europe.

One of the few remaining centres owned and frequented by West Indians in the Dale was the Mangrove restaurant. Its owner, Frank Critchlow, had run the Rio which was, in comparison, a downmarket café, part of the changing scene at the end of the sixties. But the ambitions and the reach of the immigrants were expanding rapidly and the Mangrove was a much more elegant operation. For reasons rooted in traditional attitudes to law and order within the structure of the local authorities, it immediately attracted the attention of the police.

Throughout the previous years attitudes towards the Caribbean migrants within the police forces mirrored attitudes in society at large. Most policemen emerged from the social groups who most feared the black migrants, and who were most prepared to use violence to express their fears. For petty bullies and sadists the uniform was a perfect cover. The protracted torture and murder of a Nigerian vagrant, David Oluwale, during the late sixties, was an analogy for a network of practices visited on black people by various police forces, and, generally, a widespread tradition of petty harassment of migrants was well established. During the riots in Nottingham and Notting Hill the black victims of violence were as likely to be arrested and charged as the perpetrators. It was an attitude which permeated the justice system. While sentencing a black man caught waving a knife when he was attacked by a gang of Teds, one magistrate pompously declared, 'Some of you coloured men believe there is prejudice against you.'[9]

[9] *The Times*, 15 September 1958.

Within the district most policemen shared the view that the disturbances were due to the migrants' presence and behaviour. Throughout the decade raids on premises owned by black people in Notting Dale were routine features of police procedure.

The situation was complicated by the fact that the district, as a whole, had become an important site to pop musicians, groupies and hippies, smoking and dealing in various kinds of dope. There were frequent raids on private houses, and youths were stopped, questioned and searched in the street. The Metro youth club, which had become an important venue for young black people in the district, was watched and raided, and the general tenor of relationships between black people and the local police was now intensely suspicious and confrontational. In the circumstances police harassment of the Mangrove was part of an established tradition. But times had changed, and the changes were, at least, partly to do with the nature and definition of citizenship in Britain.

In the late fifties, when the Nottingham and Notting Dale riots took place, the constitutional rights of citizens were not part of the moral landscape. Legally there were specific rights which flowed from being a British subject, but English citizenship was an informal concept, more or less guaranteed by the popular will. In this sense, when a substantial number of the white population in a particular place defined being black as a provocation, the authorities tended to take their line from the moral force of the majority consensus. A decade of legislation on immigration and race, however, had outlined the nature of British citizenship in written form and erected a formal code which was meant to apply to all citizens. At the same time, black people no longer existed in the social isolation of previous years. The police, possibly influenced by a long tradition of furtive upper-class 'slumming' in the district, were remarkably slow to appreciate this fact.

'As the Rio was closing down, I got a place about 300 yards away, and I thought upmarket restaurant. I don't like to use the word upmarket, but that's what people would say. And it was decorated nicely and, when we opened, immediately it got popular. Here you have nine, ten years later, from the Rio, from the hippy era, that people came out of hippyism, and we had the Blenheim Crescent crowd which was middle class like Professor Main, Sam Lloyd, Mary Tuck, Robin Tuck, that crowd came there. Lionel Morrison crowd, they all came there and fill up the restaurant, they take over the place. It's so packed people couldn't get in on a Friday, so they had to wait outside in their cars to get a seat. Then again we had trouble from the police. Why would they want to close a place like that? We get so much support, Lord Gifford used to be there a lot at that time. The MP was Bruce Douglas Mann, he used to be there as well. We had Sammy Davis there, we had a lot of stars there. Nina Simone, Vanessa Redgrave, Maurice Bishop, Walter Rodney, Darcus Howe. C. L. R. James used to have a lot of people, he used to take over one side of the restaurant and talking to people because everybody wants to hear. Barbara Bees. Very, very in-crowd.'[10]

'Frank never like to pay no police, you see. All the while he was running the Rio and the gambling he wouldn't give the police any money. And the life was in the Grove, you see, the strange mix of people. Colin McInnes would be sitting in the Rio, a place where you had a kind of beatnik element. The Grove always had hanging around blacks, educated, cultured, middle-class people who also liked a little seediness to life. That was a kind of magnet for people who wanted to be liberal in the days when there was so much propaganda against blacks. So when he moved to the Mangrove, they just thought, He's taking the piss now, he's just gone upmarket and occupying space.

'I was sitting in the Mangrove one day – we used to go there during the day and hang out, discuss a lot of politics, people used to. That was the nature of the moment, Black Panthers in America, Trinidad, telling them about my friends in the army who were on trial and all sorts – and they started to raid it. So, later on, Bruce Douglas Mann came, he's sitting in a corner talking to Frank; they're cooking down in the basement, preparing the food for the night. Tony Gifford comes and talking to Frank – but I don't know Frank too closely by then. He knows who I am, he knows I'm a red hot little trouble-making kind of fellow, and I'm listening to him. I said, "Listen, why you complaining to all these white people? Let's have a demonstration." He says, "Sure." I says, "Right. If you have a demonstration you're likely to lose your place, you know." He said, "So?" And I thought that rather courageous. And we printed some leaflets and 150 people came. It was a complete non-event, until you looked around and saw about 600 police, and we thought, "Hell, what's this?" All that happened really was one of the policemen who felt threatened went back and said we were planning to attack the police station. No such thing. All we were planning to do is to

[10] Interview with Frank Critchlow.

take the demonstration to every police station. And the police, Special Branch officers, everybody came, and it eventually ended up in a clash. And some of us got arrested on the day, and six weeks after my door was off the hinge, and the policeman came and arrested us and charged us for incitement to riot, incitement to kill police officers, making an affray, plus I had breach of the peace and actual bodily harm. Everybody had a standard three charges.

'So we went to a solicitor's, but when they saw my notes of evidence – which is the transcript the police give you with all their statements – the solicitor told me, "Listen, Darcus, I think you better plead guilty. I brief you, you do five." I just said, "I spend that with your wife, my friend – that five years." And I just took off my file and walked out. At the same time Richard Neville of the *Oz* lot, they had written some kind of garbage with school children and got nicked, and he defended himself, and I used to know Richard in the Grove, so I thought if Richard Neville could defend himself, so can I, and I did and also Jones did, because it would give us an opportunity to introduce a political angle, apart from the fact I was told that I was an excellent cross-examiner. And the case lasted fifty-five days in the Old Bailey. So it was well reported and the important thing was, in those days black people didn't feel they could fight and win. They feel we have to accept these things. But it's the first time the people saw you could take on the forces of power, be courageous enough to stand up for your rights.'[11]

'Demonstrations was important at that time. Very important. You had people who get together, protest. The Mangrove Nine demonstration was a good example. When we called the demonstration Black Power was around and a lot of people gathered outside the Mangrove and then we marched off into Notting Hill Police Station and then to Harrow Road. And before we got to Harrow Road there was trouble which broke out and about fifteen, sixteen people were arrested. Charges, minor charges and they were all fined or bound over. But I remember seeing the headlines in the newspaper. Maudling[12] wanted an investigation into who organised the demonstrations. I remember C. L. R. James called us in a meeting at the Metro and he hold up the newspaper and he said this is serious,

11 Interview with Darcus Howe.
12 Reginald Maudling was Deputy Prime Minister under Ted Heath in the Conservative Government of 1970–74.

and he was right. We were charged with very serious charges.
Inciting members of the public to riot, affray, threatening behaviour,
offensive weapons. Heavy stuff. And we had a big campaign. Darcus
went up and down the country talking to different groups. We had
support from the West Indies, we had support from America. And
the trial started. Big trial. At the Old Bailey. We had demonstrations
outside the Old Bailey every day. At the end of the case I was
surprised when they didn't put the jury into a hotel, when the jury
retire. We was there till about half nine. And I remember that the
court was packed. The judge allowed the court people to come into
the court as well as the galleries and every place, and that was
amazing. But we couldn't work out, because we were still downstairs,
why that was so. But we found out later that the trial got
internationally known and the police made a mess of it, really.'[13]

Even without the provocation provided by the confrontation between the
Mangrove and the police, Carnivals of the seventies would have contained
substantial elements of tension and violence. After the police raid on the
Metro in May 1971, which was followed by a series of demonstrations by
black and white youths in the area, the Carnival that year saw a number
of clashes as the police moved in to end the festivities on the last night. In
the following years police procedures grew increasingly hostile, provoking
an equal and opposite reaction from the crowds of revellers. In between
times the style of policing at various demonstrations and raids in the city
grew more and more confrontational and oppressive. Riot squads, preceded
by clouds of tear gas, now marched towards demonstrators, beating their
shields in rhythm with their batons and chanting. In between times the
Special Patrol Group, a unit which specialised in violent, aggressive policing,
scoured the streets throughout London, stopping, searching, arresting and
abusing young black men. During 1975 in Lewisham alone the SPG stopped
14,000, mainly black, people and arrested 400. This pattern was repeated
throughout all the areas where black people lived. As black unease and
anger about the behaviour of the police spread through the city, the annual
Carnival began to be a site where young black people could express their
resentment. It started to become a ritual battle as the police tried to close
down the area on the final night. Up to that point Carnival had been a
relatively predictable version of the festival in Trinidad, whose important
features were an attempt to replicate the carnival tradition. Suddenly, after

[13] Interview with Frank Critchlow.

1971, the Notting Hill Carnival became a rallying point for all the West Indians, inexorably drawn by the gathering itself, by the excitement and the rumour, powered by the noise and the gossip and the opportunity to be out in the open and part of something big. The Carnival of 1976 saw a predictable evening of violence on a large scale.

'I was arrested at midday. I was doing some work in the Mangrove and I came out because nobody was around midday. I was preparing food and things like that to put in front of the Mangrove and I came out and some police champion arrest me and took me to the station. There was a big panic, and, "What are you charging him with? He was selling drinks." I said, "It's twelve o'clock, nobody's out there, is still early days." But that's what they said, and there was hell broke loose later on and they said it could be my arrest at that time and two other reasons, which I can't remember. But that wasn't nice. A lot of people get hurt . . . because the police came down and were smashing people's heads.'[14]

'And we always went with the police commander in charge of race relations, John Thornton he was then, and he used to go round with us, and we crossed our fingers. And at one point we were in the thick of it, on a street corner. And he suddenly saw the police preparing, a hundred yards away, to charge down the street and clear it and help get the crowds go home. And John Thornton suddenly realised, Good Lord! They're banging their shields, they've got their batons, hope we don't have headlines tomorrow, "CRE [Commission for Racial Equality] Chairman and his wife injured." So he rushed and took Leslie Anne sort of under his wing, pressed her against the wall, covered her over to protect her, and the police swept past. And that's been one of our more amusing memories.'[15]

A force of 1,600 policemen, many of them drafted in from riot control squads, patrolled the area, or, locked in coaches parked in the side streets, waited impatiently in the heat. 500 people were injured and 150 hospitalised. In the years following the police treated the event as a major public order challenge. In 1979 it attracted a force of over 10,000 police, almost half the Metropolitan force. Until the end of the decade the Carnival was

[14] Interview with Frank Critchlow.
[15] Interview with Sir David Lane. Sir David Lane was Conservative MP for Cambridge 1967–76, and was appointed in 1976 to head the new Commission for Racial Equality.

to dominate the headlines during the summer recess, and the publicity became a fundamental part of justifying later arguments which began to define black people as being both criminal and disorderly. Ironically, the publicity also served to deliver another perception about the vibrancy and attractiveness of Caribbean and black culture.

'The Carnival was becoming important and it was beginning to bring more and more people into it. It is a place of life, of liveliness, and is a place if you had imagination you get things done. So artistic people started moving in, followed by the people with money, followed by the people who want to be seen or to be next to these people, followed by pop stars, followed by various other "I want to be part of that group" type of persons. So they all started moving in, and wanting to have that freedom, very much black, a freedom of expressing your feelings and your love and your likes and your dislikes, and people loved it. And all these people moved into the area, and now they're trying to turn the area into what it isn't, into what they've just left. So, maybe, in the next ten years when you come to Notting Hill, all we'll have is the Carnival and nothing else.'[16]

'That is a good platform to be on, and move on to other things, which tell about black people's presence in Britain. I mean, people come over from America, West Indians, every year. They just come because it's a West Indian thing and they want to identify it as some of them don't really go into costumes, and I think it's good. A lot are steel band tuners and they come over for the bands and things, functions like that. So it's good. It's very good. Should go on, go on and on and improve all the time as they're going along. It's something to look forward to. It's a big victory for the black community, although the local authority doesn't want it and the police didn't want it. But it's a big victory. Persistent. And I'm glad that we were part of it.'[17]

The Notting Hill Carnival was not cut to any sort of pattern. Even if one had existed it would not have fitted, because Carnival had its own peculiar origins and grew out of them in its own peculiar way.

[16] Interview with Ben Bousquet.
[17] Interview with Frank Critchlow.

'It changed when young people started to go to it and it started to
come out of the hands of some older Trinidadians. And they had to
be accommodated for one reason, that had it been exclusively that
Trinidadian set, the police would have put it in a park and some of
them guys would have taken the money. But because you had this
rush of young blood around sound systems it remained on the streets
of Notting Hill, opened up a Caribbean dimension as opposed to a
Trinidadian dimension, and makes it possible now to lift it further.'[18]

What gave the Notting Hill Carnival its unique character, was the fact that
it was, by definition, beyond control. It was more than an event. Here was
a space where thousands of people from all over the country were meeting
and mingling, a market place where everyone was negotiating the construction of a new culture in an atmosphere of anticipation and adventure.
Notting Hill had shops and restaurants and churches and barbershops and
gambling and vice and street-corner gossip and news from home and politics
and even a newspaper. The Carnival reflected all the district's radicalism and
organisation. The violent annual disturbances which occurred sporadically
throughout the seventies were not, however, a product of it. The festival
simply gathered up and reflected elements like the rage of young black
people about police harassment and legal injustice and the widespread anger
about a hopeless environment, unemployment and discrimination. Its identity sprang out of Caribbean culture, but it was never a Caribbean festival
because it was born and grew up in London. At its heart was something
other than being Caribbean. That is to say, it was focused around the
experience of coming from the Caribbean and coming to a part of British
society.

   This was a dynamic process which, for the Caribbeans, was an active
statement – we're here to stay. From the other end of the spectrum, the
Carnival was now an active element in an intensifying discussion throughout
Britain about the issues of race, nationality and citizenship. As it became
part of a national debate every summer throughout the seventies, it became
more and more obvious that what happened annually in Notting Hill over
the August Bank Holiday was undoubtedly a British phenomenon; and that
fact posed questions which could not be ignored about the total direction
of the common culture.

[18]   Interview with Darcus Howe.

22

'I think the primary difficulty was the extent of discrimination that we unearthed, and it was worse than we expected. It was taking time to do it, and we weren't getting the help we needed from senior industrialists, from politicians. So it wasn't just the police. And the press attitudes, of course, the worst of the press were very unhelpful, tiresome; the best of the press were very supportive. It was bad. It's difficult to measure. I think, in America, where the problems had been bigger, there may have been greater discrimination. But I think it was a bit worse than we expected to find it. But we were glad to be in there with the powers. We may not have made as much progress as we hoped – or not as quickly at the beginning – but, steadily, we got attitudes changing, and gradually, companies, even the Civil Service, in the end, came to see they'd got to do more, and not merely pay lip service to equality of opportunity but really tackle discrimination toughly. We did what we could to help. We were disappointed in some areas. We were very pleased with the response in others. We just wished we had made quicker progress, but you can't always do that. It's not an ideal world. But the momentum has grown, and we're glad to have set that off in the first five years when I was there. So, we could have done better.'[1]

'I think it's an extraordinary period, because what you have in that time is an extraordinary cultural, political, historical energy coming out of the Caribbean. You have an even greater wave of energy coming out of America, in the aftermath of the Black Power period, telling the world, actually, that black was beautiful; telling the world that the history and culture of African Americans was, or could be, a planetary resource, a resource for anybody who wanted to make use of it and encounter its pleasures. And, at the same time, you have a kind of demographic wave in the big cities here, where young people are looking around for the elements of a black culture

[1] Interview with Sir David Lane.

that they are going to create and negotiate, but they know that it can't be a Caribbean culture, and they know that it can't be an African American culture, although they draw elements of both and combine them in different ways. And finally – I mean, this is a long period – in the mid-eighties, probably a twenty-year cycle of cultural life, they reach a period where they no longer imitate, they no longer simply mimic things born elsewhere, but feel confident and comfortable in a culture that they've improvised for themselves, from far flung elements but also out of the texture of their own immediate experience.'[2]

Black Parents And Self Help

'Those blows that caused my heart to swell'
(Linton Kwesi Johnson)

Early on in the seventies I was living in a house in Ledbury Road with a bunch of black youths. We were all more or less disturbed in various different ways; a few were violent and unpredictable, sometimes someone sneaked in to vandalise the place. Occasionally the police raided us, claiming to be looking for runaways, and didn't leave until they'd provoked someone into the kind of anger which led to an arrest.

The house was a project which had been started by a man named Vince Hines. Vince had come from Jamaica in 1959, joined the army and served in Malaya. After he came back he decided to start a hostel for homeless black youths. When I met him I was living in a bedsit in Notting Hill, so I wasn't technically homeless, but I liked him and I wanted to be part of the venture so I became his partner in the project. At the time Vince was a leading figure in what we called the "Self Help" movement. I don't know how much it helped

[2]   Interview with Paul Gilroy. Paul Gilroy is the leading black academic and critic in Britain. His mother came from Guyana, and was one of the first black headteachers in the education system. Gilroy's reputation was established with the text, *The Empire Strikes Back*, written together with a group of young black British academics, including Baroness Amos. This was the first work to begin exploring the nature of the black British experience from the inside. He now teaches at Goldsmiths' College, University of London.

anyone because, after a while, I was completely disillusioned with
what we were doing, but it plonked me down right in the middle of
one of the dynamic strands of the culture we were constructing at
the time.

'Self Help' was possible because of a collection of government and local
authority regulations which was called the 'Urban Programme'. This
was the direct, and indirect, product of previous immigration legislation,
and it was, more or less, all that the pro-immigrant political coalition
had been able to rescue from the bonfire of Powellism. Home Office policy
under Roy Jenkins had offered legislation against racial discrimination, as
a corollary to immigration restriction. But grassroots Powellism was
expressed in a variety of outlets from television comedy to newspaper
editorials, and in popular myth the Race Relations Board had become a
synonym for the oppressive operations of a bunch of hard-faced commissars
bent on handing over power to the blacks. So the political effects of
Powellism on the ground had destroyed the prospects of a strong anti-racist
Bill. The notion of 'community relations' was in itself a dubious compromise, enshrining the idea that the discrimination that immigrants faced in
housing and employment was somehow inadvertent and dependent on their
own behaviour or on a series of simple misunderstandings. In the period
leading up to the '68 Commonwealth Immigrants Act, a group of 'community liaison officers', themselves established by the '65 Immigration Act,
lobbied the government with criticisms of the proposed Community
Relations Commission, and suggested that the responsibility for expenditure
on immigrant problems should rest with local bodies rather than with a
central body like the Commission. They were led by Wilfred Wood, an
Anglican clergyman from Barbados, who had begun to act as a conduit for
protest and new ideas between the pro-immigrant coalition and the Labour
Government. Wood and his colleagues had seen all the progress they had
made towards reducing discrimination and improving immigrant living conditions destroyed overnight by Powell's welding together of race and immigration, and the renewed respectability of racialist propaganda which
followed.

'I think what happened was that Labour took fright, and there
became a kind of Dutch auction between the two parties, each one
showing that they're likely to be less friendly to immigrants and
immigration and black people, and so on. And the Wilson government
hit upon the idea of saying, in order to safeguard good race relations
in this country, We will introduce a limit on the number of black

people coming into the country. And this despite the fact that, frankly, the number of black people had already begun to decline. But what the press and the racists had managed to do was to associate the word immigrant with black people.

'An example of what I mean, I have a very close friend who was as white as anybody can be. And one day he said, "Among those undesirable immigrant births is my sister's child, my niece." You see, he and his sister were both born in India, at the time when their father was an engineer working in India. And the definition of an immigrant birth was a child born to a woman who was herself not born in England. And so they were included in these immigrant births that Enoch was scaring everybody with. There were so many scare stories going on that, even if you were black, you found yourself wondering if they're right. One day after Enoch Powell had been complaining about this excessive number of births to black women, I found myself scrutinising every black woman I saw. And sure enough, it seemed to me almost every black woman I met on the street was expecting a baby. And it was only then I realised Shepherd's Bush Green was a terminus for a number of bus routes. And running off Shepherd's Bush Green was Goldhawk Road. At the end of Goldhawk Road was Queen Charlotte's Maternity Hospital. So all these black women came, going to the maternity hospital, on the buses. But when I was at the maternity hospital myself, waiting for my wife, I saw all these white women driving their cars in. Now they were just as pregnant as these black women who were getting off the bus, but I defy anybody to look at a woman's hairdo and tell me that she's pregnant. And that's all you could see when she's driving a car. So once you were looking for that kind of thing you could find it.

'I remember only too well a chap called Tom Stacey, who had been the defeated Tory candidate in North Hammersmith, and he wrote a devastating piece in *The Sunday Times* under the emotive heading "The Ghettos of England". And he proceeded to, as it were, put at the door of the black people all the bad conditions that existed. He wrote that to turn into Coningham Road in Shepherd's Bush is to turn into an immigrant area. And he then proceeded to describe the garbage piled up, and broken windows, the derelict conditions, and so on. Now, anyone from any part of the country reading that article and coming into Coningham Road would say "Gosh, Tom Stacey is right." What he didn't say was that parallel to Coningham Road were Stowe Road on one side and Cathnor Road on the other. And that whole area was of a piece. Only Coningham Road had black people in it. But, you see, anyone coming in would have thought that what he was saying was right. He said things like knocking on doors throughout the day you found proportionately more black men home on the dole than white. See? More black men home on the dole than white. Now, I happen to know, because I was minister in that area, that quite often I would go to a house – a room really – to talk about the baptism of a baby. And I would have to talk to the wife only because the husband was a lump under the blanket there because he was working at night. In those days the only jobs most black men could get, night time jobs. So they slept during the day and then they would come out at four o'clock, go for a little walk and then it was time to go back to work. So, as far as Stacey was concerned, the very fact that they were home in the day meant that they were on the dole. And throughout the article, he would link what you would call an ascertainable fact with a prejudice. He said he found no complaint about these conditions because they're better than Kingston's back wall. So because nobody complained to him about them, it meant that they were so happy to be living in these conditions.'[3]

In the atmosphere following Enoch Powell's 'Rivers of Blood' speech the government refused to bring in legislation which openly promoted racial equality, or which appeared to be a clear benefit to immigrants. On the other hand, it was undeniable that it had knuckled under to Powellism and it was, therefore, under pressure from a wide range of liberal opinion to deliver on its promise that the quid pro quo of immigration restriction would be an assertion of the immigrants' rights as citizens. At the same time, local authorities of every political colour were demanding help in tackling a progressive series of problems. All the industrial inner city areas were now faced with the traditional problems of housing, education and decay, compounded by the growing needs of the immigrants.

The government's response was a compromise. No new funds were granted. Instead, it collected various headings in existing policy – the educational priority areas which stemmed from the Plowden Report on education, the housing priority areas, part of the Ministry's normal

[3] Interview with the Right Reverend Wilfred Wood. Bishop Wood came to Britain in 1961 from a seminary in Barbados and was ordained a priest at St Paul's Cathedral in 1962. He has become widely known and respected in the black community for the courage and determination with which he has taken up the issues affecting the black communities.

functions, and Section 11 of the '66 Local Government Act, under which
fifty-seven local authorities received grant aid on the basis of the presence
of immigrants. All these were combined into a new description of 'special
social need'. The compromise avoided offering any kind of aid directly to
the immigrants and cast a veil of administrative and bureaucratic procedure
over any benefit they might derive. The Home Office retained responsibility
for defining the limits of the programme, and in the first phase only twenty-
three local authorities qualified, with the proviso that the funds were to be
spent on the under-fives. In the second phase, however, emboldened by the
fact the programme had so far escaped direct attack by the Powellites, the
Home Office broadened its scope and number of eligible local authorities.
Voluntary organisations, sponsored by the local authority, could now apply
for grants to fund playgroups, advice centres and a wide range of community
based projects.

> At the start of the seventies the project I was running with Vince
> was only one of several similar projects in various parts of the country.
> Ours was a kind of hostel, mainly for young men who had come
> out of local authority care, or out of periods of detention at Her
> Majesty's pleasure. The idea was that we would put them up for a
> short period while they found jobs and their own accommodation,
> and that was mostly what happened. In other towns, like
> Birmingham, for example, there were more elaborate organisations.
> In Handsworth a couple of black social workers assembled an
> organisation called Harambee which focused on a group of black
> community workers and consisted of a housing association, a
> pre-school project, a summer school, a book shop and an advice
> centre. There were similar organisations in Leeds, Manchester,
> Bristol, Nottingham and various other cities with a substantial black
> Caribbean population. Generally, they formed a loose alliance with
> the black local councillors and charitable groups working in the area,
> and their government funding tended to be augmented by grants
> from the churches and foundations like the Cadbury Trust.

The 'Self Help' projects had varying degrees of success, but were limited
by tending to be the fiefdoms of particular individuals or groups and by
the short term nature of their funding. In any case, their most successful
role was not the gaps they plugged in social services provision. Up to
that time, politics within the black communities were mostly confined to
participation in the white-led local coalitions grouped round the trade
unions or the local branches of the major Parties. By and large these linkages

discouraged the emergence of militant black responses to local crises, partly because of a series of settled alliances with various segments of the district's establishment. At the other end of the scale, the internationalist and revolutionary politics of the Marxist left were widely admired as a solution for the Third World poverty problem, but, in the context of daily life in developed Britain, they seemed abstract and distant. All attempts to create a national organisation of immigrants on the American model had collapsed. The Campaign Against Racial Discrimination, for instance, was short lived and confined to a small group of middle-class blacks and whites in London. Even the Standing Conference of West Indian Organisations was seen as part of the old island pattern and dominated by ageing elders.

By contrast, the 'Self Help' projects were grouped round the black problems for which the welfare system provided no answers: homelessness among graduates of local authority care and the prisons, the alienation of black children in schools, the harassment of young blacks by the police. In the process they created new spaces within which immigrant activists could begin living out a political programme which emerged from the experiences of their young black clients.

The ideology was muddled and ad hoc, an uneasy blend of Marxist notions and black nationalism, but the projects were like safe houses where African and Caribbean history could be taught and discussed, where information, gossip and rumour could be dispensed, and where demonstrations and campaigns could be planned. At their best moments they formed a loose network of activists throughout the country who supported each other in the inevitable battles against the police or the local authorities. To outsiders, the projects might have seemed shabby and unsuccessful, but within each locality they provided an enclave controlled by black activists which was a hotbed of black militancy, particularly among black people. Taken together, they were a national network which provided resources and support for the developing notions of a British Black Power, the idea that black people could own and control the services they needed.

All this was swept on by a rhetoric of blackness which had its roots in the experience of Africans and the African diaspora, but which addressed the conditions of life in Britain. The movement faded in significance through the seventies as the local authorities and other agencies began to repossess most of the functions they had ceded to the black voluntary organisations. Schools and colleges began recruiting speakers and assistants from the black communities, often the same people who had been teaching in the 'Self Help' projects. Black families began to move up the council lists, and more private accommodation became available for black people to rent, while the social services and housing departments of the local councils were increasingly taking on black staff, or appointing black councillors to their committees. The aspect of the projects which always attracted the biggest clientele was legal advice and, towards the middle of the decade, the law centres were set up while the Citizens Advice Bureau expanded its network of local offices and undertook approaches which were more responsive to the inner city communities. By the start of the eighties the 'Self Help' movement had had its day, but, within the space of a few years, it had helped to refine and alter local authority practices in regard to the black communities. It offered inner city youths a clear and simple explanation of what was happening in their confrontations with all kinds of authority, fuelling their urge to resist; and, by the same token, it had also made the radical politics of the black diaspora accessible to the immigrants across a broad front, giving the ideology a twist which domesticated them in the context of life in Bristol, Birmingham or Leeds.

Ironically, 'Self Help' was, in many ways, the secular version of the black fundamentalist and Pentecostal churches. They were grouped round charismatic groups or individuals. Their members shared a common identity. They acted as a refuge and a sounding board for emotions and ideas at grassroots level. By the eighties, the churches which had started out focusing on the spiritual and ethical aspects of their congregations' lives were beginning to move in a new direction, and, leaving aside the political rhetoric, beginning to pursue very much the same secular methods as the 'Self Help' projects had been doing.

'We were pretty articulate in buying properties to live in. Very important. We were, as a group of church people, very successful in buying properties to worship, and to provide the transport system that we need to get around. Yes, the influences are well known, but within that system there were no provision where people could go to and borrow money to finance their personal and family needs, whatever that might be, and when they come to the leadership of the church to ask for funds, it wasn't there. And people resorted to the door-to-door tallyman, and the money reaper on the high streets, and I felt personally that there was a need to pool some resources, pool our resources together, by which we could finance our needs. And, this long dream, this very long hope came to fruition in 1979, and I with my colleagues established the Pentecostal Credit Union, whereby we could provide some – not all – money to finance our needs. The rest is history. We just move on and go steadily in leaps and bounds. We provide money for the purchase of, more deposit and properties here, deposit and properties in the West Indies, all over the West Indies, paying off for properties here, and above all people increasing the quality of life, having central heating in their place, having a car, having a family holiday for a change together, here or in the West Indies. And the list goes on. And today we are the only financial cooperative within the Pentecostal Church movement here in Britain that provides money. We've got a lot of money. Right now.'[4]

Sometimes I'm with a friend and we hear a golden oldie on the radio or the television, and it is like a gap in my memory. I don't recognise it, or I've never heard of the band, and they say, "How come you've never heard of them? They were big in the seventies." Right there is the answer because, for most of that decade I didn't hear most of the white bands, even by accident, which was a consequence of where I was and what I was doing, because I only ever heard music from Jamaica or perhaps the USA. And that went for a long time, starting with Desmond Dekker, and it seems I was well into JA music before I even heard Bob Marley's first album that Island brought out. But when I did I was hooked because he was a great poet and what he was saying was so true. I really realised what was happening one night in Manchester. We were getting ready to go out about eleven o'clock – because you didn't really bother to go out the house before then – and next door there was this sound, one thundering bass and a kind of metallic shimmering and then this crazy voice chanting. And I said, 'What is that?' And my brother said, 'That ah Big Youth.' And it was like something started. I was down the clubs till it was getting light outside, then I had a sleep and went down Beverley's house, and stayed there till it was time to go out to the clubs again, and that was the weekend. But what I remember was being in the middle of this vibrating floor surrounded by all these other kids and the whole thing moving slowly and the sound of the bass coming through the soles of my feet and through my body till it came out the top of my head like a dream, and I wasn't thinking of anything else at all.

'Well, it was the '68 Olympics and many things was happening, and I saw three black men stood on the rostrum, raised their clenched fists with black gloves on. And it said something to me, as a person. And what it did, it actually empowered me in such a way that suddenly

---

[4] Interview with Carmel Jones.

– someone was very shy and kind of not knowing for sure what he would like to do – that particular day changed my life because, when I saw that I thought, Yes, it meant something. 'Cos I used to read Garvey. I used to read a lot of things from C. L. R. James, and it was always about strength. It's always about putting yourself in a position to affect your life and other people's lives. And I think that was a time when my life changed. Most of what I wanted to do, I became clearer, because I saw that there was black people who could stand up in a arena, in such a way that other people had never done, never dreamed of doing. And it made me realise that I can achieve certain things for myself by being the way I wanted to be, and I'm still living some of that and I suppose I never will stop living that.'[5]

For young black people in Britain in the seventies it was the start of an attempt to assert an individuality that was unique to their experience. It could be seen happening more clearly and a lot earlier in towns outside London, partly because the Caribbeans who had settled in places like Bristol and Manchester had to come to terms pretty quickly with a group of black people who were, by any standard, already British – either mixed race or from families who had been living there for a couple of generations. They found common ground partly in the experience of being young and black and subject to harassment and exclusion everywhere they went, and partly in the music and the clubs. Young people began to identify themselves by their experience in Britain, rather than in terms of how they felt about themselves as Caribbeans. It was the beginning of the development of a distinctive Black British identity, prior to which growing up in Britain had meant that you lacked some element of authenticity as a Caribbean. At the beginning of the seventies that began to change, and it became a major characteristic of the new generation which began to understand itself as being uniquely different.

Another characteristic was the fact that this generation became politi-cised in a different way to their parents. Its politics became its cultural expression, or perhaps vice versa, its cultural expression became its politics. The music, the poetry, the language all spoke of the shared experience of transformation and anxiety and defiance and hope. Young black British style became the same as the content of their protest. Both reflected the

[5] Interview with Harry Powell. Harry Powell arrived from Jamaica in the early sixties. He went to school in south London and became a professional footballer in 1971, spending seven years with second division Charlton Athletic. He later became a youth worker, running the Lewisham Way Youth and Community Centre from 1980 to the present.

same complexity, the same fragmentation, the same movement, the same disturbance. For instance, most were not Rastafarians, could not imagine being Rastafarians and never would be Rastafarians, but began to import into their daily lives different features of Rastafarianism: the dreadlocks and the language being the obvious things. The police became known as 'Babylon', everything was 'dread' or 'righteous'. We became 'I and I', and that was exactly how it felt.

Part of what was happening was a complex exchange between the generations. The seventies generation were living in a world in which all their experiences were racialised. They were conscious at every stage that their race determined how they were seen and their chances in life. The statistics alone told them this: the white kids in the classroom would have a four times better chance of finding a job when they left school. When they walked down the street the police would stop them and search their bags and pockets, and they would know that this was happening because of the colour of their skins. They didn't have to guess; most of the time the police would tell them as much in more or less abusive terms.

This generation took that experience back home to their parents, and began to racialise for their parents everything that they were going through. The difference in the generations was that Caribbean migrants in the late fifties and sixties were usually willing to take the potential for racial conflict out of the situation. For instance, when kids reported that they were being discriminated against at school, parents would typically reply with an exhortation to work harder or to see the protest as some sort of cover for laziness. For quite a long time many parents had a blind trust that all the institutions would rise above the kind of prejudice they saw in the streets. In a sense it was a deliberate and self imposed delusion. Largely, they had an intense desire to believe that a harmonious society was possible, to believe that the more they could accommodate themselves to it, the more accepting it would be. In the circumstances, they could see no other alternative.

The seventies generation began to negotiate relationships with their environment in a different way. For instance, all through that decade, most kids with a Caribbean background began to speak two or three dialects. At school they would speak the idiom of Lancashire or Bristol or broad Brummie; at home they would speak the dialect of their parents' island – if they came from St Lucia it would be a French patois; in the streets or the clubs they would speak the Jamaican/Rasta dialect which had begun to be the mark of being a black kid in Britain.

'During the late sixties, early seventies period, this is a golden period in the history of Reggae music. And I think it's in the meeting ground of Reggae music as rebel music – as Rastafari music, with the Black Power ideology and the Black Power style – that's where the really exciting things begin to happen. It's the younger generation that take the front line in the seventies, and they are a deeply troubled generation, because they feel deeply the sense that they don't know who they are. They're not British, 'cos the British don't want them; they're not Caribbean, because they've never seen the Caribbean, nothing to do with it. They called themselves African for a long time, but, of course, they'd never been to Africa, either. They are saved, spiritually and culturally, by the advent of Rastafarianism and by Reggae. These two forces make it possible for them to construct a new form of symbolic identification for themselves. Don't ask me what it's conjured out of, you know. It's conjured out of the back end of the Bible, the Bible read upside down, myth about Haile Selassie. It's conjured out of the boogie box that plays Roots Reggae music. It's conjured out of stories coming out of Kingston, you know, the Gun Court, and Trenchtown. It's conjured out of scraps, really, bits and pieces, but they manufacture for themselves a black identity that they feel proud of. They find a space for themselves.

'And my honest opinion is that that generation would have committed a kind of collective social suicide without the birth of that kind of black British identity in the seventies, because they are harassed from pillar to post. The country is in a mood of deep law and order, it's reaching for law and order at every point, wants the law to protect them against change, protect them against difference. It wants to go back to the most kind of respectable traditional values, which no black could ever enter. It's closed, bringing down the shutters on the possibility of definitions of what it would be like to be British, that any young black man or woman could actually ever get entry to. So, it's saying, "No, no, you're here, but you don't belong, you can't belong. The test now is a cultural test, and you don't pass the cultural test. You just don't fit in," et cetera. So, I mean, it's a terrible time, it's a time of almost internal colonisation. I mean, the black settlement population at the middle of most cities are being policed like they're foreign territories. Any black person moving around there after eight o'clock in the evening is in trouble, has to account for themselves. You know, carrying a bag with anything in it, they have to open it to the nearest policeman. The sus laws are used, like stop and search. You see a black person, you can hold them up against the wall, they'll be carrying drugs or they'll have something, stole something. If they're driving a car, they must have ripped it off. The stereotypes are automatic in terms of face-to-face relations between police and blacks, between the local authority and blacks, et cetera. It's an embattled situation in the seventies. And it is astonishing to me that anything was rescued from it, and, if you want a single figure who rescued something from it, it is Bob Marley.

'You know, Marley sings out of that trouble, out of tribulation, out of exile, out of being marginalised. And he makes the symbolic connection between Kingston and Handsworth. Black people feel the same. They don't know what Kingston is like, but they know Handsworth is like Kingston, both of them are being surveyed by helicopters and entered by police car, et cetera. It's the same. You are in Babylon. He provides a symbolic language with which to describe how they got like that and, in the summoning up of Africa which isn't, of course, real Africa, you know. They don't know where in Africa they came from, of course. If they went back to anywhere real in Africa, Africans would know who they were. So it's not a literal place, it's a place in the mind, but it's a place which they had to name. They could not discover who they were until they'd looked Africa in the face and said, "We are the diaspora sons and daughters of an African civilisation", as well as everything else. And until that bit of them was named – and the music helped, the re-identification with, you know, Rastafarianism, in its odd way, helped – this generation finds itself as a kind of indigenous black identity, for the first time, in the face of a great deal of local racism and police brutality, no question.'[6]

'We have our own culture. We've got our own way of life. We think different. We talk different. When I was young, the greatest thing was to be a Jamaican. It didn't matter whether you were St Lucian, Grenadine, Mauritian, Dominican, whatever, everybody wanted to be a Jamaican and everyone spoke Jamaican patois and nobody came out of the closet to say, "Well, my parents were really from Barbados", or anything like that. But it wasn't about being Jamaican, it was our way of building our own black British identity. We all had to have something that we could all identify with, that we would all come together with, and that's how we started to build something. It was like, here's the common ground, we'll all be Jamaicans. The problem was

[6] Interview with Paul Gilroy.

that we tried to like the Jamaican lifestyle for a while, until, as we got older we started to build our own little lifestyle, yes, we built our own culture and it was good. It still is good.

'I was never self-conscious of being Jamaican, I know that, because my mother's from Barbados and my dad's from Jamaica, so I always used to be stuck in the middle as to, well, What am I, Who am I? And then I took the stand that I'm a black British, and that's where I went, that's the road that I went along. Alright, I speak as good Jamaican patois as a Jamaican when I'm ready, or Bajun patois, as a Bajun person when I'm ready. But, to me, I'm my own person. I'm a black man, black British, if that's how you want to put it, but I'm a black person. It doesn't matter where I come from. I'm just black.'[7]

'The problem was racism. And my generation, we were the generation who changed things, because we didn't have the kind of constraints that our parents had. Our parents had mortgages to pay, they had to put to school, they had to find food. And when a foreman in a factory call them a black bastard, sometimes, even though they didn't like it, they would have to put up with it. My generation didn't have to put up with it, and we didn't. And it was our generation that began to change things. Not that our parents' generation were Uncle Toms or anything like that. They weren't. I mean, they resisted and fought, as they saw fit and as they could. But the responsibilities of having families put a greater constraint on their possibilities for struggle, the kind of constraints that our generation didn't have.

'For example, we would go to certain discos and clubs and found that they had colour bar policies, or they had quota policies. I remember we used to the Locarno in Streatham, and you had to get there by eight o'clock or eight-thirty because, after that, no more blacks would be let in. And so we established our own independent cultural institutions, we established the blues dance, which would be held in somebody's house on a Saturday night. We established the culture of a sound system and gave Reggae music a local agitation and a name in this country. My parents' generation had by then established little social clubs where people would meet for recreation, dances, play dominoes, domino clubs and this kind of thing. And

---

[7]   Interview with Wayne Haynes. Wayne Haynes grew up in New Cross, south London, and set out to be a professional footballer. The weekend before he was due to sign a professional contract with Millwall FC he was injured in the Deptford Fire of 1981 and is now registered disabled.

by my time now, we even had sports organisations like football teams with our own black football league, our own black cricket leagues. Even now they still exist. I think that having our own independent cultural institutions made it possible for us to cope with the alienation that we felt from British society, because of the racism and the racial oppression, institutionalised and otherwise. These things gave us a sense of our own identity, made us feel that we had something going for ourselves that made us proud and strong and independent.'[8]

'When people say safety in numbers it's not just from a physical point of view. That is one format. There's safety in feeling safe from the hostile environment around here. You get together and you play your music and you feel at one with each other because you share a common bond against the kind of discrimination that is perpetrated against you as a black person. So, as a young guy at that time, we used to get together, we used to talk about the condition, and, believe it or not, to a man, or to a young man at that time, everybody was experiencing the same condition – the same discrimination, the same approach. You'd talk about it, you'd discuss it, and it was so frustrating because there was nobody as far as the larger community to represent you. And it's like a powder keg, it builds up. At that time you used to look forward to the weekend. Come Friday night, it's party night. In those days – Friday, Saturday night – you could walk from one house to another and you find a party. It keeps your sanity, it takes you away for a while from the reality of the hostility that you'd deal with probably from Monday through till Friday. But even so, you could see and you could feel the frustration building up day by day, week by week, and there was nobody to talk to. Without the music, without the Friday night shebeen and the Saturday night parties, I don't know what we would have done as a people. It held us together. It really did. It held us together in those days, I mean, we were moving from ska into rock steady, you know, and the rock steady was so warm and sweet it take us right back to the Caribbean. It take us away. You needed something then to take you from the pressures of the climate, situation, the culture, the food, the hostility against you as a man of colour. And the music for a brief moment on a Saturday night take us way back to the Caribbean. We

[8] Interview with Linton Kwesi Johnson.

could talk, we could intermingle, we could dance, and we could just feel the groove. Very, very important, the only thing that pull us together is our colour and the music; and the only thing that take us away from the day to day jobs of life was the music on a Saturday night.

'So the music played a major part, very much so, and it still do today. I decide to go to music school, learn to play the piano, we form a band way back then, called the Black Volts, in Battersea. We used to rehearse in places like Brixton. In those days it was the Black Volts and another band from Battersea called Matumbe, and we used to play all the local clubs. We used to go Europe and, once again, it was a fantastic experience. We used to entertain black people and I mean it was strictly Reggae, trying to play the type of music that was coming out of Jamaica. So we did that for about ten, fifteen years. I remember the first Reggae promotion to be done in south London, with live band from this country, was done by us in conjunction with Matumbe. We hired a church hall in Lavender Hill and we decide to promote our first show, and we put on that show and we were playing things like "Liquidator". And the whole community turned out because, in those days, once you have a get together, everybody turned up and, believe it or not, we didn't make a penny. But it was one of our most enjoyable experience because we had about four or five hundred people in there, even though they knock the door down and they didn't pay. But they had a great night and the experience was our first as far as playing live, and it stay with me until this very day. I suppose it will stay with me for ever. And there was where people like Matumbe start coming. You walk around in south London and everybody used to call to you, "I saw you on Saturday. Wicked! Wicked!" and we develop and we start to play and we just take off from there. Those were the days when we do it, and, there weren't that many bands. They had people like ourself and Matumbe in south London. You had the Cimarons over in Harlesden, round that way, that was before people like Aswad and Maxi Priest and all these people come about. So we were the predecessor, we set the standard for these guys. In those days people were talking about, well, let's play Afro rock, and different kind of music, soul music. There were people who were playing that kind of music, but we believe in the Reggae music in those days. We stay with it, we stay with it.'[9]

---

[9] Interview with Mike Nesbeth.

23

'Police were the main problem because, as far as we were concerned, as black kids, you couldn't go anywhere without a copper creasing your collar, sort of thing, he'd be on you. Where are you off to? What are you doing? Turn your pockets out. At that time, you had the sus laws going on, and they could do whatever they want, basically, and they did. Turn you out, up against the wall, on the floor, in the back of the car. And if they didn't like your face, if your face didn't fit, or you was a bit too lippy, as most black kids are, you'd get a little kicking. Maybe then you'd get taken down the cell and get a good kicking, which quite a few of us did as well, for nothing. And that's just how it was. That's how it was in our time. What can I say?'[1]

'I walked around Brixton where I worked at the time very quickly with my hands in my pockets, never stopping because you would see people being rounded up, police vans pulling up, people just thrown out of bus queues in to the back of vans. It was something that you knew a lot about but it didn't affect me to that extent because I was sufficiently sharp to know what I shouldn't do, which was hanging around. I didn't even wait for a bus, or don't run because you automatically become suspicious. So just being black and being on a street was very frightening because you were seen as acting suspiciously.'[2]

'That's how the Black Parents' Movement came about, because we were parents ourselves, and, for example, there was the case we dealt with in Ealing, and we could not get the father to go to court. That was the other thing, the children were on their own, because their parents felt that they were bad, and they never went with them. And we have to say, "Well, you have to do that, it's important." And I remember that father coming here after being persuaded to go to

[1] Interview with Wayne Haynes.
[2] Interview with Sir Herman Ouseley.

court, and he said how thankful he was, that he didn't realise the policemen were so bad. So the parents also contributed in that way, and it didn't take long before the whole question of sus became a great issue, up and down the country.'[3]

Suspected Persons

Growing up in London the police were a natural hazard, like poisonous snakes, or attack dogs off the leash. You walked past them with care because you knew that if anything happened you would be questioned and searched or arrested. This knowledge wasn't the result of hearing rumours or gossip, or from reading books about what happened. What I knew derived from having precisely that experience repeated over and over again from the time I was a schoolboy on the way home from school. One summer evening I was on my way home from the running track and, at the top of our road, I began running the hundred yards to the house, which I was always doing, partly to see if my times had got any better. I had just got to the gate when I heard a police siren start up behind me, a police car cut in front, two policemen got out, grabbed me, threw me against the wall and began searching my pockets. 'Why did you start running when you saw us?' one of them shouted at me. After I persuaded them that I hadn't seen them at all and that I simply liked running they let me go, but that cured me of running in the street, because I knew that it wouldn't have taken much for things to have turned out very differently. Other boys I knew were less fortunate, but one way or another we were always being stopped and questioned by policemen. What made all this so hard to bear wasn't only the violence of the police, or their racist abuse and harassment. If you were a black boy, implicit in all these confrontations was the certain knowledge that you were facing a white man who could beat you, or send you to prison, or even kill you, just because of the colour of your skin, and there would be very little that anyone could do about it. But what hurt the most was their casual contempt, the

[3] Interview with Jessica Huntley.

way they flaunted their power over you and their determination to make you understand that you were less than they were.

Until I arrived at university I hadn't encountered anyone who regarded policemen without a similar apprehension, and when I began to meet such people, the fact that they saw the police merely as people in uniform doing a job, seemed to me incredible and almost miraculous. This was before the situation worsened.

'Sus' was shorthand for 'suspected person', which was the term used when you were charged under the Vagrancy Act of 1824. This allowed the police to arrest people they suspected of whatever crimes came into their heads. Police forces in London and a couple of other cities began to use the Act towards the start of the seventies and it was abolished a decade later after a fierce campaign.

Looking back on those days it is still hard to believe that the behaviour of the police towards us could have been so brutal and abusive during those times, or that it could have been as widespread and relentless as it was. For instance, during the evening at the youth club where I worked part time, or at the hostel where I lived, if one of the boys didn't turn up or was late for an appointment we started phoning the police stations or the hospitals, because it was an almost unquestionable assumption that he would have been picked up or injured by the police. In much the same way, when the phone rang you knew that almost anything might have happened.

The increasing tradition of riot policing and the use of specialist squads to patrol areas where black people lived had something to do with it. The storm of police harassment was also associated with the tabloid importation of the term 'mugging' from the USA and the typecasting of young black men as the 'muggers'. The final confirmation of the notion's importance came when Enoch Powell, in one of his periodic mischief making speeches at Cambridge, described mugging as a 'racial crime' perpetrated by young black men on the white population.

Attitudes within the police 'canteen culture' already shared many features with the National Front, and many policemen resented the Race Relations legislation which allowed black people to complain of racist harassment or brutality.

'Police cars and Pandas in those days, when they used to see me, quite a number of them would just put their fingers up to me, and although I didn't take any notice of it I was once told by one Superintendent, "Listen, my police officers can't arrest these black

youths." I said, "Why not?" He said, "Because they keep saying
that they're going to report them to you." I said, "Well, how on earth
can I stop a police officer arresting someone who lawfully needs to
be arrested? If it is unlawful and it's coming from a racist attitude,
and it's unfair, and they come to me, then I will try and help them,
see how we can best resolve it. But to say that your police officers
are frightened to arrest these youngsters because they're frightened
they're going to take it up with the Race Relations Officer, this is
nonsense." Well that was the type of thing I was seeing. I was told,
though, when I left to take up my post in London, from the person
who took over from me, when they knew I was leaving the city, the
cheer went up throughout the whole of the police stations of
Coventry. Although it's a bit of a laugh at the time, I felt it was
sad. But, nevertheless, it was a very difficult time for the police and
for me in realising that racist attitudes were just incompatible with
good policing. They now accept that, but they didn't when I was
there in '68.'[4]

'Here we face a really difficult problem, and it's one we faced
right the way from the beginning, when all this started. On the one
hand, there's the actual dynamics involved in the conflict between
young people and the police, in the neighbourhoods where they live
and move. On the other hand, there's the way in which that conflict
is represented as a national problem of race. It came to be believed
by people that conflict between young blacks and the police was
the essence, the very substance of the problem of race, for the country
as a whole.

'Now, today this might seem a laughable notion, but at this time,
there was a shift. In the early period, people had thought of black
settlers and their children as rather predisposed to be law abiding.
And yet, in a very short period of time, all of those assumptions about
the fact that we were rather less criminal than we might have been,
demographically and sociologically, was exploded. And the police, of
course, are intimately involved in creating this new expression, in
which we are suddenly thought of as being much more predisposed
to be criminal, and criminal in particular ways that actually
expressed our alien nature and our distance from the sorts of

[4] Interview with Paul Stephenson.

behavioural standards and conventions associated with the proper conduct of citizenship.

'So we're watching that idea being created. And it's created through arguments about mugging and street crime, it's created through arguments about black culture and recreation, clubs, and youth clubs, and so on, Reggae festivals, all of this bonfire night in Chapel Town,[5] the carnival in Notting Hill. All of these things fold into a large explanation which says, "Black people are generally predisposed to be criminal, and it's their culture which produces this criminality. It's their family life which sanctions it. It's the conflict between generations which reproduces it as a pathology, and we good, noble, British people, are at a loss to know how to intervene in that cycle of criminal pathology."

'The police are interesting players in this, 'cos on the one hand they throw up their hands and say, "We don't know what to do. We don't want to get into conflict with people. Our job is not to be a military force", et cetera. But, the fact is, the police are intimately involved in creating and manipulating that idea. They begin, for example, to release criminal statistics, which purport to show that blacks are more criminal than whites, that young blacks are more criminal than young whites. They put advertisements in the newspaper, *The Police Federation*, put advertisements in the newspaper to this effect, and their supporters in Parliament take this line as a representative line, speaking for the institution and, of course, the senior managers, the people in charge of the police force themselves, have a kind of dalliance with this idea, because they think they can use it, instrumentally, to win more resources and more legitimacy for the things they're trying to attempt. Now, I think that's a big story in itself, and it's an interesting one, but it's not the story of the black communities, and it's not the story of what their experience of this almost colonial relationship with arbitrary police power and police violence added up to.

'What emerges from all this is that once you've decided that you're dealing with more than just individual criminals, the question then becomes, how you manage criminal populations whose criminality can be explosively violent. I think the solution to this, partly by design, partly not, I suppose, was the sense that we might

---

[5] A reference to the famous incident of Bonfire Night 1975 in Chapel Town, Leeds, when an affray took place between the police and a largely black crowd of youths.

be able to contain these populations, we could keep them physically in certain areas where certain things might be tolerated. One of the things about the way the law works in this country is that policemen are not charged with having to apply it rigidly, they enjoy an original authority, they can be discretionary in the way they apply the law. So, they can overlook the way that things are going in this particular area, as long as another area is operating in a different way. So, the sus law was really about trying to regulate and manage a location, to keep people who were deemed to be criminal out of certain locations and confine them to others. Characteristically, of course, in London, this is about what happens when young men find themselves wanting to move into the centre of the city, to go into the West End, where their presence was not necessarily going to be tolerated in the way that it might be if they'd stayed at home in the neighbourhood where they resided.

'It doesn't have to be the sus law, actually, if you look at other parts of the country where the sus law didn't apply – in Birmingham, for example – they had another statute, passed in the aftermath of the Napoleonic wars to keep the vagrants moving back to their homes. It doesn't have to be the sus law. But what you find in each area, whether or not it's the sus law itself which is being used, is a kind of discretionary operation of police power and it's always something that's spatialised, it's always something that's localised, it's always something about keeping people in one area and excluding them from another. It doesn't matter which law lends itself to that, the mechanism is the same.'[6]

The black community's response to sus was a precise echo of its reaction to all the other crises which had been occurring over the previous years. The 'Scrap Sus' campaign drew together every element within the immigrant population with a remarkable unity of purpose and vigour of execution. Several different individuals lay claim to be the first or the most vigorous of the campaigners, but what mattered was that, in the process of the campaign the gap between parents and children began to close. At a different level, the sus campaign sketched out a role for the most energetic and well qualified professionals who had emerged from the school experience in the sixties, and blended their experience with that of the generation which had succeeded them.

---

[6] Interview with Paul Gilroy.

'Well, I came down from Cambridge, I was with the Home Office as a graduate trainee, but I always had a passion for politics, and I just was going to all types of meetings. I remember going, in the late seventies, to a conference – a national conference of black women in Brixton. It was the first of its kind, and there were hundreds of black women in the Abeng Community Centre in Brixton. I just thought it was magic and I got drawn into all types of community activity. And I got drawn into the sus campaign in particular. I mean, I was in it, Paul [Boateng] was in it, a number of us were in it. I think one of the things about the sus campaign was it drew young black people and older black people together because it was older people, particularly mothers, who could see they'd come to this country believing in a society, believing in a status quo, being brought up to respect the police and respect people with authority, and they were seeing, in their own lives, how their young children were getting harassed. And I think probably the important thing about the sus campaign was, first of all, police harassment of black youth is on the cutting edge of the relationship between black people. But it was also a campaign where, for the first time, that older generation of black people were saying, "Hey, hello. What's going on? There's something not quite right about this society." '[7]

'The Black Parents' Movement was born out of Cliff McDaniel, who was beaten up by the police in north London. It was that period when you had the stop and search all the time, that took place up and down the country, and at Uxbridge Road the police were very active. They were as active in the seventies as the National Front were. So the youngsters, when they have any problems, they would come into the book shop. And the sus campaign began in this borough, because a number of them were arrested, and they came into the bookshop and said the police have taken down so many people. At that time, we had a Black Parents' Movement, and we had *Race Today*, and we worked very closely together. So we combined, and we launched the anti-sus campaign in St James' Place, St James' Hall, just around the corner. And that is where we started the ball rolling, really to make people aware, because experiences were the same in all the boroughs. People were being picked on and people were being sent to prison. Youngsters were imprisoned on just the

---

[7] Interview with Diane Abbott MP.

evidence of the policemen, without any evidence they were accused of stealing. It was very serious. Generally speaking, you had to have evidence of a purse might have been stolen, or a watch, or a camera. But there were cases where there was no evidence at all, just the word of a policeman, and they were sent to prison.'[8]

'I was a young lawyer living in south London, a black man. One couldn't but be other than involved. It was affecting my practice, it was affecting my friends, affecting my neighbours. And a group of black women, in the main, from Lewisham, asked me to come to a meeting. And it really developed from that. Alex Lyon I remember, the MP and former Home Office minister was also at that meeting. It was highly charged. The women were very concerned. They were very together, they started the campaign and I was glad to be asked to be their legal adviser. Black youngsters, their children, were being picked on. The law was clearly unfair in itself and unfairly applied. And they wanted to do something about it. I think what was important about that meeting and, indeed, about that whole campaign, is that it wasn't black people asking white people to do something for them, it was black people organising to make sure something happened. And, in so doing, taking up a campaign really that had been waged on and off, never successfully, until that time, since the Napoleonic Wars themselves when the sus laws were first invented. So it was an enormously important campaign and those black women, really, I think established beyond doubt that it was possible for the black community, post-war, to organise effectively and to bring about change.

'I was their legal adviser, an advocate for their cause, worked with them and for them. What it meant was that in addition to my practice as a lawyer in the community defending people in court, making sure that we mounted a defence that attacked the root cause, which was prejudice and bigotry, which revealed that, in fact, many of those who were arrested were arrested primarily because they were black and young. It was important to make that clear, because by the end of the campaign we had won the support of many magistrates who wanted to see the law changed. So, it was also my job to help draft the submissions to the Home Affairs Committee, to actually appear before the Home Affairs Committee in the House of

[8] Interview with Jessica Huntley.

Commons in order to make the case for the abolition of the sus laws. That I did and it was certainly my first experience, face to face, with Parliament. It was also, importantly for me, a pretty pivotal time because I saw, again face to face, how totally unresponsive local government was to that campaign. I remember attending one meeting of a council in south London and the condescension, the paternalism, the arrogance, actually, displayed towards this group of people, convinced me that I ought to go into elected politics. I mean, I'd been a member of the Labour Party as a Young Socialist and afterwards since I was fifteen, but I think it was that time, for me, that said, well, local government ought not to be organised like this. They ought to have been more responsive, they ought to have known. They ought to be treating people better and differently. And that's what got me into local government.

'Being alongside them at the demonstrations was never a choice. It wasn't enough simply to appear inside the court. You had to be with your clients and their mums and their dads and the community when it mattered. You had to be alongside them in every way, and I didn't have a moment's doubt or hesitation about that. It was important that lawyers were there to be counted, as part of the community. Because we are just that. You know the idea that black people who have a profession, the idea that the black middle classes should somehow separate themselves from the mass of the people – or would be able to. I remember once appearing for a very bright and able young man who was the son of a very upper middle class, black professional woman, who lived in Putney. And she just could not believe, actually, that this was happening to her son. But, of course, so far as the police were concerned, he was just another black youth, and she learned from that experience – as did many other black middle-class parents – that there is no escaping from the reality of racism.

'In the end it was a triumph for the black community. It was a triumph for those women in Lewisham, those black women in Lewisham who had the notion that they were going to do something about it. It was a very important day for the black community. I never, however, kidded myself for one moment that that meant that was going to be the end of a problematical relationship between the black community and the police. But it did remove a major irritant, and I think it was the beginning of a process that did see the police themselves come to terms with the fact that, yes, there was an issue about racism which they needed to tackle. In the seventies the very notion that the police would ever admit that racism was an issue was unthinkable. And I think the success of the "Scrap Sus" campaign brought the police partially to terms with the fact that they had a problem which they had to address.'[9]

The success of the 'Scrap Sus' campaign had given the black communities a feeling of confidence which fed a new sense of belonging within the environment. It had also introduced new methods of political organisation and public relations expertise. It was clearly possible to get something from the process of political lobbying, even for a minority under pressure. It was a perception which was to move significant numbers of the newly radicalised black professionals into the political arena. On the other hand, the operation of sus and the storm of harassment through the seventies had left deep wounds, and the consequences were to fuel new crises at the start of the eighties.

[9]   Interview with Paul Boateng. Paul Boateng's father was a senior Ghanaian politician and his English mother returned to Britain in the sixties with the children. Boateng qualified as a lawyer and began his career working at law centres in Notting Hill and Paddington early in the seventies. He was elected to the GLC in 1981 and then became an MP in 1987. Presently he is a junior Minister in the Labour Government.

24

'When I signed on to do the Minstrel Show I was assured that it would be good experience. I was working in all the big clubs and the big theatres in Britain. Straight into the Blackpool Opera House, a 3,000 seater – one of the biggest theatres in the country for twenty-two weeks in 1976. Then Great Yarmouth, then Bournemouth. So these were big venues and big shows. Great experience, and you can really hide. It was that kind of thing, and people aren't watching you, they're watching the costumes and the shows and the songs. But I was a young guy, I was seventeen, eighteen when I was doing the show, and every so often it was like I was split into two and on my shoulder would be this thing of, "You know there's a fundamental problem with you being in this show, don't you, Len?" And the other side going, "God, just take the money and have a great time." But this voice on my right shoulder just got bigger and bigger until, eventually, I couldn't live with it any more. I said to the guy who was running the show, "Look, I feel very uncomfortable in this show now. I know it's normal for you guys, and this show has been running for a long time and it's very successful but, with all due respect, I've got to get out of here because I'm going mad." I'd alienated a lot of my friends who didn't want to come and see it. I would walk out on stage and there would be several black or Asian people in the audience who were there to see Len. But to me they were kind of screaming at me, even though they were enjoying the show, "What are you doing here? Why don't you do something else?" So it was hard, and I carried on with it, but in '79 I said I've got to do something else, 'cos it was killing me.'[1]

'When we were first striking out on our own, again, we were just going through that whole motion of being entrepreneurs, as it were, and we were all in control, at that point, of our own destinies and no one knew better than us, so it was again really great times, and it was where you were getting shunted and then where you weren't accepted,

---

[1] Interview with Lenny Henry.

and it was even better to go into those areas where you weren't accepted and just go on with your tactics. It was fantastic, personally, for me, being in the neighbourhood places like Finsbury Park, Hackney, Stokey [Stoke Newington], south London, but never sweeter than being up town in places like the West End, or when we used to play at a place called Peoples in Praed Street in Paddington. Because whenever you went up town it was what everybody wanted to do, and everybody wanted to adhere to that kind of life and that kind of lifestyle. Yeah, them times was really irie.'[2]

Remaking Identity

Lenny Henry and Jazzy B

The events of the seventies had drawn up a new portrait of the black communities and their goals, and the process had also begun to throw up a number of individuals who reflected its shape and complexity. They figured almost exclusively in sport and entertainment, because there was a Hadrian's Wall of discrimination barring black Caribbeans from prominence in other fields. Two of the figures who emerged from this period to become part of the cultural iconography of contemporary Britain were Lenny Henry and Jazzy B, and their different approaches to their own early careers are a neat illustration of the conflicts that the developing culture of the migrants was struggling to resolve.

Lenny Henry's career began with an appearance on the TV show New Faces. Subsequently, he joined the Black and White Minstrel Show. At the time the Minstrels were the subject of a long-running campaign because of the racist history and implications of the black face make-up which lampooned African features, and Henry came in for considerable criticism among black people. This was amplified by his backers' exploitation of his persona to titillate stereotyped expectations and, for most of the seventies, Henry was the exemplar of a black entertainer who could be tolerated by white audiences, but who presented no challenge to their prejudices.

---

[2] Interview with Jazzy B. Jazzy B's parents are Antiguan, and he was brought up in Finsbury Park, north London. He went to school at Highbury Comprehensive during the seventies. His father wanted him to be a doctor, but he became a sound system operator and DJ in the north London clubs. He founded Soul II Soul, a music co-operative whose best-known record was 'Get A Life'. Jazzy B is famous for his commitment to a black British persona and Soul II Soul is focused around that concept.

'The press took it as a huge joke. "Black comedian to be in Black and White Minstrels Show", and there were lots of pictures of me standing next to a Black and White Minstrel. I was taking his make-up off with a sponge and he'd be taking my make-up off.'[3]

Henry eventually quit the Minstrels and began transforming his persona by recreating his act to feature portraits of his friends and relatives, followed by satirical sketches of black British characters, sometimes invented, sometimes real, like the newscaster Trevor MacDonald. In the circumstances, it was a radical and imaginative move, which firmly identified him with the new black culture in the migrant areas and began making the language and the mannerisms of black Britain part of the landscape of popular culture.

'The ways out of the ghetto are sport, boxing, athletics, football, music or entertainment. Or crime. That was the way to make some serious money. I knew people at my school who were great footballers or great artists, or whatever, but it needs something else. I think it needs a tenacity and a real will to succeed. It's not just an inborn talent, it's a real sense of "I've got to get out of here. I've got to do this." That's what I had. I really wanted it with so much heart. So it's not just, "He'll get out of here 'cos he can kick a ball about." You've got to really not just be talented, but have a head on your shoulders, a strategic head.

'I remember Cy Grant, he was one of the few black people that were on television in the sixties that you would stop and listen to. I also remember the black guy in The Spinners, who was astounding. I did a joke about him in the last show I did. He was there with his finger stuck in his ear singing, "Dance, dance, wherever you may be, I am the Lord of the dance said he." Every so often they'd let him sing the West Indian song. Just once I wanted him to grab the mike and say, "I shot the sheriff . . ." But, knowing him, he'd have probably gone, "I'll go no more a-sheriff shooting, sheriff shooting, sheriff shooting." But I remember that guy. There weren't very many British black people doing it when I was growing up. There weren't very many role models – apart from American people – to aspire to. It was very difficult, I think. People needed to be shown that there was a possibility that you could do something. And I think that's what whole generations were waiting for – the ticket. "What do I

[3] Interview with Lenny Henry.

have to do to get out of here? Can I be an entrepreneur?" Well, no. It felt like we are being blocked in that way. "Can I be a top sportsman?" Well, yes, because you sort of can do that. "Can I be a musician?" Yes, I can do that.

'For a while, a lot of black performers didn't really feel that they could be comedic, because the people who went to shows in the sixties and early seventies were a predominantly white audience. So comedians thought that unless you could entertain a white audience it was very difficult for you to get bookings. People thought, "Oh well, you're just going to go out there and do a lot of stuff about being black." So the black comedians at the time just sort of told the jokes about black people that white comedians did. That was the acceptable thing. So you have to understand that Charlie Williams[4] was perfect for the time that he appeared. It was a brilliant thing, this black Yorkshireman who played football for Doncaster Rovers, who'd had the wartime experience of white Yorkshire people, who talked like them, who thought like them, but who just happened to be black. And when he came along it was astounding to hear this bloke talking like, "Eh up, flower, eh. Hey, have you ever been down to supermarket where they have the broken biscuits?" I think it was a huge culture shock for people. And Charlie exploited it to the full. He had the Roller and the big house and he was the king of comedy for a while and God bless him, good luck to him. Because at the time, nobody was doing what he was doing. He was playing the fat belly, bigoted Northern comedian at their own game, and, I think there were some jokes that he did that keep being quoted.

'The joke which we've all done – "If you don't shut up I'll come and move in next door to you" – but that joke said: "Look, I'm aware that this is what some white people think, so I'm going to say it first before you guys say it." I think quite a lot of black comedians at that time did jokes like that because they wanted the audience to know that they knew. "I know what you're thinking, so I'm going to put you at ease by saying all this stuff first." So you would do the, "I know what you're thinking. He's a big bugger." All those jokes. "Ooh, is he going to come move in next door and going to run off with my daughter or my wife?" It was all those fears of black, male domination and being invaded, being overrun by the

---

[4] Charlie Williams was a former professional footballer who enjoyed huge popularity on television in the seventies, and in the Northern clubs alongside comedians like Bernard Manning. He specialised in 'black' jokes.

immigrant. And I think those comedians exploited those fears, but also told some good jokes along the way. And I went through a period of thinking it was all bad, man, and my stuff's a reaction against that. But, actually, in the stuff that I did in the early days, I made just as many mistakes as those guys did. I just think it was the times and you did what you had to do to get by. I don't think there was any harm meant by it. I think you did what you had to do to survive in a predominantly white world.

'People in Britain watched the Black and White Minstrels and my mum would watch it, and nobody ever mentioned that these people was blacked up. It was always, "Ooh, aren't the songs lovely?" And then, "Ooh, look at those costumes. And aren't those sets great?" And people were pissed off about it, sure, but people would go, "Oh what – this is not a racial show. This show isn't a racial issue. They're just great songs." Nobody ever faced up to this fact of why are all these guys blacked up? What's going on there? Nobody was watching me, nobody cared about comedians in that show. They wanted to hear the old songs and look at the nice costumes and look at the sets. But the fundamental thing at its centre, which is why I had to leave, in the end, was this issue of nobody saying anything about the whole blacking up issue. This is something that has stuck in the craw of black people in this country for years and years and years. And nobody's saying anything about it, and I have to go, I have to leave. And, so I did leave in the end, 'cos eventually I got it.

'I think it was the pressure that I was under. I was being paid and I was staying in nice digs and all that kind of stuff. But the pressure that I felt from my friends and from my family was such that I just thought, "I've made a mistake here and I've got to get out." And the mistake wasn't in doing the show and getting stage time and getting experience and learning how to time a joke, and all that, it was just a fundamental thing of – just because this is the norm for people in this country, you are a second generation West Indian guy and they've made a miscalculation with you. And you're too young to have seen, initially, that this was a mistake. But now that you're twenty, twenty-one, you've got to move on and do something else. So once I'd reached that age, and I'd reached that maturity, I put the case forward and I split. In 1980 I did the Cannon and Ball Show and it was such a relief to go and be on a show where the audience had come to see comedy. They weren't interested in the Black and White Minstrels, or whatever, they'd just come to see funny people. It was such a wonderful release. The big, big laughs, bigger than anything I'd ever got with the Minstrels. It was like something had been torn open and I was free.

'I think it's good that I did it. Later on I did a South Bank Show with Paul Mooney, who's one of the most aggressive, pro-black comedians in America. He used to write for Richard Pryor, wrote on In Living Colour. I'm sitting with him and we were doing this routine about black face, and we were talking about the history of black face and everything. And as I was looking at myself in the mirror – and it sounds like too much of an arranged thing now, but at the time I didn't really think about my involvement in the Black and White Minstrels until I was looking at myself, wearing this black face make-up to make a point about how people in America had to do it – and then suddenly I realised that I'd done the Black and White Minstrels Show. I'd worked with people in black face too. And then suddenly there was this big "bing", this bell ringing inside me and I thought, "Oh God, I've got to tell Mooney about the Black and White Minstrels Show." And I told him. And he said something like, "Well, it's something you had to go through. This is something that we in America have had to deal with and you've had it in England and you've had to deal with it too. You've had to work in these shows and you're not the only black comedian that's been involved with these shows." Many black comedians, like Dusty Richards, I think, had to wear black face to be accepted by a bigger audience. It's something that some comedians have had to do. And it's very funny to watch the newer black comedians who are much more militant and stroppy than we ever were, talking about stuff they wouldn't do now. But maybe I had to go through that so that newer and more aggressive stuff could happen.

'My next gig on Tiswas meant I got to do thirty-two weeks of live television every Saturday morning. I'd had the Minstrels experience of learning how to do a twelve-minute set, and I'd done cabaret and pantomime, but here was an opportunity to learn how to work with a camera, to learn about the basics of television production, to figure out where I fitted and how to behave on camera. Not just to perform, but also to just be, 'cos there were many times on Tiswas where you just had to sit there and think of a funny thing to say and then say it. You didn't have to prepare a three minute thing, it was just being there and if an opportunity arose you leapt in with a line. I was working with Chris Tarrant, who is a television animal. This guy doesn't blink when he's on camera, live. He could improvise with the best of them. So, suddenly, I was with this guy at the peak of his powers. It was very, very demanding. And he didn't just want darkie jokes, actually. He told me very, very early on, "I don't want any of that stuff. I don't want any of that Charlie Williams stuff that you've been doing. You've got to think of stuff. What new stuff are you going to bring?" And for the first series I was doing an impression of Jim Davidson and Mike Reid's impersonation of how they thought black people spoke, because I knew that was acceptable on the telly. So, instead of doing an impression of my dad or my uncles, or something, I was doing an impression of what white comedians were doing in their impersonations of blacks. A really weird, screwed up situation. But Tarrant sort of shook me out of that and said, "You've got to figure out what it is you want to do, otherwise I think I'm going to have to let you go." And that was a real kick up the arse.'[5]

Jazzy B, in complete contrast with Lenny Henry, started his career as part of the Jamaican oriented culture which had been developing over the decade. His parents actually came from Antigua but, by then, black British young people whose parents had their origins all over the Caribbean, took for granted a musical heritage based on the sound systems, dub, Reggae and Rastafarianism, and rooted in Kingston, Jamaica. On the other hand, Jazzy B was always conscious of being shaped by the environment in which he grew up. By the time he arrived at school it had begun to reflect the changes of the intervening years, and transformed itself from a white working-class stronghold into a multi-racial site.

'I actually grew up in north London, Hornsey Rise, Finsbury Park is the area where I grew up. Hornsey was predominantly like a lot of black people, a lot of Greek people, a lot of Asians as well, particularly, even if you look at it now, in Stroud Green Road and places like that, predominantly Asian and black. The school I went to was definitely a similar mix of various different ethnic backgrounds, and we had quite a strong presence of a lot of black people, particularly from the Caribbean. I think it really lent a hand towards being able to understand different cultures, particularly London being that whole melting pot or sweltering pot, or whatever, and I think it helped to shape my life in the future as well.'[6]

[5] Interview with Lenny Henry.
[6] Interview with Jazzy B.

Although his parents wanted him to be a professional man, a doctor or a lawyer, he set out to be a sound system DJ or a footballer, reflecting the reach and the expectations of the culture into which he had grown. Soul II Soul was a sound system, but through the later seventies the group expanded and moved into production. Eventually they coalesced into a collective which amalgamated styles and personalities, drawing on a dazzling assembly of heterogeneous sources, and their first international hit was like a programmatic outline of the elements which went to making up the black British persona. In the video, Jazzy strolls down an inner London street, crested by dreadlocks and waving a ceremonial stick, in full Rastafarian fig. A group of mixed race children in a park play amongst the autumn leaves chanting the tag line, 'What's the meaning, what's the meaning of life?' A singer, backed up by a line of dancers in a painstakingly recreated forties ensemble repeats Jazzy's exhortations, 'Elevate your mind, free your soul.' A line-up of black classical musicians in evening dress play the harmony on violins. The collection of images is an unmistakable statement about the hybrid nature of black British identity.

'What happened in this country is that you was exposed to so many different things coming out of the Jamaican community because they were a larger community based in London, and the sound system was really such a cultural aspect of all of us growing up. I can remember times in school where you come in on a Monday, and during my day everyone was into punk rockers and stuff like that, and the man would say, "Oh, I had six pints and spewed out of everywhere, man, it was really wicked weekend", where we would say, "Yeah, I hid in a speaker box down Club Norik so they didn't chuck me out." You used to have afternoon session, used to hide in Fatman's boxes so you won't get thrown out, and they could never understand it. I think coming up to the ages of thirteen, fourteen was really where things started to become somewhat divided and more attention was probably paid on the fact of where I saw myself in years to come. For example, in the woodwork class, everybody else made a chair or a stool, we built speaker boxes. And I guess from them early days we had the ambition and the drive to know what we wanted to achieve, and the next stage was really about Soul II Soul being like an international sound system where our music will be played in as many places as possible.

'It probably was difficult to bring British music to people who listened to Jamaican music, but for me there was almost a period of time where everybody was so saturated by the whole popular music,

I actually think it helped. It helped listening to things like the Bay City Rollers and the Osmonds and them kind of a groups 'cos more than a lie, them people's music was tearing down everything. I don't remember the Beatles. I know I remember things like, I don't know, Tom Jones, and them kind of man there 'cos my mum was into that. But in my house it was more on the Blue Spot,[7] you was listening in to a couple of bluebeat tunes, and stuff like that. And then the biggest breakthrough was when, you know, Millie Small came over, "My Boy Lollipop", and I think that changed everybody. Every person who's from the Caribbean, it changed their perspective on the whole musical sphere and what was going on that the music was transcending. And obviously during that period of time there were greats from Fats Domino right through to James Brown. But I think they were just taken as almost like the wallpaper, if you like. They were the pillars of our environment, anyway, and I think the big difference was when you came through with Reggae music during that period of time. It made a huge difference, you know, and it really made people see the wood from the trees.

'When we first started out, it was very exciting. I can remember running away from Teddy Boys who was trying to duff us up, and I can remember sitting on over a bunch of skinheads and then playing some U-Roy tune and I'm being totally amazed that these are guys who try and beat us up but they're listening to our music. Well, it was just exciting. There were so few outlets, but we were enriched so heavily in our culture. Back in that day there was a lot more – and I hate sounding really old and everything, but it's true – back in them day, you were a lot closer with your cousins and a little more distant relatives. The old Wolsely or the Zodiac used to come out and you'd all pile in there and you'd break bread with a lot of people who you probably wouldn't see again until the next Easter, or whenever the pardner hand was drawn again. Those really great days around the paraffin heater, and, like, nine, ten people in a room and kind of lining up for your food. How sweeter the food was during those days, because everything from bread being baked right through to the chicken in the oven and ra-ra-ra. Them kind of things, those were beautiful times.

'I think the conscious decision with Soul II Soul taking it into

[7] The Blue Spot was the Grundig radiogram without which no Caribbean migrant home in the period was complete.

the mainstream is just simply like this: we were a sound system that were playing like seven days a week. We wanted to play more, but we couldn't. And we thought, What's the biggest sound going to be? How are we going to take on Saxon and all them kind of sounds and be better than all the sound system? Because I come from an area of people like Fatman and them guys have big sound systems, and the only other way was just to get everybody to play your record. So as well as making our own dubs and specials that we were tearing. And by that time, in the mid-eighties, we transcended from the blues scene and the community centres, through to playing more to a wider demographics and up town, up town being out of Finsbury Park, in the West End and in Old Street and playing up various places like that.

'There were great DJs in the seventies like Sir Lord Emperor and Emperor Rosco and all them people there, they were massive. And it was always our thing just to keep our interest based in the sound system, and we'd utilise all what we'd learned from being a sound and try and transcend that into our method of doing business and eventually coming out on an international vibe as we did. And a lot of that was not just myself, but there was lots of other people involved in helping us to make that move too. White people, Asian people, everybody was involved, which is the interesting thing about this scenario. We weren't stupid, we knew who made the microphone and who signed the cheque and where the cheque was going to be banked. Plus, the nucleus Soul II Soul had built, like we were a multi-cultural scenario and we still are, and we're still going to be. So it made a big difference, because we were typically black young men understanding that we were going through nonsense and knowing that for us to get to the next stage, most of the nightclub owners or people own the warehouse were all white people. The great thing that we all had in common though was the music, and when it came down to the music, the music speaks everybody's language and you know it hits us all in various different ways. Which, again, was pretty incredible for us to stumble across that factor, and at the same time appreciating all the different scenarios that we would have to be in.

'There's a great way I describe the difference between British music and American music: a pizza. You got deep pan pizza and you got thin and crusty pizza. English music is like the thin pizza, right, really light toppings, easily digestible, where the Americans is like that deep pan, cheese round the edge, or a load of dough chilling for hours and hours. And that's how I describe it, and much the same when you go to America and you eat in America, that's how it is. And I think our music is very much the same. Where our music is somewhat lighter and a little bit more avant garde, and their music is really quite heavy and you have to chew it for a lot longer. People from the Caribbean, our music is much more vibrant, much more character and I think is much more folk story oriented, hence calypso, soca and whatever they're calling it now, it's very story oriented and somewhat more quirky if you like. And in terms of the vibrantness, I think it goes with our culture as well, that we're very upward people, and where our Reggae is concerned it's just in the sensibility of how we can take something as small as it is and make it as huge as your eyes can see. And I think that's again one of the beauties of the people of the Caribbean.

'Soul II Soul's music is an eclectic mix of the Euro/colonial, because it really has the whole traces of European pop elements, laced with the very essence of roots music, Reggae background, which has been formed from being in a colonial environment. And it kind of helps to transcend itself or lends itself to various different elements, and particularly that whole thing about the story, the element of story, of folk, or whatever. I think, if you listen to Soul II Soul's music, there's no doubt about it, there is always an element of some kind of a message or some term of optimism going around in our music as well. I think that's synonymous with us, and it's to do with our cultural backgrounds as well.

'I'm in the footsteps of people like Eddie Grant, you know, Cy Munday, Loose Ends, Junior Gisk and David Joseph, High Tension, the Incognito. Gosh, the list endless. There were so many before us which we must always pay our respects to, and understanding now in the latter days we're moving on, those are the ones who gave me the inspiration to go on. Hooking up with all the people that helped to develop and make Soul II Soul which are people who have now transcended their careers on to other great and wonderful things. People like Caron Wheeler, Kim Mselbe, Toyah Wilson, James Howie, Tricky, Nellie Hooper and everybody has their input in regards to making that name of Soul II Soul what it is today. And I think it really is that eclectic mix of all the different elements that makes our music somewhat different. I think Soul II Soul is far more like a British sound than a London sound because there's been people all over the UK globe that have been involved in Soul II Soul, so I think it'd be very one-dimensional to suggest that Soul II Soul is just a London thing. We are really more of a British thing. I mean, now black Britain has all types of things to be proud of. I think I'm a bit of both really. I'm black and I'm definitely British, and that's what I am.'[8]

There is a remarkable symmetry about the way that both Lenny Henry and Jazzy B moved from opposing ends of the cultural spectrum, through equally characteristic experiences, to become focal protagonists in the movement of black British culture into the centre of popular culture in Britain. As they identified the direction in which they were travelling, they were consciously synthesising and manipulating a wide variety of influences and experiences, and using them to recast and control the way that other people saw them and behaved towards them. This represented a dynamic process which, throughout the seventies and the early eighties, was animating the progress of the black community. The vigour and creativity it released would soon begin to feed and reshape the popular imagery of what it meant to be British.

---

[8] Interview with Jazzy B.

25

—◆—

'My mother took it terribly, and she was never the same again. Rest her soul, she's passed away now. But I'm sure there are other parents like that. The Francises, their fight is never ending, it's non-stop, they're always going on. They need to know, why did their child die? Who made their child die? For what reason? Yes, and the reason I'd say for that is that nobody in authority ever really came forward to say anything. There was a fire in Ireland – it might have only been a matter of weeks after – and the Prime Minister, the Queen and everybody, they were in Ireland, fast. Sending their condolences to families of people that had died and been injured and whatever. No one ever came down to see us. No one ever picked up the phone to say, "Well, how are you? How are the children? What happened?" It didn't matter. We didn't matter. We weren't even an afterthought, because you would have thought that after going to Ireland, somebody would have said to them, "Well, hey, what about the kids down in New Cross?" It wasn't even an afterthought, 'cos nobody came to see us, nobody mentioned anything about us. The only authority that we saw was black authority, our own black leaders, who were all stepping up. I mean, nobody couldn't tell me Sibyl Phoenix is not an angel sent down from heaven to help. These people helped, and they helped a lot. But they couldn't do it all. Ros Howells, Alex Pascal, all these different people that we, as black people, looked up to at the time, they were there for us. But as far as we're concerned, black people, that's not authority. Let's deal with the Prime Minister. The Prime Minister went to Ireland, so why didn't the Prime Minister come and see us? What, do we not count? And I've got to admit, to this very day, I feel that deep, deep, deep within my heart.'[1]

'They'd planned the march very carefully. It was a long, long walk that day to pass a number of different symbolic locations that were implicated in this story. We walked up Fleet Street. People

[1] Interview with Wayne Haynes.

may not remember what kind of symbolic location Fleet Street was at that time. You don't think of the power of representation being concentrated in one place any more. But I can remember walking up Fleet Street and looking up at the people leaning out of the *Daily Telegraph* building. And I remember the noise, echoing in between the buildings, the chanting: 'Thirteen dead and nothing said." That moment is something that I will always remember.

'The next place that's really burned in my memory is walking past the Courts of Justice on the Strand, and again the kind of indictment, the intensity of the occasion, walking past this institution which symbolised all of the injustice, all of the failures of that definition of justice to reach out beyond its kind of colour-coded character. I remember the bitterness of passing there.'[2]

'Thirteen Dead, Nothing Said'

The Deptford Fire

In January 1981 thirteen young black people were burned to death when a fire took place during the course of a party at the house of a family named the Ruddocks, in New Cross Road, Deptford. This followed a decade of demonstrations by the National Front, street fighting and letterbox bombings. In the wake of an inconclusive investigation the opinion of the vast majority of black people was that the fire was a racial crime.

A few weeks after the Deptford fire another fire, at a discotheque in Dublin, elicited immediate condolences and public expressions of sympathy from the then Prime Minister, Margaret Thatcher. This was in pointed comparison with her silence after what had happened at Deptford. The difference in the response reinforced the anger and suspicion felt within the black community, particularly when the press, prompted by unattributed leaks and police canteen gossip, began to suggest that the participants had criminal records, and that the fire was the result of typically disorderly West Indian behaviour. For West Indians the Deptford fire became emblematic of the treatment that the black migrants and their children had endured for thirty years. In the ensuing campaign all the emotional and political threads which ran through the history of the migrants began to be pulled together.

---

[2] Interview with Paul Gilroy.

A massive demonstration followed, which, from the point of view of the black communities became a moral indictment, a declaration of intent, and, in hindsight, a crucial turning point in the consciousness of the black communities. One of the slogans which survived the event was a line from a poem by Linton Kwesi Johnson: 'Come what may, we're here to stay.'

'It could have been me, it could have been you'

'I think I was probably the first person to see any form of fire, from the party itself. Because what happened is that you came through the front door, that was the ground floor level, and there you had the front room, and you had the back room, where they were serving the drinks, if I remember rightly. And that's where all the adults were. Nobody was in the front room. The party started on the next floor, and they had a room up on the next floor, and then you had a room up on the floor above that. So it was basically two rooms, but everyone was sort of trying to jam into the one room on the first floor. I can't even remember the time, probably sometime after five, I decided, I'm going to come down and go and get me a drink.

'And I've come down the stairs, and as I'm coming down the stairs I've seen smoke just coming from all underneath the door and everything else. I shouted, "Fire!" And I've turned round and I've sort of run back up the stairs, gone back into the main room where the party is, trying to tell everyone that there's a fire, we've got to get out of here. It was like an old Buster Keaton movie, those black and white movies where it looks like he's doing everything under a strobe light, and it's all slow. That was like it. Nobody was really taking me on. And I went back outside, and as I looked down the stairs I could see fire now coming out of the front room, and it was, like, turn back, I've got to help these people to get out. And I've run back upstairs and I've closed the door to that actual room, and I've tried to get everyone's attention, but it was so packed, I couldn't get over to the sound system, to sort of stop the music and everything. I was shouting. I don't know. By the time I got anybody's attention, and I opened the door to that room, all of a sudden there was fire coming up the stairs and smoke everywhere. So I closed the door back, and I remember I had a big sheepskin coat at the time, and I've taken my sheepskin coat and I've laid it on the floor at the bottom of the door, 'cos the smoke had started to come through the bottom of the door.

'And at this time all hell's broken loose now. Everyone's running around and screaming and breaking windows to try and get help –

everyone trying to get out – because we was trying to push the windows up, but they wasn't going up. By this time, the heat's coming up. It was terrible. There was people there, we were pushing people out of the windows, and helping people to get up and get through the windows and everything else. And personally, in the end, it got far too hot for me to, sort of, like, go through the window, and the window frame was all on fire and stuff like that. And you could feel as though the floor was sort of going down. The strange thing is, I remember at the time, yeah, I definitely, distinctly remember at the time, taking my hands and wiping my face. It felt like I was sweating. I later discovered that it wasn't even sweat, it got so hot in there that people's skin was actually peeling. By that time, I'm sort of, like, well, I ain't taking this no more, I've got to get out. A lot of people have got out, anyway. So I've grabbed my sheepskin coat, and I've stuck my hands in it, sort of like, back to front, and stuck it over my head and pulled the door open and tried to run up the stairs. And that's how I actually got out, through going up the stairs. At the time, I felt that if I went up the stairs, by the time the fire had taken hold properly and got up the stairs behind me, the Fire Brigade would be here and I'd be out of this and safe. It just didn't work like that.

'Funnily enough, there was me and a guy named Basil, Basil Buchanan, and we both climbed out of the same window, but Basil went out before me. And Basil got on the drainpipe and I got on the same drainpipe, and the drainpipe just pulled away from the house. So I've let go, dropped straight down, and Basil's held on and he's ended up in the garden. The next thing I remember after that, I was laying on my back in hospital with about a million people looking at me. But, all the stories are crazy. Some of the guys said that people have run in, have got out and they've run back in. Me, I was found out in the back, they used to have an outside toilet. It's like a little box extension on the back of the house, and that's where I was found in the morning, unconscious and broken up. I'd gone straight through the roof and landed right next to the toilet. The same guy who was on the drainpipe with me, Basil, he ended up breaking his pelvis, and he was found in the back garden. But the fire, it's one of the great focal points of black history in Great Britain. And it's one of the great mysteries that's never been solved.'[3]

'I was coming from Greenwich, and as I turned the corner, I

---

[3] Interview with Wayne Haynes.

realised that there was, kids, really, younger than I was, jumping out of the window – the fire was blazing – screaming. It was frightening to see, because fire was something that I only came across once in my life, and powerlessness was the thing that you felt most. You couldn't physically do anything to actually change what was happening there. We didn't have a hosepipe that you could squirt. And the way in which people were screaming and laying hurt, broken limbs, it was a terrible time. Because, you imagine, you've been out for an evening yourself, you're a bit knackered, you're ready to go home and have some rest, and then you see something like that. I didn't know how to handle it, I must admit, because, you don't wish something like that on anyone. I mean, I think if they were being cut by a knife, they might have preferred that to being burned by the fire, 'cos, at least you might be able to hold the wound and stop it from bleeding too much. But with a fire, it's the whole of you. And I don't know how many people have actually spoken honestly about what they felt, whether being part of it or being in a position where they saw it happening, but, for me, the worst part of it was feeling powerless, not being able to do anything realistically to change it.'[4]

Backdraught

'I met a lady in the street, and she asked me if I heard about the fire they had at four-thirty down New Cross. So I said to her; 'No.' And she said she heard that five kids died in the house. At that time, my spirit just dropped, 'cos I know I had my three kids there. So, I went into the hospital and we went and find Denise, but then we couldn't find the other two. So, I went to the ward sister, and I said to her, "Well, you know, we had two other kids there." And she brought a policeman, and the policeman said to me to give him the description. So my eldest son, Richard, he was with us, and he knew what they was wearing, so he speak to the police, and then, within half an hour, they came back and they find David was in King's College Hospital, but they didn't find Andrew. And we went up to the hospital, and when we got there the sister said, you could see David but he wouldn't recognise you. So I went in and I had a look at Davey, and I was surprised at what I saw. Anyway, I came back

[4] Interview with Harry Powell.

out and another policeman came to me and said that he's trying to locate Andrew. And I sat there for about an hour, and then another one come again and said to me, can I go home? And somebody will come to the house and tell us about Andrew. So we just went home.'[5]

'Well, the same Sunday night, both he and David used to sleep on the bunk beds, one on top and one bottom, he was on top. I opened the door, just like that, I didn't see anything, but then gone into the room, and they had nothing belonged to none of them, but just his smell. And that was so strong, like fire was in there. And I know then that he was one of the victims.

'The Monday, they rang us and told us that they're going to move David from King's and take him to East Grinstead, 'cos in East Grinstead, they got some news that they had two others, with David. So my wife and Andrew, the one that die, his godmother, went to East Grinstead on the Tuesday morning, to see if they could identify. The one died Monday night, and the other one was still there just waiting. And neither one of them was Andrew. He was nowhere to be found. He was in the house. And when they came back from the hospital, two policemen came to the house, and told me not to bring her in the room, because they don't think that she would like to see what they saw. So, they showed me, out of a paper bag, half of a shoe, a piece of his shirt that he was lying on, that didn't burn. He had a chain around his neck, with a ring and a medallion on it. And those were dislocated but they was there. And they asked me if these were the things – I know his shoes, I know the shoes, the colour of his shoe, and the shirt, I remember the colour shirt, a kind of silk, flowered. And, the medallion and the chain he had round his neck. So, I tell them, Yes. They said, "Well, we have this body, over at the morgue, in Ladywell." He said, "Well, I would advise you not to see it." So I said, "If there's much that left, I want to see it." So, he's got Mother and myself, went to Ladywell, and what they showed us, well, it was, you know, on a stretcher, fairly long, see a bit of his shoulder, the head, not hair, not the skin, nothing, it's just like roast meat, that's what it looked to me, like. I said, I don't mind, I want to see it, show it to us through a very clear mirror.

[5] Interview with Ena Gooding. Ena Gooding came from Barbados in 1961 with her husband and settled in north London. The couple had four children – Richard, David, Andrew and Denise. Andrew died in the fire.

'The Monday or the Tuesday morning, this letter came through the door, and it says "A. Gooding". So I thought, more or less, it's one of his schoolmates from school, 'cos he used to go to Forest Hill Boys'. And, anyhow, I was shaking like anything, very nervous, but I opened the letter. And then I opened this letter now, this letter was telling me that it was a great day when all the niggers went up in smoke. And then the person said, "I went to the pub and I had a drink, and a lady was in the pub, and she said, 'Have you just got married?' And he said to her, 'Did you hear about those niggers that went up in smoke?'" And something about that he hoped it's the one that did something to his mother, something like that. The police said it's only a crank that do that kind of thing.'[6]

'The smell of that house. They were still just bringing the bodies out. And I said to the police, "What do you want me to do?" And there were people on the road, and he said, "I'd like you to talk to the people, to ask them to put the message around to anybody who they know that been at this birthday party to get their families to come forward to say who they are and to try to identify people, because there are a number of dead people in there, they're so badly burned, they're going to have problems identifying them." And I just clap my hand, and I just did like that and people just came around me, a lot of people round there knew me. And this woman said, "What happen, Miss Phoenix, what happen in there, what happen?" I said, "The police only now bring me here." I told them what the police is asking. I said, "Try and find all the people, find people who have been to the party because there's a lot of dead people in there and they said they are badly burned, they're going to have to identify them." And then the leader of the council came, the Chief Executive, and we then went down to the police station, and they then set up an incident room for people to come there. And then there were more people gathering in the street, so what I did then was to go and open the Padmore Street building. It wasn't painted yet, so I opened the building and put the urn on, and so on. And lots of people that was in the street, crying and so on, the police just brought them into the centre.

'They brought me back again to the road, because people were

[6] Interview with Orville Gooding. Orville Gooding also came from Barbados in 1961 and, at the time of the fire, worked for North Thames Gas.

there, to try to talk to people. And then it suddenly dawned on me,
Where's the mother? Well, we got some information then so we
knew then it was the Ruddocks and we knew some of the things that
were happening, and the police asked around if Mrs Ruddock has
made contact, if they found her. And they said, Yes, she was at
Lewisham Police Station. So when we did get to Lewisham Police
Station I asked to see her. They had sent her round to the old fire
station they turn into a hostel. They had given her tea bags and so
on and sent her round there. While I was talking to the sergeant I
hear the wailing downstairs. It was her. She came back to the police
station screaming and said that she want them to carry her to the
hospital, she want to get to the hospital where her children was.
And so I gave her the cup of tea, she drank some of it, and we then
went to Greenwich. And her son was there. From the hospital, then
to another hospital, and from there I brought her home here. I put
her in the bath, put a nightdress on her, and put one of the sedatives
that I had, a sleeping tablet into the coffee, because she was just
yelling into the coffee, and stick her in my bed and she went to
sleep. Well by nine, ten o'clock in the night all kinds of people was
here. The police have come earlier, but I said that she was asleep
because they wanted to have a statement then from her and I said I
wasn't going to get her up then. Later on in the night people came
from all about. By twelve, one o'clock, people were everywhere, and
people came.

'I couldn't eat – the smell of the burned people – for a long time
I couldn't keep anything down. Within, I think it was about three
months, I'd lost nearly two stone of weight. I tell you something, I
used to be afraid to go to bed, I couldn't cope with going to the loo,
and I wouldn't go in my bedroom unless somebody was there. All
I could have seen was these young people and dirt falling and
coughing, because I then had to fight not for her to have two
funerals, because the girl was dead but we knew that the boy wasn't
going to live. So we tried to hang on and after he died we tried to
get them to do the post mortem, and so on, so that she could've only
had one funeral. The first funerals that we arranged, because the
police was highly involved in this, what they didn't want was mass
funerals. I mean, the police commander used to come every morning,
we used to sort of try to look at what was happening the first week,
and so they said to me that they need my assistance to try and bury
some of them. If we can sort of bury these first two instead of waiting
to have a mass funeral, because what sort of situation it will be. I

can't say that I regret I worked with the police, but I thought I had a bad deal out of them.

'This man couldn't even identify his son, he was so badly burned. So they said it was too bad he had no dentures so they could identify it from the dentures. And I said to his mother, "Did he have his own key ring?" She said, "Yes." So I said to the police, "What did you all find? Did you find anything?" And they said, "Come to think of it, I think they did you know." So I said, "Try the key, and if it fits in the front door then it's his child." They left me at the mortuary and they went and try the key in the door. The man knew it was his son, but he had no money to bury his child, and so he was passing out all the time. It was more the distress than anything else. So we went to the undertakers and I rang the bank manager and I said to him, "We haven't got any money in the bank but could we arrange a funeral?" And he said, "It's all right, Mrs Phoenix, I understand. Don't bother about it. Arrange the funeral." Because they said they don't have to pay the undertakers, but I have to pay for the cemetery. So I wrote the cheque from my husband's cheque book for the first two funerals. I wrote different cheques for different things, and had the receipts for the funerals that I arrange. So as the nuns raised the money, for instance, and gave me, it covered those two, I gave them the receipt from that funeral undertaker, for their money. And Will Wood raise money and come and I gave him that receipt and that's how I sort of arranged to bury most of the dead. And the Methodist Church gave me money to which I did shopping for them so that the homes could have had things.'[7]

'Fairly early on the Sunday morning, we heard about it. And we started phoning round and seeing who was available to turn out, over twenty people, I think, it might have been twenty, thirty people, all volunteers. We were more or less distributed to where we were needed, whether it be actually nursing the patients, which I was asked to assist with, but it didn't really matter if we'd have only made tea all day. You just knuckled down to whatever you were asked to do.

'I was assigned to one particular girl, who was burned from the waist down. It's a very vivid memory, something that I don't think I

[7] Interview with Sybil Phoenix.

shall ever forget, bearing in mind it's over sixteen years ago, now, I can still remember what it looked like. Horrendous. Any burn is a nasty injury, but when it's that severe, it's really quite horrible to have to look at and what it must have been like for the people that were injured, I can only imagine. Yvonne, that was her. She was sixteen years old and she was a lovely girl. And she didn't realise how serious her injuries were, I don't think, and, obviously, you try not to communicate that to somebody who is that seriously injured. And she was absolutely mortified that she might not be able to sit her O-Levels. And we were saying things like, "Oh, it's alright, we can get your books brought in", and, "You'll still be able to do all that, that'll be fine." She was really such a lovely kid, she really was. And it was just a waste of a young life, because she had a lot to offer, she was an intelligent girl. And even in the adversity that she was faced with, at that young age – and that is quite young for something like that to happen, not just to you, but to have seen your friends in that situation as well – she was coping with it so well, mentally, she was doing so well. The thing with burns of the severity that she had, she wasn't in a lot of pain because the nerve endings had been damaged to the point that she couldn't feel. I mean, she was in pain, obviously, but not as much as you would expect with such extensive injuries, and she was so focused on her O-Levels and whether she'd be able to do them, she had no idea how seriously she was injured, which is just as well, I think, maybe.

'I suppose it's one of the worst I've ever been involved in. I mean, everybody in St John is used to doing things like standing on duty at the Lord Mayor's Show. I can remember being on duty at Mountbatten's funeral, and you get people fainting and crushed feet, and that sort of thing. But, as far as the injuries concerned, they were the most horrendous injuries I've ever had to witness. I think she died the following weekend, on the Saturday following the fire. I, obviously, only had contact with her on that Sunday. I wish she'd lived.

'When I think thirteen of those children died, those young people, that would be all over the newspapers, all over the TV, and it hardly made a whisper, really. I mean, people were talking about it locally, because it was a local issue, and it was in the local papers. But, nationally, it hardly made a ripple. And that's very difficult, 'cos if you were anywhere near it, it couldn't fail to touch you. And so I was quite surprised that it didn't really make much news, if you like, it didn't seem to be newsworthy. And I couldn't really understand why, because it should have been, because it was a dreadful thing and people needed to know so that it wouldn't happen again. I didn't give it much thought at the time, it was just something else that you dealt with, and you had to move on. But it disgusted me that the newspapers said they had criminal records, because that really isn't an issue, is it? Whatever somebody's background is they don't deserve to be injured or die in such an awful manner, and that's just fogging the issue, to be quite honest. It's got nothing to do with it, whether they have a criminal record as long as your arm, they're human beings. And that shouldn't have been an issue, and it shouldn't have been mentioned, even. Who knows why?

'But, certainly, going back to then, I think we've moved on apace since then. I can remember a comment that I heard, after we left the hospital, that had me flying across the table at somebody's throat because I was so horrified. We went for a drink afterwards, because we needed a drink. We'd been there from half-past eight that morning, this was nearly closing time, so it must have ten o'clock, or thereabouts. And as we sat down, me with my large brandy, which I felt I definitely needed. I heard somebody say, "Well, don't really matter, does it? They're only black." And I knocked a table over, I had my hands round the bloke's throat, and I had to be pulled off, because I couldn't handle that, after having a day of looking after somebody that had been so seriously injured. I suppose you've got to feel sorry for people that are that bigoted or, I don't know, evil almost. It felt evil to me, after looking after that young girl. And that was very much the attitude of a lot of people in the white community. I'm ashamed to say, but it was. I hadn't really thought about it until then, about the problems that black people had to face. And it was that more than anything that brought it home to me and made me really think about it, 'cos I'd not had to, and I'd never thought about it as being an issue. It certainly wasn't an issue in my life. So, yes, it was much more widespread than I realised until that moment.

'It's just like opening a book again, and there it is, all written down, only this time it's up in your head. And I had serious nightmares for about three weeks afterwards and intermittently for about six months afterwards. So it did have a really profound effect. I am a sensitive person, but I'm not, you know, a jittery person. I'm quite calm, but you could never look on anything the same again having witnessed something like that. It was that particular incident that really made me think about the issues involved. And I suppose since then I've always tried to make a difference.'[8]

The Investigation

'For my age – maybe had I been five, six, seven years older, then maybe, you know – but, for my age, I was kept in the police station for hours and hours and hours one night, just being questioned and questioned. And, obviously, I didn't know anything, and I could only tell them what I knew. But I don't know what they expected me to tell them, but I think that was pretty bad. And to look at it now, when I look back on it now I think, "My word, I can't imagine my son who, my age, eleven now, I couldn't imagine him having to sit in a police station till one o'clock in the morning being questioned about that, because, it's just not the sort of thing that you do to a child. But, at the time, you don't think of things like that. They were just asking me what was happening at the party, and I was trying to explain that, this is what I know, this is all I know. But they were saying, "Well, didn't you see a fight?" sort of thing. You know, you did see a fight. And, basically, I was giving them the statement, but it's like they were totally sort of twisting it and whatever I said didn't matter anyway. It was a long old night, that was.'[9]

'Some of them said at the start, when they questioned them, the children sign to what they write, and that the children believed that that was the truth. But the children, then, when they get to the coroner, he asked, and they say, "No, that wasn't the truth." They had wanted to get away. They tell the police what they wanted to hear, want them to say, and they told that to the police. To which I proved some of it is true, because one evening I came home from work and two of them came to my house, and they told me they want to take Denise to the police station. And while I was there, with her, they was writing, and one of them turned to Denise, while writing, and he said, "You don't tell no lies." These are the words,

---

[8] Interview with Christine Eaton. Christine Eaton was a member of St John's Ambulance Brigade and was mobilised to nurse the victims of the fire.

[9] Interview with Denise Gooding. Denise Gooding was born and brought up in south London. She was eleven years old at the time of the New Cross Fire. She was present at the party, where one brother died and another was seriously injured. Denise escaped with only slight injuries. She lives in London.

and I always remember, "Don't tell no lies, just tell us that there was fighting in the house, because six to seven other children told us yesterday." And they tell us, "If you don't tell us – remember, you have your dead brother, Andrew, in the fire, so how did the fire start?" How would she know? She didn't know. And a fight? There was not a fight. And one said to her, "Do you say there was a fight?" She said, "No." The other said, "You say there was a fight?" And she said, "Yes, there was no fight." That's how she did it. "Yes, there was no fight." You see, and they just write down that. And she was too young then, to question her like that.'[10]

'She was eleven and when the man came to the door, he brought the summons, and he knocked the door and he said, "Where is she?" And at the time, everybody was confused, 'cos, I mean, I was confused myself, you know, having one dead and one in hospital and all that then. He gave her the summons, and he said, "And do you know where to find County Hall?" And I took the summons out of his hand, you know, and after that, I thought to myself, Well, wait a minute, how could a child of eleven know how to find County Hall. And I felt I was going staring mad, but at the time, I didn't know what to do or what to say, you know, 'cos you never see no one come to assist you or to help you or to tell you what to do, so when he come and flicked the thing at her and say, "Do you know where to find County Hall?" And she took the thing out of his hand, and I said, "How can somebody come and tell a child of eleven if she knows where to find County Hall, and she have to go there on such a date?" But then, eventually, each time she go then, you know, the Bishop of Croydon, he was kind enough to go and stay in there with her, because, I mean, I was in no state of going in there to sit down with her or to stay with her. So every time she goes to the court, he had to be there to give her a little bit of comfort. So, maybe something good would have come out of that, because it started wrong, in the first place, you know, and it ended wrong. So you've just got to hope now that if they are going to do something, that some good will come out of it, although it's a long time gone. But, still, I mean, things go on for thirty, forty years and, in the end, they still find the guilty person, so you never know. We just have to live in hope.'[11]

[10] Interview with Orville Gooding.
[11] Interview with Ena Gooding.

'I was one of the last people to give evidence, and so I had to watch everyone – you know, all my friends go in and do their bit, and then it was me. And I was scared. But I used the inquest as an opportunity to let everyone know what had happened the night when the police did interview me, 'cos I felt as if they were asking me the questions and then they were answering them themselves. So I used that as an opportunity to say, Well, okay, this was what was happening. But I think the build-up to it was a lot worse than the actual day was. Bishop Wood was a big help. And he was in there with me, and I suppose I needed someone in there with me, anyway. And he was my support, really, yeah. It was an experience, for my age. It was an experience, and not one I'd like to go through again in a hurry. Yeah, it was terrible. Every morning, you'd pull up at the court and it would be sort of, like, cameramen and all that, every day.

'There were times when I did feel, especially when I was being interviewed by the police, I felt like, Hold on, I am the victim here, yet I feel as if I'm a suspect.'[12]

'The action committee – which was Darcus Howe then, and Mrs Phoenix – they wrote a letter to the Prime Minister, Margaret Thatcher, and one to the Queen. And they never get a reply until six weeks after. Six weeks after! That's when they get the reply. But, I think it was two weeks after the New Cross march, they had one in Ireland and forty-eight died. That was a Sunday, too, 'cos that happened this Saturday night, some disco, and forty-eight people die. And straight away condolence went from here to there, and we had to wait for six weeks reply. That was bad! Bad, that very bad. Something happen in your country and you write to the authorities and you didn't get no response from them. And six weeks after the time, that couldn't look good, and I felt very bad about that. That wasn't good enough, six weeks.'[13]

The Campaign

'I was in a meeting of the Black Parents' Movement. There was an alliance between the Black Parents' Movement, *Race Today*, which I edited, and the Black Youth Movement. That would be at Finsbury

---

[12] Interview with Denise Gooding.
[13] Interview with Orville Gooding.

Park, around John Larose[14] and the New Beacon Bookshop, and we were there on Sunday night and a phone call came, I think it was via Sibyl Phoenix, to tell us that this terrible thing had happened on the Saturday. And the first thing we did was to stop the meeting, adjourned it, and went. And we met Mrs Ruddock and Sibyl Phoenix and they invited all of us down on the Monday to the Moonshot Club, youth club. And we thought, or I certainly thought, Well, we're going to meet a committee of about ten people. When we got there there were three hundred people. John and I were, by and large, two of the major figures in that alliance, so I said, "John, this is trouble. This is it." But, you see, I wasn't surprised that much, because the black people were starting to gather. And then we decided to have a public meeting. This is Monday, for Saturday, and when we went down there were about three thousand people.

'The suspicion was that it was a racial attack. A lot of that was happening in the country at the time, in the East End of London, everywhere. So it seemed perfectly reasonable to believe the place had been fire-bombed. I genuinely believe that, and everybody believed that at the time. A policeman told Mrs Ruddock on the night of the fire that there was a fire-bomb – from his mouth came the words. And we started to meet every Tuesday. It was a kind of black assembly – hundreds of people came every Tuesday. John Larose was chair. We had a committee which I was on, the officers were officers of *Race Today* in Brixton, by which time we could organise. We took a political decision to do that, for one simple reason: every single week you would hear clashes between the police and blacks all over London and it was becoming something of importance. There were other issues at large, and I said, "Well, if they're going to kill so many kids in a fire, we have to mobilise and show them we got some power in this place, and only way to do that is to call a general strike of blacks." That was at the back of my mind. I discussed it with *Race Today* people. I said, "Let's see how it goes 'cos I think we can pull this one off."

'So we decided to call a day of action, the meeting, and they decided it should be on a weekday, a working day, and I thought, "Well, let's see how it goes." They appointed me organiser and I went from Liverpool, come right down to Luton, going and see the

---

[14] John Larose came from Trinidad in the fifties and started the New Beacon Bookshop and Independent Publishers. He became a well-known figure in the community as a result of his involvement with black and left wing politics.

different black communities, mobilising people, with a knapsack on my back and working at it. And I was away from home for about a week, eight days, and when I came back I thought ten thousand people, sure. And then when I went round London, I was doing a lot of the public speaking, I thought fifteen. And I think that's by and large where we reached.'[15]

'At the time, it was said that it was a racist thing. I think that's crap. It was very hard for there to be a party in a house, in New Cross, at five-thirty, six o'clock in the morning, for a white person to come up and throw a petrol-bomb through the window and nobody didn't see him. It's not happening. Secondly, the forensics have made us know that the explosion, or whatever took place, the heat, blew the glass out, but if somebody threw a petrol-bomb through the window, why isn't the glass inside? Stuff like that. You see, I think that's a load of crap, personally. If there was a white person that had come and thrown a petrol-bomb through that window, somebody would have seen them. Whether it's something to do with someone that was in the fire, or not, I don't know. I mean, I've got my own theories which I'll keep to myself. But, as far as I'm concerned, it wasn't a racist thing. I think it was an accident that went totally wrong. I think that a lot of our black politicians at the time saw it as a way to further their careers, and they jumped on the racist aspect of it and everything else to help further their careers. I won't call any names, but, at the same time, there's a lot of them out there that are still working now, that have made their money, they've made their names, they've made their fame, and a lot of them made it out of the New Cross/Deptford fire. As far as I'm concerned, they've made it off of the back of fourteen dead children.'[16]

'As the days rolled on you began to hear different things – that it wasn't a fire-bomb, that the fire had started inside. And what was strange was that nobody in any official position had begun to understand what had happened in the black community, that thirteen children had died in a fire. And I think the first thing we began to feel was the isolation inside this large country. And I remember people like Darcus Howe, Wilfred Wood, John Larose, and people like that

[15] Interview with Darcus Howe.
[16] Interview with Wayne Haynes. The actual number of deaths was thirteen.

coming down and the people were like lost souls. You didn't have to say there was a meeting, people were there, people kept coming to the Moonshot Youth Club, wanting information, what had happened, what was going on. But the press didn't seem to see there was a tragedy. It was then I began to realise that the country didn't seem able to accept that something like an attack on the black community could happen, therefore there was a sort of denial syndrome about the whole thing. My role was merely about caring for those people because we began to want to bond with people, to feel that, My God, nobody cares about us but ourselves. Sibyl and I were going to families, and people were distraught, people whose children had gone to the party, high hopes, high expectations, the child was only young, the young people were only there to enjoy themselves and have fun. We were absolutely shocked when the reality of how the British public and press and those in authority reacted.

'I can compare to something happening in a youth club somewhere where some children got burned, and the Royal Family had sent a telegram and sent messages of condolence to those families, and nothing came to us at all. The churches were silent. It took the energy of the black people to begin to put pressure on them, to say something, to do something. I don't think Sibyl had ever politicised blackness, and she probably thought that by talking to people and saying, "I hurt, I hurt, this is a pain". That she would get results. I think people like John Larose and Wilfred Wood and Darcus Howe, it was something about black people taking responsibility for themselves and saying, "You don't care about us, but we are a force to be reckoned with and we will come out". And, I think, for a lot of people the march which resulted was also something about people being able to do something, 'cos we felt so helpless within the country. And I think it's the very first time that the black community felt the need to come together as a force. I think, by the time I got to the march I was so angry, that it didn't matter how long it was, I was with the young people, and the more you looked at them, the more you realised they could have been killed in that and nobody would care. I think it's the lack of care that kept me going. It was important for us to bring London to a standstill, to say, "We're here. Look at us. We're here. We're hurting, and you're not doing anything about it, you're pretending it hasn't happened." It was that lack of appreciation of our presence, I think, that hurt us, was for me the most painful.

'And the white community appeared not to be concerned with

what had happened that morning. Whether it was a deliberate attack
on the black community or not that was how it was seen. And I
think this is the point, that nobody was brave enough to investigate
it thoroughly to see whether it was or it wasn't. I mean, there was
a bomb at another house in Forest Hill, so there was a history, there
were marches on the street, so, yes, it didn't appear as though that
was in isolation. There was a lot more pain than the fire in the
marches. People suffering harassment, about being victims of racism
in this society was coming out of that. So whether that was a political
movement, whether anyone had any special agenda was not
important at that time. What was important was black people was
coming out together.'[17]

The Black People's Day of Action (2 March 1981)

'Masses of people, masses and masses of people. It was real. God,
it was unbelievable to see that many people coming out in support
of the families. Basically, it was real – makes you wonder, would
they do it again? Would they do it today, now? There was just so
many people, and there was all these banners and people were
coming out with all these, I don't know if you call them chants, or
whatever. We joined it from Camberwell, and I went to school in
Peckham, and as the march approached Peckham and passed the
school, all the kids were jumping over the fences. And, as far as I
can say, when I went to school every day, it was like, well, "There's
Denise, she was in a fire." That's it. I never realised how many
people actually was in support of us until I saw them all scaling these
fences, basically, and joining in the march, and that was touching,
because you never see your peers as being real interested in things
like that. That's sort of a big people thing. It was awesome, it was
just amazing to sort of like be there and see that many people. People
were very angry and you could sense that the black community
were angry. There was definitely a feeling of anger there from the
people in the march. It's like they were out there for a reason. They
wanted an answer, basically, and sixteen years later, we're still
waiting.'[18]

[17]   Interview with Ros Howells.
[18]   Interview with Denise Gooding.

'If people stopped and really thought and dug really into their minds – why were they getting on this case of thirteen kids that ninety-nine point nine per cent of the nation never knew. No skin off my nose, it's not my child, that's how people think. But now there was a chance that, well, we've got loads of people getting together now. We can now air our views and now be heard, stand up and be counted, for a change. We can maybe make a difference, and if we can help to make a difference with this, it might make a difference for the next person that comes along and the next tragedy that happens. And that's why it wasn't just about the fire. It wasn't just about the people that died, the people that were injured. It was about people's underlying feelings from way back when, from the troubles up in Notting Hill and whatever, not that my mum and my dad used to tell about. Never had any place to air our views before. Our people have had pent up anxieties and this was a chance for us to get them out. I mean, the riots and everything that came afterwards were – nobody can't tell me any different – they were a direct result of the fire. It was people expressing themselves and letting out all the anger. I know a lot of people that have been beaten up by police, beaten up by skinheads, that have been sent to gaol and they didn't do the things. All of these things, they feel as though the system has let them down. And when you feel as though the system's let you down, who do you go to? How do you fight the system? You can't fight the system by yourself. So when people see a chance for me – here's my chance now to release some tension, release some anger, direct something at the system. You need a whole body of people, a big body, to even attempt to fight the system. Here's their chance. It's everyone's chance to use that particular thing to fight their own cases, to fight their own causes. That's the way I saw it.'[19]

'It was a very moving and very powerful statement about how the black community saw itself. Come what may, we're here to stay. I was struck, first of all, by the numbers, the vast numbers, who were assembling in south London, in Lewisham, on that day. The sense of purpose, the meeting of friends, whole families involved, young people, older people, the involvement of white people in a way in which they didn't feel threatened, but in which we were

[19] Interview with Wayne Haynes.

undoubtedly, as it were, as black people, in the leadership of the march. In the main, if you look at street demonstrations, even street demonstrations around issues that affect black people, you get a sense that white people were somehow in command of events. They'd organised it. This was black organised, black led and you felt that. So it was very much a black community event. And then the numbers who joined it, that was significant, as you went along. But also in some parts of the march the hostility, directed by people who were undoubtedly racist. And then as we came up Fleet Street there, the taunting and the abuse that rained down upon us from the *Express* building in particular, I will never forget that.'[20]

'The start of the demonstration was in a valley. You came down a hill in this little valley. And I was there, commander in chief, really, on the day, dealing with the stuff. I was in charge of the big truck, and I was in charge of the mike. So I was settled in. I was there on time, and beautiful weather, not cold, just temperate, bright sun, and waves and waves and waves and waves and waves of black people coming down that hill. It was a Charge of the Light Brigade. And we gathered, and the police wanted to start at eleven-thirty, and I pulled one of them across at eleven, said, "Let's go." So whatever plans they had along the route, I'll upset it. It's kind of military kind of thinking at the time. And off we went: "Thirteen dead and nothing said." That was the slogan. "Thirteen dead and nothing said." So the whole organisation of the march was around the fact that we can't get an explanation from anybody.

'All the time, inside of it, relationships between the parents were deteriorating and it was around some kind of infidelity. So there was tension within the families, with the two sets, so that was difficult to deal with. That was a problem. But we held it together by and large. We come across Blackfriars Bridge. No demonstration had crossed that bridge since the Chartists and, suddenly, the police threw a cordon across the road and say, "You are not going anywhere." And the driver, I insisted the driver was a member of my organisation, of that huge wagon, and I said, "Drive!" Just leant towards him. "Drive that." Brrrrm! And the police ... "What? Are you going to stand before a truck?" I don't know any police officer that brave. And we crossed the bridge into Fleet Street, running. We came in

20 Interview with Paul Boateng.

running into Fleet Street. And do you know those huge buildings? And the noise is bouncing off: "Thirteen dead and nothing said" A huge echo. That was the high point. And we went to Hyde Park. Now, the media, all through, it was an arm of the police. It's not like that any more; the *Daily Mail*, the *Evening Standard*. Strange how I wrote for them after, it's a whole new regime. I was interviewed and I thought, "Okay, this is a moment of triumph, instead of being modest." They said, "Mr Howe, what do you think of the demonstration?" I said, "It was a good day." The following day in the *Evening Standard* they showed a police officer, blood streaking down his face: "Darcus Howe says 'It's a good day.'" And I from that then, I thought we could only draw this fight, can't win it.

'There was one black policeman that turned up around Blackfriars Bridge. I don't know that those who ran the police force was so stupid to bring him there by sheer accident. In those days, to have a black policeman around was pretty well a serious thing to do. The young people just went berserk. But at the time the police didn't understand quite what was happening. I think it is from then that they too had to assess what policing blacks meant. I think everybody after the demonstration had to assess who they were; what side they were on; how long would they be part of this force of black durability; how long we would continue to be uncompromising. In fact when I was getting a bit over-hyped with it, my uncle C. L. R. James was my political mentor, said to me, "I think you ought to retreat. Just calm down, take two steps back, because this is big stuff." I said then we needed some overview to moderate extreme and violent instincts, because there was a violence that was obviously beneath the surface. It manifested itself weeks after that demonstration.'[21]

'At the time I was the local councillor for the area where the fire happened, and I was involved in working with the council to see that the council's response was as positive as possible, and also liaising with people like Sibyl Phoenix, who were supporting the families, and also those involved in the work on the various defence committees that sprung up at the time. So it was almost like a bridge between community and town hall, that's the sort of role that I tried to play.

---

[21] Interview with Darcus Howe.

'The response at the time was difficult to fathom, because one would have thought that with such a tragedy there'd be an attempt made to understand the circumstances and to try to deal with the issue of the families and how they were dealing with it, but it was almost ignored. It was just a by-line, just a short little note in many of the papers, very little interest nationally on the scale of the tragedy, given the numbers of people involved. So, it was quite a revealing moment to understand the operation of the British press and the British institutions at the time. It didn't come as a complete shock, it was just sad, really, that here was an occasion when a better than average response would be appropriate and we couldn't have that.

'There was a big debate as to whether it would take place, and, if it was to take place, which route it should take, and all sorts of discussions about whether the stewards would be able to manage the size of the crowd, whether the police should be involved directly in stewarding, how many police there should be. All of these issues were still being discussed right on the day of the march, right up until it actually took off. I remember the march itself passing through New Cross, south-east London, parts of south London, where black people wouldn't normally go for fear of being attacked, but the march went through those areas. In the Docklands area, there was re-building taking place. And some of the building site workers were hurling racial abuse at people on the demonstration. I mean, we would be shouting back, which, again, was significant, 'cos you wouldn't do something like that unless you had a big group of black people. So, that was the type of thing that was happening at the time. We also had some abuse from people standing by, usual sort of things. I can distinctly remember it around the Docklands area, but, elsewhere, things were, like, people would immediately shut their shops if they saw that there was this demonstration coming, and the response would be very cold and negative as we went by.

'There was clearly sympathy coming from onlookers who were black or people passing on the bus, or anything like that, if they were black people. But I would say that the majority of sympathy certainly was not with the march. The press had built it up as this horrific thing that was going to happen anyway, and created a division between those of us marching and those who were onlookers, and that was very difficult to break down at the time. And all the way up through Blackfriars and up into Fleet Street, the reactions were mainly hostile from onlooking crowds. There was an edge of unreality about the whole thing, about people marching, about people trying to explain why they were marching, people responding to this in a negative way, and a sort of edge of panic around the whole thing, a feeling that it shouldn't be happening but yet it was. And amongst those of us involved, it was a sort of liberating experience, because we were doing what we wanted to do. We wanted to show solidarity with the families. We wanted to demonstrate that this is something important to our community, this is something meaningful to us, rather than accept the imposition of those who wanted us not to do it. And that was, for a lot of us, a liberating experience, and showed that with determination amongst black people we can achieve things a lot more than maybe we thought was possible in the past. The point it made was that the black community could organise at a political level, and that was a revelation for a number of people. Maybe we just didn't think, previous to that, that it's something we could do. But that proved the point. It can be done at the community level. The individuals involved, the families themselves, received an awful lot of support, much more support than was the case before, from the local authority and from people generally. That was, I think, one of the really good benefits of that demonstration. And none of those things would have happened if we'd done what people wanted to do at the time, which was to have like a church service, and it would have really been a great shame had people not gone ahead to organise that demonstration and participated in the event.'[22]

'I remember walking through the West End as we approached the destination point of the march at Hyde Park, and being pleased at that point that there had been only minimal kind of conflict, that nothing had come out of the day which could undermine the seriousness and dignity of our purpose. That was very important. And, as I remember it, the march was reported as a riot. It was reported through the episodes of windows broken in the West End after the demonstration was over as people made their way back. I wasn't present at that point, so I can't judge, but I remember getting the newspapers the following day and seeing that it was, "Black Mob Rampage Through West End", kind of thing. And, in a sense, nobody could have been surprised by that because we knew those were familiar patterns, actually, although we were, I think, deeply

[22] Interview with Russell Profitt.

disappointed that the justice in our claim, and the tragedy itself, was still considered to be secondary to this sort of sensation.'[23]

'There was a sense in which we weren't really concerned with what impression we were making. there was a sense in which we were almost talking to ourselves. It was a feeling of solidarity. I was wearing my cassock and collar, just as I would be in church. And marching with arms linked with some other people, and I remember hearing a woman saying, "That's Reverend Wood and he's told us we mustn't be afraid." Now that is one of the great moments of my life, and I can close my eyes now and see her trudging along, a woman in her late forties or early fifties, a short, bustling woman. And she said, "That's Reverend Wood and he told us we mustn't be afraid." It was wonderful. One of the highlights of my life. There was a tremendous feeling of togetherness that we knew who we were and that there was a purpose in what we were doing. Because I think, instinctively, we knew that this was not this particular incident, but that we were living in a watershed age in this country. That something had happened which had never happened before. There'd been waves of immigrant groups, and so on, but we were going to leave a mark on this society in a way that had never been marked before. That from now on you could not assume that when you spoke about a British nation, or even the English people, you were white, blond, blue-eyed people. And we knew that our children would not particularly want to be anything other than what they are. And that is why, when I addressed the 10,000 people who were there, I quoted the words from Martin Luther King that either we live together as brothers, or we perish together as fools. And then I went on to say but, in any case, the important word is together. You know, 'cos that's how I felt about it. And I think that's the case now.'[24]

'The Deptford Fire and the period leading up to it is a very special event, expressing the changes, the wider changes that are going on. Remember, the Deptford Fire comes at the end of a long sequence of conflicts with the police. A long sequence of conflicts with the police involving young people, which are also represented in the

---

[23] Interview with Paul Gilroy.
[24] Interview with Wilfred Wood.

press and in the media in a certain way, which is explicitly hostile to the idea of the black community and its political integrity. So when a tragedy arrived, that appeared to share certain superficial characteristics with this sort of stereotype of the Carnival in miniature, destroying the peace and quiet of our leafy suburban life, the very best you can say is that they didn't know how to handle it. The worst you can say is that they were callous and indifferent. What happens next is that people, at many, many levels in our community, which is no longer merely localised, reach out to the families who had lost their children in that conflagration and decided that they are going to have to do something that will highlight the indifference and the callousness of the media and the press, but also put pressure on the police and the same institutions of law and order that had been telling us we're all criminals, when we become victims of a crime.

'So, the demonstration that follows was a very important moment, too. People are always surprised when we turn up and invade the public domain, because they think of us as being on another planet most of the time, because of our physical, spatial concentration, in our neighbourhoods, in our communities. We don't necessarily move out very far, but when we invade the whole kind of public domain of the nation, people begin to jump around as though our membership, our affiliation to this country is something that is a sort of hidden secret. I would look back to that aspect of the demonstration, especially.

'It's very clear from the research that was done on the police immediately afterwards that they viewed this demonstration, this eruption of anger by the black communities in this country as a kind of symbolic defeat for them. I remember reading the Policy Studies Institute survey which said policemen were complaining in south London that after that demonstration, the blacks in Brixton had a swagger in their step. And it was decided that street crime operation, Swamp '81, was going to be launched as a way of dealing with, of course, the problem of black criminality. But I think it's something more than that, as a way of restoring the proper mode of symbolic authority. And it's that response by the police which leads into the next phase of conflict, with the Brixton riots a few months later.'[25]

[25] Interview with Paul Gilroy.

Postscript

'Sibyl Phoenix, it's through her that we had the memorial service
and the plaque. But then, what she had wanted was a plaque, we
didn't want that – didn't like that. So we said, we wanted something
that can be placed on some government building, with all the names
on that. We did agree to, and that's what we got, that's what we
got. And we had a service, at the end – I think it was the nineteenth,
'cos the date is the eighteenth, but the nearest Sunday to it, and that
last one we had, was the nineteenth, and that was very good. And
then, on the tenth of February, we had the plaque, the laying of the
plaque, at Catford Town Hall. Now anybody can go and see it.
Turned out one thing that helps us. And Sibyl Phoenix, she was
from the beginning up to the end, she's still with me. She's still there.
And next year now, we're planning another memorial service. So,
through her and the councillors from Lewisham and Catford, they
still sponsor everything for us, they help us with everything, so I
can't complain about that lot. That was very good, those people. I
appreciate and thank them very much.'[26]

---

[26] Interview with Orville Gooding.

'Police over-reaction is causing a siege mentality in black people: Who is really on the rampage?'

The chief constable of Manchester, James Anderton, has in recent months been loud in his complaints about the 'campaign of vilification' against the police. But there's little doubt that the reputation of the police in the North West stems from public reaction to their methods and approach. One incident which took place recently in Moss Side, Manchester, demonstrates the way that police methods either are designed to keep the local population in a state of terror and confusion, or else display a remarkably low commitment to good community relations.

The story begins with the rumour on a Friday that the Troops Out Of Ireland movement was due to hold a demo on Saturday. They had in fact booked a hall near the district shopping precinct and announced that they would hold a meeting at the Polytechnic, to be followed by a march to an undisclosed destination, which most people took to be Moss Side. The National Front responded with the threat to be on the streets with a counter demo. As it turned out, neither took place. Troops Out had a small picket near the university, and the action between the NF and anti-fascists was confined to a few small scuffles, and a broken window at the Royal Northern College building, where a man took refuge. On the other hand, there were some scuffles near the centre of the town, and a number of arrests were made.

By contrast, Moss Side itself, according to everyone passing through the area on Saturday morning, and up to the time the police moved in, was 'dead'. No one appeared to have noticed any unusual activity. There were, however, a number of black children playing on the empty turf between Alexandra Park gates and the shopping centre, a length of grass running for about a hundred yards along the road, which is used as an unofficial playground by most of the kids from the neighbouring estate.

At about 3.30 p.m., two West Indians, a community worker and a local teacher, were driving past the green when they saw a large number of police vehicles approaching Alexandra Road. When they stopped to see what was happening, they noticed 'several policemen and dog handlers driving the kids off the street. They were shouting at them to go home and chasing them with dogs'. The men asked the boys what had happened and were told, 'I don't know. We were just playing and they appeared and started chasing us.'

One of the men then approached a dog handler and asked why this was happening. He was told that there was a crowd of two hundred black youths 'rampaging'. But the only thing like a black youth that any of the eye witnesses could see at the time was the frightened schoolchildren, and subsequent inquiries have failed to locate the rampaging two hundred.

A white youth approached the community worker while he was speaking to the dog handler and said, 'It's a waste of time arguing with them.' He was subsequently arrested. His younger brother, who came up to say that his brother hadn't done anything, was also arrested. The middle-aged white woman whom the brothers were visiting nearby spoke to the police, and claims that one of them said something about her son Tony, who had recently hanged himself in Risley Remand Centre. She was being 'restrained' on the ground screaming, 'My Tony's dead', when the community worker, on his way over to see if he could help, was struck on the back of the head. After hospital treatment, he was arrested. The hysterical woman's other son was later arrested. Of the people that were arrested none could be adequately described as 'rampaging black youths'.

Police actions on this scale, inspired by relatively tiny incidents, are now commonplace in Manchester and other large cities. In London during the same week, police in Paddington were called to the Mozart estate, which has a large black population, and is in the constituency of John Wheeler MP (of 'sus' committee fame). The call was the result of a domestic dispute, and it took seven policemen to arrest one grey-haired black man in his fifties. After radioing the station for handcuffs, which none of the officers possessed, they took him away. But a large number of policemen remained. Within ten minutes a scuffle developed with a black youth, whom the police chased through the estate and arrested. By this time there were over thirty policemen and dogs present, and they arrested a white woman before they left. A bag of three, stemming from the original domestic quarrel.

All this passes without comment in the national and local press; but the continual occurrence of incidents of this kind has produced a siege mentality in the inner cities, especially among the black community. The editorial of a black magazine recently told the story of how the editor had taken his niece and nephew to a museum, when the fourteen-year-old nephew wandered off for a few minutes. The nine-year-old niece apparently began to show strong signs of anxiety the moment her brother was out of sight, and insisted that he should be found quickly; 'the police might pick him up'. (Mike Phillips *New Statesman*, 27 June 1980)

War!

1980-85

There is one crucial point to grasp about the disturbances which marked the first half of the eighties. Predictably, during this period the Powellites trotted out for another airing of the claim that 'Enoch was right', and that the violence was his 'rivers of blood' come true. But they had, by now, lost their ability to unsettle the political culture, if only because everything about the riots which raged through the early part of the eighties differed from what had happened during '58 in Nottingham and Notting Dale. Those had been massive attacks by white residents, racists and delinquents on black people's lives and property. In contrast the battles of the eighties were not inter-communal 'race riots' pitting blacks against whites. Indeed, the same kind of young white men who had attacked in Notting Dale and Nottingham twenty years previously were now participating eagerly on the side of black youths.

In hindsight, after 1958, the conditions which had produced the race riots had changed so much that there was never the slightest prospect of a repeat, and it was only the commentators' and politicians' obsessive focus on race which made such a thing seem even remotely possible. To begin with, the pool of generalised white working-class resentment which had been focused and exacerbated by the 1957 Rent Act, had been dissipated by relocation, and by the new building stimulated after the 1964 Housing Act. By the late sixties many of the whites who might have taken their troubles on to the streets were dispersed into new housing estates or dormitory towns, and, for the moment, they could defend these new enclaves with a barricade of estate agents and local council regulations. In much the same way the Caribbean migrants had begun to be dispersed, with a new breed of middle-class resident moving into the spaces which had been cleared.

At the same time, the life of the Caribbean migrant communities were marked by a gradual, but unmistakable, coalescing of resources and expertise. It is true that the style of young black people who had gone through the school experience in Britain determined the domestication of black culture in the seventies, but parallel to this was an equally vigorous movement into local government, public administration, the trade unions and business. Powellism slowed down the migrants' progress, but when you look back at what was happening the picture is surprisingly complex.

The popular narratives which tell us what happened during these times are stories which paint with a broad brush, editing out the contradictory details. The story which identifies a gap between the generations of Caribbean migrants has developed over twenty years and presents a portrait of the community in which the immigrants before the decade of the seventies are quiescent and menial, isolated and marginalised, humbly accepting their lot, until the following generation which has grown up focused around the Reggae/Rastafarian culture boldly strides into the arena and rejects its racist limitations by rioting during the eighties. Accounts of this kind feed an increasingly racialised view of history, and create a narrow focus through which we can see only a small part of the landscape. For example, later commentators began to describe the '58 riots as the work of racist Teddy Boys or as a spontaneous eruption of white rage, depending on the intentions motivating their account. But neither of those things was entirely true, and without a variety of factors which linked them together the riots could not have taken place.

In much the same way, reading the history of the preceding years through the prism of the eighties disturbances disfigures both those events and the process which led up to them. The description which separates the Caribbean migrant generations seemed to be validated by the events of the early eighties, but has largely been extracted from the work of black commentators, notably Stuart Hall and Paul Gilroy. In 1979 Ken Pryce, a Caribbean sociologist, published his PhD thesis under the title 'Endless Pressure'. It was a study of a group of young black people in Bristol and noted the differences between them and the generation of their parents, and the new pressures imposed on them by their educational experiences, their relations with the police and the discrimination they faced in employment. He argued, also, that the young people's resulting drift into alienation provoked parents into 'rejecting them completely'. When the disturbances which opened the eighties occurred, at the Black and White café in Bristol, Pryce's descriptions seemed to have been predicting the event and locating it within the nature of the black community. Similarly, since then, academics, journalists and entrepreneurs of every sort have filleted the work of black sociologists for references which compartmentalise the experience of succeeding Caribbean generations, and which could be used to relocate the responsibility for the 'rebelliousness' of black youths within the structure of the black community.

In fact the period which runs from the mid-sixties to the late seventies is also to be characterised by the energy and determination which Caribbeans across the different generations bring to the task of coming to terms with their newly racialised identity, and with the problems of establishing footholds within the environment. The conventional view, in some quarters a dogmatic article of faith, is that the Caribbean migrant community has consistently lacked 'leadership and organisation'. This is a view decisively influenced by comparisons with the television and movie imagery of African America. During the sixties, to be 'black' was to be American. For generations reared on the notion that 'black' leadership was defined by a King or a Malcolm X, or that 'black' organisation could only take the form of a Black Panther movement, the forms of black leadership and organisation which emerged in Britain were ramshackle and unimpressive. This is a view propagated and amplified by generations of white commentators whose interest in 'black politics' had originated in their study or experience of the American Civil Rights movement.

On the other hand, the re-invention and domestication of a black culture within Britain cannot be explained merely by reference to the part played by Reggae music and the Rastafarian religion. As Paul Gilroy has consistently pointed out in his work, Caribbeans were marked by the ability to be more than one thing at the same time. The Caribbean migrants who were imbued with the sense of being British at the moment of their arrival also brought with them a determined black nationalism, shaped by a society which originated in the nightmare of black slavery. It was this same society which had fuelled black nationalism and anti-colonialism all over the globe in the person of Marcus Garvey, followed by internationally renowned activists as diverse as C. L. R. James, George Padmore and Frantz Fanon. The same Caribbeans who were later to be described as 'Victorians', carried with them folk memories and descriptions of legendary rebellions, from the Maroons and Paul Bogle in Jamaica to the series of slave martyrs all over the Caribbean who bore African names – Quashie (Akwesi), Quackoo (Akweku) Cuffee (Akofi), all leaders of slave rebellions in the Caribbean.

This was a strand of Caribbean identity which was, by tradition, more or less hidden, communicated by folk tales and oblique references. In the sixties, however, its emergence was symbolised by the naming of the Huntleys' book shop in west London, Bogle L'Ouverture. The names of the enterprises utter a similar rhetoric – Harmbee, Dashiki, Back-ah-yard. Over the next decade the existence of this 'hidden' strand of blackness was of equal importance in shaping and defining the response of the Caribbean migrants to their environment.

In any case, for many Caribbeans, travelling to England constituted a short circuit between two kinds of status in the Caribbean itself. By the end of the sixties it was apparent to most of them that their future, whether it involved a return or not, depended on the extent to which they could engage in various different ways with British society. This is the point at which most migrant families are settled in their own houses or living in secure accommodation. In the workplace they are engaging in the trade unions or challenging their exclusion. In local politics they are standing for elections, attacking discriminatory policies and constructing projects which claim a share of local expenditure. Even at the height of Powellite hostility and the most vicious phases of 'sus', black Caribbean migrants were clearly asserting their independence, their engagement with British institutions and their intention to breach the limits imposed by discrimination.

In 1968, for instance, one of the records which reached the top of the charts was The Equals' 'Baby Come Back'. The group was made up of five boys, two whites and three blacks. The singer/songwriter was a twenty-year-old youth from Guyana, named Eddy Grant. Eddy wanted to be a doctor until sidetracked into music, but, unlike many previous and subsequent black musicians his success wasn't frittered away into drink, drugs or the pockets of white promoters. Fuelled by a fierce determination to be his own boss, he began planning for the time when the hits would dry up. In a few years he had built his own recording studio, leasing it to other black groups like Osibisa for their recordings, and he had started marketing his own music in the Caribbean and Africa. His brother Rudy made his own records for their Ice label under the name The Mexicano, and the youngest brother, Alpine, acted as general manager, with a staff that included a white local government councillor from Basildon and the white members of the now defunct Equals. By the start of the eighties Eddy had made his million and moved his operation to Barbados, where he wrote music for Hollywood movies and played host in his new recording studio to luminaries like the Rolling Stones. Alpine, twenty-one years old in 1978, wanted a career as a property developer, so he began buying dilapidated houses around Islington and renovating them with his friends during the weekends. One of them was bought by a doctor who worked with musicians and it eventually ended up being sold to Tony Blair.

Or take Jo Whitter who, during the same period, bought substantial blocks of property in south London and was on his way to becoming a millionaire. Even the portals of Conservative politics in south London were not immune from the energy of the West Indians.

Basil and Stuart's ball

Britain's ethnic newspapers over the last few weeks have been carrying a number of full page adverts for a 'Spring Ball', which was held last week at the Grosvenor Hotel. It was a typically Tory event (carriages at 2 p.m.), but the participants were mainly West Indian. The whole affair was part of the continuing Conservative attempts to woo the immigrant, which have gone unnoticed by most people, both black and white. This is because the thrust of Tory self-advertisement, in the case of the West Indian community, is carried by two Jamaican businessmen,

Basil Lewis, a Haringey travel agent and councillor, and Stuart Weathers, owner of the Clapham plumbing firm, Help.

The dynamic duo are notorious for vying with each other for Conservative favours and, as the immigrant vote emerges in certain marginal constituencies as more and more important, they find themselves in greater demand at Central Office. So far Lewis has been thought to be ahead in the race for Tory esteem. He is a fervent admirer of Margaret Thatcher and during the last election in Haringey, to the embarrassment of the Tory candidate who was trying to play down such issues in front of immigrant voters, he was loud in his support of law and order policies. He is, however, a small, quiet man, eager to organise community events.

Weathers, on the other hand, is a flamboyant character, whose claims are as dashing as his suits. Some time ago he was said to be feeling disillusioned after failing to be elected to the executive of the local party, and he caused the Tories some embarrassment by kicking up a fuss when he was ushered to what he said was an obscure table at a Conservative function. He is also ostentatiously proud of his contacts with leading Conservatives, and pictures of himself with Heath and Thatcher adorn his office wall.

But there was no sign of coolness last week at the ball. A large proportion of the West Indian business community turned out to see the fun. They were treated to a fashion display; they were awarded prizes provided by Caribbean Airways and by that sturdy arm of reactionary Jamaican business interests, the *Gleaner*, and they were entertained by the spectacle of plumber Weathers wandering about with a large snake draped about his neck.[1]

The Minister's speech was the expected exhortation. He said that the onus was on blacks to make their requirements known to the government, and this could only be done by taking part in politics. The crowd of potential Conservative politicians took this less enthusiastically than might have been expected. As law-abiding, middle-aged, anti-welfare state business persons, they found it hard to understand why the Tories hadn't sent along a spokesman from Trade and Industry, or an expert on small businesses, or even a tame peer to lend the event some social cachet. What they got was Patrick Jenkin, Secretary of State *for the Social Services*, and as if to ram the point home he was accompanied by John Wheeler, chairman of the Commons sub-committee, which reported recently on the sus laws and black youth. As one businessman commented after listening to Patrick Jenkin: 'Perhaps they're trying to tell us something.' (Mike Phillips, *New Statesman*, May 1980)

Such characters and events were regarded as irrelevant and ludicrous by more radical elements at the time, but they were laying down prominent

---

[1] Stuart Weathers was in the habit of taking his pet snake draped round his neck to Conservative occasions, and he once held it out to Mrs Thatcher and asked her to stroke it. There is no record of her reply.

markers about the presence and the reach of the Caribbean migrant community. After all, Weathers was also a super hustler who had invented twenty-four-hour plumbing, and thereby become rich by exploiting a loophole in the market which no one had previously spotted. His career, therefore, prefigured the iconography of 'black success' which came to rule 'black culture' later in the eighties.

Taken together, these trends create a space which expands the boundaries within which young black people can make choices. This process, at one and the same time, outlines their frustrations, while at the same time freeing them to imagine new futures.

The Deptford Fire and the Black People's Day of Action showed the immigrants a map of what they had become. After the fire itself the black migrant welfare network, exemplified by Sibyl Phoenix and Ros Howells, moved into place and provided the necessary services and mediation. They were supported by the black clergy like the Reverend Wilfred Wood, and local councillors like Russell Profitt. The most powerful political organisation in the locality, *Race Today*, interpreted the events and organised the subsequent action, using the national support of the self help groups and projects, while harnessing and re-directing their black nationalist instincts. The black newspapers and radio stations publicised the events and imposed an explanation which amplified the views of the black people on the ground. In that sense, it was an impressive display of the community's ability to deliver a consensus based on the leadership cadres and the internal organisation which had been built up throughout the preceding decades.

The disturbances of the early eighties were certainly triggered by the pressure visited on young black people by the police and other authorities, but it was as much a confrontation between traditional racist barriers in the society, coming face to face with the growing expectations of the entire community of black Caribbean migrants.

The point was not whether parents approved of their children's style or language or street manners. Such matters were significant, but not crucial. What was crucial was the sense that the community now possessed a confidence and capacity which called for a new status as citizens, which implied a new protectiveness towards its members, and which conferred a kind of approval on a resentment which had been nurtured and handed down through the generations. It was no wonder that black youths walked south London with a swagger after the New Cross march. The point was not entirely lost on the police themselves. After the Brixton disturbances in 1981, the Police Federation, in its evidence to Lord Scarman's enquiry, blamed 'well educated activists' who were 'getting young blacks to believe they are victims of police oppression'. White commentators, generally, conditioned to look for evidence of an organised political will in the emergence of figures like King or Malcolm, or in the sight of blacks in some kind of 'militant' uniform, had no idea what it all meant.

The first skirmish took place in Bristol on 2 April 1980. At 3.30 p.m. thirty-nine policemen raided the Black and White café in St Paul's, which was the haunt of the city's black teenagers. They were looking for cannabis and evidence of the illegal consumption of alcohol. They found the alcohol, arrested the owner and questioned and searched the customers. While they were humping the drink out to a police van, bricks and other missiles began to be thrown. The police took refuge inside the café and radioed for reinforcements. A column of 100 men with police dogs arrived and were bombarded as they attempted the rescue of their comrades inside the café. More reinforcements arriving found themselves under attack and their vehicles overturned and burned. At the height of the disturbance the police were faced with 2,000 youths, some of them white. At about 7.30 p.m. the police withdrew leaving the crowds to loot the stores to their hearts' content. Round about 11 p.m. the police returned and were in control of the area by midnight.

'The sus laws were very difficult and, throughout the seventies resulted in a build-up of tension – not just in places like Brixton but elsewhere – because of the indiscriminate way in which they were applied, no doubt the police felt pressurised into arresting people and charging people and very often they arrest people but not charge them but treat them very badly. And there was a build-up in which you could sense the people saying, "Well, we are not prepared to go on taking any more." And something like Operation Swamp, when it emerged in '81, was really not just pushing people up against the wall but trying to push them through it, and at the end you always sense that people are saying enough's enough. And throughout the whole period of the seventies there were tensions which could have resulted in a some full-scale disturbance. It was surprising it didn't come before and although there were some in Brixton in 1980, the way in which 1981 arrived was I think frightening to people who didn't realise what was going on, but not to those who knew that people were being picked on and picked up, and if not imprisoned or charged were actually being treated extremely badly. There would come a point where – as I think the disturbances show – people were settling old scores. It was all about settling scores which were building up over a long period of time. So the sus laws made a major contribution to that huge resentment, not just against the police but the way in which authority was being seen in British society.'[2]

'It was a combination of all the pressure that young people were feeling there, and something went off and everybody was going and all pour their grief over the period that they have been suffering. And that was it. There was nothing led. It was a spontaneous situation. It wasn't a situation where people sit at home and plan it for two or three or four week and we have some great leader there, exposing certain things that, okay, we're going to do this. It happened. There was nothing planned. It was from the vindictiveness that had been shown to young black people in those days by employers, by the police to a certain extent, by the frustration of the condition that they find themselves in. Sometime it was the condition at home that they see that's being inflicted upon their family.'[3]

On Friday 10 April a policeman on foot patrol along Atlantic Road in Brixton tried to stop a youth who turned out to have been stabbed in the back. He resisted, and after a struggle escaped to a nearby block of flats, where the white occupants of the house he approached dressed his wound and called him a minicab. As the cab left it was followed by a police van which stopped it. The police examined the wound and called an ambulance, but by this time a crowd of up to fifty black youths had gathered in a suspicious mood. They seized the wounded youth, and flagged down a passing car to take him to the nearest hospital. Then they ran off, pursued by the police, who shortly came under attack themselves. Reinforcements and riot shields duly arrived, with about forty policemen facing a hundred youths. It ended at about seven-thirty that evening, but the scene had been set for real trouble the next day.

'And now this Operation Swamp '81, you can see that something more is going on in this just from the name. Swamp '81, this was a kind of acknowledgement, I suppose, for me it seemed, they were remembering the things that Mrs Thatcher said just before the election two years ago when she said, "People are really rather frightened they might be swamped by those of a different culture." This is, in a sense, a sort of revenge swamping. They wanted to swamp the streets

[2] Interview with Sir Herman Ouseley.
[3] Interview with Michael Nesbeth.

of Brixton, they wanted to target young men in particular. And the hostility and the violence, I guess, latent or manifest in the way that operation was conducted compounded the bitterness that was already there. It compounded it, it amplified it, it multiplied it. So I think that the connection is very, very, very clear, between what happened in April and what happened earlier.'[4]

That Saturday afternoon I was standing outside Lambeth Town Hall with a few other people. It was a good vantage point where some of the heavy action took place next day. Everyone knew that something was going to happen after the Friday night. This wasn't because it was planned, but because when you put together the mood of the youths, and the viciousness of police behaviour, it was obvious. A lot of politically active people who I knew from west London, other parts of south London and Tottenham in north London were there, too. A few had come down from Liverpool, Manchester and Birmingham. They weren't there to get involved, just to check out what was going on and to size up the police action, or visit some of the projects like the Melting Pot Foundation.

There was an intense throbbing vibe in the air, like feeling the bass on some incredible sound system pounding into action, but the vibe was more like excitement than anger. Among the people I knew there was always a lot of rage about discrimination and the nasty attitudes of some white people, but nobody was talking about attacking whites. In fact there were a couple of white reporters along with me, we were all working for the Guardian *and, although that weekend the newspaper reports about 'outsiders' starting it all had pissed off everyone in Brixton, everyone who came along outside the Town Hall treated the white people who were around with an almost exaggerated courtesy and friendliness. The strangest thing was that there were people walking about who didn't know or believe that something was going to happen. Later in the afternoon, after it had started and you could hear the shouting and the banging from down past the railway bridge, a white man came up, gave me a nervous grin and told me that he was working on the census and he wondered whether it was worth his while carrying on that afternoon. That was the best laugh I had all weekend. It seemed downright crazy that he hadn't noticed anything until that point. But, in a way, that*

[4] Interview with Paul Gilroy.

wasn't too surprising because apart from this strange vibe in the air, the atmosphere was sort of cheerful, everyone chatting to everyone else as we stood there in front the Town Hall waiting for the action to begin. That's how it felt, a bit like the Carnival on the first day.

The disturbance started properly on Saturday afternoon when two plainclothes policemen of the Swamp squad decided to search a minicab driver in Railton Road. They claimed to have seen him concealing drugs in his sock. It turned out to be where he kept his money, but instead of leaving they decided to search his car, drawing out the whole procedure, even though a crowd of angry young black men had gathered round them. Soon the inevitable happened. One of the officers found his way blocked by a black youth, a confrontation developed and ended in a struggle during which the youth was manhandled into the waiting van. As the van left, the youths began to throw bricks at it and at the policemen on the scene. A number of minor scuffles ensued, arrests were made, the crowd grew bigger and erupted. A police dog van was overturned and set on fire, so was another police car. The police drew their truncheons and charged, but the crowd simply dispersed and gathered again in nearby Leeson Road. From this point the crowds were simply out of control. An orgy of burning and looting took place that night. The George pub, the Windsor Castle and a local school building were burned, while firemen and ambulances were prevented from getting through to the sites of the blazes. Brixton didn't settle down until the following Monday when there were minor skirmishes, and by Tuesday it was all over.

Mike Phillips on the build-up and failure of a strong-arm strategy in Brixton

It couldn't happen to the Met

'Get Duncan.' the kids yelled, as the reporters went past. 'Interview Duncan!' They were referring to a PC Duncan, whose activities appeared to have earned him considerable unpopularity in the area. This was, in its way, a symptom of the tight, narrow circumstances which gave the spark, if not the fuel, to last weekend's riots.

The speed and spontaneity of the development was impressive. Over the weekend at least four different youths claimed that it had all started in a different place — Kellett Road, Railton Road, Chaucer Road. The truth was that it had started in all those places, at almost the same time. Nowadays, a clash with police half a mile away, or even in another town, angers and excites black youths who hear about it, almost is if it had happened to them. And the macho style of the culture is frequently equalled by the style of the police. On Sunday night a force of about three dozen officers, on foot and on horseback, chased half a dozen white youths into a building site, and 'hammered' them. Coming back, one police sergeant smacked his truncheon into this hand and remarked in tones of deep satisfaction: 'First time we've got 'em in a corner. They won't be coming back for more.' One of the boys who'd been hit over the head and shoulders with truncheons was only thirteen. Elsewhere, a black youth who had been arrested claimed to have been hit in the face by a policeman: 'I began to cry,' he said, 'and as I was crying I told him, "because you are the first white man ever to hit me without me hitting back".' Even if there had been no other contributing factors, attitudes of this kind on both sides would sooner or later have produced a large-scale version of what usually takes place every weekend in the district.

After two days of rioting, explanations vary from theories about deprivation, through police harassment, to frustration against society. All of these may be true – unlike Sir David McNee's dark hints about 'outsiders' orchestrating the affair. True, there were whites with cameras present. But consider the sheer number of young people around London who are keen amateur photographers unwilling to pass up the chance of snapping such a remarkable event. And as for the story of men with faces hidden in balaclava helmets, it is worth noting that anyone who didn't want to be recognised later by a local policeman would have had good reason for hiding his face. Who on earth could the outsiders be anyway? Tariq Ali? Carlos the Assassin, perhaps? On the streets of Brixton they are saying that McNee's statement merely underlines his contempt for blacks. 'As if we couldn't have put on a riot without a white outsider to show us how. It's typical.'

Similar hints were touted after the recent Black People's Day of Action when thousands marched in protest at the New Cross [Deptford] fire. The *Express* was so far off the mark as to suggest that a group of predominantly white journalists called the Campaign Against Racism in the Media had started it. In fact, on the Day of Action, it was only after intense argument that whites were allowed to take part in the march at all – and then they were told to stay at the back of the procession. Then, as now, the suggestion that white outsiders were behind the trouble was simply a fantasy through which racists could assimilate the nature of the disturbance.

The Brixton riots have put the Metropolitan Police in deep trouble. After what happened in Bristol, senior Met policemen were saying both publicly and privately that it couldn't happen in London – and, anyway, if it did the lads would sort it out. London's Special Patrol Group were already veterans of clashes with black youths, and in each case (the Metro, the Mangrove, the Carib, Southall, Lewisham) police had been seen to be containing the situation. As McNee commented after the Bristol riot, there would be no 'no go areas' in London. The Bristol police were ninnies for their withdrawal, inefficient for their failure to bring in reinforcements, and undermined by their concern about community relations. The Met wouldn't let it happen.

But the two days of Brixton rioting fatally damaged that kind of confidence. The Hammer, as they're saying in the streets, has taken a hammering. And one white resident demanded: 'What good did all those policemen do? If they were here to protect our property, they failed.'

Local residents in Brixton suggest that, since the Day of Action, police operations in the area have been stepped up. Most blacks who live there have been familiar for years with the SPG vans, with the risks of being picked up on 'sus', and with the fear of being injured on arrest. But the police presence throughout March and early April was unusual. Even 'respectable' residents commented on it. Last week, the police launched Operation Swamp, timed for completion at the weekend. This was to foreshadow Operation Star, a London-wide production. Brixton had been chosen for the experimental run. Uniformed police officers were pulled out and sent in again in plain clothes. A thousand people were stopped and questioned in the four days immediately prior to the riot. The police claim that Brixton was chosen because it has high figures for street crime. But to young blacks in the area, the operation was a show of police strength – a boast (after the New Cross march) that no one but the Met would rule the streets. It was calculated that the people of Brixton would accept it, as they had accepted the SPG, with anger and protest, but without wholesale revolt.

Black activists link the behaviour of the police with the Nationality Bill, which is presently before Parliament and with the economic climate, which is biting hardest in the areas where black people live. If the Bristol riot was caused by a combination of deprivation, social despair and rage at a racist environment (as most commentators suggest) the same combination of factors surely prevail in a number of British cities. Yet the government failed even to appoint a special inquiry into the Bristol affair. With predictions of trouble proliferating as dole queues lengthened, it's hard to believe that there was a complete absence of strategy for dealing with similar conflicts in the future. Most blacks maintain that there was indeed a strategy, and that it consisted of a crude reliance on the police to contain trouble. It was precisely that strategy which sparked off the riots in Brixton.

By comparison, US cities faced with similar problems in the sixties had – while not conceding the basic structure of discrimination – tightened police regulations, relaxed drug laws and withdrawn patrols from black areas; even more effectively, they had pumped funds into an infrastructure of community participation agencies, which gave the better-educated blacks a position of relative power, to be converted into a system of local patronage, changing the colour of local firemen, police officers, housing inspectors and teachers.

In Britain, the nearest equivalent has been the granting of a larger number of training places for young people in Brixton than elsewhere; but these last only for six weeks, and then turn youths back onto the streets, still jobless. After the weekend of riots, a meeting was held between the Labour council leader, Ted Knight and a group of local traders and community workers – the talk was all about money. An attempt by one activist to refer to the political dimension was quickly glossed over. To some people, such as Community Liaison Officer Herman Ouseley, the essential job was 'not rebuilding, but building a better Brixton'. David Lane, head of the Commission for Racial Equality, was expected to visit the area shortly: there were angry mutterings, suggesting fears of a switch from reliance on police strength to a handout in which the CRE and its local representatives could scoop the pool. 'Next time', one local resident remarked, looking at the ruins of the Post Office (as if there could be no doubt that there would be a next time), 'the fire will be hotter'. (Mike Phillips, *New Statesman*, 17 April 1981)

The Brixton riots in '81 had startled and alarmed the authorities. There had been no significant enquiry after Bristol, but this time an enquiry under a respected judge, Lord Scarman, was set up and for a while it appeared as if the problem had been solved within the framework of traditional practice. On 3 July, however, Southall erupted when a group of racist skinheads were bussed into the area for a concert by the band Oi at the Hamborough Tavern, and marched through the High Street smashing windows as they went. Asian youths, already organised by west London's Asian Youth Movement, and incensed by the concert in what was now their town, laid siege to the pub. The police intervened, and there were over a hundred casualties, sixty-one of them policemen. On the same night police in Liverpool chased a black youth on a motorbike. He fell off and they caught him, but he was then rescued by a crowd of about forty black youths. Two hours of fighting followed, and on the next night, a Saturday, police were lured to Upper Parliament Street by an anonymous report of a stolen car, then attacked. A crowd of nearly two hundred youths, both black and white took over the district, burned cars and shops and began looting. On the Sunday the rioting went out of control with the police calling in reinforcements from all over the North West to make up a force of 800, but they were still overwhelmed by a crowd of black and white youths. In the meantime the local community poured out to loot everything they could. They were pushing shopping trolleys and prams and filling them up as they went. They drove vans into the area like a regular shopping trip, picking up refrigerators, electrical goods, carpets, the lot. The rioting didn't end until Monday. On Tuesday 7 July, rioting broke out in Moss Side, Manchester. The local police station was attacked and damaged, but Manchester marked a watershed in police violence. James Anderton, the chief constable, had never been patient with the idea of policing by consent and his solution was to send fifty-four vans speeding through the area on the third night of rioting, with their back doors hanging open and filled with snatch squads in crash helmets who leapt out to crack heads and drag their targets away. 'Nigger, nigger, nigger – oi, oi, oi', the cops shouted as they went, beating their truncheons on the side of the vans. In spite of the new tactic, the disturbances took until the Saturday to quell. The violence spread round Greater Manchester during that time, leading to a final tally of 475 arrests, of whom the majority were white.

Around Moss Side the joke was that the black youths would start the trouble and as soon as the elderly white folks living along Whalley Range and off Moss Lane heard the noise, they would get out their prams and their shopping trolleys and get ready to go out and get what they needed from the shops.

Wood Green in north London, a stone's throw from Tottenham where the most serious riot of the decade was to take place years later, had exploded on the same night as Moss Side when a crowd of 400 youths went on a spree of smashing and looting in the shopping centre, but that died down almost immediately. At the end of the week fighting broke out in Brixton again. In Woolwich, Lewisham, Stoke Newington, Balham and Fulham crowds of youths went on the rampage, smashing shop windows, looting, overturning and burning cars. On Friday of that week, 10 July, there were disturbances in Reading, Ellesmere Port, Nottingham, Sheffield, Wolverhampton, Hull, Preston, Slough and Handsworth in Birmingham. Southall blazed with burning cars, while black and Asian youths stoned the fire engines trying to reach the fires. There were more disturbances everywhere on the next Saturday night. In addition to the places where there was already fighting, trouble spread to Bradford, Halifax, Huddersfield and Leeds, and even to places like Knaresborough and Cirencester in Gloucestershire where a police car was fire-bombed. In Blackburn 500 youths broke shop windows and the same in Preston, Blackpool and Fleetwood in Lancashire. In Handsworth the crowds were only dispersed after the police had staged baton charges. In Wolverhampton, Enoch Powell's constituency, petrol-bombs were thrown, some of them by the sort of white youths who had once supported him. In Leicester there were attacks on the police, said to be coordinated by boys on bicycles using CB radios. There were disturbances in Southampton, Portsmouth, Luton, Derby, Nottingham and Sheffield. The worst violence took place in Chapel Town in Leeds where police battled with rioters for five hours in the early hours of Sunday morning. By this time there was rioting in High Wycombe, Birkenhead, Aldershot and Gloucester. On the day after, Monday, there was more trouble in Huddersfield and Battersea, where a crowd of youths on roller skates attacked and injured three policemen. In Leicester riot police clashed with crowds throwing petrol-bombs and acid.

The night of 14 July was quiet, and on 15 July, incredibly, the police staged a raid on eleven houses in the heart of the front line in Brixton's Railton Road where the hottest fighting had taken place. They had warrants for bomb-making equipment, but didn't find any, although they succeeded in smashing the furniture and appointments with axes and crowbars. The raid took 176 policemen with 391 standing by, and it netted five people charged with possession of cannabis and one with obstruction. A night of rioting followed.

After this the country went quiet again, until 26 July when rioting started in Liverpool while Michael Heseltine was visiting the city. This time a disabled man was killed by a police Landrover using the Manchester police's hot pursuit tactics, and the riots took three days to subside.

The riots of '81 effected little immediate change in the methods and approach of the police forces towards the black community. When the worst riots of the period took place in 1985 at Broadwater Farm in Tottenham, the flashpoint was located in precisely the same corridor of confrontation between the police and black youths as the one which featured in Brixton during '81. On the other hand, the riots of '81, along with the disturbances which followed it for the next four years, had a clear and discernible effect on the status and the clout of the black communities as a whole, and on the ability to influence their relationships with the institutions which controlled the environment in which they lived.

'People were crying out, like, Come down here and look at us down here, for Christ's sake. Come and find out what is happening to us. We are here, we want to be law abiding citizens but we are not allowed to live the way a human being should live. We were crying out to the politicians to come and recognise and have a look and try and understand what is happening. That was it. It was the whole condition and it was the whole agenda.'[5]

'I don't think you can realistically, as an individual, believe when you hear stories that people are just being picked up and rounded up for no reason unless you experience it, or you know of people who have experienced it. In the aftermath of '81, many people of both black and white were saying, "I didn't realise what was happening

5 Interview with Michael Nesbeth.

until I heard all the stories and now I know for sure." It wasn't just people shouting racism, and a few bad eggs or a few bad apples in a barrel, it was a deep institutional problem that had to be grappled with, and that was a defining moment. Immediately, what I detected was a recognition on the part of some institutions, particularly local authorities, that discrimination was happening, that they were actually perpetuating it and engaged in it, that historically they've contributed to a situation directly or indirectly, and that they had to start to take action to reverse that scenario. It meant that over a period of four, five years you started to see a new politics emerging, more black elected members on local authorities, a recognition that you can't tackle institutional racism within those institutions unless you really scraped it all out. Not the bad apples but the whole barrel, you put in special arrangements within those local authorities to deal with the problems of under representation, the problems of policies and practices which are discriminatory – and that was one immediate effect.

'Another was the realisation that people's attitudes needed to change, people particularly who were making decisions about black people, whether it's in social welfare and social care, or it's about housing allocations, or employment opportunities. Whatever it was, particularly in relation to public services, there had to be training that dealt with the issue of racism and racial awareness, and that started to explode on the scene quite considerably, peaking around the late eighties. And also there was clearly a recognition that the economic situation was one in which there was a paucity of black economic development, largely once again as a result of a variety of discriminatory measures where the banks were failing to lend to local authorities, not giving planning permission or support programmes, not actually encouraging and including black and other ethnic minority people. All those things were very significant in the way it had to change as a result of the riots and the fallout from that. So there was a recognition then that black people needed to be seen to be part of the wealth creation, part of the economy, and to be encouraged to be business owners, business leaders, employers themselves, and that started to gather a head of steam during the mid-eighties.'[6]

---

[6]   Interview with Sir Herman Ouseley.

27

<hr>

'In terms of real politics I think the first thing that happened was
in 1978 when Russell Profitt created the Standing Conference of
Afro-Caribbean and Asian Councillors, whereby we were able to
start bringing our people directly any legislation that affected them
and how it affected them. So we were politicising the people. The
second important thing was the BTUSM, Black Trade Union
Solidarity Movement, which is the brain child of Bernie Grant. That
too was very important, because it made an attack on the Trade
Union movement, and showed black people that they can actually
through mobilising and organising themselves, they could go to the
Trade Union movement and they could probably push the Trade
Union into areas it had not been looking at. The third one was the
black sections movement, and the idea was that we should look
seriously into black politics and to take to the Labour Party – because
we were all members of the Labour Party – its racism, slam it into
its face and say, "It's all right you pointing your finger at everybody
and saying they're racist, but how about you? What are you going
to do for the black people, with thousands and hundreds of thousands
of black people who voted for you?" And for the first time the
Labour Party actually had to look at itself and decide to do something
about it, instead of calling everybody racist, to do something about
it. Although I must say it was the ordinary members of the Labour
Party who did it, not the hierarchy in the Labour Party who tried
to water it down by turning it into something called the Socialist
Society, whereby the black people could not organise themselves
unless they organised themselves with other groups. But they allowed
women's groups to organise themselves. There was the Jewish
Society already in the Labour Party. They had the women
organisations already in the Labour Party, and for the Labour Party
to turn around and say that black people could not organise within
their structure and that was being unsocialistic, well, I felt was
dishonest.'[1]

<hr>

[1] Interview with Ben Bousquet.

From The GLC
To Thatcherism

1980–87

Whatever the causes or the effects of the riots had been they were a graphic demonstration of one thing – black people and their interests were no longer marginal. Widespread racial discrimination was still a feature of British life, but for a few weeks, young black people had led a movement which not only gripped the entire country, but drew in young whites and inspired them to imitation. Even though the newspapers were generally hostile and made no bones about supporting the police and their polemic about black criminality, no one was in any doubt that what young black people claimed about harassment and injustice on the streets was true. After the riots, public opinion polls showed that the credibility of the police forces had declined considerably, and even Powell climbed back into the arena with apocalyptic warnings and appeals for repatriation. The public response, in comparison with '68 was, more or less, indifference.

At the same time, alongside the rage and riot of the eighties another movement was taking place, which was to prove equally crucial for the future shape of the black communities. This was the climax of a trend which had begun back in the sixties, when the *Windrush* migrants began standing for election to the local councils. Since then the approach of the Caribbean migrants to the political culture had been gathering shape. Towards the end of the seventies the different strands of trade unionism and local government politics coalesced into a campaign to infiltrate a black agenda for action within the Labour Party.

'I was one of the first black councillors in Lewisham and probably amongst the first black councillors in Britain, at the time. Getting a position on the council seemed a very important thing to do for the community. But it was not at all easy to get that message across to local politicians, and, in fact, in national politics. The British political parties all wanted to adopt what they say was a colour blind approach, i.e., it doesn't matter what colour you are, what matters is whether you get good services and, at the end of the day, it's that which matters more than the fact that you're of one colour or the other. Totally wrong. You cannot look at society as one great big lump, you need to be careful that you understand the differences between people otherwise the services that you're offering will not pick up those differences. And, at the time, there was always that struggle to establish that fact in every political forum that I'd have been in or other black councillors would have been in. And it took a long time to change that situation, so a number of us became involved in joint working across London, and nationally, through the creation of black councillors' forums and the like, so that we could understand how we can draw up, almost an agenda for action on the issues that we thought would be important, that we needed to get across to local and to national politicians. That took a long time to be established and to get the message through.

'The Labour Party didn't like it, and the Labour Party did its best to stop black political organisation in Britain at the time. I can well remember Neil Kinnock pointing his finger in my face and saying, You are evil, you have got to be stopped. And that's the sort of pressure we were under. Roy Hattersley saying to me, You would never be selected as a Member of Parliament, over my dead body, and that sort of thing. At that stage I was trying to become a Member of Parliament, and when I was nominated by local parties my candidature was often blocked by headquarters and, if I ever asked them individually why it was, those were the sorts of answers I would get. I was, at the time, the Chair of the Labour Party Black Sections, which was seen as one of the splinter groups that was fractionalising the Labour Party at the time. And Kinnock was famously involved in a campaign to quash all of the splinter groups. So, I suppose, in that context, I was one that had to be quashed as well. We stifled all of that at the time, and we can say it now 'cos these figures don't matter. You can say, thank goodness, the Labour Party's changed, but changed for what? I'm still not clear that the Labour Party understands the sort of questions we're talking about, even now, even though we have black Members of Parliament, I'm not sure the issues are understood. But at that time, the pressure was severe on those of us involved to stop the debate, because it was uncomfortable.'[2]

There was very little hope, at the time, of gaining acceptance for an agenda constructed by representatives of the black community, if only because the Labour Party, like the rest of the political culture, had not yet emerged

[2] Interview with Russell Profitt.

from the trauma of Powellism. All the politicians were sure of one thing –
being seen to be 'soft on immigrants' was the electoral kiss of death, as the
Powellites were always popping up to assure them. The anti-racism of the
left had never focused on equality of opportunity for blacks. Instead it had
been based on opposition to the racists' fascism, within which racism was
simply one outstanding element. At the coal face of race relations in the
Labour-controlled industrial areas, it was frequently difficult to tell the
difference between the stalwarts of the Labour movement and the supporters
of the National Front.

'Largely by historic coincidence, where black people settled when
they came to this country in the post-war period, it happened to be
mainly in areas which had a fairly dominant Labour presence.
Equally it was in the relatively poorer areas you found well qualified
black people competing with poor white people for jobs which are
available within the economy. And clearly in areas where there was
opposition to black people you would find a lot of working-class
white people involved in that and Labour and trade union movements
involved in that. If one traces the history of a borough like Lambeth,
back in the fifties and the sixties there was a pattern of deliberate
discrimination to exclude black people from social housing, getting
on to council waiting lists, segregating and dispersal policies were
prevalent.
  'All of these things were deliberate policies in the same way as
the government had a deliberate policy to slow down the numbers
of people coming in to the country. And so it is not surprising to
understand what was happening in the sixties and the fact that it was
Labour-controlled authorities who were discriminating. Equally,
one would say that in authorities which were Conservative-controlled
the problems were less magnified and not necessarily on the same
scale, but the discrimination was also occurring.'[3]

When it came to racial issues the Labour Party had become accustomed to
treading a careful path between the rhetoric of racial equality and the
Powellite instincts of some of its members. As a result the route by which
the issues affecting black people were to move closer to the centre of national
politics faced an immovable barrier in the centre of the Labour Party, and

³   Interview with Sir Herman Ouseley.

the activists had to begin canvassing ways of bypassing the Parliamentary political culture.

On 7 May 1981, a matter of weeks after the Brixton disturbances, the County Council elections delivered a Labour-controlled Greater London Council. Representing Walthamstow, the black lawyer, Paul Boateng, was only the second black person to be elected to a county council. Boateng had a white mother and a Ghanaian father, but he had from the start of his career been closely identified with the Caribbeans and the issues which affected them in London. In the West Midlands James Hunte, who, during the previous decade, had led the campaign against pyramid sales[4] in the district, was elected to represent Handsworth, along with a Guyanese in Aycocks Green, and two Asians in Coventry and West Bromwich. If nothing else, these successes demonstrated that the riots had not alienated the electorate at large, and they hinted at greater possibilities for black politicians. Above all, they signalled the start of what became known as municipal anti-racism, a programme deeply influenced by the agenda that the black local government councillors and their allies had drawn up over the previous three or four years.

'The time when the GLC came into being in '81 was a really important time, because it was round about the time of the Brixton disturbances that the new GLC was elected. But it's quite important to recognise that it was already in their manifesto, the incoming Labour administration said that it recognised institutional racism existed and it was going to do something about it. So there was a clear recognition that here was this huge strategic authority in London, that had no relationship at all with the black and ethnic minority communities in and around greater London. So people like Paul Boateng, Ken Livingstone, John Carr, leading members who had a focus on the issue, were instrumental in putting in place arrangements which would lead to new policies and practices, an ethnic minorities committee, the ethnic minorities unit permeating the whole organisation, new policies and strands which related to communities at risk which included the ethnic minority

---

[4] Pyramid sales were a method of recruiting people to sell the products (often non-existent) of a company. Recruits had to pay for a position in the company and pay substantial sums for the products they were meant to sell. In Birmingham banks and finance companies lent money for mortgages to large numbers of people who then found themselves deep in debt with no way of repaying. James Hunte was a 'self help' activist who formed an association of victims of pyramid sales and instituted court proceedings for compensation. Hunte came from Barbados, joined the British Army and served in Malaya. On leaving the Army he settled in Birmingham.

communities. Therefore, the notion of black people identifying with
the GLC became a reality towards the end of 1981 and '82. As a
large employer, employing over 22,000 people, it was quite important
because it was able to move quite significantly and dramatically in
attracting people from all backgrounds, including black people, and
trying to put them into positions relative to their ability, qualities
and skills, and I think because of its size, because of its budgets to
profile its work, because of how it was perceived at a time, because
of the way the media saw it as a demon, race and ethnic minority
issues and black people's involvement became a high profile of the
GLC's work. It was a very important part of the process of public
bodies becoming sensitised to the needs of black people and tackling
the issue of institutionalised racism and how it was rooted in policies
and programmes that propped up the status quo.'[5]

'What the GLC did was what we had been attempting to do on
a smaller scale locally in Haringey and elsewhere, which was to bring
to the attention of the British people that there were certain groups
within society in London that were severely disadvantaged and that
in order to equalise the opportunities for everyone, there was a need
for them to take some positive action to ensure that those people
were given some help, some resources, in order for them to reach
a level from which they can begin to take off. And I think that's
basically what the GLC did for black and minority ethnic people in
London, because their rate base was so large and they could raise so
much money by putting a penny on the rates of the city and all the
other big institutions. What the GLC did was to use that money from
the City in order to encourage and to assist women's groups, black
and minority ethnic groups, lesbian and gay groups. And the GLC
opened up a whole new world for us, because what the GLC did
under Ken Livingstone in particular, was that the GLC went into
areas that no one thought possible. We had all been accustomed to
the whole way in which politics has been run in Britain – Labour,
Conservative all doing basically the same thing – and what the GLC
did was it went to the people and it opened up the GLC so it was a
people's palace, so that on Saturdays and so on there were festivals
for the people, festivals along the South Bank. The GLC began to
give people the feeling that they could actually make a difference

[5] Interview with Sir Herman Ouseley.

to their own lives. I think this is what the GLC did that was so important, that's why Mrs Thatcher had to stop them. Because, of course, it began to spread to other metropolitan authorities – Manchester, Birmingham and so on. And if it had been allowed to continue there would have been quite a revolution in British society. So they had to be stopped. But, basically, they ingrained in peoples minds that your life was your own, that there are a number of things that you can do. You didn't have to wait for handouts from anyone. That if you had the resources, and if you were independent and clear thinking, that you can go a long way and this is basically what happened.

'I became the leader of Haringey Council because, for a number of years, I and a number of other people, including people like Jeremy Corbyn, who was a councillor at that time in Haringey, led a faction against the leadership and our contention was that we wouldn't make cuts in the provision of public services for the people of Haringey. Cuts that the government wanted to impose on us. So that it all came to a head at the special meeting of the council that was to set the rate, which went on all night and there was a lot of argument and eventually a rate was set. But the leadership of the council resigned because what they did was against the Party's wishes and against the wishes of the people of Haringey. So there was a vacancy and I was asked, as one of the leaders of the alternate group, whether I would become leader of the council, and I accepted.'[6]

'I think the importance of the GLC to London, at that time, in the eighties, was it gave London a voice. It celebrated and didn't see as a problem the fact that we were a multi-racial community. I remember once a great event of music and culture and politics, led by Stevie Wonder. I mean the fact that a local authority could bring Stevie Wonder over and, at the same time, be bringing over black leaders, municipal and political leaders, religious leaders from the United States, all to participate in a conscious effort, actually, to say we are a multi-racial London, yes we want to celebrate that, but also there are issues of disadvantage and discrimination which we have to address. And also, to put the black struggle for civil rights and for liberty and for justice within a global context. Because, don't forget, it was the GLC that first brought Oliver Tambo to the

---

[6] Interview with Bernie Grant.

attention of a wider audience saying, "This is a great man, he represents an authentic liberation struggle in southern Africa. He needs to be recognised. And rather than simply welcoming P. W. Botha and a succession of white racist apartheid leaders from South Africa, we ought to be honouring this South African, we ought to be honouring Trevor Huddlestone, a great prophetic white Christian leader. These are the true voices of a multi-racial South Africa who need to be recognised in London. And London needs to be saying something about opposing apartheid." Now that was a very radical, but a very necessary stance to take at that time.[7]

The GLC and the other municipalities which took their lead from it, clearly had a huge symbolic influence in putting forward and forcing acceptance for the notion that the migrants were now entitled to all the rights and benefits of civic life in Britain. On the other hand, it was unarguable that they did not possess the resources or the authority to deliver a programme which would have effectively promoted racial equality to the blacks within their boundaries. They didn't control the police, for instance, and couldn't call them to account. They couldn't control discrimination in employment, except for their own employees and contractors. They couldn't reshape the attitudes of the major national institutions which sat around them in London.

In some ways the black people got the worst of both worlds. On the one hand, the newspapers and saloon bar gossip maintained that black people were now privileged by statute, and the tabloids delighted in trumpeting the news of every GLC award or every regulation they could represent as benefiting blacks 'unfairly'. On the other hand, the funds which actually went to black community groups were an infinitesimal fragment of the total budget. Another problem was its effect on the identity of the black communities. Under the rubric of the GLC, the communities which came from Caribbean, African and Asian roots, became 'ethnic minorities'. For the white politicians and bureaucrats who ran County Hall, the identity of all these groups was now determined by the shape of their relationships with white racism, rather than by their own history and development. The Caribbeans were worst affected, since this view coincided with a period of intense interest in opposition to apartheid, in the post-Civil Rights relationship of African Americans with government programmes, and in the adroitly marketed glamour of Jamaican popular culture. The white radicals in

[7] Interview with Paul Boateng.

County Hall tended to assemble their view of 'blackness' from these elements, so when it came to the Caribbeans everyone looked abroad for models and policies, a lesson which the community was not slow to learn. For a period of five years the developments within the structure of black politics and organisation began to slow down and freeze, as every new group and most of the old reshaped their agenda towards winning support from the GLC Ethnic Minorities Unit. The radical thrust of black organisation became rhetorical.

'What happens is that the, supposedly, most radical local government elected in the history of London in the form of the GLC under Ken Livingstone arrives on the scene, and arrives on the scene at a time when the politics of race and conflict over criminal justice questions and over the life of the streets of this city is absolutely prominent. So the question of race, while having been seen to be a sort of marginal thing that people can just ignore or forget about, is actually suddenly catapulted into the very centre of official, formal political institutions where there is some sort of political will to connect. Now this is a novel situation. The new ways in which the struggle over race had become suddenly relevant to the political mainstream, interrupted the processes that were going on at community level. A simple example might be that whereas before in the organisation of the march, people had to raise that money for themselves and print those things for themselves and go round on the train or the bus speaking to different groups and so on, suddenly there was a group of specialists like almost paratroopers, charged with the job of acting on these things, who were being delivered into the core of those communities to address their needs in relation to questions of education, to raise the issue of policing, and so on, and to work against the way that racism was operating in the city.

'Suddenly all of that was made available, and I don't think anything was the same after that. So, just at the time where we would have been trying to calculate where to go next, a new situation is created, a big change in the weather that actually requires new skills, new disciplines and a new kind of political interface with the mainstream. The emergence of a sort of local authority anti-racism and municipal anti-racism was a very mixed bag, and there's some really wonderfully exciting developments, but there was also a kind of loss involved too. I don't want to be sentimental about the days when we didn't have any resources to do the things that we wanted to do, but I think that there is a sense in which the institutional life of the politics became almost more important for many people than what was going on in the sort of immediate places where those struggles were being waged. Sometimes they were very successfully joined together, but sometimes they weren't.

'I think it becomes a very difficult political challenge when you stop thinking of racism as being only to do with the activities of, you know, fascist groups or the sort of particular violent local cultures that they create in certain areas, and think seriously about what it might mean to organise the municipal government of London along lines which were not just neutral, but which were positively engaged in the struggle against racism in the city, and nobody had a blue-print for that. Even attempts to use the commercial power of the local government to ensure that people who supplied things and provided services were acting in ways that were consistent with existing legislation were stamped on, and produced an incredible hostility. So it was a very, very mixed bag. There were also some problems about the form that official anti-racism took. It got a little doctrinaire, a little bit formalistic, a lot of guilt was kind of summoned up but, actually, not enough. So the effect can be paralysing. You suddenly realise that this is a huge, huge problem which has tentacles going in all sorts of directions, and you also know that you don't have a recipe that you can apply to it. What it means to work in a school and change a school is not the same as what it means to work in a police station and change a police station. So I think there was a mistaken sense in which the real hard long work of doing something about these things got trivialised as a result of that municipal anti-racism.

'Of course, I'd like municipal anti-racism back, and perhaps I was too critical of it before. Now the best we've got is a bit of privatised anti-racism with Nike and Benetton and these other people taking on the large-scale sort of symbolic interventions that local government was prepared to dabble in under the GLC, but I think there was the danger of trivialising it that troubled me.'[8]

'The problems then came in trying to transform the fortunes for black and other minorities within their areas, how quickly they would do that and who would be doing it. I think there was obviously a

---

[8] Interview with Paul Gilroy.

different approach being pursued by Labour authorities compared to Conservative- or Liberal Democrat-led authorities, a lot of the high profile gains were made in Labour-controlled authorities, the three leaders of local authorities were all Labour when we had Brent, Haringey and Lambeth at different times having black leaders. There were no leaders emerging in any Conservative-led councils. So there were successes and gains and achievements in Labour-controlled authorities which were high profile and there were lower level successes in other authorities, but at the same time there were also greater expectations on the part of black people for change and for equality which were often directed at Labour-controlled authorities, and therefore pointed fingers of failure at the same time as those authorities were pursuing change."[9]

The GLC was abolished in 1986. The Prime Minister, Mrs Thatcher, was incorrigibly opposed to its politics and its policies, and she had, in any case, been whittling away at the powers of local government for most of her period in office.

The demise of the GLC was generally viewed as a disaster for the black communities, but there was a curious sense in which it had already prepared the Caribbean migrant communities to adopt a Thatcherite approach to themselves. Within the culture of the GLC there were a number of important elements leading this trend. First was the use of 'black culture' as a way of defining black identity. This had to fit what the white left knew or believed about blacks, so certain elements of the culture blacks had begun to create were now privileged. Music, dance and performance became the touchstones of black identity. ('Black music', 'black dance' and 'black performance' that is.) Black authenticity was also guaranteed by class references – the Rastafarian-tinged 'black dialect' was now the correct form of black speech. The black 'generation gap' was now also a privileged concept, with older black people redefined as conformist and 'Victorian'. A number of policies were also driven by the notion of a diaspora in which black people shared similarities which were more important than their environment, so there was a brisk trade in the import of black authority figures from the USA, the Caribbean and Africa, reinforcing the imagery of blacks as an outpost of an alien culture in Britain.

Oddly enough, all these elements were crucial in the first stage of recreating British blacks as captive buyers for the products of an American domi-

[9] Interview with Sir Herman Ousley.

nated 'black culture' controlled and marketed by a network of multi-national companies. What followed in the next stage of the effect of Thatcherism on the black communities was the mythology of 'black success'. Set over against the GLC ideology in which the state would re-invent the community's independence, was the Thatcherite idea which suggested that you could pull yourself up by your bootstraps, and that the intervention of the state weakened your will and your capacity to achieve material success. It was a seductive idea for a community which had started in the reckless adventure of sailing over the sea looking for a future. But the avenues to success for black people were strictly limited by discrimination. However optimistic you were about the future, that was one factor that you ran up against sooner or later. There was only one resource that black people possessed which the white market wanted, and that was the music, the style and the bodies which exemplified these things. Following the trends in the international market for black culture, black people set out to recreate as a marketable commodity the only things they could produce and be sure of making a sale.

'A third element is the period of Thatcherism itself, in the eighties. In a very funny way, because of its sort of radical attack on a number of established traditional British institutions, it sort of opened some spaces, it sort of made the society slightly more permeable. Now, it made it more permeable at a cost, only for a minority, and only if you really went after success of a very individualistic kind. And I think, actually, the black British identity is an identity of that kind, it is very individualistic. It's lost a lot of its sense of collective politics of the seventies and eighties. It's not waiting to pool the whole society, you know, through equal opportunities, up alongside it. It's making time for yourself. It's built on what I would call the hustling elements of black culture, you know. Mrs Thatcher's "enterprise culture" and black hustling are sort of cousins under the skin. They really say, Carve it out for yourself, you know, open it up. And what I think is wonderful, it's a minority only, of course, everybody is not successful. I don't want to overdo this in any way, but what is marvellous about that minority of black kids that have managed to move into some of these spaces is their tremendous confidence. They just occupy them, they just say, We're here, we've arrived. They're equipped with their mobile phones, they're in touch with New York or Los Angeles and the record company and they have fifteen deals going down. They're just manipulating the society, they are moving it. They're not moved by it any longer, they're not held in place by it, they are moving through it. And this gives it a particular cast, and it's a cast which sometimes one doesn't like so much, it is very hustly, it is very me, me, oriented.'[10]

Here's the problem with Mrs Thatcher. At the same time as she was thumping the tub of white nationalism, she was destroying some of the bases on which it stood. Her attack on traditional Toryism, for instance, opened the door for people who came out of the next to bottom drawer. There were so many contradictions. Her chief anti-immigrant hitman, Michael Howard, was an immigrant himself. She made a great noise about British culture, but the identity of her main men was defined and dominated by international money. She raised money in the Far East from Oriental millionaires. Her poll tax provoked riots and united the country against her in the way nothing else did for a long time. She smashed a network of working-class cultures when she smashed the miners' strongholds, and when she did so she set off a fragmentation and decline of one of the most reactionary and insular groupings in the Labour movement. She managed the same thing with the power of the trade unions. After she had finished with them the ground lay bare, which meant that outsiders like us could walk in, without being repulsed by organised interests. She took away the sense of belonging and certainty from huge swathes of the British, but, then, the truth is that we immigrants had never known those roots, and that left us free to join in the re-building. She laid out a set of criteria which defined a good citizen, like hard work and thrift and enterprise, and whether or not anyone believed she meant it, they were a kind of benchmark which anyone could aspire to, no matter where they were born. She made it clear that if you had money there was a ticket you could buy. She was the great She Elephant in whose path nothing stood.

'But, this Thatcherite style has very positive things. I think you see it more especially in black women than you see it in black men. I think black women are more successful at it and at a tremendous cost. They're looking after the kids, they're holding families together, they're holding down a job, they're going to college, they're taking a course at work, they are just putting themselves on the line, hour

[10] Interview with Stuart Hall.

after hour after hour. But they're determined that they will live a better life and get a better job, and have better rewards than their parents did. Black men, I think, are in slightly more trouble. I think the defensive resistance culture around black men, especially in schools, sometimes prevents them from really exercising their skills and capacities in quite that success-driven aspirational way. But I think the generation as a whole is so much more confident. This is the generation that came out of the wars of the seventies. They were minted in the seventies, they were being born in the seventies, and they have come through with a tremendous confidence about themselves. Now, of course, right around them, our kids are not doing well, not doing well in school. Huge numbers of them excluded, large numbers of them in unemployment, on the edge of crime, being criminalised. I don't want to underplay that other element, that is the majority story, still. But, we have to talk about the different stories, what I sometimes call the front line and the back yard stories. And now black experiences and black identities are more complex than they were. There is no one story that encapsulates the black experience, there is no "the black experience", any longer. There are black experiences, there are a rich variety of ways in which blacks are now deeply part of the fabric of British life.'[11]

---

[11] Interview with Stuart Hall.

28

'It was very difficult for me to survive. I got a job at the Charing Cross Hotel, then I got pneumonia and got in the hospital coming out the hot kitchens. Now, in the hospital, I didn't want to live. I was ready to throw the sponge in, I really didn't want to live. This was 1940. I came out determined to get back to Bermuda, my nice comfortable little island. Fate had it that it wasn't to be, like God said, No, no, no, I want to teach you something. So I got a job on an Egyptian ship which took me to Calcutta and then for the first time I saw suffering. I saw humanity at its lowest depth of poverty. I couldn't believe what I saw, really. I saw mothers who would gouge out the eyes of their children in order to get money. Literally gouge out the eyes of their children so they can beg and people have sympathy for them. When you came off the ship and you walked down the street you got a thousand people, "Wanna sab, wanna sab" and it was like that all the time. I saw the worst kind of suffering that could be. Then I'd see some Maharajah drive past in his Rolls Royce and not even know these people existed. So I realised the injustice of this planet I lived on. So the stuff in England fell by the wayside. That was nothing compared to what I had seen. So coming back to London, on that train from Liverpool down to Euston Station, I suddenly looked back and I thought I was coming home, strangely enough, and I'd only spent then about less than nine months, ten months in London before I went out to India. I like London, to be honest. I like London very much.'[1]

'West Indians, they've learned, over the years, to select an area or a town or a city that is progressive. A city that has got industries. You don't find West Indians living in Scotland. In general, they don't live in Herefordshire, they don't live in North Wales, they don't live in Northern Ireland. They live in Birmingham, Manchester, Leicester, Bristol, where there's industries. So that is one thing that you learn through experience. Coventry, yes, but not Herefordshire.

[1] Interview with Earl Cameron.

Nothing there, nothing there. They want a town where they've got a lot of industries, a lot of factories, they can change jobs if they want to. Now, talking about towns, don't mention Liverpool to me, because Liverpool is the graveyard of all black people. No black people in Liverpool ever make anything out of their lives, because of the history of Liverpool. As far as the blacks are concerned – and I wouldn't advise any black person to even set foot in Liverpool to ask for a job. They won't get it.'[2]

Change And The City

The story of how the Caribbean migrants came to this country and became British is a story about cities. It isn't to do with a specific city, although London plays a major part in what happened. It is something to do with the nature of cities, but it is a little more than that. To begin with consider this story of July 1948, discovered by accident while reading Ministry of Labour reports about the *Windrush* migrants. The story was outlined in a letter from one C. D. Bellamy, Works Officer. It concerned a group of Jamaicans who had been hired out as agricultural labourers to farmers in the Romsey district in the county of Southampton. The farmers who employed them had refused to have them back and the district was asking for their removal. The Works Officer's impression was 'that it is their object to be unsatisfactory in order that they may be drafted to some other industry where they may earn higher wages ... I do regret to have to report on them in this manner, but have to admit our failure to extract anything like a day's work from any of them.'[3]

On first reading, this letter was mentally filed, almost automatically, as a typically prejudiced account. Then came the questions. Taking Mr Bellamy's words at face value you were left with the riddle of why these men who came from a country where farming was familiar and instinctive found it so difficult to do the work. Two possible answers occurred immediately. The first was that this was a more routine, industrial form of agriculture than they were used to, which might well have been true. But then, men like them had been migrating for generations to do similar work all around

---

[2] Interview with Euton Christian.
[3] PRO LAB 8/1816.

the Caribbean basin. The second answer was that they had not come all this way to set themselves into the familiar rural patterns. They had come to live the industrialised life of the city, and they were doing everything they could to get there.

The same could have been said about all the people who had come from the Caribbean. They weren't simply migrating to Britain. Their colonial relationship with the mother country was the means which gave them a legal and moral permit, but it was the life of the city which called to them and which they had begun to crave. This was, in any case, part of the workings of great industrial cities like London or Birmingham or Manchester. Britain had been the first, most intensely industrialised nation in the world and it was her cities which led and which encapsulated that process. By the beginning of the twentieth century the city had begun to be an instrument which defined the social nature of industrial life. Industrialisation meant urbanisation, and it was the operations of the city in the twentieth century which outlined the content and the shape of modern life. The constitutional relationship which governed Caribbean lives gave them a stark choice. Given the political and economic circumstances of the region, staying there made it impossible to engage with the broad currents of modernity which the wartime experience had shown them. The only option was to migrate.

The cities to which they came, might have, if they could, been crying out for their presence. Post-Powell accounts of the migrants' role, driven by an obsession with race, pictures a homogeneous community forced into making a reluctant space for newcomers. Ironically, however, it was precisely the indigestible nature of the new migrants, which set in train the process of remodelling and modernising British cities. Take the matter of housing, for instance, where it is arguable that, far from inhibiting building and renovation, it was the migrants who accelerated it through the sixties. In London, for instance, the districts where Caribbeans settled had nearly all been declining and rundown since the nineteenth century. Inevitably the tendency to suburbanisation had shifted the most energetic and restless of the native population out to the borders, and it was the Caribbeans who revalued huge swathes of the inner city. But the changes went wider and deeper than this, at every stage and in every location in the life of British society. Everything which symbolises the presence of Caribbean migrants, for instance, faces in two directions. The Notting Hill Carnival is an obvious example. It began as a unique analogy for our situation in Britain. In the same streets through which we'd been hunted by baying crowds we assembled to dance and sing and to say that we were celebrating being alive and being here. As the festival continued it also began to demonstrate the hybridity which proved that it was an integral part of our identity, and an emblem of our presence and our belonging. At the same time it became an emblem of a new British identity. When William Hague, the new leader of the Conservatives, went to the '97 carnival and had himself photographed enjoying it, he wasn't merely making a gesture to the West Indians. His intention was also to signal his wish to look towards the future rather than the past, and to symbolise his membership of a new conception of British citizenship. Ironically the Notting Hill Carnival was probably the only public event through which he could send that message.

On the other hand, the Caribbeans themselves had to go through a fundamental series of changes in order to live and flourish in the city. Analyses which take race as their starting point fail to see what was happening and, in that sense, underestimate both the strength and creativity that the Caribbeans brought to the process, and the role played by their interaction with urban life in the delivery of those changes. Caribbeans came to terms with the individualistic anomic structure of urban, industrial life early on, substituting networks and strategies which enabled them to survive and master it; and slowly but surely, the cities began to reflect the shape of that struggle. Unlike the African Americans, for instance, we could not retreat to the isolation of a 'black' quarter. We lived for the most part cheek by jowl with whatever other individuals the city turned up. This meant that the Caribbeans who arrived fifty years ago, and during the following decade, had to become individuals who shared the tempo, the regularity and the order of industrialised urban life. The culture we created allowed us to face towards the Caribbean and towards the African diaspora, but it also opened a doorway into some of the deep structures of British life. British 'black culture' from the beginning, therefore, was dynamic and ambiguous, swapping values between four or five different sources, tapping whatever roots were available and useful. In that sense, what the black British became was little to do with biological characteristics determined by skin colour, or with mystical connections to the African diaspora, and it was not exclusively shaped by resistance to white racism. Black people have used those notions where and how they need to, but the dynamic of the culture they have built is everything to do with following the logic of their escape from the Caribbean, towards the process of managing a hostile urban environment and infiltrating its structures. The product which has resulted is unique and unmistakable, but also marked by the ambiguity and many-sided quality of black British life.

'I play a game every time I go to the Caribbean, to Tobago, to Jamaica. I could watch a black person walking down the road, or on a beach and say, "Oh, she's from England." Different personality.

They're a much more thoughtful, less hurried, more rooted in what you're doing at this moment. "I want a drink from that bar, and if somebody's making any trouble I'm not going to get too much tied up with that, I'm going to get it because I'm going back into the sea with my wife and daughter." That way of standing in a queue. If you see somebody at a bar you go stand behind him. You don't want to stand next to them to be asking anything because it's going all end up in disorder and it will take a longer time to get what you want. The normally quite simple things that we do spontaneously, unknowing to ourselves. When you hear the inflexion in the voice, anger is as far away as you can see. Urgency and immediacy is not there. It's a take our time to get somewhere. And I can spot them, how they walk – I used to do it with, with my wife on holiday in Tobago. I say, "English." I say, "What part of England are you from?" "How do you know that?" "I just see you, man." I'm not saying it's superior to anything else, but that's us, that's what we have become: a kind of match and mix between two cultures which are very similar.'[4]

'The point of Soul II Soul, was about saying to the population of black people in other parts of the world, particularly in America, that a black English culture was operating that was convincing on its own terms. Many of the black Americans who were touched by that music didn't know that it came from England. That only strengthens the point. It was the first time that a sound had been born here which was not traceable back to an inferior copy, or a copy at any rate, of something that black Americans had done. That's the first thing. The second thing was that by trying to combine elements of soul and Reggae and to do that in a way that didn't damage either and yet remained faithful to both, Soul II Soul gave us a kind of example of how contamination between different cultures was something that was enriched, something that was positive. The other thing that you have to say about Soul II Soul is that it was the expression of a very particular local scene, a local possibility within London. Soul II Soul didn't come from Brixton, didn't come from Hackney, it came from a part of north London where it was easier to make those connections. It was easier to play with the elements of the culture and improvise something creative out of it, and I think

---

[4] Interview with Darcus Howe.

that's another pattern, as this community matures and as its history grows more complex, you will see much more uneven development between different places. Not just within one city of course, between, say, north, west, east and south London, but also between the life of black culture in places like Manchester or Birmingham or Liverpool or Leeds and the things that are going on in London. And I think what we're looking for now is to find some institutions which measure up to the job of translating between histories and experiences that are much more radically localised than they have been in the past.

'The producer of Soul II Soul was someone who came out of the Bristol scene, because Bristol was very much a place where they weren't bonded to anybody else's definition of what you could do under the sign of black culture. There was nobody standing over them saying, "Well, actually, that's not black enough so you better not do that. You have to stick to the script." They made their own script, and the life of Soul II Soul is about taking that script up and selling it on a world-wide scale. So I think there's also a sense in which a black culture coming out of Europe is able to speak to a number of different global constituencies in a different voice than the one that an African American culture would find. And there's also the aspect of the novelty involved in being European, in being people working out of a British context, and that opens different doors. In a sense, in marketing terms and music terms and youth culture terms, people think they know everything about African American culture already, there's nothing new to learn. So I think that Soul II Soul also represents the novelty factor involved of being based in Europe and speaking, therefore, in a different register and a different voice.'[5]

The period in which the Caribbean migrants were transforming themselves was also a time when Britain had to come to grips with the end of Empire and with the decline or fragmentation of its industrial power and structures. The two movements met in the cities and the ripples spread outwards. Powellism, for instance, had been an attempt to adjust to the decline by defending a quasi-historical, pre-industrial and racialist outline of English identity. But this was finally undermined and defeated by the dynamic structures of urban life. The nature of urban living maintained a distance

[5] Interview with Paul Gilroy.

between groups and individuals, but the instinct of the city was to centralise services and administration, to equalise choices, to level out differences between consumers and producers. So the essential job of the city was to put people together: and as rural structures declined in importance, it was the character of the city which came to define the identity of the nation. As a result, once the Caribbeans had arrived, and settled themselves in the major cities, it was already too late to isolate them effectively from the developing concept of Englishness. The consequence has been to radicalise public discussion about the identity of the nation, which is, in itself, a sign of how far things have changed.

'I made my maiden speech on the subject of human rights, which is very close to my heart, and fits into the kind of issues around race and gender discrimination which I've worked around over many years. So I was very pleased to participate in that debate. I think the other thing about doing a maiden speech on human rights was that I was speaking on the same platform with a number of people who had campaigned on human rights for a number of years as well, and who I have a great liking for. So, that felt very good. The other thing was that everybody's very kind to you on the day that you do your maiden speech, and everybody says that your maiden speech is very good, and they're very positive about it. So it was a day on which a number of people came up to me, welcomed me to the Lords, and also were very positive about the maiden speech that I had made. From a personal point of view, I felt that I had made a significant contribution and I was pleased about that, because that's one of the reasons why I agreed that I would like to go there. I do want to make a contribution. I want to want to make it work. And I was pleased that I could make my maiden speech so early. I made it in less than ten days of being introduced. Its importance was the recognition of what the black community has achieved in the UK, a kind of recognition that we have skills, experience, expertise. That we can actually bring to a place like the House of Lords – and this very much came as a result of the kind of positive feedback from people – a recognition that British society has changed, that it has matured, that it is, in a way, more ready to think about the reality of diversity and inclusiveness as two different sides of the same coin, if you like.'[6]

---

[6] Interview with Baroness Amos.

'One of the things that I get irritated by is this constant harping upon what is being done to us, as though we haven't changed, as though our capacity to respond or be pro-active is not dependent on how we have changed. Now, what I find quite simple to say is that we have an ease of presence in this country. If you have a demonstration now, you never hear the slogan, "Come what may, we're here to stay – here to stay, here to fight." If you hear that you look around, say, "What's, what's wrong with them? Of course, we're here to stay." That has now been completely accepted and you do not go around with something in the back of your head, which all of us have had over a period of time – not all, but some generations, the early generations – is that we could all be deported in the twinkling of an eye. There was no absolute certainty. Enoch Powell could frighten us into believing that. There was no relationship between governments and black people, except to pick up some votes and join the Labour Party and be a Trades Unionist, mildly so. But now, who we are is different, so how we fight is going to be different, how we contribute is going to be different. In fact you'd find more of a willingness to be part of here, and to be part of the English cricket team, to be part of LWT, to be part of Channel 4, to be part of the *New Statesman* without reservation, committed to these institutions. I mean I'm committed to Channel 4, and its development and its success, and the *New Statesman*, and I'm not committed to *The Voice*, not because I'm against it, but simply not.

So that kind of change where you can make choices and not be hemmed into a little gang that is only together because some white people doing something to us. There's no life like that, and there is no excellence. You can't excel, you can't be a novelist, you can't be a serious poet, easy with the metaphor and the simile of the land, if constantly you have to say, "The police and them are murderer; we can't get no furtherer", or whatever was necessary to say at one time. I mean we gotta write like Dickens, man, we got to – we can do it, we're creative people, and the way they bop along, it's like they're going somewhere. What's behind you will take care of itself: let's go. You get that kind of feeling particularly among working-class kids, man. They bump and move, they're not looking behind their shoulders. "If you want to come, you come, see what you get." And the whole fashion. I see some guys wearing some trousers round their thighs. Well, I say, "Hell." Even though we were fashionable in our time, there was always something deeply conservative: we did not want to be noticed, because to be noticed too much is to be a target. Now you find they say, "Hell, let's go. Let's go for it. Let's make it here." And they have not lost the ease of rice and peas, either. They haven't lost that. There are some things that they have which their parents made absolutely sure that makes them distinguishable from a bland mass. I have brought up seven, and I make sure that they are distinguishable from some mass of faceless wonders. And that's what parents do now. Now it's not watching to see you don't get in trouble. It's watching you to see you don't lose that thing.'[7]

In the post-war days when the *Windrush* sailed into Tilbury, the linkage between race, nationality and the rights of citizenship in Britain seemed firm and indissoluble. A few years ago Lord Norman Tebbit, then a Conservative peer, proposed a 'cricket test' as a touchstone of British citizenship. Britishness, he argued, should be defined by examining the West Indians' loyalties when the West Indies team played England.

'This sense of the inability to conceive of identity, of national identity as a complex phenomenon; the inability to see that people's allegiances might be multiple and that, actually, to see their encounters with difference, their encounters with otherness not as danger, not as jeopardy, but to see them as something that was potentially enriching to the life of a national community: that was what struck me as peculiar. What troubled me more about the Tebbit remarks was that people in our own community would actually buy into that model of thinking of identity as well, that somehow or the other they, as a consequence of their rejection, as a consequence of their emiseration and their marginalisation, would begin to say, "Yes, it's true, actually. You can't hold to a complex identity, you have to be either one thing or the other, and if we are externalised, then we will be external, we will be other." That seemed to me to be more worrying. Norman I would have predicted that from; but I didn't like the idea that people were so depressed and so squashed and so boxed in by the ways in which their life chances were undermined that they too would accept that sense, that truth about themselves, that black people have no future in this country over the long term, that the only way to escape those pressures is to leave. Now a number of us generationally, politically, and so on, have

[7] Interview with Darcus Howe.

rejected that option. We didn't necessarily predict a rosy future, but we knew we weren't going to go anywhere.'[8]

The truth was, however, that Lord Tebbitt's remarks attracted practically no serious interest, a demonstration of how much Powellite nationalism had faded. Shortly after William Hague was elected Conservative leader he showed up at the Carnival, as if pointedly rejecting Lord Tebbitt's implication about the alien nature of the Caribbeans. It is clear that during the last fifty years the Caribbeans have become an integral part of British society and have fundamentally altered Britain's image of itself, but the existence of the black British remains conditional.

'Well, I've called it fragile on two grounds. One, it's fragile because it's a minority rather than a majority experience. You could not look at the position of black people in British society and say that it's a majority success story. That is not the case. And those communities remain vulnerable, because they're poor, and remain vulnerable 'cos they're marginal and unemployed, and remain vulnerable because they're black. So I want to insist on the double sided nature of this. It's partial and it's temporary because some will make it and some will not. And those being left behind are in serious trouble, and we have to think about them alongside the success stories. But it's fragile also because it depends on what happened to Englishness and British society itself, which has been transformed by their presence, but which contains deep roots of racism, which contains a long imperial history, you know, which could swing back the other way. I don't think any of these things are permanent. I'm not a permanent optimist in that sense, you know. I mean, if there were floods of black refugees coming out of a Europe which had gone a different way from Britain – say we didn't join the EMU and all that – and a really strong anti-foreigner climate began to develop in Britain, perfectly possible, that would have its spin-off in attitudes towards the indigenous black population, too. So, none of these battles are forever, they're not won completely. What I think has happened is this kind of tilt in the balance of forces, and the tilt has been towards the opening – the possibility – of being black and British. That's as far as I think one can say it has gone.'[9]

[8] Interview with Paul Gilroy.
[9] Interview with Stuart Hall.

29

'Coming here, I felt British. I knew I wasn't English, I know a whole lot of black people think they were English, because they had English in their mind, but they didn't realise, to be English, you had to be born here. But I resent not being classified as British. I think I've done what the country asked of me. I've come here as a naive Jamaican, I've learned their ways. I'm not saying I'm diplomatic, because I have to keep part of me. But I am British, I am loyal, I've learned to speak out and say what I feel. And I love the country. I love to see the patchwork and, furthermore, I love the history of England. They skipped over it at school, gave me bride story readers to read because I was supposed to be stupid. They didn't give me the complete book of *David Copperfield* or *Great Expectations*, just a chapter. Only when I went to high school, I got the complete book. And I have read and read. I did English history at school and English literature, which I love. Every place that I can identify in history, and every period, I have read. I used to hate Victorian history at school, and now, what I'm doing is reading Victorian authors, who have researched it and make it more simple for me, right? I've been all over England. I go to battlefields. I go to places like Bamburgh. Why do I go to Bamburgh? 'Cos my mother sits there telling me, Grace Darling, rowing out in her lifeboat to rescue people, so I want to see what it's like. And everything I can see, I see and I like. But, at the same time, you can take me out of Jamaica but you can't get it out of me. And so I've become two people. And sometimes both come together.'[1]

'The idea that black people in this country who came from this *Windrush* generation, that they were sort of fundamentally different on any level than the white people that they worked with, fought with, whose lives they negotiated day by day, week by week, was always absurd. So again, it's not a surprise to see this. If you look at the history of this country and you look at what happened in the

---

[1] Interview with Tryphena Anderson.

eighteenth century over there, some people would argue that demographically there were equivalent numbers of black settlers, although perhaps the population then was much more skewed towards the male than it has been this time around. But similar patterns of connection and intermarriage and so on were visible then, too. So I mean, this is an old British script you're seeing reworked.'[2]

Ali: Black kids are the best fighters in this school. They are also the best footballers and they've got the most women . . . I think it's because they're bigger and they can bully us around.[3]

The Irresistible Rise

Take a view from the dance floor. Flip through a fashion magazine. Look at the music programmes on TV. Black is sexy and we all know it. 'Black culture' is beat music, dance, athleticism and violence, the stuff that gets the girls going. Black is a jazz musician pouring out emotion through the ends of his fingers. Black is a fighter, bulging with muscles, arrogant with physical power. Black is a boy with a gun, or a knife, scary eyes and dreadlocks. Black is dance fury shimmering with supple agility. Black is movement, fast as the wind. Check out the line-up of footballers and athletes, irresistible bottoms in cute little shorts. Thrill to the Lycra thighs on those guys as they flash down the track. Gimme some! Black is beautiful. We're born that way, like a cheetah is born fast or a tiger deadly, with a sense of rhythm and a fantastic body that the average white wimp can only dream about. Listen to any game involving a black sportsman and sooner or later you'll hear the commentator call him 'a natural athlete'. That's how it is.

What you gain on the roundabouts you lose on the swings. By the end of the eighties the transformation of the Caribbeans was complete. In 1987

---

[2]   Interview with Paul Gilroy.

[3]   Tony Sewell, *Black Masculinities and Schooling: How Black Boys Survive Modern Schooling* (Staffordshire: Trentham Books, 1997), p. 184.

the first black MPs in modern times entered the House of Commons and for most of the British public the event marked a watershed in the status and the place of the Caribbeans in British life. And if you looked at the thing from a distance the changes were remarkable. Round about this time the news media stopped speculating throughout the summer about whether there would be trouble at the Notting Hill Carnival and started calling it 'Europe's biggest street festival'. Trevor MacDonald started to become the nation's favourite newsreader. At the Olympics black athletes wrapped themselves in the Union Jack every time they won something. Black footballers gained a foothold in the nation's most popular sport and started campaigning against racism on the terraces. When Mrs Thatcher stepped down the 'blackness' invented during the defensive years of the seventies and the early eighties had become a valuable commodity in the cultural big bang which had occurred, and it had become a commonplace, highly prized, marker of post-Caribbean identity.

'Teach some West Indians and some English people, kids, and you'll see who influences whom, in Archbishop Tennyson and them schools in the inner city, see who influences who from the point of view of fashion, from the point of view of style, from the point of view of slang, from the point of view of dialect. See who influences whom, and who's carrying the sway. The power of West Indian spontaneity and English caution has produced a generation of little children who are quite remarkable in the way they approach things.'[4]

A Martian watching British TV at the start of the nineties might have been forgiven for thinking that there had been a complete turnaround in the fortunes of the community founded by the migrants who had come on the *Windrush*. A closer look would have told a different story. Black men, most of them Caribbean, or from Caribbean parentage, made up seventeen per cent of the prison population. Black male school leavers were four times less likely to be employed than their white counterparts. After four decades of living in Britain the Afro Caribbeans were among the most economically vulnerable groups in the population, easily outstripped by almost all the immigrants who had arrived later. 'Blackness' had become a cornerstone of British 'multi-culturalism', a quality which could confer the manna of proletarian vigour to politicians and media networks, and was being brandished as an emblem of the 'new Britain'. At the same time, it had become

---

[4]   Interview with Darcus Howe.

a device which justified widespread discrimination, accentuated by developments in the workplace at large.

> 'Black men are finding themselves marginalised within the labour market. One thing that's happened in the British labour market has been the collapse of opportunity for blue collar, male workers in general. Unskilled male workers don't have a role in the modern labour market approaching the millennium. But that's hit our black men harder than white men, really. Whereas women, black women and white women, they've got keyboard skills, they have the service industry skills and they're much more, generally speaking, much more employable.'[5]

The contrast between the two different outcomes of 'blackness' was an outline of a paradox. The defensive culture which had evolved throughout the seventies, that had forced the pace of change in the eighties, and then become a capital asset for the migrants, now threatened to become a trap within which the grandchildren of the *Windrush* generation would be imprisoned. In a recent study of Afro Caribbean schoolchildren Tony Sewell outlines the process by which Afro-Caribbean children are reduced to two extreme choices: 'the (acting white) MacDonald man and the rebellious Yard man.'[6] Those who fail to stay within the collective boundaries of 'blackness' are regarded as 'white', and he lists a rigid schedule of behaviours, which involve habits of speech, tastes in music and dress, along with approaches to learning and relationships in the school. This self conscious labelling has further consequences.

> The majority of Afro-Caribbean boys were excluded not for breaking explicit rules, but for 'crimes' that were open to interpretation. For example, violent and disruptive behaviour. What was key in the perception of many teachers was that African-Caribbean boys were the ones who broke most of the school regulations or had the propensity to do so. The irony for most of these boys was that their convictions were rarely for breaking any 'explicit' rule. They were trapped by the techniques of power which had regulating effects. Put simply, African-Caribbean boys were in a double bind that principally involved their teachers and their peers. They suffered a disproportionate amount of disciplinary power, which their

---

[5] Interview with Diane Abbott.
[6] Sewell, op. cit. p. 185.

teachers (prison guards, courts, psychiatrists, police) justified by their imagined perception of black masculinity.[7]

Looked at from this perspective the history of the Caribbean migrants and their successors is no success story. Instead it is an ambiguous, many sided and continually evolving event.

In the old days – this is when we would be sitting in a corner listening to the grown-ups talk – they used to say, 'I don't want to leave my bones in this country.' A lot of people went back, though not as many as you would imagine. For every one who went back to Jamaica or Trinidad or Guyana, another went to the USA or Africa. Sometimes they only stayed in the Caribbean for a while before departing for Canada or the USA. Mostly, the ones who stayed in the Caribbean didn't give up British citizenship and even when they went back to live they left something of their hearts in London or Manchester or Leeds. They kept their UK passports too.

'I left on 29 November 1990, and it wasn't too bad leaving. But when I had to give my key up for my house, oh, that was a shock. And then, when I got on the plane, I just got emotional. I couldn't stop crying, I just couldn't stop crying. I left my family and my friends, I don't know if I told Arthur about this, but I met somebody on the plane who knew me. And the tears wouldn't stop. So, it was quite emotional, leaving. After all, I'd spent a long time there, so it was difficult. There are certain things that you don't just return and say, all is well. We found the discipline, in certain areas a little bit difficult to accept. Sometimes you go into a shop and, the bank or wherever, and, it's not what you're accustomed to, the time you take to get through certain business that should have been done, and I get a little bit edgy. And, they know me so well when I go into the bank, and if there isn't sufficient tellers, and the queue is so long and I'm watching the clock. I'm standing twenty, thirty minutes and the line is not moving. I'll open my mouth, because I am the type of person. "What's going on here?", you know. "We need some more tellers. I'm here too long." And they have a saying here that it would appear all the people come from England are mad. So, sometimes I capitalise on that, to get things moving. Here is a mad woman, here, you'd better get things moving, you know.'[8]

---

[7]   ibid., p. 186.

[8]   Interview with Cherie Byfield. Cherie Byfield came to Britain from Jamaica in 1961. She trained as a nurse and settled in Manchester where she met and married Arthur Byfield. They returned to Jamaica in 1991 and became farmers, employing twelve people and growing local produce.

*   *   *

'Some of our friends here, when I say "friends", fellow Jamaicans, they look upon the returning people, rather puzzlingly. How are you going to adjust here? How are you going to behave towards us? Have you got a lot of money? And things like that. Or assuming that we have a lot of money, isn't it? When you return. Are you from the United States or what? And it is for you, the returnee, to take the initiative and go to them, and say, you know, "We're the same people. Let us find a way of working here." And we find it quite, happy to work, for instance, in this neighbourhood here. We work with our fellow neighbours, and most of them are returning residents, as we call them, and largely from the United Kingdom. And we form things like neighbourhood watches, community associations. We meet and know each other and try to continue the good community life. When it comes to the people who work on my farm, from our experience in England as employees, we know what we expect from the employer, how we tried to practise good employer-employee relationship, so it works well, we benefit from that experience and it's worked well, so we have no regrets."

'Many of them are going to live in rural Jamaica and in Mandeville, which is the capital of the Parish of Manchester, very interesting. I asked someone who facilitated that particular movement, why do they go to Mandeville? And he said, "Well, it's England, it's cool, you know." And, in fact, people used to refer to it as the "Cheltenham of Jamaica". And lots of people are coming back with their homes. You have had a number of housing, building societies, at least two, that have done tremendous business in Britain with those early migrants who saw their sojourn in Britain to be temporary. Of course, this is of value to us as well, because their pension is paid back here in foreign exchange, which we need badly, so that is a help. Some people feel, of course, that we need the energy of the people, not an old people's home. With migrants, usually they sometimes live in a time warp, not realising that things have changed, and Jamaica has changed considerably since 1948. The younger ones find it a little difficult, they see their accent is usually

---

[9]   Interview with Arthur Byfield. Arthur Byfield came to Britain in 1961. He settled in Manchester, worked in a factory in Trafford, then on the buses. In the seventies he took his A-Levels and went to Manchester University where he trained as a teacher. He taught in Moss Side where he lived until retiring to Jamaica in 1991.

laughed at. But, in fact, on the whole, they are welcome. I, myself, have found a number of them who work as secretaries to be very, very disciplined, very industrious, and apply themselves marvellously. I've always been impressed by that. And, of course, we have two fellows on the football team, Reggae Boyz, who we have re-imported, and one of them has been the scorer of the goals. They're different. Their speech pattern is different. It's funny to hear a sort of Midlands accent or a Cockney accent coming out of somebody with so much melanin in the skin. But then, of course, I remembered travelling to Africa many times and speaking English, and the Yoruba taxi driver couldn't understand how I couldn't speak Yoruba, so it makes sense. It's just a difference.'[10]

The latest population figures tell us that the number of people in Britain who describe themselves as Caribbean or Afro-Caribbean are declining. The people who came on the *Windrush* have been dying in increasing numbers since the seventies. Others have left. But the declining number of 'Caribbeans' may simply mark the extent to which their grandchildren now describe themselves, when they have to fill in the forms that ask who you are, as 'English' or 'mixed race' or 'black other'. If you were born in the Caribbean and shared that moment of arrival, and lived through the dreams and the changes, it gives you a peculiar little shiver to think that when your children look past you they don't see the colours of the Caribbean, bright green and vibrant red and the endless blue of sea and sky. What they see is England. When anyone asks us, we say that we're from the Caribbean. That's where our origins are. Our children's origins are in us.

'Not that I feel British, I am British, I come home. I am not one of the West Indian, or whatever you might label me, as someone who come here to make their fortune and go back home. I left Guyana to improve and better myself. And this is what immigration is all about. Many of us came here with an "indefinite reason", to return some day. There's no place like home. But for the work that I have done here, consistently, for forty-four years, or even that, is not the same country that I left. And I wouldn't be able to fit in, because nothing stands still. I mean, ask me, going back home, is where I come from, it's not the same. It's a different place. And the only place I know is Britain, Shepherd's Bush. Sorry to say that. But I live here

[10] Interview with Professor Rex Nettleford.

for forty consistent years. I go back home on vacation. I have another family at home, you know, I've got two sons, a few granddaughters, I'm welcome. They're in a very good position. But, at my age, or even younger than my age now, I couldn't fit in there because it's a different environment, different type of youth. Their values are different, you know, all over the West Indies. Everywhere, nothing goes backward, everything goes forward.

'Wherever a child is born, you are a native of that country, whether you're black, Chinese, Asian or what. And many of us confuse our children by telling them, every day, I'm going back home. They haven't done anything for the child that was born here, that belongs here. They haven't done anything, because their whole object, to go back home. And when they go back, they'll be taking the children home, who does not belong to where they were born, and haven't made any foundation for them while they're here. So when they've gone back home, the children can remain here, confident that they are black British and British subjects. I came here to improve myself – no – nothing goes backward – to improve myself. When I was mayor, the press used to follow me, as usual, and asked me, "Did you think you were going to be mayor? What did you expect?" I said, "I expect to carry on from where I left off, you know." Just carry on from where I left, and that's what I do today. I came here, I make a contribution, to myself and the country that I live in, quite happy, quite satisfied. I realise, I mean, the things that I have done here. And I become an old man, and prepare, when the Good Lord call me. I don't want to be taken back home.'[11]

'Britain is where I live. Is Britain my home? I don't know, not until the British tell me that they accept me as being part of their country. I cannot just be part of the country when they want me to be and when they don't wish me to be. It was made plain to me by Mrs Thatcher that I had to pay for citizenship of a country where we was born a citizen. So if I have to pay for the citizenship, which I have not done, then Britain is not my home because I'm not a citizen. If I'm accepted as a citizen, we're not happy to pay for something which I already had, then Britain is my home. I know I've already decided that I will probably spend the rest of my life here. I hope to spend my life here knowing full well that I would

[11] Interview with Rudy Braithwaite.

have loved to have been a citizen of this country, but if I have to be afraid, no. So, altogether, I am not sure that this country really wants me, but it's got me and it's got to do what it can with me, 'cos I ain't going nowhere. And that's where I am.'[12]

'So that's fifty-three years. 3 June gone, fifty-three years. Well, when I come to myself, taking a stock of my life, I have come to the conclusion, say, well, no, I didn't regret. I haven't done too badly. I get the privilege to travel around, meet different people with different outlooks of life, and the other thing, I was offered a job back home because I wanted to go back home to pass on some of the knowledge that I got in this country, pass it on to my people. But due to my wife's illness, 'cos when she had this MS you see that changed, so I had to change my mind and stay on. And I have no regrets. I visit whenever possible, but not to go back to settle down. I would never do that. England is my home.'[13]

'In the early years I had thought of going back. But, by and large, I must be quite honest to myself that I know that staying here I would be able to provide a better standard or quality of education for my children than if I had gone back out there. Education and higher education out there in those days, you'd have to pay for it. And for me to go back with a wife and family and start from scratch and develop, it would have been a hopeless travel. And so, eventually, my wife and I, we decided, Well, look, this is home for us. And, we have been out to Jamaica on a few occasions, on holiday, and I look around. And I have no doubt that, at the time, we made the right decision to stay here. And I would hope that because of that decision we have made, several other, not just West Indians but other minorities have benefited from it, from a professional point of view, from my work, and from a voluntary point of view as well.'[14]

'I have really had various upsets, but nothing too detrimental to my state of life, to my perception of life. I had to go through a lot of different times of difficulties, but I tried to put that area of mishaps beyond my achievement and beyond my thought. I always tried to

---

[12]   Interview with Ben Bousquet.
[13]   Interview with Cecil Holness.
[14]   Interview with Eric Irons.

get in the thought of progress and put away the bad points to an area of experience or adventures. And I concentrate on the areas of success more than anything else. And I haven't got any upsets at all, I have upsets in a way where it was trivial, nothing to give me any animosity about life, nothing about being revengeful to anyone. It was just a period of infiltration. On the whole, I find that I've got quite a comfortable and happy life in Britain.'[15]

'The thing is I thought, that having paid my taxes since the age of fifteen, I've paid into a system. There's no way I'm going to walk away from my due. Plus, my family here, my wife, my children and grandchildren. They don't want to go to Jamaica so, unless they go as tourists I'd have to go on my own, and there's no way I'd do that. I'm entitled to the benefits that I've paid into, and I'm here to stay. Of course, it's part of my wish that when I die I'm cremated and my ashes are spread in Africa, 'cos then I would have gone home. But, until then, I'm here to stay.'[16]

Postscript

When we began to write this book, part of what drove us was the feeling that this story was part of the tale that we had to tell about ourselves and our own family. The other thing we felt strongly was that the people of the *Windrush* had been forgotten, their real characters, intentions and behaviour obscured by our need to reinterpret and change them to fit whatever kind of assurance or validation we needed at the time. For fifty years they had stood, silent in the photographs, unable to resist the narratives which were heaped round them by the politicians, villains and fools who found them useful objects. But as we spoke to them about that moment of arrival, we re-discovered many things that we had forgotten or had driven to the back of our memories. For instance, the language they used, whether they were speaking dialect or standard English, was softer, sometimes more formal and, always, more individual and poetic than the idioms which emerged from our experience in the cities. They were tougher too, enduring, with a cheerful stoicism, conditions which would make many of their English contemporaries weep tears of frustration and anger. They weren't

15   Interview with Laurie Philpots.
16   Interview with Vince Reid.

brought or brainwashed or deceived by phoney promises. If anything was phoney it was the structure which they fled with the clear understanding that they were going to the other side of the moon, and that they would do what they had to do in order to make it serve their needs. They were straight, meeting life head on, whether they were thieves or jokers or honest workers, and they were full of confidence and belief in their own strength and capacity to take the blows that life would undoubtedly hand out.

Our father seemed like that, and our mother. Nowadays we neither remember nor care whether they were too strict or too poor or that we spent so much time apart. Talking with the people of their generation who, like them, had walked the streets looking for shelter, or worked through the night for years at a stretch, brings them back to us, and gives us a sense of a continuity which stretches far beyond anything we can remember or know about. Our hope is that this book goes some way to setting the record straight. Forgive our mistakes and accept our respect.

Biographical Notes

Diane Abbott MP was born and brought up in London. After a degree at Cambridge University she entered the Civil Service, then worked for the National Council for Civil Liberties, before becoming a reporter and television researcher. Later she worked for the broadcasting union, the ACCT, and became a prominent member of the Labour Party, and one of the leaders of the campaign for black sections in the Party. She was elected MP for Hackney in 1987.

Eddie Adams has lived in Notting Dale since he was born in 1936. He was a Teddy Boy in the fifties, worked at Fords in Dagenham, Essex, then at the local Law Centre until retiring.

Valerie Amos came from Guyana at the age of nine and went to school in Kent. Later, she was part of an influential group of young black British academics whose best known work, *The Empire Strikes Back*, was a polemic which called attention to the views of the generation which had grown up in the sixties. In the mid-eighties she became head of the Equal Opportunities Commission. She became a Labour Peer, Baroness Amos, in 1997.

Tryphena Anderson came from Jamaica in 1952. She landed at Liverpool and went to live in Nottingham where she trained as a nurse.

Jazzy B's parents are Antiguan, and he was brought up in Finsbury Park, north London. He went to school at Highbury Comprehensive during the seventies. His father wanted him to be a doctor, but he became a sound system operator and DJ in the north London clubs. He founded Soul To Soul, a music co-operative whose best-known record was 'Get A Life'. Jazzy B is famous for his commitment to a black British persona and Soul To Soul is focused around that concept.

Randolph Beresford came from Guyana in 1953 at the age of thirty-nine. He was a carpenter by trade and became an active trade unionist. He went into local politics after the Notting Hill riots and was elected councillor for the London Borough of Hammersmith and Fulham 1974–5 and Mayor in

1975–6. He organised a fund for the Kelso Cochrane memorial in Kensal Green cemetery. He is now retired and lives in London.

Paul Boateng MP Paul Boateng's father was a senior Ghanaian politician and his English mother returned to Britain in the sixties with the children. Boateng qualified as a lawyer and began his career working at law centres in Notting Hill and Paddington early in the seventies. He was elected to the GLC in 1981 and then became an MP in 1987. Presently he is a junior Minister in the Labour Government.

Ben Bousquet came from St Lucia in the eastern Caribbean, and arrived in Britain in 1957. He settled in Notting Hill, became an active trades unionist, a North Kensington councillor and a prominent anti-apartheid activist.

Rudy Braithwaite came from Barbados, arriving in 1957, and is now a self employed osteopath.

Gary Bushell is a hugely popular tabloid columnist and broadcaster, a major figure in popular culture in the nineties.

Arthur Byfield came to Britain in 1961. He settled in Manchester, worked in a factory in Trafford, then on the buses. In the seventies he took his A-Levels and went to Manchester University where he trained as a teacher. He taught in Moss Side where he lived until retiring to Jamaica in 1991.

Cherie Byfield came to Britain from Jamaica in 1961. She trained as a nurse and settled in Manchester where she met and married Arthur Byfield. They returned to Jamaica in 1991 and became farmers, employing twelve people and growing local produce.

Earl Cameron was born in Bermuda, came to Britain in October 1939 as a seaman and joined the Merchant Navy. Later on he toured with ENSA. After the war he became the best-known black film actor in Britain, appearing in some of the most notable 'problem dramas' made at the Ealing film studios, such as *Pool of London*, *Sapphire* and *Flame in the Streets*.

Euton Christian joined the RAF in 1944. He took part in the legendary battle of Manchester, when West Indian and African Americans together with white British servicemen fought a 'pitched battle' through the centre of the city against white American troops who were trying to impose segregation. He returned to Jamaica in November 1947, after signing up for another four years in the RAF and, after his leave ended, embarked on the *Windrush*. After leaving the RAF he settled in Manchester, becoming a town councillor and the city's first black magistrate.

James Christian was Kelso Cochrane's cousin. He came to Britain in 1957 and returned to Antigua after thirty-three years.

Arthur Coats came from Cardiff and was the cook on the *SS Empire Windrush*. The journey from Jamaica, which ended in June 1948 at Tilbury, was his last voyage on her.

Frank Critchlow came from Trinidad in 1953 at the age of twenty. He worked on the railways before opening the Rio Coffee Bar in Notting Dale in 1959. In 1969 he closed the Rio and opened the Mangrove Restaurant in All Saints Road. As a result of frequent police raids he went through a succession of court trials – the Mangrove trials of the sixties and seventies. He still lives in Notting Hill.

Ulric Cross came from Trinidad, joined the RAF and flew bombers during the Second World War. He featured in a BBC wartime propaganda film as Flying Officer Ulric Cross. He flew eighty missions and crash landed seven times. After the war he qualified as a barrister and worked as a talks producer for BBC radio. He went to Ghana in 1956 when it became independent to work in the Attorney General's Office; then to Cameroon as Attorney General. Subsequently he went to Tanzania as a High Court Judge and Dean of the Faculty of Law at the university. In 1974 he returned to Trinidad as a High Court Judge.

Ivor Cummings was a principal in the Colonial Office. He was himself of mixed race origins, his father a Sierra Leonean and his mother a white Englishwoman. He was a central figure in the decisions and arrangements made within the various Civil Service Departments with regard to the migrants' reception. He was a fastidious, elegant man, with a manner reminiscent of Noel Coward – he chain smoked with a long cigarette holder, and addressed visitors as 'dear boy'.

Arthur Curling ran away from home in Jamaica to join the RAF at the age of sixteen. He lied about his age and was admitted. He returned to Jamaica in 1946 but could not settle down, coming back to Britain on the *Windrush* in 1948.

Oswald 'Columbus' Dennison sailed from Jamaica on the *Windrush*. He was the first of the *Windrush* passengers, according to the contemporary press, to get a job. After leaving the deep shelter at Clapham Oswald Dennison settled in Brixton, where he worked as a street trader until his retirement.

Carlton Duncan arrived from Jamaica in 1961. He had to repeat his school qualifications while working in the evenings as a dancer before gaining the grades he needed for university entrance. After seven years' experience he was appointed deputy head of a school in Coventry. He was subsequently appointed to the Rampton Committee, later the Swann Committee, which had been commissioned to prepare a report for the DES on the situation of migrant children in the education system. He was appointed to his first headship in Bradford and is now head of a grant maintained school in Birmingham.

Christine Eaton was a member of St John's Ambulance Brigade and was mobilised to nurse victims of the Deptford Fire in 1981.

Johnny Edgecombe arrived in Liverpool in 1949 as a merchant seaman. He lived in Notting Hill and ran various enterprises on both sides of the law, but is most famous for his romance with Christine Keeler, which sparked off the Profumo scandal. He was jailed for firing a gun at Keeler. He now lives in London with his family.

Larry Ford owned the restaurant Fiesta One, on Ledbury Road, which was one of the earliest and most important social venues in the district, frequented among others by Keeler, Ward, Rice-Davies and their friends. Larry Ford came from Trinidad and is a furniture maker by trade. He now conducts one of the major steel band troupes involved in the Notting Hill Carnival.

Paul Gilroy is one of the leading black academics and critics in Britain. His mother came from Guyana, and was one of the first black head teachers in the education system. Gilroy's reputation was established with the text, *The Empire Strikes Back*, written together with a group of young black British academics, including Baroness Amos. This was the first work to begin exploring the nature of the Black British experience from the inside. He now teaches at Goldsmiths' College, University of London.

Denise Gooding was born and brought up in south London. She was eleven years old at the time of the New Cross Fire. She was present at the party, where one brother died and another was seriously injured. Denise escaped with only slight injuries. She lives in London.

Ena Gooding came from Barbados in 1961 with her husband and settled in north London. The couple had four children – Richard, David, Andrew and Denise. Andrew died in the Deptford Fire of 1981.

Orville Gooding came from Barbados in 1961 with his wife, Ena. At the time of the Deptford Fire, in which he lost one of his four children, Andrew, he was working for North Thames Gas.

Bernie Grant MP came to Britain from Guyana. He studied engineering at Heriot Watt University in Edinburgh. Subsequently, he worked for the Post Office and became a full-time official of NUPE, the National Union of Public Employees. He was elected as a councillor in Haringey and became the leader of the council. He was elected MP for Haringey in 1987.

Cy Grant came from Guyana and joined the RAF in 1941. He was shot down flying a mission over Germany and spent the rest of the war as a prisoner of war in Germany. After the war he qualified as a barrister, but, instead of practising, became an actor. During the fifties he was an international star, performing with such actors as Richard Burton and Joan Collins. Subsequently he became a household name as a result of his nightly appearances on the BBC's *Tonight* programme.

Stuart Hall arrived from Jamaica in 1951 as a Rhodes Scholar to Oxford University. In the sixties and seventies he became a leading figure among radical sociologists, a recognised leader in the interpretation of the new schools of Continental philosophy, and founder of the *New Left Review*, a highly influential journal of the British Left. He went on to head the Centre for Contemporary Cultural Studies at Birmingham University, subsequently becoming Professor of Sociology at the Open University.

Alfred 'King Dick' Harvey came to Britain in 1954 as a stowaway. He now lives in London.

Wayne Haynes grew up in New Cross, south London, and set out to be a professional footballer. The weekend before he was due to sign a professional contract with Millwall FC he was injured in the Deptford Fire of 1981 and is now registered disabled.

Lenny Henry was born during the fifties to a Jamaican family in Dudley. After school he became a stand-up comedian, achieving enormous popular success on television. He is the best known and most influential black entertainer in Britain.

Cecil Holness joined the RAF from Jamaica in 1944 and after the war re-joined for another four years. He went back to Jamaica and returned to Britain on the *Windrush*. His wife Claire was the daughter of West Indian parents who had lived in Britain since the First World War, when his father-in-law had joined the British Army. He settled in London after leaving the RAF, worked as a motor mechanic and is now retired.

Darcus Howe came to Britain from Trinidad in 1961. He worked in Notting Hill at the Mangrove Restaurant and was famously one of the nine victims of a police raid which gave rise to a series of trials at the end of the sixties, a cause célèbre in its day. Later he was editor of *Race Today*, and organiser of the New Cross March in protest about the circumstances surrounding a fire at New Cross in 1981 when several black children died. Recently presenter of The Devil's Advocate, a talk show on Channel 4, a columnist for *The New Statesman*, and independent television producer.

Ros Howells came from Grenada, arriving in Britain during 1951. She settled in south London, where she worked as a counsellor.

Eric Huntley came from Guyana in 1957. An anti-colonial activist who intended to return to Guyana after a breathing space of a few years in Britain, he settled in north London and worked in the Post Office, then in insurance sales, as well as being engaged in the work of the publishing house Bogle L'Ouverture and the Black Parents Association. He now lives in London and edits *Caribbean Watch*, a magazine devoted to ecological concerns in the region.

Jessica Huntley came from Guyana in 1958 to join her husband, Eric Huntley. Both were committed political activists in the region and did not intend to stay very long in Britain. In the sixties she founded the independent publishing house and book shop, Bogle L'Ouverture, and published a stream of works from Caribbean and African writers, including Andrew Salkey, Walter Rodney and Linton Kwesi Johnson. The Huntleys were part of the Black Parents Movement which had its origins in the campaigns over Educationally Subnormal Schools and the 'sus' laws. They still live in London.

Eric Irons grew up on a farm in Jamaica, joined the RAF and came to Britain at the age of twenty-three. He stayed in the RAF after the war, serving in Malta and Egypt, then settled in Nottingham and worked at the MOD's Central Ordnance Depot at Chilwell. Subsequently, he worked for the WEA and, in 1962, was appointed as a magistrate in Nottingham.

Linton Kwesi Johnson is the acknowledged poet of the seventies generation of black British youth. His first book of poems, *Dread, Beat and Blood*, became a bestseller in Britain and was widely read internationally. The phrase 'dub poetry' was coined to describe his performances of his work. During the marches and riots of the early eighties it was his voice and his performances which came to represent the style and the emotions of black British youth.

Carmel Jones came from Jamaica in 1955 and joined the Pentecostal Church in 1959. He became a Pentecostal Minister, and then Chief Executive Officer of the Pentecostalists' umbrella organisation, The New Assembly of Churches.

Clem Jones CBE was editor of the *Wolverhampton Express* and *Star* during the time of Enoch Powell's 'Rivers of Blood' speech. He was a friend of Powell's from the time of his arrival in Wolverhampton in 1959, sharing an interest in literary figures like A. E. Housman and George Borrow.

Mervyn Jones was a staff reporter on the *Tribune* in the fifties. He covered the Notting Hill riots in 1958.

Sam King came from Jamaica and joined the RAF, arriving in Britain in 1944. After the war he went back to Jamaica, then returned to Britain on the *Windrush*. He joined the Post Office and became active in local politics. He was elected to Southwark Council in the early eighties, becoming Mayor of Southwark in 1983.

Sir David Lane was the conservative MP for Cambridge, 1967–76. Subsequently he was junior home office minister, 1972–4. Later on, he was appointed first chair of the Commission for Racial Equality, 1977–82.

Connie Mark joined the WRAC in Jamaica and worked as a medical secretary until she came to Britain in 1954 to join her first husband, the professional cricketer Stanley Goodrich. Subsequently she worked for the NHS in west London until retirement.

David Mason OBE is a Methodist Minister who set up home in Notting Hill after the '58 riots and started a race relations project, supported by Donald Soper, the leader of community welfare tendencies in the Methodist Church.

Lloyd Miller came to Britain from Jamaica in 1949 and worked as a builder in Notting Hill.

William Naltey came from Jamaica to join the RAF in 1943. He served as an air gunner with Coastal Command. After the war he joined the Civil Service. At the time the *Windrush* docked he was living in Wandsworth.

Michael Nesbeth came from Jamaica at the age of fifteen. A well-known keyboard player, he performed with Matumbi and Dennis Bovell. He is the older brother of the boxer Frank Bruno.

Professor Rex Nettleford came to Britain as a Rhodes Scholar in politics at Oxford. He is now widely acknowledged as the leading intellectual, cultural critic and creative artist in the Caribbean. He is Pro Vice Chancellor of the University of the West Indies and also the founder, artistic director and choreographer of the National Dance Theatre Company of Jamaica.

Sir Herman Ouseley came to join his family from Guyana in 1957. He went to school in south London and later worked in local government, eventually becoming chief executive of Lambeth Council. Subsequently he was appointed Chairman of the Commission for Racial Equality. He was knighted in 1997.

Professor Ceri Peach is an Oxford Professor of Geography and the author of a number of landmark studies about West Indian migration.

Laurie Philpots joined the RAF and came to Britain at the age of eighteen in 1944. After the war he lived in Nottingham and qualified as a linotype operator. In the late fifties he moved to Welwyn Garden City after the Nottingham riots, then worked for the Mirror Group in London's Fleet Street until his retirement.

Reverend Sibyl Phoenix MBE came to England from Guyana in 1956. She worked in the fashion industry for a time, but became famous as a source of help and advice for young black women in south London. She started the Moonshot Club, a youth and community centre which was then burnt down by arsonists. She was ordained and made an MBE during the eighties.

Harry Powell arrived from Jamaica in the early sixties. He went to school in south London and became a professional footballer in 1971, spending seven years with second division Charlton Athletic. He later became a youth worker, running the Lewisham Way Youth and Community Centre from 1980 to the present.

Russell Profitt came to England early in the sixties to join his family. He went to school in north London, and became a primary school teacher. As deputy head of Deptford Primary School he became a local Councillor in Lewisham, and in the seventies stood as a Labour candidate for the City of London and Westminster South.

Vince Reid travelled to Britain on the *Windrush* at the age of thirteen. In London he attended a secondary modern school and left without qualifications two years later. Subsequently he joined the RAF, served overseas in the Far East during the period of insurgency in Malaya, and achieved the rank of NCO before buying himself out. He later studied at Sussex University, then qualified as a teacher and taught in London until his retirement.

John Richards came from Jamaica on the *Windrush*. He had been a farm worker in the USA before setting out for Britain. Subsequently he joined British Rail where he worked until his retirement.

Aldwyn 'Lord Kitchener' Roberts is a Trinidadian and one of the best known and loved calypsonians in the Caribbean. After working in various parts of the region he embarked on the *Windrush*, settling later in Manchester. He returned permanently to Trinidad in 1962.

Mike Steele was Liberal Party candidate in the 1974 General Election. He established the Ladywell Action Centre in Lewisham in 1969. Formerly a member of the Police/Immigrant Sub Committee on the Lewisham Council, he has been a lobby correspondent for several newspapers and still works at the House of Commons.

Paul Stephenson was born in 1937. His father was West African and his mother came from a mixed race English family. In 1963 he initiated a boycott of the Bristol Bus Company because of its refusal to hire black workers. Subsequently he worked for the CRE and sat on a number of quangos, including the British Sports Council and the Press Council.

Dudley Thompson came to Britain from Jamaica in 1940 to join the RAF. He flew missions as a bomb aimer and navigator. He bombed Nuremberg during a 'fearsome' raid in which ninety-three British aircraft were shot down. In London he met and became friends with a number of personalities in the Movement for Colonial Freedom, such as Kwame Nkrumah, Jomo Kenyatta, George Padmore and T. R. Makonnen. As a result he was first chairman of the legendary Pan African conference at Manchester in 1945, at which the leaders of the anti-colonial movement began outlining their plans. After the war Thompson went back to Jamaica, but returned to Oxford as a Rhodes Scholar in 1947. Subsequently he entered politics in Jamaica and became Minister of Foreign affairs under the first Michael Manley administration.

Rene Webb came from Jamaica, having joined the RAF at the age of twenty-two. He was stationed at Biggin Hill and settled in west London before moving to Brixton. He was an ILEA youth worker, and was awarded the Jamaican Badge of Honour by the Jamaican Government for his services to the black community in Britain. In the seventies he started the Melting Pot Foundation in Brixton, one of the earliest 'Self Help' projects, and became chairman of the Lambeth Community Relations Council. He is retired and lives in Brixton.

Ivan Weekes came from Barbados in 1955. He settled in Notting Hill, living in a Rachman property and later on becoming a tenant of the Notting Hill Housing Trust. He served as an alderman on the Kensington and Chelsea Council during the seventies, and was one of the first black people in recent times to be appointed as a magistrate.

Jo Whitter came from Jamaica in 1954, and became the first black property magnate on a large scale. He returned to Jamaica in 1980 and went into business there, but he still owns substantial property in Britain and his five 'English kids' have remained here.

The Right Reverend Bishop Wilfred Wood came to Britain in 1961 from a seminary in Barbados and was ordained a priest at St Paul's Cathedral in 1962. He has become widely known and respected in the black community for the courage and determination with which he has taken up the issues affecting the black communities.

Index